RICASOLI
AND THE RISORGIMENTO
IN TUSCANY

Bettino Ricasoli

RICASOLI

AND THE RISORGIMENTO
IN TUSCANY

by W. K. HANCOCK

NEW YORK

Howard Fertig

1969

First published in 1926 by Faber and Faber

HOWARD FERTIG, INC. EDITION 1969
Published by arrangement with the author

Library of Congress Catalog Card Number: 68-9603

PRINTED IN THE UNITED STATES OF AMERICA
BY NOBLE OFFSET PRINTERS, INC.

to

ANTONIO CECCONI

of

ROCCA   CIGNATA

this book is dedicated

PREFACE

A STUDENT who goes to Florence to investigate the history of that city and of Tuscany in the nineteenth century will doubtless be asked, sooner or later: ' Why did you choose to study this dull period? ' The question will sound like a reproach, and Florence will herself appear reproachful, for all the beauty which the traveller sees around him beckons him insistently to forsake the modern world and to lose himself in the Middle Ages or in the period of the Renaissance. The question, nevertheless, has its answer. Florence is supremely interesting in all ages; she is, as the title of a recent book describes her, ' a flower which is ever renewed '. The history of Athens makes a fascinating study even in the period of Macedonian supremacy; and Florence, similarly, has an interesting life that is peculiarly her own even after the leadership of Italy has passed northwards to the Piedmontese.

In the nineteenth century, also, old motives of her Renaissance history reappear, as if they had been lingering on as an undertone throughout three centuries. The easy-going enjoyment of life to which the citizens had given themselves in the time of Lorenzo de' Medici is challenged again by the earnest, evangelical spirit of Savonarola. The favourite maxim of the chief minister of Tuscany that ' the world gets along by itself ' expresses in prosaic form the theme of many of Lorenzo's poems; while the letters of Ricasoli are full of that scorn for all activity which has no conscious moral end, that indignation against those who are content with seeking mere knowledge, mere pleasure, or mere beauty, that passion for a political order embodying certain principles of morality—which gave form and power to Savonarola's sermons. It is true that the visions and acts of Ricasoli were less dramatic and startling than those of Savonarola, and that the life of the ' Earthly Paradise '—as Tuscany was named in the earlier part

of the nineteenth century—was more moral, less beautiful, and far less creative than Florentine life in the
time of the early Medici. It is nevertheless interesting
to watch the old struggle between two contrasted sides
of the human spirit once again fighting itself out within
Florence, as it had been fought in those same streets
and palaces three centuries before.

To those who are interested in the nationalist movements of the nineteenth century, the history of Tuscany
is a specially valuable study. The story of the *Risorgimento* of Italy has usually been told as a story of
courageous struggle, in which a suffering people, ever
true to the sacred principles of Democracy and Nationality, cast from off its neck the yoke of a wicked and
tyrannical Empire. Such an interpretation of the
Risorgimento is too simple to be altogether true. It may
at first be rather disappointing to discover that in Tuscany
there was nothing which had the least resemblance to
tyranny: that the people was contented and happy: that
the Grand-Duke was a mild, studious person who
attempted with pathetic perseverence to keep the love
which his subjects had once given to him, and who was
repaid at the last with scorn, hatred, and bitter accusations which were untrue. But disappointment will give
place to curiosity. When it is discovered that in Tuscany
there were none of the usual obvious causes which
produce revolutions, there will be a new interest in
tracing the growth of the revolutionary-nationalist spirit.
This spirit will be seen taking shape among different
groups of men, sometimes hostile to each other, sometimes conservative, sometimes radical, sometimes, but
not always, courageous and honest. Nineteenth-century
Tuscany was rich in personalities. In Tuscan history
throughout these years appeared every type of nationalist hero, apostle, politician, agitator, charlatan and
knave. In the end, the character of Ricasoli asserted
itself in domination over them all. The story of his life
is told in this book because it forms a connecting thread

between the various episodes of the nationalist movement, because it illustrates the nobler aspects of that
movement, and because it is finally merged in the
history of the new Italy. Ricasoli has also a fascination
of his own in virtue of the contrast between his intellectual limitations and his moral grandeur, his feudal spirit
and his nineteenth-century ideas, his sincerity and his
self-deception, his narrowness of understanding and his
depth of character. His spirit was essentially Puritan. It
is curious to see how his unconscious faith in Predestination clothed itself in political wrappings, and in
1859–60 made of him a dictator and a diplomatist of a
type which Europe had scarcely known since the days
of Cromwell.

Ricasoli's rigid obstinacy in these years wore down
the resistance of Napoleon III, and by carrying the
Kingdom of Italy across the Apennines made inevitable
the union of the whole peninsula. The history of
Tuscany for eleven eventful months became an important part of the diplomatic history of Europe. In
this book, however, diplomatic history has been given
no more attention than was absolutely necessary; because
it has been often chronicled in other works, and because
the more important questions of what people thought,
of how they were driven and influenced, of their interests,
their hopes and fears and motives—have been unduly
neglected. The author hopes that his book will be a
contribution to the knowledge of Italian and European
history in the nineteenth century, inasmuch as it attempts
to give a careful account of the development of opinion,
during a critical period in the history of a small State
and of a large Nation. An attempt has been made to
understand and explain the thoughts and actions, not
only of those who made the revolution, but of those
who opposed it; not only of cultivated people, but of
the illiterate; not only of the great leader Ricasoli, but
of Ricasoli's peasants. To a peasant in a remote corner
of Tuscany the book is dedicated.

The author must express his thanks, first of all, to the Baronessa Giuliana Ricasoli Firidolfi, for the hospitality which she courteously gave him in the Ricasoli castle of Brolio, and for the readiness with which she placed the family Archives at his disposal. His thanks are also due to the Barone Ricasoli Firidolfi for permitting him to consult the same Archives, and also the *Carteggio Lambruschini* in the *Biblioteca Nazionale* at Florence. He is grateful to the Director of that library for the facilities granted to him in his researches, and to Mr. K. N. Bell, of Balliol College, Oxford, who read through his manuscript and made many valuable suggestions.

CONTENTS

Chapter		*Page*
	PREFACE	vii
I	FLORENCE AND BROLIO	I
II	THE EARTHLY PARADISE	17
III	THE PURITAN OF BROLIO	54
IV	'SONGS ABOUT FREEING ITALY'	86
V	DEMOCRACY AND REACTION	125
VI	YEARS OF PREPARATION	164
VII	RICASOLI AND TUSCANY	196
VIII	THE DICTATOR	227
IX	THE PLEBISCITE	266
	EPILOGUE	291
	SELECTED BIBLIOGRAPHY	296
	INDEX	309

ILLUSTRATIONS

BETTINO, COUNT RICASOLI   *Frontispiece*

' THE EARTHLY PARADISE ' AT PLAY   *Facing page* 18

THE CASTLE OF BROLIO   *Facing page* 60

THE ROSE-WATER REVOLUTION   *Facing page* 200

RICASOLI
AND THE RISORGIMENTO
IN TUSCANY

CHAPTER I

IN the ancient *Centre* of Florence, which a bare half century
ago remained a mediæval labyrinth of narrow streets and
dark courtyards, littered with the odds and ends of petty
commerce, and glorified, here and there, by some mediæval
craftsman's masterpiece (now resting in the cold order of
a museum, its preordained destination) a pompous arch
looks down on a bronze Piedmontese horseman, the first
king of Italy, who rides on a great pedestal where the
hucksters of the old market used to chatter beneath their
awnings. Across the arch runs an inscription in heavy
capitals, proclaiming that this ancient centre of the city
has been restored to ' new life ' after centuries of squalour.
The arch, the inscription, the square itself, with its characterless architecture, its clean pleasant cafés, its threatening
bandstand, typify the age which was born from the labours
of nationalist revolution. Florence had brought to Italy
the gift of her priceless beauty; never doubting, in the
exaltation of her devotion, that a new and richer life would
spring from the old stem. In the past she had created so
much beauty, and power was stirring in her again; Italy
would be her inspiration. Perhaps she was too impatient,
too arrogant, and then, too easily disillusioned. The age
of struggle passed suddenly into an age of politics; politics
that seemed as base and dull as the struggle had been
glorious and romantic. Italy, which had been an ideal,
half hid herself in a machine, a thing of taxes, roads,
standardised education, clerks and administrators. It was
said in Florence that too many of these administrators
were Piedmontese, and that the Piedmontese were dull,
unimaginative, not at all like Tuscans, almost like Germans.
. . . Whispered jealousies grew in a few months to open
rivalries. Then the capital came to Florence. For a time
she was the centre of the state, a modern state, and very
large. Uneasily, half conscious of some virtue that was

I

passing from her, the old city proclaimed her new greatness. She proclaimed it in bronze and stone, hoping that the free genius of her artists would rise again to illustrate worthily her latest struggle for freedom. Before her old churches, in the new piazzas to which she denied native Tuscan names, she raised monuments to her own leaders and to the heroes of Italy whom she had made her own. Must the age be judged by the failures of its artists? They failed to lighten their marble with the faith and enthusiasm of the statesmen. Before the church of San Spirito, Ridolfi, a melancholy figure in a long coat, seems only to brood over the reckless little boys who play beneath him and run to a peddling confectioner with the pennies that should have been locked away in a savings bank; in the Piazza dell' Indipendenza, another liberal leader, Peruzzi, is portrayed in low-relief, making speeches to groups of respectful but uninterested citizens. Were the statesmen really like this? And were the soldiers of Garibaldi like that staring figure in the Piazza Mentana, who supports his dying comrade while he fires into the windows of the National Fascist Party? Not very far away rises the great Palace of the Republic, and before it Donatello has immortalised in the figure of Judith the defiance and victory of his city. There Florence appears serene, in harmony with herself, secure of a greatness which the artists of the *Risorgimento*, with all their straining, could never capture.

It was, nevertheless, the spirit of a great past, as well as the dream of a splendid future, which moved the man who in the last great crisis of Florentine history disciplined the hesitations and misgivings of the city, and nerved her with the resolution to defy Europe and give herself to Italy. No one could deny to a Ricasoli the right to speak with authority for his country. The family[1] was the most ancient of all the ancient houses which survived in Tuscany; genealogists confessed themselves unable to trace

[1] L. Passerini, *Famiglia Ricasoli*, and G. Tiribilli, *Famiglie Celebri Toscane*. Repetti, *Dizionario della Toscana* (Brolio, Trappola, Meleto, etc.).

its origin,[1] but it emerged in the eleventh century already rich, powerful, and long established in the mastery of a great domain. It had held sway in the Mugello, but its position for eight centuries was based on its control of the Chianti. The family split into three branches, one of which kept its original name of Firidolfi (the name traces back to a Ridolfo, who flourished early in the eleventh century, and whose descendants are described in Latin documents as *de filiis Rodulfi*); while the other two came to be called, after one of the family castles, Ricasoli. Of the Ricasoli, one branch entrenched its power in the castle of Meleto, the other in the neighbouring castle of Brolio, half way between Siena and the Arno. With the smaller castles and watch towers which they held through the hills of the Chianti, the Ricasoli dominated that most important tract of country on the frontiers of Florence and Siena. At the beginning of the thirteenth century they were still Ghibelline lords, allied with Siena against the Guelf city; but they changed sides just in time to share the discomfiture of Montaperti, and for the rest of the history of the Florentine Republic they served it constantly in war and peace—most frequently and most signally in war. The house was at first hostile to the rising power of the Medici, but an astute piece of policy on Cosimo's part won over the lord of Brolio, who a little time before had been fleeing for his life to the southern stronghold, and from that time the Ricasoli were among the staunchest and most valuable supporters of the Medici. Those same walls which ring the castle to-day withstood for three weeks in 1478 the assaults of the armies of Naples and of Rome, while in Florence the power of the Medici seemed likely to fall before conspiracy. The Ricasoli kept faith in days of adversity, and when the Republic had been subdued for the last time, and the Medici held their power unchallenged, they were treated as no ordinary subjects.[2] Opportunities for men of the sword became less frequent;

[1] Passerini, *q.v.* [2] *e.g.* in 1646 their dependents were exempted from a law forbidding the carrying of arms.

one baron was a gentleman of the chamber to Cosimo III ;
another satisfied his military ambition with the captaincy
of the guard of the lancers. But till 1777 the Masters of
Brolio kept the power of feudal lords in their own domain,
making and executing laws like princes in their little
state. They were the only barons in Tuscany. Other titles
had been conferred upon them; but, says the historian
of the family, they were ' more satisfied with the pride
of being the sole barons of Tuscany than Counts Palatine,
equal in condition to many houses of most vulgar origin'.[1]
Most of the noble families of Florence could trace their
greatness to the counting-house, but the Ricasoli had
once been conquerors.

Their pride of race was never so strong as in the last
baron of the direct line of the branch of Brolio, who, born
into an age of mass movements, adopted the ideas of
Liberty and Nationalism, strange for one who expressed
regret that he had not been born in the thirteenth century.
An opponent wrote of him: ' His is a feudal spirit which
survives by anachronism in the body of a modern, the last
product of a race of castle-lords. His true element . . . is
his castle of Brolio, where he surrounds himself with
homage, with liege service, with memories of the past,
with contradictions to the present—this head of a liberal
party, this instrument of a national revolution'. [2] The
fortunes of his life brought him into contact with princes
and emperors; conscious of his ancestry, he felt himself
at least their equal. If his rigid judgment condemned their
conduct, he refused to do them honour, for, as he said of
himself, ' he had never been obsequious to any individual
unless he embodied in himself a great Principle of social
salvation'.[3] In 1859, when the diplomatists of the French
Emperor were straining every nerve to impose on his
country a settlement which all his pride rejected, he said
to one who took leave of him to go to Paris: ' Go and say

[1] *Passerini*, 195.   [2] An anonymous journalist, quoted A. Valle, *Studi Storici*, Vol. XXI, p. 292.   [3] Autograph note to Dall' Ongaro, *Ricasoli*, p. 26. (See bibliography.)

to those gentlemen that I have twelve centuries of existence;
I am the last of my stock, and will give the last drop of
my blood to maintain the integrity of my political programme'.[1]

His contemporaries always thought of him as the ' iron
baron ' of Brolio; they were never able to think seriously
of the man without summoning some vision of his castle.
The road from Siena to Brolio leads across the Arbia, once
colorata in rosso, but 'more rich in fame than in water';
from the valley it rises sharply towards a high rough range
which divides the hills of Chianti from the valley of the
Arno. On a hill broken off from the range, lower than it,
but six hundred metres high, a square of grey stone walls
encloses the high palace of red brick which symbolises
the restored wealth and power of the family. From the
ramparts, and from the grey fourteenth-century keep, one
looks down on the hills which spread out like a vast undu-
lating plain, till they rise far to the south in the great mass
of Monte Amiata.[2] Fourteen miles away can be seen the
towers of Siena, and many times the watchers on the walls
have marked the approach of the armies which issued
from the gates of the hostile city to assail the feudal champions of Florence. The castle keeps something of the spirit
of the middle ages. It speaks, like all its kind, of old forays
and sieges and ambitions. But the voices of the long past
are faint; the spirit which rules at Brolio is the spirit of
the baron who died there forty-six years ago. And this
is in despite of his own will. He tried to restore the castle
in mediæval fashion, but the architect built the central
palace in a ' mixed ' style which ingenuously betrays the
period. On the walls of the great stairway are painted in
fresco the portraits of generations of the Ricasoli, but the
artists were of the nineteenth century, summoned to
Brolio to do the will of the reigning baron. In the hall is
a collection of ancient armour and weapons, worn, not
only by those for whom they were made, but by their

[1] *Dall' Ongaro*, p. 50. [2] *Lettere e Documenti*, VII, 190. Ricasoli describes
this wonderful view.

nineteenth-century descendant, who tried his strength
against theirs, girding himself in their ponderous armour,
that he might the better recapture their spirit.[1] It was
this same baron who made in the crypt of the little chapel,
where for years he heard daily mass, a tomb for his family;
but the simple name which marks his own resting-place
records the greatest of his house. The more he strove to
make the past live around him, the more he made the castle
a monument to himself, even to his own worship of a past
which he could not re-create.

Bettino Ricasoli was born on the ninth of March, 1809.[2]
Within the next five years were born his two younger
brothers, Gaetano and Vincenzo; the father died when
Bettino was seven years old, and the mother at once sent
the two elder boys to a religious school at Prato.[3] Four
years later the three brothers were sent to a similar school,
of good reputation in Florence—the *College of the Angels*,
where Bettino remained from 1820 till 1824. At school
he had from the very beginning taken his own line and
gone his own way. He declared his independence in his
first year at Prato, when he was seven years old, and his
master ordered him to express repentence for some misdeed
by making with his tongue the sign of the cross on the
floor. ' This is a thing for beasts', the small boy answered,
' I shall never do it'. He did more or less what he liked.
His teachers learnt not to bother him with memory work,
and he neglected classical exercises. He kept very much
to himself, and did not share even in the sports of the
other boys. They on their part let him alone, though the
tradition of Florentine schools was in favour of persecuting
anyone who showed himself a little strange.[4] He lived
his own life, not because he disliked the others, but
simply because he loved solitude ; there were things

[1] Dall' Ongaro, p. 13, told this story, and Ricasoli wrote in the margin,
Verissimo. [2] His baptismal names were Bettino, Maria, Giuseppe, Luigi,
Gaetano, Gaspero. [3] For Ricasoli's childhood see Gotti, *Ricasoli*; Ch.
I. Gotti collected some information from Ricasoli's contemporaries,
especially Vincenzo Ricasoli, whose letter to him is in *Brolio MSS.*,
Cassetta A.C. (1886). [4] Tabarrini, *Vite* (Life of Capoquadri).

in his own mind which he wished to examine, and he developed early the habit of writing down in little note-books summaries of what he read and accounts of what he thought.

He was happier when he was taken away from school and allowed to study chemistry, physics, entomology, botany, and similar subjects, under the supervision of professors. Drawing pleased him, but he turned it to utilitarian purposes; he had a tutor for music, but did not care for it; he consented to fence and to play *pallone* (his bats remain to this day at Brolio), but he professed contempt for frivolous relaxation and for all artistic pur-suits which had no serious end. In 1827, when he was sent to improve his mind by a journey through Italy and as far as Vienna, he jotted down in a little diary an account of expenses, including details like tips, the price of a cup of coffee, the charges of a porter.[1] For once an official report on a young man was not far from the truth, when in May of 1829 the department concerned decided to grant Ricasoli the rights of his majority some ten months before he came of age, on the grounds that he was ' wise, well-behaved, respectful, devoted to study, aloof from idleness and pleasure, conscious of the disordered state of his family affairs'.[2]

It had been decided in family council that Bettino must take charge of the Ricasoli estates. His father had been a good spender and a bad administrator; his mother had been unable to shoulder the burden of management. Everything had been left to the *fattori*, or managers, and a Tuscan proverb records the prevalent opinion on the honesty of these persons in no complimentary terms. ' The economic fortunes of the estate', said Ricasoli many years later, ' were altogether in the hands of Provi-dence'.[3] A new power, less benevolent to the servants of the Ricasoli, now appeared, insisting on rigid economies. This was only half the battle, which was fought throughout long years. The same man who refused respect to a prince,

[1] *Brolio MSS.*, A. 2. [2] *L. & D.*, I, 1–2. [3] *L. & D.*, I, 493.

unless the prince stood for a ' principle of social salvation',
and who throughout his life disliked court dress, decora-
tions, and empty ceremonies,[1] could not brook the thought
of being the possessor of a great title unless the title carried
with it great power. Florence was full of nobles who had
sunk from wealth and dignity to the most distressing
poverty; Giusti[2] maliciously pictures them carrying away
in their pockets remnants from some godsend of a dinner,
and forming a queue outside the house of a vulgar money-
lender who had offered his elderly ugly daughter, with a
handsome dowry, to the most noble bidder on the marriage
market. . . . Many of the nobles who retained their
inherited wealth had chosen the road which would destroy
their greatness, like the three elder brothers of the Ridolfi
family, who resolved together to ' give themselves a good
time . . . to enjoy the world each in his own way, and to
hope that their life would not last longer than their inherited
wealth'.[3] Others were following the same path unconsciously, giving over their estates to the *fattori* through
mere inefficiency, and reluctance to leave the chatter of
the stuffy reception rooms of Florence for the isolation
and dullness of their country houses. Ricasoli looked with
disdain on such frivolity, and when he was just twenty-
two he gave signs of a trait that remained constant with
him, the passion of moulding other people to his own
serious standard of duty. ' I weep', he wrote to his
favourite brother,[4] ' to see the degradation of this my
country, and am almost ashamed of being born into it;
it grieves me to see the young men of the best families
involved in vice '. He considered that the decadence of
the youthful nobles of Florence sprang in part from the
decay of ancestral fortunes, in part from the ignorance in
which they had been brought up. He himself had chosen
professors as his only boon companions, and expressed
the opinion that Natural Science was ' the thermometer

[1] See for example *Lettere Politiche* (Zanichelli), Nos. XXIV and XXXI
and autograph note to Dall' Ongaro, p. 44.   [2] Giusti, *Poesie, Il Ballo,*
and *La Scritta.*   [3] L. Ridolfi, *Cosimo Ridolfi,* p. 10.   [4] *L. & D.,* I, 3.

of human civilisation'. But he had a plan for saving these young nobles who seemed lost (many of them may have been his schoolfellows). In his own house he had established a museum of natural history, ' collections of minerals, shells, fossilised bones, skeletons, marine products, insects, plants, geology, and finally a chemical laboratory'. He had taken counsel with his old tutor, Professor Targioni, and the two had resolved to open a school in the museum for adolescents of good family. As guardian of his brothers, he had taken their education seriously, and sent them off for three years' travel in Europe; the youngest of the three, Vincenzo, was showing himself a keen student of botany, and the elder brother encouraged him with the dazzling project of the chair of Botany at Pisa University. So many of his aspirations, at this time, seemed professorial!

Yet, as soon as he had come of age, he had married. This was perhaps part of the plan for the restoration of the family power, for his bride, Anna Bonaccorsi, brought him a dowry which was considered large for the times.[1] In the later history of agricultural and human experiment at Brolio the Baroness Anna had a part to play, but when she married she was not yet nineteen, and Bettino interpreted his relation to her, as to everyone else, in terms of duty; she was another soul to educate. In 1831 she bore him a daughter, Elisabetta; they had other children, but none of them survived, and it was upon Elisabetta that his passion for education concentrated itself for many years. ' I am consecrated to this task', he told his brother later; ' I am consecrated to it for duty, for affection, for hope; perhaps it is the one way in which I shall be able to help my country in some very small degree, giving to it a woman of noble character'.[2] He looked on the position of father as a profession. When, years later, his country called for his services in another field, he felt a baffled impatience as if his real work were being interrupted;

[1] L. Grottanelli, *Il barone B.R. . . . . da ricordi personali*, in *Rassegna Nazionale*, Oct. 1, 1905, pp. 396–425. [2] *L. & D.*, I, 63.

in 1847 he professed himself ready to spare it a little time, but not too much, for he had more important duties. 'I am Father and Educator of my daughter'. [1] He kept notebooks in which he jotted down precepts on the theory and practice of education; notions of the right method to teach children geography, grammar, ideas on Antidiluvian Fauna, and simple explanations of the planets and the terrestial system, all by question and answer.[2] He prepared with his own hand lessons on mood and tense and the cases of nouns and adjectives, taking care to supplement the exercise of memory with material for reflection and comparison, and adding a flavour of moral training 'through procuring that the propositions for grammatical analysis should be also a successive judgment on good and bad'. A lesson on the possessive pronoun aimed at teaching the little girl the meaning of *my* country, and a lesson on nouns explained the meaning of Sobriety, Abstinence, Frugality, and Temperance. He took as his guide a maxim which he jotted down from Montesquieu: 'Imperfection in education comes to the same as not educating at all'. His own precept was that education had three essential parts, physical, religious or moral, intellectual; a good education would achieve the greatest possible harmony in the three branches.[3] The task, he wrote, was slow and difficult, but success brought endless compensation to the father and teacher.

He decided that the harmony he sought could not be achieved while he was dividing his time between Brolio and Florence, and that the air and influences of Florence ran counter to his dreams for the little girl. His wife showed some reluctance when he first broached his plan for retiring altogether to Brolio; in the end she was persuaded and threw herself into the scheme; but more than half a century later a friend of Ricasoli and of his family

[1] *Brolio MSS.*, O. 2. To Ridolfi. He told the Grand-Duke, when he was offered the position of *gonfaloniere* of Florence, that he would dedicate to his fellow-citizens 'any remnant of time' not absolutely necessary to the education of his daughter, *ibid*. [2] *Brolio MSS.*, B. 8. *Ibid*. C. 49. [3] *Ibid*. B. 7.

thought it necessary to confute curious rumours which pictured the baron as a sort of mediæval ogre who had dragged his gentle lady to imprisonment in his mountain fastness.[1]

'Our retirement into the country', he wrote after the death of his wife, 'was the result of a preconceived design. In that seclusion the action of the mother, and I shall say the action of the parents, fulfilled itself without disturbance; physical development was more than an appearance, the infiltrations of moral and religious education occurred as it were of their own accord, thanks to example and the opportunities of the time'.[2]

The family moved to Brolio in 1838.

Other influences had contributed to this decision. Four years previously his success as a serious agriculturalist had been recognised in the inevitable manner at Florence, by his election to the Academy of the *Georgofili*. He was already engaged on the researches and experiments[3] which made the wine of Brolio unequalled among the vintages of the most famous wine district of Tuscany. He regarded his achievement with complacency, and when in 1847, as a good free-trader, he presented Cobden with a dozen bottles of Brolio '41 (Cobden, however, used to mix water with his champagne!), he declared that he would not have let them go for any King upon the earth.[4] But the problem was not merely one of agricultural technique, and from some notes which Ricasoli jotted down from 1833 till 1835 in one of his little books,[5] it is apparent that he was beginning to see it, as in the end he saw everything, as a problem of education. Tuscan agriculture, he told himself, was in a state of anarchy. The peasant, on whom all depended, was left to himself to struggle with his fear of poverty; as a result he sought first and foremost for the greatest immediate return from his farm, exhausting its power with his primitive assaults upon its productiveness. Little could be done while the land-owners looked upon

[1] G. Finali, *La vita politica dei contemporanei Italiani*, Ch. I. Cf. R. Lambruschini, *Elogi e Biografie*, p. 202. [2] *L. & D.*, II, 203. [3] *e.g.* Notes on Viticulture in *Brolio MSS.*, C. 1, 54. Ricasoli perfected Brolio wine through his studies of Bourgogne and Bordeaux wines. [4] *L. & D.*, I, 191. [5] *Brolio MSS.*, C. 1., 54.

the country as a few days' solace from the heat of the city
and the tedium of society, instead of a battlefield where
the earth was conquered and character tested. But he
warned himself to be cautious. ' Take good care not to
begin lightly and without pondering an agrarian enterprise and reform of any kind '. ' It is easier perhaps to
organise the government of a nation than a perfect rural
economy '. [1]

Ricasoli did not exaggerate the complexity of the task
which faced a progressive Tuscan landowner. The soil
of Tuscany was not in the main fertile; the lack of a
hydraulic system had for centuries closed the plains of the
Val di Chiana[2] and the Maremma to agriculture, and
confined it to the hills where every burst of rain threatened
to wash away the scanty priceless layer of soil. Even to
this day, on the estate of Brolio, the surface rock has
literally to be lifted away before it is possible to plant a
new vineyard. The land was greedy of capital, and
demanded at the same time the endless, day-to-day attention of patient labour attending to the needs of small areas.
To meet these needs had arisen the co-operative system
known as *mezzadria*, which became the most permanent
feature of Tuscan history, lying at the base of life in every
changing system of government. The legal rights to the
soil belonged to a proprietor, who drained it, prepared it
for cultivation, supplied it with houses and farm buildings,
furnished implements, manures, and vessels for wine
and oil; supplied as a rule half the seed, shared
with the *colono* the expenses of cultivation, and paid the
taxes. The *colono* gave his own labour, supplied the implements of minor importance, and shared a few of the capital
expenses; his tenure was customary, and the verbal
understanding between him and the proprietor recognised
the latter's right to dismiss him at the end of any year.
In practice a good peasant enjoyed almost complete
security, for the ordinary proprietor could devise no other

---

[1] *Brolio MSS.*, *C.* I., 54. [2] By Ricasoli's time the conquest of the Val di
Chiana was complete. For the Maremma see Chapter II.

means of using the land, and had no inducement to make capricious changes among the peasantry on whom he depended for the half share of the produce that was his right. Thus the same families remained in the same solid stone houses (Capponi asserted that they were the best lodged peasantry in Europe) from generation to generation. Their needs were simple. They lived chiefly on bread, beans, oil, and wine; meat was the rarest luxury. Thus it was that a holding (*podere*), whose normal size was ten hectares, might support a family of ten or fifteen persons.

The two main marks of the system were first, as between proprietor and family, the co-operation of capital and labour in a particularly harmonious and simple manner; and secondly, the stress laid on the family as the economic unit in the cultivation of the land. The link between the proprietor and the family was the *fattore*, who acted as the lieutenant, and too often as the captain of management. Neither the *fattore* nor the proprietor had any official relations with the adult worker as such, but only with the *capo di casa*, or *capoccio*, who represented the family in its contractual relationship, and exercised within it a modified *patria potestas*. The whole family—from the little boys and girls sent into the vineyards to drive away birds, or into the woods to mind the goats and swine, to the old withered grandmothers, who would not be happy unless they spent some hours of the day picking olives or gathering prunings and twigs to crackle under the pot—shared in

On the system of *Mezzadria*, which is here only sketched, see Capponi, *Cinque Letture*. Also *Atti dell' Accademia Reale dei Georgofili*, especially Vol. 29, p. 92 *et seq.* (Ridolfi) ; Vol. 12 (Capei) ; and *Nuova Serie*, Vol. 1, 355 *et seq.*, 543 *et seq.*, 613 *et seq.* (Ridolfi and Poggi) ; Vol. 2, 93 *et seq.*, 210 *et seq.*, and 475 *et seq.* (Rossini, Salvagnoli, and Digny). Also *Giornale Agrario*, Vol. 7, 293 *et seq.* (Gasparin) ; R. Lambruschini, *Lettera al Marchese Ridolfi* (Firenze, Cellini, 1857). G. Pelli Fabbroni, *Del Sistema agrario di colonia parziaria* (with bibliography), Firenze, Tip. Galileiana, 1855. For more recent descriptions of the system see bibliography in Francesco Serragli, *La Mezzeria e i vari sistemi della colonia parziaria in Italia* (Hoepli, 1895), and M. A. Martini, *La Mezzadria Toscana nel momento presente* (Firenze, Libreria Editrice Fiorentina, 1910).

the labours of the holding. Within the house the *massaia*,
usually the wife of the family's head, ruled domestic life
and controlled the women.

The advantages which led to the growth of the system,
and which explain its persistence to the present day, lay
in the inducement which it offered to industry and to
contented labour. 'The cultivator', said Capponi,[1] 'is
always on the spot, always careful; his constant thought is,
" This field is my own". He works for his own advantage,
not as a mercenary or as a slave or as a machine . . . he
gathers together the manure that has fallen on the roads,
that it may contribute to his dunghill'. Giusti[2] said that
the landowner who employed day-labour might for a
time appear a gainer; but before long he would find paths
across his vineyards, and his terraces neglected; the
labourer, if his spade struck the root of a vine, would
break it, for it was not his own, but the *mezzaiuolo* would
carefully avoid it. Every writer who dealt with this favourite
topic congratulated himself that, so long as the system
endured, Tuscany need never fear communism. In answer
to those who bewailed the slowness of agricultural development, they pointed to the happy human results of the
system. Capponi urged its critics to study landlordism and
poverty in England, and suggested that the principle of
mezzadria might provide a solution of the industrial
problem.

Yet even this doughty champion of co-operation
admitted that all was not well in the Tuscan agricultural
economy. 'The erroneous self-sufficing system pervades
everything, even to the extent that a single field should
produce everything, that one man should do everything'.[3]
Compared with manufacture, the land yielded a poor
return to capital; often the proprietor could have bought
a farm many times over with the money he had sunk in
it; very often he failed to receive that half of the produce
which was his right. Towards the middle of the century

[1] Lecture 5.   [2] Quoted M. A. Martini, *Mezzadria*, p. 15.   [3] *Cinque
Letture*, p. 40.

one of the most famous of Tuscan agriculturalists raised a ' cry of alarm'. From eight of his best farms, declared Ridolfi, he had received in recent years only one tenth of the produce, the rest being necessary for the livelihood of his peasants; the peasants were usually in debt to the proprietor; the system was hostile to the division of labour, hostile to scientific improvements, incapable of supporting any sudden crisis.[1] The good sense of thoughtful proprietors saved them from panic. They reflected that the adverse conditions then affecting agriculture would operate equally under other systems, and that centralisation of responsibility would be the ruin of the majority of landowners, who knew nothing whatever of their own business. Ridolfi had, nevertheless, drawn attention to an important fact: the system was, from its very nature, unadaptable, conservative, hard to move.

Nothing could be done unless an assault were made against the prejudices of the peasants. They had a shrewd commonsense of their own; they knew every inch of their farms, and handed down from generation to generation, in their ancestral proverbs, a ' manual of practical wisdom'[2] for all occasions, seasons, crafts, relationships. Throughout the proverbs there breathes a cautious scepticism, a distrust of the passions, the allurements, the indiscretions which might destroy a hardly-won security. ' If debts were good, everyone would lend something '—a score of similar proverbs caution the imprudent against the secular scourge of peasants. ' There's no need of a hammer to open a lawyer's door'. ' Litigation is the lawyer's harvest'. Lawyers were the snare of the grown man, women of the youth; a mother could warn her son in a hundred rhymed adages which defy translation that ' a beautiful head is often without brains', that ' he who once marries badly

[1] *Atti* of the *Georgofili*, XXIX, 392. In these years (the 'fifties) the Tuscan vines were suffering from a fungus called the *crittogama*. For replies to Ridolfi, who urged a ' suspension ' of *mezzadria*, see *Atti*, Nuova Serie, I and II, and especially a letter of Capponi's, *Lettere III*, 156 *et seq.*

[2] Giuseppe Giusti, *Proverbi Toscani*. Others are collected by Giuseppe Stefanini (*Il Clima Toscano*) in *Monti e paesagii della Toscana*.

grieves it for all his life', that ' he who has a bad wife has hell on earth'. The father might in moments of exasperation choose other ancient proverbs on the wiles of women.

' Donna si lagna, donna si duole,
Donna, s'ammala, quando la vuole'.

But with all this cynicism there went a sober appreciation of family life, of charity, of neighbourliness. ' Better are scraps of bread with love, than fat chickens with grief'. ' The smoke of my house is worth more than the smoke of others'. 'Alms make nobody poor'. ' Charity is a good act, even to the devil'. No virtue, it is true, is more insisted on than parsimony, which in youth lays up a store for a secure old age; but no vice is hated more than avarice, the ' queen of vices', through which men make their money first, and their conscience afterwards.

Many of the Tuscan proverbs, like those of all peoples, contradict each other. One strain, however, runs through the most diverse—the strain of conservatism. ' He who leaves the old road for the new, knows what he leaves, not what he finds'. [1] Ricasoli was right in judging that the management of an estate of *contadini* was a task as difficult and intricate as the government of a nation. Since he admired the Tuscan peasant,[2] and since he was determined to assail the peasant's conservatism, he found himself once again launched on a work of education.

' My friend', he wrote to a sympathiser in Florence: ' Tuscan agriculture needs head and heart; to me it seems an apostolate. . . . The Tuscan proprietor is born a missionary'.[3]

[1] Chi lascia la via vecchia per la nuova
Sa quel che lascia, e non quel che trova.
[2] See Chapter III. [3] *L. & D.*, I, 22. To Vieusseux.

CHAPTER II

THE EARTHLY PARADISE

In 1824, the same year in which the good Prince Leopold succeeded to the throne of Tuscany, there came to Florence one of the most notable figures in the literary world of the time, exiled from his city of Piacenza by the comparatively mild government of Napoleon's widow, Marie Louise of Austria. The exile, Pietro Giordani, knew that, since the Carbonaro revolutions of four years ago, Tuscany had been the asylum for liberals who had compromised themselves with the governments of Naples, of Lombardy, or of Piedmont; but he was little prepared for the welcome which awaited him in Florence. He found the company so good that he could snatch no time for study and writing; he was besieged with invitations to join this society or that; the government itself appeared to him ' adorable', ' sacred'. ' One could never end speaking its praises'. The head of the police was more interested in his literary than his political opinions, the high officials of public security hovered round the door of their chief hoping to be introduced to a writer famous throughout Italy; nobody seemed able to grasp the fact that he was an exile. And if the government was good, reflected Giordani, good also, nay, excellent, was the country. It pleased his fancy to write to his friends from ' The Earthly Paradise', and the name which he then gave Tuscany became famous.[1] It was not till a generation had passed that one of the Tuscan liberals who had welcomed Giordani reflected that the Earthly Paradise had neither the Tree of Knowledge nor the Tree of Life.[2]

Few of the dynasties that ruled in Europe had such claims to the gratitude and affection of their subjects as the Austro-Lorraine dynasty of Tuscany could advance. In the age of Enlightened Despots, the Grand-Duke, Pietro

[1] P. Giordani, *Epistolario*, Vol. V, 275, 284, 294, 304, 311, 355, 360.
[2] G. Capponi, *Scritti editi ed inediti*, II, 106.

Leopold, had been the most enlightened and the most successful. His son, Ferdinand III, was loyal to the tradition of his house; and if, after the wars of the Republic and of Napoleon, he was unaware that a new spirit was abroad in Europe, he was at least sincere in his appreciation of the most liberal maxims that had inspired the most liberal governments in the eighteenth century. Napoleon, after turning him out of Tuscany, had established him as master in the little principality of Salzburg, but he disliked the climate, grumbled because he could never hear Italian, and came back joyfully to Tuscany in 1814. His subjects were equally glad to see again their rightful prince, and when a marquis of French leanings showed his disdain by appearing ' clothed in a shameless fashion, with long red and white trousers, and a green coat, and a knotted walking stick', and by ' holding seditious discourses with a person unknown', the crowd promptly burnt his carriage and hunted the marquis home to dress himself in a more fitting manner. As for Ferdinand, he was determined that the rancours of the past twenty years should be forgotten for ever. To one who sought to please him by boasting that he had never served Napoleon, he replied, ' You were wrong; I have served him; you too could have done so'. His council of state, after the brief episode of Murat's occupation of Florence, reported that it would be politic and magnanimous to ' raise a hand of clemency ' for any who in those days had misjudged the future and compromised themselves in one way or another. He, himself, when presented with a list of suspected Jacobins, answered simply: ' They are my subjects, they are my children'.[1] Much of the legal and administrative system which had been introduced by the French was swept away by the restored government, but in this work of demolition the action of the prince and his advisers was less reactionary than the temper of the people,[2] and probably none of the faithful subjects of Tuscany were so discon-

[1] Marcotti, *Cronache Segrete della Polizia Toscana*, pp. 11, 13, 16.
[2] Francesco Forti, *Istituzioni Civili*, Lib. I, Section 5.

'THE EARTHLY PARADISE' AT PLAY

From a picture by Giovanni Signorini

Photo Alinari

tented as the servants of the Palace, where a new regime of economy imposed penalties for the waste of light, and initiated drastic reforms in the royal kitchens.

Ferdinand's son, Leopold, inherited in 1824 from his father a kingdom that appeared fabulously prosperous, a yearly surplus of three million lire,[1] and advisers of experience, culture, and tolerance. Before he had been long on the throne his subjects understood that they had a sovereign of the same stamp as Ferdinand, with a little less dignity, a little more earnestness, and the same benevolent intentions. In polite language he came to be known as ' the excellent prince '; on ordinary occasions he was called ' Daddy'. He had little of the appearance of royalty; he kept his head bent, his lower lip protruded; he was short-sighted and seemed always to be sleepy. He lisped, and his tailor (the same tailor who cut for the palace officials) never quite managed to get his measure. His servants never spoke of His Imperial and Royal Highness; to them he was always ' The Master'. And, at the Carnival, affectionate but irreverent subjects would recognise him beneath his mask and call out: ' Good night, Leopold, I know you! ' . . . or to the Grand-Duchess: ' How pretty you are! Isn't he happy! ' Leopold merely laughed at the sallies. He was content with the good-humoured affection which his subjects gave him, and his chief ambition in life was to promote their happiness.[2]

He began his reign by a notable reduction of taxes, though Tuscany's fiscal burdens were comparatively light. He encouraged his government to eat up the surplus and turn it into a deficit in the attempt to drain the Maremma,[3] a problem which he himself studied and of which he could

[1] Zobi, *Memorie Economico-Politiche*, Vol. I, p. 166. [2] On Leopold II see Montazio, *L'Ultimo Granduca ;* Guerrazzi, *Ritratto Morale di Leopoldo II* (in *Scritti Politici*) (both hostile); Baldasseroni, Conti, F. Martini (*Confessioni e Ricordi.*) In the memoirs of the time there are many anecdotes and descriptions of him. [3] See Zobi, *Storia*, Vol. IV, 336–381, and Appendices 39, 40, 45. *Baldasseroni*, p. 72 *et seq.* By 1840 the Maremma had cost the government 15,954,529 lire, and the returns had been 414, 261. (Baldasseroni's Rendiconto of 1847).

speak with real competence.[1] Like George III of England, he experimented with the breeding of sheep, and like Louis XVI of France he was interested in mechanical contrivances. He had been a student, and published from his own private press a rich edition of Lorenzo the Magnificent's works in four volumes; later, he promoted the publication of a complete edition of Galileo. The most nationalist of the Florentine publishers appreciated him as a patron of science and literature,[2] and the most respectable of the degenerate school of Tuscan sculptors revered him as one who was in fact the father of his people.[3] He himself, as a youth, knew enough to be suspicious of Carlo Dolci as a painter, which perhaps was rather extraordinary at the time.[4] He sent to the booksellers for works which his government had forbidden in Tuscany, he was ready to patronise scientific congresses, he gave personal attention to the founding of a chair of agriculture at Pisa,[5] and later chose the professor, a liberal noble who would have been suspect in any other Italian state, as tutor for his son. In every calamity that overtook his people, whether it was a disastrous flood, or an earthquake, or the cholera, he expressed his sympathy by words, by his presence, and by undoing his purse strings. For the first twenty-five years of his reign he was loved; for the last ten he was derided, and perhaps disliked. Later, the nationalists tried to stir up hate against him as the author of a savage plan to destroy the city which he had loved; and perhaps (for there is no limit to the achievements of propaganda) they actually convinced a large number of their fellow countrymen that Tuscany had been groaning for more than thirty years under the oppressions of a bloodthirsty tyrant. This was the greatest injury which an unkind fate could do to Leopold.

[1] *Lettere Scientifiche e Familiari di. F. Puccinotti* (Firenze, 1877), p. 404. [2] G. Barbera, *Memorie di un Editore*, p. 157. [3] G. Dupré, *Pensieri sull' Arte*, p. 203. [4] *Lettere inedite di Leopoldo Principe di Toscana* (Guido Biagi) Firenze, 1911. [5] *Carteggio Lambruschini*, Cassetta 14. Giorgini to Ridolfi, Jan. 5., 1841 (R. Biblioteca Nazionale, Florence).

Between the Grand-Duke and his ministers there was almost complete harmony of ideas. For thirty years following the restoration, the prosperity of Tuscany was in the hands of two veteran administrators, Neri Corsini, and Fossombroni. The spirit of the first appears in a minute which he wrote for the police in the year 1831, when Europe was full of plots and the Austrians were acting as police in the Duchies and the Legations: 'Better that these persons should be punished less than their deserts, than that a resolution should be taken which does not seem justifiable before the law'.[1] A Roman exile, one of the few men who kept a balanced and serene judgment in the years when passion and patriotism dominated Italy, considered him 'more liberal than many liberals by profession'.[2] It was, however, his colleague, Fossombroni, who most of all attracted the attention of his age and gave to the government its peculiar character. ' C'est un géant dans un entresol', Napoleon had said of him.[3] He was a scientist of reputation, and was elected to the Institute of France; he was able to make for himself the engineering plans necessary for public works in Tuscany, and he was a respectable master of the free trade economics of his day. He carried the ideas of self-regulating liberty from the sphere of economics into that of politics; he believed more or less in the free circulation of ideas (a species of merchandise), and it was his favourite maxim that the world got along by itself. *Il mondo va da se.* He hated people who ranted, and worried, and got unduly excited, and he paid a hack writer thirty *scudi* to belittle the tragedies of G. B. Niccolini.[4] The story is told that once, when a secretary spilled a bottle of ink over some important state papers which had just received his signature, and exclaimed in alarm—' What now? ' the minister answered unruffled—' Now, my dear fellow? Now let us go and have dinner'. ' But the business? '—' To-morrow, my dear

---

[1] Zobi, *Memorie*, I, 146. [2] E. Masi, *Memorie di F. Ranalli*, p. 25.
[3] G. Capponi, *Scritti editi ed inediti*, II, 422. [4] Gualterio, *Gli Ultimi Rivolgimenti*, I, 252. For Niccolini, *vide infra.*

fellow, to-morrow. Dinner will burn, but the state will not'. There are numerous anecdotes of the same tone which illustrate his sceptical, reasonable, even temperament, and show him as a sort of early nineteenth-century Giolitti, a master at managing men so long as they remained temperate and reasonable, but intuitively opposed to ideals, passions, and exaggerations whose advent would inevitably mark his own downfall. ' We are sceptics born',[1] declared the Tuscan satirist, and Fossombroni's success was due to his perfect understanding of the good-tempered, indifferent strain in the character of his countrymen. But sooner or later most people, and especially Italians, get tired of being governed by irony, and perhaps Fossombroni himself saw signs of an approaching age when government would have to change its methods.[2]

Any description of the government of Tuscany which stressed the machinery of the state rather than the characters of the men who guided it would miss the mark and fail to account for the prosperous and happy condition of the Grand-Duchy. The liberals themselves made it their chief complaint that ' government here rests upon men, rather than things',[3] and complained repeatedly of the lack of harmonious institutions. ' We live among the rubbish of all the ages', Ricasoli declared later. Technically, the Tuscan government was an absolute monarchy, for the dynasty held its title by European treaty and patents of the imperial house of Austria recognised by treaty.[4] There was no legislative body to share the sovereignty vested in the Grand-Duke; all legislation was by royal decree, which, according to legal theory, modified the fundamental basis of Roman law. The administrators were responsible to the prince alone; there were three departments of state (war

[1] G. Giusti, *Epistolario*, III, 50–51 (Dec. 7, 1847). [2] Zobi, *Storia*, Vol. IV, Appendix No. 47. [3] Capponi, *Lettere*, II, 290. Cf. *Scritti editi ed inediti*, II, 106. [4] See *Baldasseroni*, pp. 3–9, and Zobi, *Storia*, IV, Appendices 15, 16, 17, for the Treaties and Patents in Question. Also Vienna Settlement, Article 100. Political propagandists were wont to appeal to the immemorial rights of the Florentine Republic filched away by the Medici, but the argument had no legal validity.

and foreign affairs, finance, and internal affairs). The
three departmental heads, to whom later was added a
minister without portfolio, met together as a council of
state. Despite this institution, and despite a sort of primacy
given to one of the ministers as 'first director of the royal
secretariats', the great defect of the system was its lack of
unity. The various interests of the government were divided
in a haphazard manner among the various departments,
the council of state did not meet regularly to discuss and
decide questions of policy, and responsibility was scattered
among heads of sub-departments—*capi d'ufficii* and *soprain-
tedenti*—who had access to the sovereign and went along
the normal tenour of their ways without any reference to a
central controlling body.[1] Still more serious was the large
measure of independence enjoyed by the institution known
as the *Buon-Governo*, which performed all the functions of
' police ' in the widest sense of the word. The heads of
the administrative divisions of the state (governors, com-
missaries, vicars, *podestà*) were all members of the ' High
Police', under the authority of the President of the *Buon-
Governo*. It was their duty to report to the president all
that concerned the good government of the state and the
well-being of the citizens. For the efficient performance
of their duty they depended on the services of the ' Low
Police'—*sbirri*, organised in squadrons under a *capo-
squadra*, to whom were entrusted the rough day-to-day
executive work of public security, and *agenti*, persons of
rather more importance, who, through their chiefs, were
allowed direct access to the president. Neither was a
regular disciplined force, like the *gendarmerie* to which
the Tuscans had become accustomed under the French
regime. They had no uniform, and it was their duty to
perform all the tasks of the spy—in which they sometimes
received aid from high quarters.[2] The service was generally

[1] On the machinery of government see especially Zobi, *Storia, passim,*
and L. Galeotti, *Della Consulta di Stato.* [2] Del Cerro, *Misteri della Polizia,*
Ch. IV. In 1836 the expenditure on espionage in Florence was about 2,000
l ire a month. [3] *Marcotti*, p. 92.

regarded as a disgraceful one; it was the practice to draft
into the ranks of the *sbirri* customs-officers who had been
guilty of disreputable conduct, and the miserable level
of their pay was a constant temptation to small knaveries
and injustices. Their investigations extended to everything. They reported the gossip of the cafés, the chatter
of the theatres, the meetings held at private houses, the
number of letters which various persons received in a
day, and the postmark on them; the articles which appeared
in journals imported into the country, the books that were
to be seen on sale, the conduct of foreigners in the city.
Thus their weekly reports have afforded to various writers
material, not only for a history of opinion, but also for
pictures of the shadier side of Tuscan life. Nothing was
too trivial for their notice. It is, for example, not beneath
the dignity of the official archives to record that the minister
of a certain foreign state resigned his embassy because his
wife became 'too frank in her gallantries', and that the
lady, on being informed of his decisions, promptly fell
into convulsions, tore her hair, and then fainted; or that
a Leghorn lady of different class set herself at her window
resting on a pillow surrounded by flowers, and squirted
water on acquaintances who showed signs of passing on
unmoved by these seductions. Into signs of political
disaffection their inquiries were equally minute, and in a
list of over a hundred Florentines who showed signs of
treason when the Neapolitans entered in 1815 occur
items such as the following: 'Bianchi: although he
cannot read or write, he boasts of having correspondence
with all the cabinets of Europe'. 'Savi: praised the fine
appearance of the Neapolitan troops'. 'Picchi: the
morning the Neapolitans arrived in Florence, got up early,
which is not his custom'.[1]

   In the lack of newspapers, of a central representative
system, and of adequate municipal institutions (the restored
government had committed one of its most serious mistakes
by destroying the spontaneous character of local institu-

[1] *Marcotti*, p. 164.

tions which had existed under Pietro Leopold)[1] the reports of the police authorities were the only means through which the government could hope to get any idea of what its subjects were thinking. The defects of the system were all the more serious, in that the *Buon-Governo* had what was called ' the Economic Power ': that is, the right to inflict punishments on the persons whom the *sbirri* or the spies had reported to it, after a trial conducted by its own agents. The Economic Power enabled the High Police to deal, not only with offences defined by the law, but also with matters of mere suspicion or intent. Its penalties were arbitrary and uncertain, and the only guarantee which the defendant had was that his accuser, with whom he was never confronted, swore, on an image of Jesus Christ, to tell the truth. The penalties, it must be admitted, were as a rule mild, and there were certain classes of the disreputable which blessed the Economic Power, not only for its mildness, but also for its happy lack of publicity. Nevertheless, the system, when it dealt with matters of opinion or politics, was essentially vicious; and had it not been for the men who controlled it, could have been an engine of tyranny as hateful as that existing in any Italian state.

As it was, Tuscany only had one president of *Buon-Governo* who had the ambition to copy the methods of the Neapolitan Canosa, and when his intentions became plain, the government first revived a half-forgotten law circumscribing his powers, and shortly afterwards dismissed him.[2] The only death which can be traced to the police occurred through an unfortunate joke of Fossombroni's; the minister suggested that the police, who had intercepted letters between Neapolitan and Tuscan conspirators, should forward the letters to their destination with an official *visto* on the envelopes, and one of the recipients, whose head was full of the usual stories from Plutarch, worked himself into the agonies of despair, and, in the

---

[1] Zobi, *Storia*, IV, 39 *et seq*. *Galeotti*, Chapter IV cf. *L. & D.*, I, 140.
[2] The president Ciantelli. Zobi, *Memorie*, I, 166.

worst of bad taste, took his own life.[1] The leniency of the
Tuscan authorities was always a source of grievance to
the other Italian governments, and especially to the
Austrians. In 1821 the Austrians were spreading their
net in Lombardy and Venetia for all who had been concerned in the abortive Carbonaro conspiracy; and they
thought that if the Tuscan government would allow them
to examine the papers of Gino Capponi, they might find
material which would help their case against the Milanese
Gonfalonieri. They would, indeed, have discovered a
number of letters in which the two nobles discussed the
possibility of reforming Italy by 'enlightenment';
then, wearied of that hope, agreed that speculative ideas
came to nothing, that Italy's real need was self-sacrifice,
that reformers should think less of liberty and more of
independence, and that revolutions would only be made
by the masses.[2] Their request, however, met with a flat
refusal.[3]

Then the exiles began to flock in increasing numbers to
Tuscany, and Corsini replied blandly to the Austrian
protests that it would be easier to watch them if they were
all gathered together in one place.[4] Francis of Modena was
no more satisfied than were the Austrians; he kept his
own spies in Florence, and instructed his envoy at Vienna
to stir up the government against Tuscan 'indolence'
in this matter.[5] There was indeed quite a large flavour of
indolence in the system of Corsini and Fossombroni.
When there came to Florence the liberal, Borelli, who in
1820 had been president of the short-lived Neapolitan
parliament, he was at once informed that he must leave
the state within three days. He stayed, and was given
twenty-four hours. He lingered, and was ordered to be
gone within a month. Finally the minister Corsini took
matters into his own hands; he instructed the police that
an order should once again be served upon Borelli, but

[1] G. Stiavelli, *Le Società Secrete in Toscana*, p. 24.   [2] Capponi, *Lettere*,
I, 73, 105, 109.   [3] Capponi, *Scritti*, II, 32.   [4] Gualterio, *op. cit*. I, 250.
[5] Bianchi, *Storia della Diplomazia Europea in Italia*, II, 162.

that nothing more was to be done if he remained obstinate.
. . . The Neapolitan remained undisturbed to enjoy the
good company of Florence.[1]

Against such conduct all good friends of authority, and
Austria in particular, were furious. In 1820 Metternich
was 'beside himself' with anger at the obstinacy of the
Tuscan government. 'Enemies', he exclaimed, were easy
to deal with, but friends! . . .[2] More than ten years
later Leopold II was dubbed by the Austrian envoy
'traitor, infamous criminal, apostate, unworthy to belong
to the Imperial house and to bear the name of Archduke
of Austria'.[3] The dynastic position of Leopold made his
conduct all the more shocking. At the time of his accession
Austria had tried to impose upon him the control of her
family system, and had been defeated only by the dexterity
of Fossombroni;[4] from time to time she had her eye on
the possibility of securing the 'reversion' of Tuscany.
Metternich did not hesitate to warn Leopold against
conceding reforms which would force Austria to safeguard
her interests on Tuscan soil, and to remind him that, as
a simple tenant of an imperial patrimony, he had no right
to alienate the rights of complete authority and jurisdiction
which belonged to the house of Austria.[5] Any state which
stood outside the friendly league of repressive governments
threatened the Austrian power in Italy by encouraging the
aggressive ideas which in the end might beget force greater
than the force of the Empire. That Tuscany in particular
should protect these ideas was especially disquieting, for
Tuscany was the neighbour of Piedmont, a potential
enemy of military importance, and through Tuscany ran
the main roads that led across the Appenines to Rome and
the south. Whenever revolution stirred in Italy, Metternich
thought of Tuscany. In 1821 he sent the Austrian troops
across her territory to Naples, and the Tuscans, though
resentful, could not say him nay;[6] in 1831, while the

[1] Del Cerro, *op. cit.* p. 138. [2] Metternich, *Memoires*, III, 463. [3] *Bianchi*,
IV, 21. [4] Zobi, *Storia*, IV, 297–8. [5] *Bianchi*, V, 36 and 91. [6] See the
dispatches of the French envoy, De Maisonfort, in *Gualterio*, I, Appendix 13.

Austrian soldiers were stamping on the embers of rebellion
in the Duchies and the Legations, he offered Leopold
the security of armed intervention. The Grand-Duke replied
that he was strong in the love and fidelity of his subjects,[1]
and enrolled a citizen guard. Such conduct, on the part
of an Archduke of the house of Austria, was nothing less
than treason!

'Since we can't be lions, we must be foxes':[2] that
was the maxim of Leopold and Fossombroni. But ruses
and evasions cannot put off the clash of great issues for
ever. As an Austrian Archduke and an Italian prince
Leopold was overshadowed by a Fate which one day
might call him to choose between his family and his people,
marking him out as a victim in the irreconcilable struggle
between the old dynastic order fortified with all the sanctity of Treaties, and the uncompromising claims of revolutionary nationalism.

But for the first twenty years of his reign there were
only faint mutterings of that storm, and Tuscany was still
the earthly paradise. The very tranquillity and contentment
that reigned there roused the impatience of the liberals.
Leopold was to them the Tuscan Morpheus; the government was a thing 'of IF, of BUT, of PERHAPS—
more a parish-pump government than a Tuscan one, not
Italian, even in dreams . . .'[3] Capponi, who had been
saved from the Austrian police by the reasonable tolerance
of his government, found that tolerance at times intensely
provoking. 'We are somnambulists', he told Foscolo,
'and though the limbs are in motion, the mind sleeps'.[4]
To Confaloniere he lamented the very happiness of his
country, and its good nature; 'the people is tranquil and
rich, and has happy ease, and that accursed, poisonous
gift of tolerance'.[5] A Pisan professor and a romantic
novelist of Leghorn, both of whom were destined to win

---

[1] *Bianchi*, IV, 13–14.   [2] *Ibid*. III, 183. Prince Poniatowski to
Cardinal Lambruschini.   [3] Giusti, *Memorie*, p. 6.   [4] Capponi, *Lettere*, I,
105.   [5] *Ibid*. I, 109.

some prominence as revolutionaries, joined in complaining
that the government stifled the people with narcotics.[1]
But none of these Jeremiahs were themselves stifled, and
if the majority of the people was asleep, they were free at
least from those nightmare dreams which tortured men's
minds in Naples or the Romagna.

Life was easy in Tuscany. It was not only the ' truly
adorable ' government which attracted thither exiles from
all parts of Italy. A young Piedmontese came to Florence
to make his fortune as a publisher, and was able to rent
an excellent room for 15 *paoli* (about 7 shillings) a month;
he paid 56 *centesimi* for an ample dinner with two meat
courses, and 28 *centesimi* for a lighter supper.[2] La Farini
wrote to his father in 1837 that he had secured a well-
furnished bedroom and an excellent sitting-room for
50 lire a month, with 7 lire a month extra for the service
of a woman who attended to him for more than seven
hours a day; for a dinner of 6 courses he paid $3\frac{1}{2}$ *paoli*.
Translating the Tuscan figures into terms of Italian
currency, the final result is 106 lire a month for all living
expenses and a more than moderate amount of comfort.[3]
Wine cost four or five *crazie* for a large *fiasco;* in seasons
of great plenty it was almost given away. The Tuscan
cigar (Florence, it was said, was famous for three things:
the campanile of Giotto, the hospitality of her citizens,
and the Tuscan cigar) cost a *quattrino,* or 3 *centesimi.* The
Tuscans were content with the products of their own
soil. The nobles drank native wines, and on the hot summer
afternoons entertained each other with iced-watermelon
in the shady gardens of their villas or in the courtyards of
their cool palaces. In a land almost entirely agricultural,
great fortunes were hard to achieve, and there was no
class of new-rich. The Russian prince, Demidoff, outshone
in splendour the court of Leopold, and the dinners and

[1] Montanelli, *Memorie,* I,13. Guerrazzi, *Scritti Politici,* 106.   [2] Barbera,
Memorie, 42.   [3] F. Martini, *Ricordi ed Appunti,* p. 50. The Tuscan lira
equals 84 Italian centesimi.

receptions chronicled in the *Gazetta* were almost without exception gatherings of *forestieri*.[1]

The population of the country in 1837 was just under a million and a half; of that number less than a quarter of a million lived in the towns. Florence had nearly one hundred thousand inhabitants; Pisa and Siena about twenty thousand each; Leghorn seventy-five thousand. The smaller cities such as Pistoia, Arezzo, Volterra, Cortona, were, then as now, hardly more than market centres; and even in the larger there was little manufacture. Criminals were employed in making cloth in Volterra and carpets in Florence; there was a straw-hat industry, especially round Prato; the manufacture of silk was in the main a domestic industry. There was some mining of different kinds: iron in Elba, potash, borax and alabaster in the district of Volterra. Wages were low; the straw workers of Prato received $2\frac{1}{2}$ *paoli* a day, or something just over a shilling. Given the low cost of living, this was enough for food and lodging, and middle-class writers waxed virtuously indignant over the extravagance of labourers. A few were tormented by the bugbear which Malthus had raised,[2] but the young labourers cared little, and married in time to give a respectable welcome to their first-born, begotten as a rule without the sanction of the Church. Paupers were well cared for by the state—too well cared for, according to respectable economists; but for the first twenty years of Leopold's reign Tuscany enjoyed a succession of good seasons, the country districts were almost self-sufficing, and in the towns there were no economic crises. Tuscany was the only state of Italy where emigration was unknown. The export trade was very small, and, with the possible exception of the traders and

---

[1] For a picture of Tuscan life in this period the most useful books are Conti, *Firenze Vecchia;* various writings of F. Martini; a chapter in Guido Biagi, *Fiorenza, Fior che sempre rinnovella;* Collodi, *Occhi e Nasi;* Stiavelli, *Antonio Guadagnoli;* Giusti, *Poesie;* Bowring, *Report on the Statistics of Tuscany;* Zobi, *Manuale.* See also bibliography. [2] Digny, *Cenni sui pericoli sociali in Toscana,* Firenze, 1849.

labourers of Leghorn, there was no class which could
have any economic motive for wishing to merge the Grand-
Duchy in a larger unity.

Florence, too, had not yet been surrendered to the
tourists. Wheeled traffic had not yet begun its remorseless
offensive against the pedestrian, and it was something of a
novelty, when in 1824, six cabs for city service took up
their stand in the Piazza del Duomo. All foreigners were
understood to be ' English '; a servant once announced
to his master—' Some English have come, but I am not
certain whether they are Germans or Russians'. Grass
grew in the Via Larga (now the Via Cavour), and a map
of 1843[1] shows the city only gradually creeping out along
the main arteries towards its last circle of walls. The small
boys, whose delight it was to annoy the peasants who
came into the city for market on Tuesdays and Thursdays,
could find also peasants even within the walls; and on the
pretext of looking for lost balls would jump down to
forage among the carrots, celery, radishes, cabbages and
watermelons which occupied two thirds of the space
between the third and the fourth circles. At night the gates
were shut; notice was given at the stroke of one, and for
the five minutes' grace that followed there was a wild
homeward rush of stragglers; for those who were late
had to pay a *grazia* to the gate-keepers, unless they happened to be near a certain spot by the Arno, where it was
possible to clamber over.

The citizens, indeed, seldom went far from the city.
The landowners left for their estates only at one or two
seasons of the year, to shoot little birds and to supervise
the grape-harvest, and it was matter for admiration and
prolonged leave-taking when a member of a middle-class
family set out on a trip to Leghorn to broaden his mind
by seeing the sea and the Tuscan navy—a prehistoric
vessel called the *Giglio*, and a couple of cock-boats. Florence
seemed all that was desirable, though the firemen whose

[1] *Raccolta di antiche Carte—della Citta di Firenze*, Firenze, 1824
(Istituto Geografico-Militare).

task it was to clean the streets found that they had more
to do than they could manage, and each capo-squadro of
sbirri was given by the municipality an extra ten lire to
make sure that dead dogs and cats were cleared away.
The water from the roofs descended full on the heads of
the pedestrians, and the marvel of gas-lighting (it did not
come till 1846, and the cautious municipality ordered that
it was not to be used when there was a moon) was yet
unknown.

The citizens did not feel any tedium of life, for in
Florence conversation was, and is, a recreation; and on
summer nights they would pull their chairs out into the
streets or join each other in the cafés. Then there were the
theatres; for people of taste the Alfieri or the Cocomero,
or the Pergola, if they wanted music; for others the
Quarconia or Borgo Ogni Santi, where it was perfectly
in order for the spectators to bombard each other with
apples. The great recreation of all classes, however, were
the religious festivals, poor survivors of the *feste* of Medicean
days, perhaps, but full of variety and excitement and colour.
At Epiphany there was the carnival; on Ascension Day
families led out their children to the Cascine to hunt the
cricket and bring it home in a little wicker cage; for
Corpus Domini there was a great procession, with soldiers,
and the Grand-Duke, and the court, and all the high officials
of Church and State, and the children of the parishes led
by their priests. For the feast of St. John, the patron saint
of Florence, there was on the first day a race of chariots
in the Piazza of Santa Maria Novella; and, in the evening,
fireworks on the Ponte alla Carraia, with two skiffs full of
good swimmers to rescue the little boys who fell into the
Arno. On the day of the saint himself there was a horse
race round the north wall of the city, with the stretchers
of the *Misericordia* ready to collect the injured riders and
carry them off to the hospital. The popular and joyous
character of the Florentine Catholicism is shown best of
all in the events of the season of prayer and fasting. Lènt
began as a rule with an indulgence mitigating the rigours

of the fast, on the ground of the high price of fish, the unhealthiness of salted foods, the shortage of vegetables, and the fact that 'the greater part of families are composed of old men, children, and invalids, incapable of supporting abstinence from meat'. It was a season of fairs; on Ash Wednesday there was the fair of dried fruits by Santa Maria Novella; on Sundays there was the fair of walnuts at the Porta San Gallo; at the Porta Romana was the Fair of Contracts, a peasant marriage-market where young men paraded to show off their points and their elders haggled over the dowry. The Thursday of mid-Lent was the day for which rude little boys waited most impatiently, for it was then their right to lie in wait behind corners and porches for wretched old ladies, steal after them on tip-toe, pin a paper ladder to their backs and hiss and jeer—' *Now you've got it*'. On Holy Thursday the Grand-Ducal family communicated in pomp, and afterwards, in the Pitti, the Grand-Duke and his attendants washed the feet of twelve poor old men, and the Grand-Duchess and her attendants washed the feet of twelve poor old women; then the twenty-four sat down to eat, waited upon by the royal family and the chamberlain. This was not a display for Florence at large, but compensation came at Easter, when the archbishop at the High Altar set fire to a dove which carried a sacred flame down the cathedral to a car clustered with fireworks supplied by the Pazzi family, one of whose ancestors had brought back to Tuscany authentic relics of the Holy Sepulchre.

At all these festivals part of the attraction was the Grand-Duke himself, transformed from the unassuming citizen who went through the streets with an umbrella into a real general with an enormous cocked hat. The soldiers were there, too. Nobody imagined that they could have duties more serious than the embellishment of festivals, and liberals were wont to grumble that twelve battalions of infantry, three squadrons of cavalry, and one or two pieces of artillery made an army that was too big for Tuscany.[1]

[1] Capponi, *Scritti Editi ed inediti*, II, 108.

The true brain and hope of Tuscan liberalism, said Giusti, was in the Academy of the *Georgofili*.[1] The aim of the Academy, as set out in the reformed constitution of 1817, was 'the progress, encouragement, and propagation of theoretical and practical knowledge concerning agriculture and any other branch of Economy'. It had been founded in 1753, and had accepted the economic gospel of the Physiocrats; to the end it was in spirit a product of the eighteenth century. Its members were composed of scientists, of educationalists, of benevolent nobles who, like those nobles of eighteenth-century France with whom Arthur Young made friends, had felt the call to sacrifice some of the amenities of city life, and, for part of the year at least, look to the management of their country estates. They embodied the fruits of their studies or experience in papers which they read to each other. The best of the papers (some of them were really excellent, and form a useful record of the economic life and ideas of the time) were printed in the *Acts* of the Academy. When a member read more than the one paper to which he was obliged under the constitution, he was rewarded by his grateful colleagues with a medal.[2]

The Marquis Cosimo Ridolfi must, during the period of his membership, have received something like one hundred medals. From the year 1816, when he read his first paper, till the year 1853, with which the index compiled by himself comes to an end, his discourses were the most constant feature in the history of the Academy. In one year he read as many as nine, and during the whole period he read seventy-six. His character and ideas may be taken as typical of those of the Academy, which for years honoured him as its president. The dominating note of all his activities is an earnest faith in Enlightenment and Progress (he himself, with a sort of reverent awe, would have written the words in capital letters). In 1816

[1] Giusti, *Memorie*, 25.   [2] The Constitution, countersigned by P. Strozzi, is in the Biblioteca Nazionale of Florence. See also M. Tabarrini, *Academia degli Georgofili*.

he began to pioneer the cause of gas illumination in Florence; it was almost a crusade. He was an enthusiast for the schools of mutual instruction on the English model of Bell and Lancaster; he established one in his own house, and the example spread among his friends. Ridolfi was in the main satisfied with them, ' though they left something to be desired in the teaching of arithmetic'.[1] In 1825 he was placed by the Grand-Duke at the head of the Tuscan mint; in 1828 he was put in charge of the workhouse. A few years later, after a discourse in praise of the virtues of self-help, he instituted the first savings bank that was known in Tuscany. ' Who knows where we shall finish', wrote one of his associates to Capponi, ' if God gives us life ? '[2] There was much to be done in Tuscany, and Ridolfi never tired; he was a pioneer of bridge-building and joint-stock companies, a leading figure in the science congresses, the founder of a school of agriculture. He started many good men along the road of intelligent hard work, and superficial observers might have thought that Ricasoli had taken him for a model. But Ridolfi saw no reason to doubt, as Capponi had come to doubt, that ' Enlightenment ' would usher in the new age for which Italy was waiting. His fellow Academicians shared his assurance. Guerrazzi said of them after gathering a handful of little foundlings into an asylum they would exclaim: ' Let us go to render thanks to Jove, thundering on the Capitol'.[3]

Liberalism of this brand, which was purely Tuscan and in spirit a thing of the eighteenth century, was encouraged rather than opposed by the Grand-Ducal government,[4] and Ridolfi himself was entrusted by Leopold with the education of the heir to the throne. Trouble arose when the

---

[1] Luigi Ridolfi, *Cosimo Ridolfi e gli Istituti del suo tempo*, p. 42, and *passim*.
[2] Lambruschini to Capponi, quoted Tabarrini, *Capponi*, Ch. VI. [3] Guerrazzi in a letter of 1840. (Appendix to Giusti, *Memorie*, p. 247). Giusti, *Memorie*, 25. ' An Academy remains an Academy, and the oak does not bear citrons'. [4] *L. & D.*, I. 171. *Ridolfi*, op. cit. 55 *seq*. The freedom of the Academy was respected.

liberals began to weary of Enlightenment, and became conscious of spiritual desires which could not be satisfied by gas, roads, bridges, and savings banks, or which invested these very objects with a new significance. For some reason or other the Earthly Paradise began to pall on many generous minds, and Tuscans were ceasing to find complacent satisfaction in contrasting their happy state with that of their fellow Italians across the border in Umbria or Parma. Giusti sang of making with love and prudence Italy's 'boot' all of one piece and all of one colour. Years before this, the vague longing to spend his devotion on a country which could call for it and inspire it (the most that Tuscany could inspire was content) had come upon the Marquis Capponi. His close knowledge of the classics and of three modern languages, the breadth of mind which made him later the most understanding of Italian historians, and a voyage to England where he was for a time the guest of Jeffrey of the *Edinburgh Review*,[1] had combined to give him a peculiarly detached attitude towards his own country. He doubted whether he had a country at all; none, certainly, he told Foscolo, to inspire the sentiments which should be joined to that name.[2] He sighed for the intellectual freedom which he found in England, drew up a careful scheme for the foundation of a paper[3] which would make him the Jeffrey of Italy, and on his return found that he lacked the practical ability to found it. But while he was in England a 'certain Genevan' had set up in Florence a reading-room where could be found 'the most respectable papers of Europe'.[4] The Genevan's name was Vieusseux; he had travelled in three continents, read little but observed much, and for all his forty years had the enthusiasm of a youth. He had, too, a flair for the work of literary *entrepreneur*, and arriving at

[1] Tabarrini, *Capponi*, 65 *et seq.* [2] Capponi, *Lettere*, I, 29. [3] *Ibid.* I, 23 and 38; III, 499; V, 93–112. [4] A. Vannucci, *Niccolini*, I, 446. On Vieusseux, N. Tommasèo, and Lambruschini; Prunas, *L'Antologia*, etc, Cian in *Nuova Antologia*, CXXIV (consult Bibliography). Almost every collection of letters in the period gives material for his biography.

the time when two journalistic enterprises had just come to grief and Capponi's venture was dissolving into a dream,[1] he gathered up the wreckage and founded the *Antologia*.

He undertook the work, ' not as a speculative venture, but as a task of disinterested propaganda'. He could not afford to pay for articles, except with the exquisite courtesy and tact of his thanks, the occasional gift of a book, or literary information which might be invaluable in those days of incomplete bibliographies and publishers' notices. Nevertheless the *Antologia*, which began in 1821 with a predominating array of cuttings from other papers, soon gathered to itself the aid of all the best writers in Italy. All the Tuscans, from men like Ridolfi to Enrico Meyer, idealist educator and friend of Mazzini; the Neapolitan, Colletta, who wrote his history of Naples in a villa lent him by Capponi, and his fellow exiles, Poerio and Pepe; the scattered writers of the *Conciliatore* of Milan, who flocked to Florence after 1821 and began their work anew; the Dalmatian, Tommasèo, who came to Florence in 1827 and sometimes tried the harmony of Vieusseux's group by his uncertain temper; Leopardi, who was enticed there by Giordani, and even Mazzini, who gave two articles to the *Antologia*—worked together under the reconciling geniality of Vieusseux. Many of the best articles of his review were born in the weekly gatherings where he presided over the conversation of his diverse literary family, and where on occasion occurred those events of literary history famous as the meeting of Manzoni and Leopardi.[2] From these meetings and from the day-to-day ferment of ideas there was born of necessity a new and ideal liberalism. The calm waters of the Tuscan lagoon were invaded by currents from outside, and gradually, unmistakably, the change began to make itself apparent in the pages of the *Antologia*. In setting out his programme in 1820, Vieusseux said: ' It will be always our care that the voices of Humanity, Philosophy, Love of Country,

1 Capponi, *Lettere*, IV, 442. 2 *Ibid*. I, 231.

shall not be silent'. The Tuscan government did not
object to the voices of humanity and philosophy, but
Fossombroni might well ask whether love of country
might not become a passion which would stiffen the
pressure of Austria and sweep away the good-tempered
indifference with which his tolerance had been recipro-
cated, and which was necessary to the continuance of his
system. Would these intellectuals be content to let the
world 'get along by itself?' In 1830 the *Antologia*
announced that it 'aimed to make Italy known to strangers
and to herself, to defend her glories, to encourage her
forces . . . to point out to the thoughts of Italians a
goal not merely municipal'. All this talk of Italy! Fossombroni's fears were realised when the Austrian minister
formally complained of the *Antologia* as 'a journal of
dangerous and revolutionary tendencies'. From that time
its days were numbered.[1]

Into the University of Pisa nationalist excitement came
suddenly, like a disturbing wind. Giuseppe Giusti lived
there among two generations of students, for his father,
dissatisfied with his progress, had taken him away in 1829,
and did not let him return till 1832.[2] In the first generation
the undergraduates had found sufficient entertainment in
the mannerisms of their professors (one of whom had
astonished a class by delivering a lecture on heat in impro-
vised Latin hexameters) and in their own 'rags'. Their
hero in those days was a certain Arcangeli of Pomerance,
a genius at organising buffooneries and a fertile author of
dirty verses. When his impudence passed the limit and the
Buon-Governo was forced to consider his punishment, it
was decided that he must not be sent as a conscript to
Elba, on the grounds that he was not sturdy enough to
support the rigours of barrack life, and that he would
corrupt the virtue of the soldiers. . . . But when Giusti
returned in 1832, adolescence had found new scope for

[1] See Del Cerro, *op. cit.*, Ch. 28, and Prunas, Ch. 5.   [2] For the following
see F. Martini, *Giusti Studente* in *Simpatie*.

fervour. There had been revolutions in France, in Poland, and in Italy herself, and the police reports were now full of the plottings of professors, students, and citizens. The reports did not say what the traitors were plotting, but it seemed that the revolution was due to break out in all Europe on a given day at 4.30 p.m. precisely. The police struck at the disaffection of the students by suppressing their magazine, and then, turning their attention to the professors, suspended the physiologist, Pigli, for teaching maxims ' contrary to religious beliefs'.[1] The students revenged their professor as best they could. When his successor appeared and began to lecture, they noisily and unanimously cracked chestnuts, then shouted to a tune: ' Pigli! Pigli! Pigli!' beating time with their feet. The police thought it wiser to bow before the storm; Pigli returned, and that devotee of pure scholarship (Giusti said that he found Italy in the pineal gland[2]) saw the chance of making a sensation. His first lecture, which was crowded, began with a ' discourse on generation'; from generation he descended to treat of the brain, from the brain he passed to thought, from thought to duty, and then, having found a subject sufficiently physiological, he concluded that the first duty of a citizen was to love his country. At this conclusion there was tremendous applause, the students crowded round their master, cheered him, clapped him, kissed him—fervently, as students are accustomed to kiss professors. Next day, after a private interview between Pigli and the police, it was announced that the professor was indisposed, and for a time would have to discontinue his lectures. The sick man was brave enough to defy the doctors, and for a time walked about the streets of Pisa, enjoying the adoration of the undergraduates; then the government found work for him elsewhere. It was an unpardonable interference with the liberty of education!

The government, nevertheless, was kind to the University. By 1841 a general reorganisation at Pisa and Siena

[1] E. Michel, *F. D. Guerrazzi*, 77. [2] Giusti, *Memorie*, 159.

had increased the number of chairs at the former seat of
learning from 33 to 46,[1] the salaries of the professors had
been raised, and among the distinguished Italians whose
services were sought was none other than Gioberti.
Patriotism was still a sure road to popularity. One professor, Centofanti, could claim the achievement of bringing
out a seventy-page introduction to the study of Dante
which only once mentioned the alleged subject of his
essay; all the rest was reflection on civilisation, progress,
the moral function of poetry, 'lyrical flights, auguries
and vaticinations', including a hymn to Rome where the
nations would one day hold the elections of religious
thought.[2] An admonition from the government in 1846
did something to modify these rhapsodies. The progress
of revolution did more, and when stormy days came upon
Tuscany, Centofanti sought to still democratic propaganda by explaining in a long article what Rousseau really
meant by the sovereignty of the general will.[3] Of a temper
less fundamentally cautious was the new professor of
commercial law, Giuseppe Montanelli. He had been an
ardent youth of precocious genius; he entered the university at the age of thirteen, and at fourteen had composed
a number of sonnets and sapphic odes on The Nativity,
The Annunciation, Spring, David killing Goliath, and
similar subjects.[4] At eighteen he was a doctor of law, and
at twenty-seven he was a professor. He was pale, he had a
melancholy appearance and a black beard, and the patriotic
enthusiasm which fired his discourses on commercial law
won such applause that his veteran colleague, Carmignani,
exhibited a jealousy 'unworthy of his gray hairs'.[5] To
Giusti, this enthusiastic young man, among the grave and
learned Pisan professors, appeared like Christ among the
scribes and pharisees of the Temple. He became the idol
of his students. In their letters to him he was Giuseppe,

[1] *Baldasseroni.* Ch. XXII.   [2] A. D'Ancona : *Confessioni e Ricordi*, 216.
On Centofanti's philosophy, see G. Gentile in *Gino Capponi*.   [3] Zobi V,
appendix 70.   [4] Printed in appendix to A. Marradi, *Montanelli*.   [5] *Ibid.* 185.
Letter of Niccolini to Montanelli.

they were 'Beppo or 'Poldo; he was their master, their father, their political and religious guide, and at last their comrade in arms. ' Thy voice will defend me', wrote the young Cempini when he was exiled for work in which he had been Montanelli's lieutenant, ' for I proclaim it at this moment, I am thy creation, thou art my second father. . . . Be certain that I shall be worthy of thee'. [1]

The secret of Montanelli's appeal to the youth of Pisa lay in his enthusiasm, his courage, the vague ardent idealism of his evangelical mind. From 1832 he had been a devotee of the Saint-Simonian Gospel, and when after a decade his mind began to rebel against the fantasies of this doctrine, scepticism gave him such acute melancholy that he contemplated suicide. Then appeared Gioberti's *Primato*, which had the wide sweep of emotional generalisation for which Montanelli hungered. He pondered it till one day he experienced a sudden conversion to Catholicism, after which he reassured himself with the reflection that, after all, ' Dante, Savonarola, Pascal, and other eminent minds ' had given him a precedent of orthodoxy.[2] He had found a faith to preach which seemed to suit the times. In ' orderly liberalism ' he found the necessary application of Christian principles; Christians must set themselves to the task of removing artificial inequalities, and work for the substitution of physical force (which, of course, had to be destroyed) by moral force.[3] This benevolent programme lasted him for a few years, but in a critical period of Tuscan history he changed again, pursued a new plan with the old fervour, and caused not a little confusion. His enemies nicknamed him Beato Angelico.

In these years propaganda invaded every intellectual field. While the professors were turning their chairs into tubs for patriotic oratory, writers were surrendering the liberty of their art to further the liberty of their country.

[1] M. Gioli, *La Democrazia Toscana*, p. 81. [2] Montanelli, *Memorie*, I, 88. [3] Montanelli, *Discorso . . . dopo la legge Toscana del 6 Maggio 1847*.

Even Capponi, a conscientious historian, came to his
subject with the preconceived idea that it was his patriotic
duty to upset the theory of a Teutonic origin for the
institutions of mediæval Italy.[1] In drama, the uncrowned
king of the age of the Risorgimento in Tuscan literature
was to be G. B. Niccolini. His culture was founded on a
severe study of the classics; to that he had added erudition
in history and mythology, and, as a professor in the *Belle
Arti* at Florence, he was able to inculcate the principles of
republican virtue by lecturing on Michelangelo.[2] In
1825 he inherited a legacy, retired to the country, and
devoted himself to dramatic poetry. In 1830 he won his
first great triumph with *Giovanni da Procida*. When one
of his characters compared the rumbling of Etna to the
wind of liberty sweeping over Italy, the audience broke
into frantic applause; and when the hero proclaimed that
the Frank would become a brother of the Italian when he
had gone back to his own country across the Alps, the
Austrian ambassador whispered to the representative of
France: ' The envelope is addressed to you, but the
message is for us'.[3] Niccolini continued to write tragedies
of increasing patriotism, but the government thought it
well to postpone their production in Florence.

One other name must be mentioned in illustration of
the more extreme developments of liberalism which were
to sweep away for ever the Earthly Paradise which Giordani
had found so perfect and the Florentines so amusing:
the name of F. D. Guerrazzi, lawyer and novelist of
Leghorn. Guerrazzi was wont to claim that he embodied
in himself the robust vigour of his city; in later days, when
Leghorn was in bad odour with the Florentine liberals,
and he himself was denounced by all Capponi's friends as
a scourge, he pleaded with Capponi to remember that no
one could live so long in a place without acquiring some
of its virtues and its vices.[4] The British statistician who
reported on Tuscany declared that Leghorn was one of

---

[1] Tabarrini, *Capponi*, 255.   [2] Vanucci, *Niccolini*, I, 39.   [3] Del Cerro,
Misteri della Polizia, 210.   [4] Guerrazzi, *Lettere* (Martini), 283.

the most important ports of Europe. Its trade in 1834 amounted to nearly two million pounds.[1] Its population, barely 60,000 in 1828, had passed 80,000 twenty years later. The number of ships which visited the port was steadily on the increase, but it would seem that trade did not quite keep pace with the growth of population, for Genoa had reformed her system of port duties, and her competition was felt seriously by the Tuscan port; while both Genoa and Leghorn were losing to Marseilles, which was flourishing on the monopoly of the Algerian trade. The government of the Grand-Duke did what it could, and hoped much from treaties with Turkey and America, but many thought that the real evil to attack was the fiscal barrier laid across the hinterland by the governments of Parma, Modena, and Rome.[2] Thus the city gradually drifted into a suspicious discontent when everything which the government did for it became a grievance; it felt itself alien from Tuscany, and complained that it was exploited like an estate which brought the government a good part of its revenue.[3] Leghorn, indeed, was not in spirit a Tuscan city. Capponi denied that it was a city at all, in the Greek sense of the term, or even as the Italians conceived it. Leghorn remained merely 'a collection of men brought together by chance and time, haphazard persons of every nation, who every few years change, merchants always ready to shift their persons and capitals to another place . . . and beneath these a *plebs* ignorant and fierce, agitated always by the fluctuations of trade and the uncertainty of wages'.[4] What a contrast to the stability and security of Tuscany, where life was untroubled by fierce competition and by crises! But, for that very reason, there was not in Leghorn that over-ready tolerance which Capponi had called poisonous. Strange and disturbing to

---

[1] Bowring. Report cited. For a summary of Leghorn statistics see *Baldasseroni*, Allegato No. 9. [2] Zobi, *Storia*, IV, 290 et seq. [3] See for example Guerrazzi, *Scritti Politici*, 210 et seq. A good example of money spent on the city to the indignation of the citizens was the enlarging of the city wall. [4] Capponi, *Scritti*, II, 103.

the liberals of Florence, the city was Italian rather than
Tuscan. A port seldom lingers in a past age, and Leghorn
was among the first of Italian cities to be distracted by
the vulgarities, the sufferings, the fevers, the ideals, of the
nineteenth century.

Both the parents of Guerrazzi were natives of the city.[1]
His father was a wood carver and sculptor, a great reader
with an enthusiasm for Plutarch and Dante, from whom
he had learnt a deep hatred of all that he thought to be
tyranny or servility. When his son was twelve years old,
the elder Guerrazzi solemnly opened the room where he
kept his books, and let the small boy pick his way among
Homer, Ossian, Voltaire, Ariosto, Plutarch, and the
Arabian Nights. As a father he adopted a habit of republican aloofness and austerity; when Francesco came
crying home with a cut forehead after a battle with the
urchins of the quays he would say: 'People who
have glass heads should not throw stones'. His
mother on such occasions would abuse him and give him
more reason for weeping; and if Leopardi's ruined health
and melancholy can be traced to the cruelty of his mother,
some at least of Guerrazzi's angry bitterness may derive
from a similar source. 'What are the consolations of the
child?' he wrote later to Capponi: 'Those that come
from his mother. . . . Ah, I have never known them.
I carry in my left thigh a wound inflicted by . . . my
hand trembles to write it'. . . . His mother had in a
fit of ungovernable temper hurled an iron at the wretched
little boy. It was one incident of many, and in later days,
when Guerrazzi was wont on occasion to claim Christlike
virtues, he ascribed it to these that he did not hate her.

The father and mother between them, and his own strained,
super-sensitive pride, drove him out of the house at the
age of fourteen to fend for himself. For a year he picked
up a precarious living by teaching boys older than himself,
by doing odd pieces of translation and literary hack-work.

[1] For the youth of Guerrazzi see his *Note Autobiografiche* and *Memorie*,
and A. Mangini, *Cenni e Ricordi*.

He learnt what it was to be hungry and to sleep on the
pavement, and he discovered a friend, a happy-go-lucky
genial youth, Carlo Bini. Guerrazzi's character was de-
veloping along its own lines and in accordance with an
artificial ideal which he was fashioning from his study of
the classics, the Cinquecento Italians, and the characters
in Byron (Byron himself had already come to Leghorn);
and often in the evenings he would look for his friend from
tavern to tavern, and in the end drag him away to the
austere pleasure of reading Livy.[1] Then came a reconciliation with his father and some years at the University
of Pisa, where he found ' no instruction, much persecution,
weariness of men and life, growing melancholy'.[2] The
melancholy and the weariness were in part sincere, in part
a pose which became habitual and twisted his character.
At Pisa, too, he had his first brush with the police,[3] and
acquired a doctorate in law; but his profession did not
attract him; he regarded it as ' a chain on the leg of a
galley slave'.[4] His interests led him towards literature and
political agitation. He developed a style of his own, a
tortuous, egoistical style in which the influence of Byron
and his slipshod classical education gave direction to the
fire, bitterness, and scepticism of his own self-centred,
restless, impetuous spirit. Manzoni's romanticism was too
serene for his passion; at Pisa he had given way to a
curious fascination which led him to the operating theatre
in the hospital, where he had shuddered at the pain of the
sufferers and the callousness of the surgeons; but he
nursed his own repulsion and disgust—and came to watch
other operations. It became habitual with him to see
everywhere the misery and the foulness of the world, and
a sort of dramatic insincerity crept into his attitude to
the most common things of life. He wrote to the bride of
one of his faithful friends: ' Woman, I charge you,
trembling: if your child, flesh of your flesh, should one

[1] *Memorie*, p. 32. [2] *Ibid.* 33. [3] Guerrazzi, *Apologia*, 58. Mangini in
Archivio Storico Italiano. Fasc. III, 1908, p. 142. [4] Guerrazzi, *Lettere*
(Martini), I, 63.

day mount the gallows, look to the crime, not to the
punishment . . . forget never that one of the titles of
the mother of God, perhaps the most grand, certainly the
most pitious, is that of the mother of sorrows'.[1] Life
tormented him; he told his friend, Puccini, to whom more
than any other he opened his heart, that he looked on it
as 'a morsel given to him to gnaw'.[2] For men, and
especially for Italians, he felt at times, a fierce disgust.
'We are the offspring of the Romans . . . as the vermin
of a battle-horse a month dead'.[3] Yet he was affectionate
in his friendships, and his devotion to his two fatherless
nephews was unwearying; stories are told of his kindness
to children, and he possessed a fascination which later
broke down the prejudices of the Grand-Duke and which
swayed Capponi in the days when Guerrazzi was anathema
to all the moderates.[4] It is hard to judge him from what he
said and wrote, for his words are always full of exaggerations, contradictions, and insincerities. Yet fundamentally
he was sincere. Capponi said in a flash of insight that he
was too much steeped in Macchiavelli and Byron to be
himself; that ' he sought always in public life the satisfac-
tions of the artist'. He sought them in private life as well,
he posed eternally to the world and to himself, he nursed
his own emotions, and their bitterness gave him satisfaction. He was the actor, and, at the same time, far in the
background, the cynical disillusioned spectator of his own
acting. But there was one theme where his action was his
very life, and where he rose above his own cynicism.
There was no trace of insincerity in him when he declared:
' I, who have doubted God, have never doubted Italy'.[5]
Italy was the one thing to which he gave himself, for his
loves were brief and turbid. To Italy he devoted his literary
aspirations. Like so many others, he twisted his art to
propaganda; but his propaganda was more passionate,
more direct, than any which had yet been heard. There is

[1] Mangini, *Cenni e Ricordi* (1920), p. 21.　[2] *Lettere*, I, 101.　[3] *Ibid.*
141.　[4] Capponi, *Scritti,* II, pp. 44 and 155.　[5] *Lettere* (Martini), No.
307 (July, 1848).

that famous passage in his first popular novel, the *Battaglia di Benevento*, where eight Italian champions meet in combat eight French. Six of the former fall at the first onslaught. The two survivors do not know each other: one asks . . .

'Are you an Italian? '

' I am'.

'And what do you intend to do? '

' Conquer or die'.

Emilio Bandiera wrote to a friend before the brave sacrifice of his Calabrian expedition that this dialogue had wakened in him the conviction that he, too, must conquer or die for Italy.

To the mild guardians of Tuscany such a man would appear a serpent who had found his way into the Earthly Paradise, for the Leghorn novelist embodied in himself those enthusiasms and passions which were at deadly war with Fossombroni and all his works. Guerrazzi, on his side, regarded the Tuscan government, not with hatred, not with the helpless despair which Capponi had sometimes felt, but with a curious, contemptuous irony. He could not take it altogether seriously. He wished to bait it, to shock it; and when he found it clumsily protecting itself against his insulting defiance he was filled with an angry surprise, an indignant sense of injustice that the thing which he so much despised should have the power to spy on him, to silence him, to imprison him.[1] In February of 1830 it suppressed his paper, the *Indicatore Livornese*, which he had started in the previous year and which had printed a good deal from the pen of Mazzini. Immediately he struck back by reading at a dull academy a patriotic eulogy of the Livornese Cosimo del Fante, who had fought with glory under Napoleon. The governor of the city, the bishop, all the high functionaries and respectability of Leghorn were present, and listened in dismay while the orator gave vent to his ardent Italian sentiment.

[1] For the period of the plots there is an accurate study by E. Michel, *op. cit.*

The governor himself was taken to task by the government for failing to protest against a discourse ' in which
is abused every human belief'.[1] He put forward the plea
that he had been asleep, but the police insisted that he had
been awake part of the time at least.[2] This argument, had
he known of it, would have incensed Guerrazzi more than
his punishment; but he remained in merciful ignorance
and was marched off for six months' seclusion in Montepulciano. There Mazzini came to see him, and Guerrazzi
read aloud some of the early passages in a new novel he
had begun, *L'Assedio di Firenze*. As he read, he bathed his
face from time to time with a sponge. Both men, however,
realised that great differences lay between them, and it is
probable that Mazzini refrained from unfolding all his
plans.[3] When the last minute of his six months' captivity
had passed, Guerrazzi snapped his watch shut and marched
out of the hill town; came back to Florence with schemes
of plots in which he tried to draw Capponi;[4] devised new
plans for annoying the police. He was accused of belonging
to a secret society whose members called themselves the
Children of Brutus. No evidence was found against them,
but a nervous president of the *Buon-Governo* denounced
him as ' the most terrible of all the liberals of Tuscany',
and proposed to shut him up for three years in the island
of Giglio.[5] This the government would not allow, but he
spent another month at Montepulciano. Two years later,
in 1833, when the government was forced to strike at
secret societies of more serious intention, Guerrazzi was
sent with his friend, Bini, to prison in Portoferraio.
Guerrazzi claimed in his writings the sufferings of a
martyr. He ' felt his blood boil ' when the prison clerk
came to offer on behalf of the government to bear the
expenses of his lodging in durance vile; the most natural
and conciliatory of offers was to him an insult. ' The
government can harass me, it cannot degrade me; say to

[1] *Apologia*, 63 seq. [2] Del Cerro, *op. cit.* 57. [3] Guastalla, *La Vita e le
opere di F.D.G.*, I, 349 seq. [4] Capponi, *op. cit.* II, 43–44. [5] Del Cerro,
op. cit., 73 seq.

him who sent you that he can offer me charity when he
I ask it'.[1] It was mortification to him that tyranny should
veil itself in him in so mild a form; but he would not be
robbed of the glory of suffering, and in his memoirs he
recorded with indignation the brutality of his gaolers, his
miserable room, the mental agonies of a lost liberty. It
was all imagination. Carlo Bini's geniality and humour
made it difficult for him to imitate this pose, but in the
Manuscript of a Prisoner he did his best with a contrast
between the elegant life of a gentleman-criminal and the
agonies of the needy wrong-doer. Unfortunately, his
private letters were published in the same volume after
his death, and in one of them he told his parents that the
prison officials were really charming. ' We are treated
with all consideration; we can read, we can write, and as
regards the comforts of life, everything for which we ask
is given us on the instant'.[2] Another prisoner declared
that the conspirators were ' victims in sugar'.[3] Guerrazzi
employed his time in writing his *Note Autobiografiche* and
continuing the *Assedio di Firenze*, a novel of fervid patriotism, called by Mazzini the ' most energetic, the most
ardent protest that I know'.[4] ' Here was born', said the
author himself, ' the *Assedio di Firenze* . . . a protest
from a spirit dishonourably tortured, conceived as a defiance,
written as one fights a battle'. ' That book', wrote Giusti,
' tells you the man. . . . Grief, bitter and desperate, of
one who has lost faith in men and things dictated that
book. It goes in leaps as a great pulse'.[5]

Guerrazzi, said Capponi in after years, had ' become
among us a hero of legend; he was looked on by enemies
and almost by admirers as a demon, a serpent, an eater
of babies'.[6] In this year of his prison he had not yet built
up such a reputation in Tuscany as a whole, but the police,
at any rate, regarded him as the evil genius of the country,

[1] Guerrazzi, *Memorie*. [2] *Scritti editi e Postumi di Carlo Bini* (Livorno
1843), p. 246. [3] *Vittime Candite*. The *mot* was Salvagnoli's. [4] Letter in
appendix to Guerrazzi, *Memorie*. [5] Giusti, *Memorie* 110. [6] Capponi, *op.
cit*. II, 140.

personified in him all the terrible things of which it was afraid. How much reason was there in its fears? The mistakes of its agents were often ridiculous. They were on guard against the influence of revolutionary France, but their ideas on French revolutionaries were sometimes a little vague; they sought to prevent the circulation of caricatures against Louis Phillippe,[1] and descended in suspicion on a circle of Frenchmen who turned out to be scandalised legitimists.[2] They sent to the President reports of plots which had no existence; they bribed Leghorn labourers to hiss the most patriotic of the exiles who came to the city for asylum. As for Guerrazzi, they shadowed him everywhere, and it is not unusual to find him reported, on his devilish errands, in two different places at the same time.

Their reports, therefore, must be used with caution. Guerrazzi, in his *Apologia*, practically denied the existence of secret societies in Tuscany; the police, he said, would not have found them without a microscope.[3] But Montanelli's Memoirs gave one or two chapters to the societies as a serious factor in the history of the country. Many of them were mere masquerades, the playground of adolescents like the young student of Siena, who said pleasantly but inaccurately at lunch: ' How much nicer this bread would be, if dipped in the blood of kings ! '[4] Typical of this type of plotter are the Children of Brutus, whose rules the police succeeded in discovering. When one child of Brutus met his fellow, he was to make himself known by wiping his forehead with his handkerchief, by bending his head to his right hand, feigning agitation, beating himself on the right breast, and pretending to throw down a card which he had drawn from some part of his person. These marks of identification were considered sufficiently definite to elicit the question: ' What is the matter with you? ' ' I am in grief through not finding my brother', the first child of Brutus must reply. ' I am one of them',

---

[1] Michel, *op. cit.* p. 8.   [2] Martini, *Simpatie*, 60.   [3] *Apologia*, 64.
[4] Martini, *Simpatie*, 66.

the other would answer, and then: ' What do you want? '
' Liberty or death! ' was the proud rejoinder (had it been
adapted from Guerrazzi's novels?), and the allies were
now free to discuss the killing of tyrants.[1]

Organisations of this sort, however, with all their
absurd ritual, sometimes existed for an idea of potential
revolutionary force. The *Milti Apofasimeni* were a band of
' Knights', named, each one of them, after a hero of the
Republic; on the anniversary of Cæsar's death every hero
donned a ' cockade of large size ' and assembled to keep
republican festival. There were not many Knights, but
their oath was a serious one: ' I swear in the sight of
Almighty God that I enter this society, with no intention
of favouring any particular interest but only that of ren-
dering Italy one, independent, and free'.[2] Mazzini's idea
was evidently finding a few followers in Tuscany; his
famous letter to Charles Albert circulated comparatively
widely, and the victims of the year 1833 were genuine or
reputed associates of Young Italy or the half-affiliated
society of the True Italians, founded by a descendant of
the great Michelangelo. But Mazzini himself admitted
that Tuscany was not good soil for his propaganda,[3] the
government acted decisively against plotters in 1833 and
1836, and as the echoes of revolution died down in Europe,
the poor energy of the Tuscan societies dwindled away.[4]
Even Guerrazzi threw himself into his profession, aiming
at material compensations. The government might claim
that the serpent had been expelled or charmed from Eden.

[1] E. Michel, *op. cit.* 59. [2] *Ibid.*, p. 170. [3] *Epistolario* di G. M. (Firenze
Sansoni), I, 619. Letter to J. Ruffini. [4] The subject of secret societies in
Tuscany has attracted attention disproportionate to its importance. The most
complete account of them for 1830–5 is given by Michel, *op. cit.* For the
Carbonari, who had two sickly lodges in Leghorn, see Scaramella, *Spirito
pubblico, . . .in Livorno,* 1815–21. A summary account of the societies is
given by F. Martini in *Nota XI* to the *Memorie* of Giusti, and G. Stiavelli
in *L'Italia Moderna,* Anno IV, Fasc. 23. It is not worth while to enumerate
them, but it may be interesting to note that Professore Pigliwas 'pontiff'
in the *Carbonari Riformati* and Professore Montanelli in the *Fratelli
Italiani* (1843), which was a very moral organisation.

The crisis had only been postponed. In these years the system of Leopold and his ministers had suffered an assault more disastrous than any which Guerrazzi could bring against it. In February of 1833 the Austrian ambassador presented a protest, couched in the most general terms, against the *Antologia*.[1] The government gave one of its customary evasive replies, but the *Voce della Verità*, a reactionary journal subsidised by the Duke of Modena, maintained a constant attack against the *Antologia*, and the censorship of Tuscany reacted to the pressure. Vieusseux, in despair at the hindrances which met him on every hand, wrote to Corsini demanding a definite statement of the government's attitude towards his review; he received a most reassuring answer. Then, when he was away in Genoa, appeared two articles (both passed by the censor[2]) which raised a storm in the Modenese paper. One of them was considered an offence to Russia, the other (an article by Tommasèo under the initials K. X. Y.) an insult to Austria. The ministers of the two countries protested; and, according to Tommasèo, the alarm at the Palazzo Pitti surpassed that of Vieusseux himself. The *Antologia* might have been saved if Vieusseux had revealed the names of the offending writers. Tommasèo himself wrote at the last minute to the Grand-Duke, begging him to ' impose on him alone the condemnation inflicted on the entire *Antologia*'. Vieusseux would not allow him to despatch the letter.[3] The *Antologia* was suppressed.

It was a revelation to Tuscany that the liberties she had enjoyed were held on a tenure even more uncertain than that of Grand-Ducal benevolence. It seemed that, in the last resort, it was Austria who governed in Florence, as she governed in Milan. In a large issue which admitted

[1] For what follows see Prunas, *op. cit.*, Ch. V, and Tommasèo on Vieusseux, p. 135 seq. [2] Tommasèo notes that the censor had made fourteen corrections. [3] See Prunas, Appendix VII, for Vieusseux's notes of his conversation with Corsini. Tommasèo's letter is in the *Carteggio Vieusseux*, not in any official records; the inference therefore is that it was never sent.

no evasion the government had given way. Leopold had shown that the demands of his house must, in a crisis, override his own will and the will of his subjects. The duke of Modena, whose onslaught against Vieusseux had prepared the way for the final disaster, had, everyone knew, thrown in his lot with Austria. Was the Tuscan government the victim of an Austrian vassal? Among the many bulletins which were distributed in Florence at the time, there was one which stated the position with remorseless precision.

'The Grand-Duke of Tuscany has had the baseness to obey the lieutenant of Austria ! . . . Tuscans ! ! Either we are under the government of Modena, or the Grand-Duke of Tuscany is another Duke of Modena'.[1]

There was no escaping from this dilemma. The government could only hope that such a cruel proof might not come again. In the years that followed, despotism was as benevolent as it had ever been, and Tuscany made a brave show of independence. But the Earthly Paradise had lost its glamour. Giordani himself had at last been remembered as an exile and a dangerous liberal, and had been expelled from Florence. Liberals were closing their ranks in a common desire for independence from Austrian control. Any chance incident might force Leopold to choose again between the aspirations of his most active subjects and the claims of his house.

The country, however, enjoyed good seasons, and the majority of Tuscans cared for none of these things.

---

[1] Prunas, *op. cit.* Appendix IX, prints this and similar protests.

CHAPTER III

THE PURITAN OF BROLIO

In the agitation which disturbed the police of Tuscany in the early 'thirties, and which seized on the occasion of the suppression of the *Antologia*, Vieusseux himself had no part. Politics to him were of secondary importance; he interpreted civilisation in cultural and economic terms. ' The questions of political reform are nothing', he told Ricasoli, ' the social questions are everything. . . . Industry, labour, wages, pauperism, labouring and intellectual proletariate, education . . . these are tremendous questions, and are all embraced in the great question of agriculture, especially in Tuscany'.[1] Ricasoli believed him. Working slowly outwards from a centre, consolidating every inch of intellectual ground which he gained, he felt all his energies absorbed in the education of Bettina and his ' apostolate ' in the Chianti. His one great fear was that he should fall short of the task which he had chosen.

' There is one thorn which ever torments me, and brings tremendous oppression to the ardour of my spirit. . . . In the divine decrees is it written that I shall reach the final goal of the plan that I have conceived? Or is it decreed that, amid the best of my work, I shall see myself . . . constrained again to annihilate myself in that city of Florence? '[2]

He escaped the annihilation which he feared, and six years after he had taken the great resolution was able to recite to the *Georgofili* a history of difficulties vanquished and success achieved.[3] The peasants, when he came to Brolio, had all their eggs in two insufficient baskets. ' It did not occur to the *contadini* of Chianti that there were other riches than those that came from wine and the fattening of pigs'. In an age of low prices, this traditional economy gave small returns. There were, it is true, the

[1] *L. & D.*, I, 24. Cf. I, 28, on Science Congresses, ' Let us pray God that such slow but secure progress be not disturbed by politics'. [2] *L. & D.*, I, 24–25. [3] *L. & D.*, I, 493.

olive groves, but their productivity had been ruined by ignorance. There had been insufficient control of the water that came pouring down the mountains, so that the soil round the roots was washed away, and the roots exposed to the burning summer sun; manure for the trees was almost unknown, and pruning neglected or performed ignorantly. There was the same blundering and ignorance in the treatment of farm stock; it hardly occurred to the peasants to grow their own fodder, and the beasts were expected to thrive on straw and leaves.

Ricasoli described the technical measures which he had taken to redress this state of things, but he made it his main concern to lay upon the right shoulders the blame for past neglect. He would hear nothing against the peasants.

'When I hear people sympathise with the peasants, or abuse them, I cannot avoid thinking that the pity is usually empty, and the abuse unjust; it is not the people's fault that it is ignorant and uneducated; it lacks the opportunity rather than the will'.

Least of all could the Tuscan proprietors blame the peasants, for either they stayed away from their estates altogether, or went there only 'for the uneducative pleasures of the chase'. Nor could the clergy, for the Tuscan priests were remarkable neither for education nor for evangelical zeal. This is the theme to which Ricasoli often returned. Only a year or two earlier he had written in the *Giornale Agrario*[1] that the contadino, always abused, could be made the nerve of Tuscan agriculture, while the blind and foolish neglect of him by the landowners made him instead its bane. ' Who instructs him, to be able to say that he does not want instruction? Who educates him, who shows for him sympathetic and prudent care, to stamp him as ungrateful?' . . . and he went on to praise the good *fattore* who knew how to read to the people the open book of the fields.

' Let us remind ourselves how much we spend to educate ourselves', he urged the *Georgofili*, 'and how little we do for the education of the

[1] *L. & D.*, I, 485.

people'. 'We compassionate poverty, and the misery that comes with it, but we forget the real affliction of the poor man, his real poverty . . . the lack of that second creation which forms the heart'.

His own sovereign rule in dealing with the peasants was patience. He had determined to proceed by degrees, to change practices step by step 'as heart and mind adjusted themselves'. The peasants must be under no illusion as to who was master—'I felt that many times I should have to be severe with them'—but granted the two essentials of firmness and patience, the rest was simply a matter of time. The baron was able to address his listeners with the prestige of a famous success.

The miscellaneous records of management which remain at Brolio illustrate more intimately Ricasoli's methods and mind. A notebook of Economics and Statistics[1] shows him at work on the technical side of management, writing down everything that related to his task; various notes on machinery, a receipt for making punch and *vino aleatico*, considerations on the nourishment and custody of cows, on the cultivation of potatoes, and methods of ceramic art, precepts on domestic economy, including the mystery of cooking. Another notebook is given over to the technique of pruning, illustrated by beautifully clear designs.[2] Another records his personal supervisions of the various farms of the estate in alphabetical order, with his criticisms on their economic position, and the moral and intellectual state of the families.[3] There were seventy-eight scattered farms which demanded supervision, and the good proprietor must know every fruit tree from which he had the right of toll, and every child whose future was in his charge. . . . When the master was dead his old peasants sometimes believed that they saw him riding over the rough, wooded hills through the wind and rain, as he had ridden so often in those years when he first came to live among them.[4]

[1] *Brolio MSS.*, C. I, 52. [2] *Ibid.* C. I, 54. Cf. *Ibid.* F. 34 (potatoes), F. 39 (grain and fodder), F. 39 (beet), etc. [3] *Ibid.* E. 43. [4] G. Finali, *op. cit.* p. 39.

In the complicated task of administration much had to be left to subordinates. Ricasoli made his power felt through his agents,[1] as later he imposed his will in every corner of Tuscany by directing the activity of carefully chosen prefects. Order throughout the estate had as its first condition discipline and harmony in the castle; to this end he issued to the servants of the household and the agents of the estate printed instructions which called upon them to see in what he ordered, the unshakeable expression of his will, and at the same time a testimony of his bene-volence. In the document[2] appear with bewildering rapidity of change, the spirit of a mediæval baron, of a modern man of affairs, of an evangelical preacher. The servants have first of all a duty towards God:

'Have religion simple and sincere; religion in words and acts. Religion is comprised in the ten commandments of God. Stamp them on your hearts'.

They have also a duty towards their master:

'Regard the property of your master with as much zeal and care as if it were your own'.

In faithful service of God consists the faithful service of man, and both demand the exercise of simple virtues:

'Do not be hypocrites, of those who before the master are sheep, and with others become vipers. I hate such people; they are viler than reptiles'.
'My dear people, hate idleness. Idleness putrifies the body and destroys the spirit. Hate idleness. Postpone old age by an active life. So will you keep health and freedom of spirit. . . . Go to bed early, and acquire appetite with exercise'.

He promises them that such habits will secure them 'discreet' desires, will save them from bad dreams, and keep them content with their station in life, so that 'with plain and sufficient fare, a peaceful bed, and health, you will count yourselves happier than kings'. Ricasoli only demanded from others what he performed himself. If he fought idleness in his own dependents, he loathed it even

---

[1] For characteristic instructions to the agent of the fattoria see *Brolio MSS.*, E. 23, E. 26. [2] Published in Gotti, *Ricasoli*, pp. 30–41.

more in persons of his own class;[1] from his earliest days
he had made himself an apostle of serious work.

There were other virtues almost equally important:

' Be careful of cleanliness . . . water costs nothing . . .'

' Each of his own accord will look after the cleanliness of the bed and
of the room assigned to him'.

' Before going out he will make his bed, clean the vessels which have
served for his use. . . . Twice a week he will change the towels; the bed
linen he will change every fortnight'.

' Every room will be furnished: with a bed, and mattress, a chest of
drawers, a washstand, with basin and jug, a night-vessel, four chairs, and a
Portrait of the Blessed Redeemer'.

It is a complete system of benevolent despotism! And the
baron, like a crowned prince, claims to be the father of his
faithful subjects. He will have order first, but he will
rule by love, and will give affection as the reward of
obedience. He tells his servants that they may trust in his
justice and moderation, and that ' they will find in him a
father rather than a master'. He returns to the same
theme again and again:

' Regard the master as your own father, and the master's house as your
father's house'. ' My house should be a single family'.

But, in order that this may be so, the servants must themselves be brothers one with another.

' You will be brothers one with another, and if you will not be, I tell
you in truth that you cannot be mine, nor I yours. Jesus Christ died for us
men to redeem us from sin, and will you not love each other, aid each other,
suffer each other, bear with each other? '

His servants must be in their dealings with the peasants
as he is in his dealings with them: first, they must be
unflinchingly just, and then they must win the love of
those who are under them by kindness and understanding.

' If you win the reputation of being just, you will obtain respect and
love, and even the guilty will bend their heads to your reproof, and make
no complaint'.

' Because you are poor, do not believe that charity is not for you. You
are wrong. You have this prejudice, because you believe that charity consists
in giving food to others without benefit to anyone. . . .'

[1] See C. I, and *Brolio MSS.*, C. 19 (notes on the duties of the rich).

The baron proceeds to a panegyric of charity as glowing
as that of the apostle Paul:

' The true charity is that which teaches, which sweetens, which corrects,
which directs the man, and teaches him to go by his own power, and puts
him beyond the need of the aid of others. Jesus taught the poor. Here is the
true charity'.

And so this extraordinary document of benevolent despotism goes on, and the baron appears now as the martinet,
now as the preacher, now as the man of business, always
as master. He is a Lycurgus ordering his little state; in
the end he launches to his agents an ultimatum calling on
them to accept his system within three days, or else get
them gone for ever.

From time to time he posted up bulletins on the castle
wall, like the captain of a liner at sea. Some of them have
to do with the seasons and the needs of the soil:

' The Master notifies the peasants that this is the time to put lime on
corn. Lime is a secure protection against the Fox. . . . Anyone who has
his corn *foxed*[1] in the coming year, if he has not taken lime, will pay the
penalty'.

Others, like the following, seek to stimulate the peasants
by precept, or by arousing them to a spirit of emulation.

NOTICE !

' The Master of Brolio values the good peasants; those, that is to say,
who, living like Christians, are religious, enemies to idleness and to sloth,
friends of labour, of industry; those who have improved their holdings . . .
those who have lived honourably on the product of their labour, and not at
the expense of the Master. . . .'
' In proof of the above the Master of Brolio institutes ten prizes to be
conferred one every year on the head of the family which unites the following
excellencies: . . .'

The virtues necessary included Christian reputation,
economy in the use of time, industry, dutifulness towards
the master, a good order in cultivation, the satisfactory
care of farm-animals, freedom from debt. The prize was
of fifteen *zecchini*, and two local priests were to be the

[1] *Volpato. Brolio MSS.*, E. 24. Cf. E. 25, E. 39 (b).

judges. Perhaps the reward was too small, or the virtues demanded too difficult of attainment; at any rate, a note of Ricasoli records that the prize was given one year, and that afterwards the competition lapsed for lack of competitors![1]

There came a day when Ricasoli, like a Tuscan Napoleon, codified all the laws of his domain. In the *Regolamento*,[2] as he named his code, he starts bravely with a preamble.

' A good culture of the farms will have as its chief end the annual increase of the fertility of the soil. . . . We live a few years; after us come our children. Accursed be that master, or that peasant, who exhausts the earth, eating as it were the bread of his sons'.

There follows an enumeration of the proper methods of working the soil, of tending vines and olive trees, of using manures, of storage, of the use of water, of the nurture of animals, of the care of implements, of every detail that concerns economy and efficiency of cultivation. Then comes a declaration of pains and penalties, through which the master enforces good manners, good morals, decency and gravity of conduct, with the minuteness of a Calvinistic dictator. The Administration will take steps against all those peasants who do not keep in their holdings a well-ordered garden; who do not rise early in the morning; who do not give adequate attention to the condition of their implements; who do not dress with ' that simplicity which befits a peasant'. It will take measures against those heads of families who do not assert their authority over all members, or who are guilty of favouritism towards individuals; against all those families where there is no instruction in the Christian religion, where there is evidence of the vice of blasphemy, or neglect of the virtue of charity. It is announced that the master will not concede to any maiden the so-called right of dowry, unless he is satisfied that she is fit to be a good

[1] *Brolio MSS.*, E. 40 (b). In Tuscany the *zecchino* was equal in value to a florin. [2] Regolamento Agrario della Fattoria di Brolio, 1843. It was reprinted at Siena (Tip. dell' Ancora di G. Bargellini) in 1873. Copious extracts are given by Gotti.

THE CASTLE OF BROLIO

wife and a good mother (Ricasoli used to address the
mothers of his estate on the dignity and the practical
duties of their calling[1]) and until she has undergone an
examination in Christian doctrine. . . . And, after an
accumulation of rules which read now like a mediæval
sumptuary law, now like an Act of Uniformity, and now
like the regulations of a factory-owner in the nineteenth
century, the document changes suddenly to the wistful,
pleading tone of a gospel.

‘The ruin of families occurs where there is not given early to the children
the education through which alone can be developed their good qualities.
Through education they are made religious at heart, moral, fit for their
work, and sound of body. To have a good and sound plant, to what else do
you resort but to education? To have a fat beast, what else do you do than
give guiding care? And you take care of plants, and beasts, and will not take
care of the child, of the peasant?’

The man’s ardour did not content itself with written
rules and instructions. On Sundays, when the baroness
and her daughter were holding school for the children,[2]
Ricasoli gathered the adults together, and gave them
that instruction which, he complained, was so criminally
neglected by the priests. There remain among his papers
written sermons which formed part of a weekly course.[3]
Each Sunday there were questions concerning the parable
which had been expounded in the previous week, and
after ‘ some rather free discussion ’ the evangelical
master spoke to the congregation with his written discourse before him. He explained to them in simple Tuscan
the parables of the sower, of the lost sheep, of the lost
talent, with their lessons of filial duty and love, of the
dangers of bad companions, of the saving grace of penitence,
of the goodness of God.

‘God’, he told them, ‘has created man for the sake of man, which
means that we should assist one another. God has created the earth for man,
and I shall say more; it is the soil which joins me to you; there is consolation

[1] *Brolio MSS.*, C. 15. *Consigli alle Donne circa all’ ordine indispensabile
nell’ andamento della famiglia.* [2] Gotti, p. 65. Cf. Lambruschini, *Elogi e
Biografie*, 205 *et seq.* [3] *Brolio MSS.*, E. 21. Three of the sermons were
printed, and are noted in Gotti.

in the thought that all of us are bound together in one sole interest, common to us all ! It is a happy thing to know that my will ought to be your will, since that which I will is to do you good in every way'.

In later years he defined government as ' doing good to the people who are entrusted to us'. [1] His conviction that ' my will ought to be your will ' re-appeared in the great crisis of the destinies of Tuscany and Italy. His will was the ' real will ' of the Tuscans, as it was the real will of the peasants; it would lead them along the roads of freedom and greatness; none but an enemy of the people's will could withstand it. Ricasoli doubted none of those things.

Some of the sermons returned to the old theme of idleness, and the preacher terrified his listeners by calculating that an hour lost a day amounted to two and half days a month, and thirty in a year; that, with the return of a day's labour standing at a lira, this implied the loss of 30 lire in a year and 1200 lire in forty years. The audience was overwhelmed with the figures. Then, before it could recover, it was dazzled by a different calculation; the good worker who stayed in the fields this extra hour, and deposited his gains in a savings' bank, would have at the end of the same forty years a sum amounting in principal and interest to 2956 lire. To drive the moral home, the preacher printed one of his favourite sermons, and at the end of it appended eighty precepts for the young peasant whereby he might make his fortune. They were the same precepts urging early rising, cleanliness, saving, sociability, filial duty, the hatefulness of sloth, the value of time. Many of them might have been adapted from the proverbs with which each generation of peasants put its sons upon the narrow path of parsimony and virtue. The most sage of them all is a reflection upon poverty:

' Poverty is not a vice, but it is not a virtue; see then that you flee from it; see that you are virtuous, and with the aid of work, of order, and of economy, it must follow that poverty will flee from you'.

[1] *L. & D.*, IV, 119.

It is a misfortune that the history of enterprises such
as that which Ricasoli undertook at Brolio, can, as a rule,
be told only from the side of the active and strenuous
reformer. Only the tradition of the fields stores up the
thoughts, the hesitations, the fears and the hopes of those
who are led or driven to throw aside old practices, to
perform new and strange duties, to 'leave the old road for
the new'. A friend of Ricasoli's, who used to visit Brolio
after the death of its master, and found time to move
about among the peasants, discovered that they remembered the baroness Anna as 'the good lady'. When he
asked the old men who had known the baron, whether he
had been loved by those whom he had championed and
persuaded and drilled, they used to answer:
'Ah, sir, he was a powerful man'.[1]

  .   .   .   .   .   .

Throughout these years Ricasoli had been engaged on
another labour as endless and absorbing as the ordering
of his estate, the struggle with conservative peasants, or
the education of his daughter—a labour within his own
mind. His fear of events that might call him to 'annihilate' himself again in Florence was not only a dread of
leaving his 'apostolate' half finished, it sprang from his
spiritual craving for a solitude in which he could concentrate his mind upon his task and upon himself. 'I am the
product of meditation, of solitude',[2] he told his brother.
'Thy mind ever works upon itself in solitude', a friend
wrote to him,[3] almost in compassion. In his latter years
he felt the need of 'thoughtful, active solitude';[4] and in
the disappointments of life he sought an asylum within
himself.[5] Man, he believed, was a stranger upon this
earth; his task was to prepare what was alone eternal, his
character.[6] Nothing was more absorbing to Ricasoli than
his own inner life; no faculty of man seemed to him of
more supreme importance than the faculty of conscience.
Every evening he asked himself: 'Have I lied to myself

[1] Finali, *op. cit.* p. 45.   [2] *L. & D.*, VII, 17.   [3] *L. & D.*, I, 36.   [4] *L.
& D.*, VII, 248.   [5] *L. & D.*, VII, 243.   [6] *L. & D.*, II, 137.

in thought, in action?'[1] He believed that 'a man's conscience is infallible, if rightly questioned'.[2] He had the
temper of an English Puritan, ruling and testing his own
life according to his own standards, indifferent to the
judgments of the world, to the criticisms of friends or
enemies. 'Between me and God no one can enter'.[3]

From the contemplation of his own soul he turned to
the contemplation of the world, expecting to find in it
the same principles which held sway within his own being.
He read books of history and philosophy, and he made
summaries of what he read;[4] he collected facts of every
shape and character. But in all that he read and in all that
he wrote down for his own contemplation there was not
a grain of disinterested intellectual activity—nothing but
material for moral judgments, nothing but illustration of a
principle.

'My spirit', he wrote to a friend in Switzerland,[5] 'takes pleasure in
thought, in reading, in conversation, only when it is of a nature calculated
to fill the heart and the spirit. Everything that nourishes this need, a little
restless, of interior life, which makes it felt incessantly within me—life of
the heart, life of the soul, life of the spirit as detached from every connection
with what is material—constitutes my greatest pleasure'.

All this labour on his own mind, which he carried on
in his solitude, was a labour to discover the meanings
which most men dismiss as simple. Ricasoli was one of
those men who feel the need of probing for themselves
the truth of truisms. He could not grasp the meaning of
anything until he felt it. In the end, after all his toil, he
found that he had garnered just a few simple ideas. Their
value was fixed, not by the laws of exchange, but by the
labour which had gone to the making of them. They were
not theories; they were convictions and rules of life. He
clung to them, brooded over them, used them as the
touch-stone which would test every work of man, the
standard by which his conscience would judge every work
of his own.

1 *L. & D.*, VII, 243. 2 *L. & D.*, VII, 235. 3 *L. & D.*, I, 360.
4 *Brolio MSS.*, B. 12, B. 14, B. 21, B. 30. 5 *L. & D.*, II, 227.

' The rule inflexible of every act, every word of mine, is principle, only principle'.[1]

In every task to which he was called he had a plan of action, mapped out beforehand; there was one right way, and all other ways were wrong; from the right way no power on earth could shift him.

The introspective, moralising character of his spirit is illustrated by his correspondence with a friend whom he discovered in the early days of his apostolate. Despite his passion for solitude, he needed a friend with whom he could share his spiritual experiences; his mind worked incessantly, but never joyously; his thought trod always the same circle and came back to the same starting point; his brain grew weary. He could commune with God and with his notebooks; this was communion with his own spirit. He was fighting a battle with loneliness.

Raffaello Lambruschini[2] was well fitted to give him the religious friendship for which he craved. Lambruschini's training as a Jesuit might have led him, as it led his uncle, to the cardinalate; but an evangelical conception of Christianity and unorthodox ideas on the question of authority made ordinary Church discipline impossible for him. He fled from Rome to a quiet farm at Figline, in the Val d'Arno, where he experimented on the rearing of silk worms and meditated on the problems of Church reform till Vieusseux dragged him from his retreat to play a large part in agricultural and educational propaganda in Tuscany and Italy. His religious ideas can be summarised in a few propositions: hostility to the mediævalism which clung to the Church; belief that religion must reconcile itself to the scientific and political ideas of the century; elevation of individual intuition (not reason, which he distrusted) as the medium of true religious experience; and with it all a faith in the universal mission of Catholicism.

' General principles are the same for all, but the method of grasping them, of conceiving them, and expounding them, is altogether individual'.

[1] *L. & D.*, I, 397. [2] G. Vannini, *Raffaello Lambruschini;* Tabarrini, *Vite;* G. Gentile in *Gino Capponi* (the quotations are taken from this last.)

'Truth lives historically, adapting itself and conforming itself to the incessant development of the human spirit'.

'All attempts to discover with our reason the nature of God . . . are vain and rash . . . Jesus Christ has told us of God all that it is necessary for us to know'.

'From now on', he wrote to Niccolo Puscini in 1848, ' as far as I am concerned, I believe that the time is come to raise again the banner of Jesus Christ, that is, of true Catholicism; and what I write or say shall be to this end. Either they will burn me as Savonarola, or I shall do some good for Italy and for the world'.

In all Lambruschini's writings there appears the same reiteration of fundamentals, the same insistence on a few central principles, which had marked the solitary meditations of Ricasoli. Each found in the other a kindred spirit; their friendship reached the point of ardour. 'Take good care', wrote Lambruschini when there had been on Ricasoli's part some slackening in the correspondence, ' do not put me any more to trial; remember that I am human, and that you are such a friend, that I cannot suffer in peace to be forgotten by you'.[1] The baron received his friend's affection and moral reflections with a sort of ecstasy.

'Oh my friend, how your thoughts have penetrated my soul! Yes, I firmly believe that our characters are alike in many points. I feel the same need, I experience the same desire, and yes! I share an inconceivable good, a balsam restoring to my heart, since my mind expands itself in thine; oh! why are we not near enough to be able to take counsel together more often!'

Contrasting the spiritual truth of Lambruschini's principles and his own with the baseness of his age, Ricasoli exclaimed:

'And in this age of vile materialism and guilty egoism, can there exist two spirits which really *feel* ? Yes, my spirit feels, and feels profoundly, and if I assert it, I know that I am not led to this by any human pride, but by the need to find a similar soul'.[2]

Under the touch of sympathetic friendship the lonely meditations of Ricasoli flowered into expansive sentimentalism. It almost appears as if he were losing some of the sturdy independence of his character through an excessive deference to the nice scruples of the older man.

[1] *L. & D.*, I, 15. [2] *L. & D.*, I, 38.

He sought his counsel on the sermons which he should
preach to the peasants, and accepted as guide a book of
homilies written by a country curate;[1] he asked and was
given advice on the bounds within which it was legitimate
to call simple folk to religion and hard work by exhorting
them to venerate a peasant-saint.[2] Here he raised many
points for intricate moralising, and Lambruschini wrote
at length on all of them. Ricasoli paid humble attention.
He bowed his head in contrition, too, when his friend
reproved him for delivering a sermon which appealed
over-much to the worldly ambition of those committed
to his spiritual care.[3] If one judged from this correspondence alone, it would seem that Ricasoli's worship of
' principles ' was degenerating into hair-splitting, and
that his character was being enervated by excessive sentimentalism. But there was an opposite side to his nature.
To another friend he had declared that he felt himself
made only for *action*.[4] Ricasoli was not able to spin his
thoughts into elegant essays, as Lambruschini could; but
he was capable of spending day after day in the saddle and
night after night in the laboratory. Here only was he really
happy, for sooner or later his own musings always
became nauseating to him. Thus it was that his
life became darkest when the old methods of action
lost their savour;[5] and that he was most supremely
happy when he could translate his moral reflections into
practical instructions to the prefects under his control, and
apply his principles in the hundred day-to-day details of
government.[6]

Throughout these early years at Brolio his interests had
gradually expanded from their chosen centre. Idleness,
thrift, poverty, education, religious teaching, were general

[1] *L. & D.*, I, 30. [2] *L. & D.*, I, 39 *et seq*. Ricasoli chose Saint Isidore
as the theme of a discourse, and told the peasants that he had become a
saint, because he was a good son and a good father, and worked hard, and
was content all his life to remain a peasant. Lambruschini held that there
could be no moral objection to calling on the peasants to venerate the saint,
so long as this was not done *inside* the Church. [3] *L. & D.*, I, 58.
[4] *L. & D.*, I, 33. [5] See Chapter VI. [6] See Chapters VII–IX.

problems not limited to Brolio; as gonfaloniere of the
little commune of Gaiole he saw in microcosm the machine
of Tuscan government. The particular, as ever, was to
Ricasoli an illustration of the general. In some notes
written before the disturbances of the late 'forties,[1] his
thought shows itself passing from considerations on the
decadence of Tuscan agriculture and commerce to a
general criticism of public morality and the government
machine. ' Governmen there means *laisser-faire* and *laisser-
aller*. He blamed in the government its lack of a clear
design, and he blamed the inertia of the government
officials: ' public weal is entrusted to men who have
neither love for it nor understanding in advancing it'.
He complained of the neglect of local administration, and
traced all these ills, not to any superficial causes, but to
the lack of institutions which might educate the citizens.
He was at war with the whole system of Fossombroni;
he had rallied to the political faith of Capponi. And, just
as the problems which surrounded him at Brolio re-
appeared in the same form in Tuscany, so the questions
agitating Tuscany appeared part of great movements
which were passing across Italy and Europe. A journey
to France in 1844, during which he attended the Paris
exhibition, sent his daughter to study botany in the Jardin
des Plantes, and studied for himself viticulture in the
Bordelais, reminded him of principles and ideals which
still had explosive power. He thought of France[2] as ' a
fire which burns those who rashly get too close to it, but
can give pleasant heat and can satisfy the need and desire
for warmth when we stand before it as we should stand'.
He saw in the spread of railways the sign of an irresistible
force which was drawing mankind towards a larger and
freer life. The project of a Sienese company excited him
with the thought that it would be possible ' to be at the
same time at Brolio, Siena, Florence, Pisa, Leghorn, Lucca,
High Italy . . . and all the world, so that Brolio and

1 *Brolio MSS.*, C. I. The date is uncertain; it may be 1847, when the
disturbances were beginning, and is certainly no later.   2 *L. & D.*, I, 91.

Paris may become just one'.[1] He himself took the initiative in the formation of a company which would send a line down the Val di Chiana and in the end would link Arezzo to Ancona.[2]

'God be praised', he exclaimed, 'for this and similar happenings, which take place every day throughout the world. . . . It is a power of Providence which draws men with them, taking no notice of the reluctant, the timid, the obstinate'.

This idea of a 'power of Providence', an irresistible spirit of the age which must draw men and governments in its train, became with Ricasoli a serene conviction. If he had been asked in what this power, this spirit, consisted, he would have replied: Liberty. Liberty, he would have added, was the same as progress; it was the assertion of human dignity, the triumph of spirit over matter, the law of the moral world.[3] As for himself, he never doubted that he was an humble instrument of Providence, a servant of Liberty. It was in the service of Liberty that, thirteen years later, he stilled all voices of protest and loosed every force of propaganda till he had planted among the Tuscans the faith that their destinies lay 'in a strong Italian kingdom under the constitutional sceptre of Victor Emmanuel'. It was in the service of Liberty that he had drilled, ordered, persuaded his peasants to throw aside their prejudices and commit themselves to the strange ways of scientific agriculture. Always, in the days when he held supreme power in Italy or in Tuscany, as in the days of his apostolate at Brolio, he found it 'a happy thing to know that my will ought to be your will, since that which I will is to do you good in every way'. He had learnt his idea of Liberty in the years of dictatorship and meditation among the lonely hills of the Chianti. The decrees of Providence were nothing more nor less than those 'principles' which he had discovered in the daily examination of his own conscience, and declared in his letters to Lambruschini.

[1] L. & D., I, 102. [2] Brolio M.S.S., H. 9, 10, 12, 19 (1845–6). The venture broke down. [3] L. & D., VII, 144; I, 309.

He did not yet dream that he would be called upon to
leave what he considered his real work, and to serve the
spirit of the age in a wider field. Yet, once his mind had
been turned to the consideration of the greater problems
in the world beyond Brolio, it was inevitable that the
same weariness of mere reflection, the same passion to
mould men and things, would drag him from the retreat
to which they had originally driven him. He distrusted
his own ignorance and narrow culture, and for a time,
without realising it, nourished the hope that he
might play a part in the world of affairs by directing the
genius of another friend, whom he had discovered at the
Science Congress of 1841.

Vincenzo Salvagnoli was at this time thirty-nine years
of age, and was one of the cleverest of Tuscan lawyers;
he was also an ardent liberal, who in 1833 had been sent
to prison by an 'economic process' at the same time as
Guerrazzi. On being released, he was ordered to be of
good behaviour, and to have nothing to do with suspected
persons. 'Have the goodness to tell me who they are',
he answered, 'and I promise to have nothing to do with
them'.[1] It was a request with which a timorous police
found it difficult to comply; Salvagnoli, if for the future
he eschewed conspiracy, remained as ardent a liberal as
ever, and found suspected persons like Capponi a little too
conservative and academic for his taste.[2] His genius was
of a French rather than an Italian character. His education
had been almost entirely French; he was a friend of
Thiers and Mignet, and had a good acquaintance with
the French writers of his own day and of the eighteenth
century. He had the detachment and the delight in things
purely intellectual which Ricasoli lacked, and was perhaps
the most brilliant talker in Florence. 'The first time that
I heard him speak', recounts Ferdinando Martini, 'was
one evening at home; he maintained in burlesque, and to
the great scandal of a priest of Valdinievole who took him
seriously, that stealing books was not only justifiable, but

¹ Martini, *Simpatie*, p. 219.   ² Tabarrini, *Capponi*, p. 258.

praiseworthy . . . with a wealth of Latin, French and Italian quotations that astounded me, and not only me'. On another occasion he gave, on the spur of the moment, the plot, the chief characters, and some of the purple passages of a play which he had never written, and never intended to write; and the small boy, who had met Giusti and remained cold, could think of no one save Dante with whom he might compare Salvagnoli.[1]

It must have been the unwavering constancy of Ricasoli's mind which attracted the more errant genius of the older man. Salvagnoli found, too, in the attitude of Ricasoli and Lambruschini to the Church, a special bond of union; for he had the true liberal's impatience of spiritual authority, and greeted the Giobertian propaganda with disdain. Ricasoli, on his side, admired and at times distrusted the brilliance of his friend; and almost unconsciously adopted towards him the attitude of a moral director standing behind a genius which seemed to him too unstable.

'I beg of you', he wrote to Salvagnoli after they had become political allies,[2] 'to sustain always the dignity of the orator. . . . If you do this, you will be the greatest orator of Tuscany. . . . I urge on you constant calm; not to make people laugh; not to make anyone angry; always to be simple and sincere'.

For years previously the two men had exchanged letters in which the one hid something of his brooding introspectiveness, and the other (who could make epigrams to Ricasoli ?) modified the free play of his fantasy. But Salvagnoli had surrendered to the obligations of intimacy.

'Friend, arise !' Ricasoli besought him; 'Friend, desist from declaiming against the impotence, the invading corruption, the abominations which grow and gain ground; have faith in the future; work, but work for the public; I have told you before, work, work, but work for all. . . . Friend, arise, arise, and do not hide yourself; oppose yourself to the current; truth is never impotent, except when she is hidden; declamation with one's friends is little, is nothing; you must act, act, act'.[3]

'I desire only', he wrote again, 'that there should be kindled in you that sacred fire which enflames Lambruschini, by which he is sustained by

[1] Martini, *Confessioni e Ricordi*, p. 37 *et seq.* [2] July 19, 1848. *L. & D.*, I, 372. [3] *L. & D.*, I, 80.

a hope of the future . . . and by which his faith is nourished, and through which he works to make things better'.[1]

Once in the clutches of such a friendship, Salvagnoli could not escape a surrender to the earnestness of Ricasoli. In compensation, he helped to draw the recluse of Brolio into the currents of Florentine liberalism. The baron's visits to Florence became more frequent; he followed more closely the events which were maturing in Italy. He was hoping that Capponi's history, when it appeared, would have printed on it 'a character, a sentiment, an action, which will awake Italian hearts to admire again this dear country of ours'.[2] He copied out with his own hands an article in which Capponi denounced impartially the folly of Romagnol conspirators, and the infamy of the Papal government which made continuous revolt a necessary feature in the history of the Romagna.[3] Another Italian, D'Azeglio, had written a famous little book on the same subject. Early in 1846 he was in Florence, carrying with him, everybody knew, the promise of the Piedmontese king that, when the occasion came, his life, the life of his sons, his arms, his treasures, his forces, would be at the service of Italy. A number of Florentine liberals prepared in honour of D'Azeglio a banquet; it was in the nature of a political demonstration. Ricasoli could not attend, but he wrote to his brother, Vincenzo:

'Grasp D'Azeglio by the hand for me, and tell him that Providence watches over Italy, and that the day must come when this will be made known'.[4]

One year later Ricasoli journeyed to Florence on a mission which began his political career. He sought an interview with Cempini, the chief of the Grand-Duke's ministers, and opened it with the brusque declaration:[5] 'The honest man ought to speak the truth, cost what it may'.

. . . . . .

[1] *L. & D.*, I, 84. [2] *L. & D.*, I, 102. [3] See Capponi, *Scritti*, I, 43. *Sui moti di Rimini.* [4] *L. & D.*, I, 112. [5] *L. & D.*, I, 127 (from Ricasoli's own notes, *Brolio MSS.*, M. 28).

For two years Tuscany had been stirred by the clatter of machinery and the clamour of protesting voices, which together invaded her peaceful towns and valleys; in those two years the quiet and indifference of the Earthly Paradise were drowned in the flood of a new age. The railways had come, hailed with enthusiasm by all patriotic liberals;[1] private companies were pushing the lines from Leghorn to Pisa and on to Florence; from Pisa to Lucca and from Lucca to Pistoia. With the railways came the telegraph; the service between Florence and Leghorn was ready in time to be a new toy for an amateur dictator, to carry the extravagant messages which Guerrazzi in 1849 sent flying from the seat of government to his own turbulent city. And, as if they were conscious that the advent of new machines and new ideas was closing the era of tranquillity over which they had presided, the veteran statesmen, Corsini and Fossombroni, had passed from the scene. Capponi[2] believed that their passing was Leopold's day of grace, a heaven-sent opportunity for overhauling the state, and ensuring its preservation by means of institutions in harmony with the ideal forces of the country. But the government neglected its own preservation; it remained a 'government of men', and the new men were inferior to their predecessors.

Giusti recounts that the names of the new ministers were announced to a gathering at Capponi's villa on an evening of November, 1845, and that Salvagnoli turned pale, and exclaimed that this news meant the ruin of Tuscany.[3] His fears were justified by events. Some months previously a conspirator named Renzi, a miserable scoundrel who made a business of patriotism,[4] had come fleeing across the mountains into Borgo San Sepolcro with a few followers, pursued by the Papal forces whom they had

[1] They denounced however the powers given to private companies: see Pettetti, *Delle strade ferrate italiane*, Capolago, 1845; and G. Carmignani, *Apologia delle concessioni sovrane per le strade ferrate in Toscana*, Pisa, Nistri, 1846. The first concession was made in 1841. [2] *Scritti*, II, 106 et seq. [3] Giusti, *Memorie*, 31. [4] Zobi, *Storia*, IV, 603 et seq., for the Renzi case. For the Treaty of 1827 *ibid.* appendix 61.

defied at Rimini. To the indignation of the Roman government, they were given safe-conduct through Tuscany, on
the condition that they should leave the country immediately. The leader, Renzi, broke the compact and came
back to Florence to prosecute intrigues of love and politics.
The Roman envoy demanded his surrender under the
terms of a treaty of 1827. When the government tried to
hedge on the matter, the envoy himself pointed out the
house where Renzi was hiding.[1] There followed a battle
between the government, bound by its treaty obligations,
and public opinion, which saw in the Papal demand a
threat to the independence of the state and a manœuvre
of Austria. The liberals hailed Renzi as a martyr, and
Salvagnoli, who was chief organiser of the campaign in his
favour, brought Renzi's often-betrayed but loyally-weeping
wife into the presence of the Grand-Duke. Mismanagement,
such as Fossombroni would have known how to avoid,
raised the affair into a burning question of principle. The
surrender of Renzi was widely hailed as a sign that Leopold
had once more bowed to a ' Lieutenant of Austria', that
the semi-independence of Tuscany was at an end, and
that the Tuscans must join the rest of the Italians in a
common resistance to a common enemy. Montanelli shut
his books on commercial law to study the problem of
organising nationalist propaganda in a country that had
no free periodical press.[2] ' Why should not the people
hear from the walls', he asked, ' the peaceable and
effective voice of reason?' He sought the words which
' most concisely and urbanely would express the feelings
aroused by the restitution of Renzi'; and his favourite
combination, DOWN WITH THE JESUIT MINISTRY, began to
shout its message of reason and urbanity from every
convenient wall in Pisa. Nearly six months before the
election of Pius the Ninth, Montanelli had started the
reformist agitation in Italy.

Before indignation at the surrender of Renzi had time
to wear thin, the government gave Montanelli a new

1 Baldasseroni, 185.   2 Montanelli, *Memorie*, I, 131 *et seq.*

occasion for action by authorising the Sisters of the Sacred Heart, whom all liberals regarded as ' the cranes who are wont to announce the flock of Jesuits',[1] to establish a convent in Pisa. Deliberately disregarding the law, Montanelli prepared a petition of protest, and for two days walked bare-headed through the city, openly urging the citizens to give their signatures. Pisa was in a ferment, and golden days opened out for the students. A month or two later the English ambassador reported them returning from the funeral of one of their professors to visit the houses of his surviving colleagues and greet them with cheers or hisses; then to march in a body to shout anathema to the Jesuits and acclamation to Italy before the palace of the Grand-Vicar of Pisa; then to the palace of the Archbishop to receive his blessing.[2] Throughout the previous month Montanelli had been stirring up passion by means of secretly printed bulletins. This new venture of his was excellently organised; there was a press at Pisa, and a reserve press safe across the frontier at Lucca; and a regular business-like treasurer, Rinaldo Ruschi,[3] to manage the financial side. The success of the Pisan experiment encouraged some of the younger liberals of Florence, among them the son of the minister, Cempini, and the banker, Carlo Fenzi, to set up a press in league with that of Montanelli. The Sienese liberals followed suit, and though Capponi and his friends would have nothing to do with this clandestine propaganda, respectable leaders like Salvagnoli, Niccolini, and Giuseppe Giusti lent it their support.[4] It had not yet occurred to the moderate liberals to think of themselves as a party, nor to denounce Montanelli as an extremist; as late as October in this year Vieusseux wrote to Ricasoli that he had acquitted himself with

[1] Giusti, *Epistolario*, III, 41–42. A. Marradi, *Giuseppe Montanelli*, Documents, VIII, IX, X. Gualterio, I, 36. [2] Parl. Papers, 1849 [1097], Part I Italian Correspondence, Hamilton to Palmerston, May 10. [3] A. D'Ancona, *op. cit.* 251 et seq. For the press see Montanelli, *Memorie*, C. XXII; and Gualterio, Part II, Vol. I, C. III; and Appendix 25 (many examples of bulletins). [4] Montanelli, *Memorie*, 209, 221, 228. Giusti, *Memorie*, Note 17 (Martini).

much dignity and wisdom towards the government.[1] The programme of his organisation, nevertheless, was radical for the time. In a bulletin entitled ' The Tuscan Liberals to the Tuscan People', it accused the government of ' hostility to all the ideas which constitute the moral need of our country', and summarised Tuscan needs in two propositions:

(1) Union of Italy against the Austrian.

(2) Internal institutions, suitable to the civil conditions of the time and of Tuscany—including the right of petition, municipal reorganisation, a reformed jury system, a periodical press under reasonable censorship, and a national guard. This pamphlet and all the others were distributed by a band of resourceful young men—the same who later fought with Montanelli at Montanara and Curtatone— who rained sheets down from the galleries in the theatres, passed them from hand to hand in the streets, left them in the Grand-Ducal ballroom, and sent them regularly by post to the Grand-Ducal ministers. The police tracked them down; some were arrested and exiled, but there were always others left to fill the gaps. The secret press boastfully called itself ' The new Hydra'.

The agitation was in full swing when news came that an obscure cardinal had been chosen to succeed Gregory the Sixteenth, and had taken the title of Pius the Ninth. Italy, as a whole, hoped little from the change. Jerome Bonaparte wrote to Farini that the election was due to Austrian intrigue, and Farini himself thought that Pius would do little to alter the miserable position of the Papal States.[2] A few believed erroneously that the ex-cardinal of Imola had once been a Carbonaro, and hoped that something might therefore be expected from him,[3] but in Tuscany there were not many who hoped anything. The Giobertian ideal of a liberal papacy had won few converts; Montanelli, himself an ardent disciple of Gioberti, recorded that the ardent young men preferred the anti-Guelf doc-

[1] L. & D., I, 120. Cf. Marradi, op. cit. Doc. VII.　[2] Farini, Epistolario per cura di Luigi Rava (Bologna, 1911), I, 467.　[3] Zobi Storia, V, 232.

trines of Niccolini.[1] Capponi's friends did not know what
to expect, till gradually rumours multiplied the new
Pope's virtues and whispered that ' he wished to change
everything into something better'.[2] The rumours received
startling confirmation with the publication of the famous
amnesty.

It is doubtful whether even the apparent incarnation of
Gioberti's ideal really convinced a majority of Tuscan
liberals that Italy would find salvation through the Papacy.
Salvagnoli remained sceptical and Ricasoli unenthusiastic.
Lambruschini wrote that it was madness to seek salvation
in the Temporal Power, that it would still be madness if
Pius were a thousand greater than his own goodness.[3]
But Montanelli had faith, and even those who doubted
were grateful for ' the wind which carries us on and
blows in the face of our enemies'.[4] The agitators who had
been fighting an uphill battle seized on the name of Pius
as a heaven-sent war-cry; ' the friends of liberty began to
make of him a support, the enemies a scarecrow'. Niccolini,
who had spent all his life preaching a different doctrine,
shut himself up in his villa in a rage. Either all the world
is mad, he said, or I am mad; and in contemplating this
dilemma he made himself ill.[5] One of his admirers recorded
a visit which he paid to the patriotic dramatist when the
neo-Guelf propaganda was at its height. The servants told
him that he would find their master locked up in the
library; he went to the door and knocked twice; no answer
came. He knocked again:

' At last I heard inside a rumbling like thunder in the distance, and then
a slow shuffling of feet approaching the door, and the rumbling grew louder.
Suddenly it stopped, a moment later the door was thrown open, and there
fell upon me so violent a tempest of injurious imprecations shouted at high
pitch, that I bent my head, and stood waiting till they should end'.·

Niccolini had mistaken his visitor for Montanelli, who
used to come to preach to him the reforming Papacy and

[1] Op. cit., I, 77.   [2] Giusti, Memorie, 67.   [3] L. & D., I, 123. Cf
118.   [4] Giusti, loc. cit.   [5] Masi, Memorie di F. Ranalli, 35; Vannucci
Niccolini, I, 74.

'drench' him in holy water like all the other imbeciles'. He was full of apologies when he recognised the visitor as a faithful Ghibelline.

Towards the end of 1846 the unfortunate government of Tuscany was faced with disturbances of a new kind. In the previous year the long succession of prosperous seasons had come to an end; the winter of 1846–1847 promised to be a severe one, and for more than three months the temperature was almost constantly below freezing point.[1] An unreasonable fear of famine began to spread through the country; men made pessimistic calculations of the harvest, and speculated gloomily on the effects which the adoption of free-trade in England would have on the flow of foreign corn to Leghorn. The government did what it could. It sacrificed nearly half a million lire of import duties, with the result that 1,773,000 bags of grain were imported within nine months;[2] it instituted public works to provide for the unemployed. But a normal wage of one lira a day is not conducive to philosophic detachment in a period of rising prices. It needed only the obstinacy of a village housewife and the greed of a local engrosser to start a succession of riots in the villages of Tuscany. Everywhere the authorities 'put their tails between their legs and came to terms with the robbers', and each success was the sign for a new riot.[3] Another and less respectable secret press began to champion the Poor Man, and in Florence respectable persons began to fear the spectre of communism. Then nationalist feeling, as ever, raised the cry of foreign gold, and patriots began to talk of the hidden hand of Austria, working secretly to 'give a body to the phantom of insurrection', that it might be grappled with and despatched before it grew to size and power. 'The food riots', declared Montanelli's press on January 22, 'have been disproportionate to the cause. . . . A few men caused the trouble in village

[1] Zobi, *Storia*, V, 41, et seq.   [2] Baldasseroni, 212.   [3] Giusti, *Memorie*, 73, et seq. Giusti was a witness of the first riot, which broke out in a village of Valdinievole.

after village; sometimes they were priests, with Austria behind them'. Whatever truth there was in this accusation against Austria,[1] it was serious enough to capture the attention of British diplomacy.

Moderate liberals were anxious at the course which events were taking. In the old days, when they had imagined the Earthly Paradise waking out of sleep to move in the stir of the modern world, they had never doubted that they themselves would be the unquestioned and honoured leaders in its onward march. Things were now happening in a very different fashion. While they themselves were held back from underground agitation by honourable scruple, unknown persons were driving on the people and snatching control from the rightful leaders. The government, they felt, was very foolish; by maintaining the laws which kept them silent it was crippling the one power which could promise it salvation. . . . Misgivings such as these prompted Ridolfi and some of his friends to approach the government and demand for themselves a special exemption from the existing laws which restricted journalism.[2] If their request were granted, they proposed to found a newspaper which would uphold the economic policy of the government, reassure the people against all fear of communism, stimulate activity in the municipalities, spread information on the progress of philanthropic works and education, discuss contemporary civil history—carry out on a grand scale, in fact, a day-to-day propaganda in favour of that Progress which Ridolfi had served for thirty years. . . . To their surprise, they found that the government had already decided on measures more far-reaching than those which they demanded.

· · · · · ·

[1] See appendix I. [2] See Gualterio, *op. cit.* Part II, Vol. I, Document XXVI; Zobi, *Storia*, Vol. V, appendix 5. Ridolfi, *op. cit.* 140 and appendix 10 (for a Memorandum of April 28, 1846, that had declared his general opinions). For very similar opinions see Capponi, *Lettere*, II, 287. (Letter to Baldasseroni, March 5, 1847).

The interview with the chief minister of state, which Ricasoli opened with his uncompromising truism—' The honest man should speak the truth '—was considered by contemporaries looking back upon two years of revolution as an event of great historical importance.[1] There seemed something dramatic in the descent of the Tuscan baron from his fastness to lecture the government on its short-comings, and something profound and original in the Roman sternness of his discourse. In fact, Ricasoli had simply overwhelmed the minister with the whole mass of precepts accumulated with such pain in the last ten years, adding some not very complimentary reflections on the recent conduct of the government. He, who lived among the people, knew that it was at heart sound; all its vices sprang from bad example and defective education; lack of schools,[2] lack of a learned and evangelical clergy, lack of efficient government, lack of leadership in harmony with the spirit of the age. He denounced ' the imprison-ment in which it is desired to hold the spirit', the veto which prevented men like himself from appealing to the sterling qualities of the people and thereby saving the government. As it was, the prince was profoundly un-popular; the people, who sought in him a Father, could see only the vassal of Austria who had surrendered Renzi.

'I know it, I know it only too well', broke in Cempini, '. . . the prince is become unpopular, and we cannot find the reason, for in everything he acts with angelic virtue, and we, we try to carry out his aims, we are martyrs of labour; and look how we are treated !'

' Ah ! If I were only twenty years younger', he exclaimed, when Ricasoli had finished expounding the principles whose adoption would win immortality for himself and his master.

---

[1] An account of it was first given by Gualterio, who printed his memoran-dum. Ricasoli's notes of his conversations with Cempini are printed in *L. & D.*, I, 127, *et seq*. [2] In 1838 about 1 child in 69 attended school, as against 1 in 12 in Lombardy and Venetia. Out of 284,200 children of school age, 21,300 actually attended. Bowring, *op. cit.* 57, *et seq*.

The baron had left behind him a memorandum[1] which treated in detail the arguments which he had sketched. It reduced the causes of anarchy to three. First were the hindrances to moral order, and in particular the lack of a sense of duty among the people, for which he blamed the deficiencies of the Church and of education. The regular clergy was neither learned nor moral, and was too numerous; the friars instructed neither themselves nor others, there was no teaching of true religion, but only a multiplication of festivals and ceremonies for the sake of gain, and as a result ' Society is without a foundation'. As for education, the lack of elementary instruction made of the University a ' pyramid without base'. ' Tuscany has more need of culture than any other country. . . . She has her glory and her strength in a most ancient civilisation, which she cannot repudiate without bringing infamy and ruin on herself'. She was already on this road of infamy and ruin.

The second disease of the state lay in the inefficiency of the governing machine; the inferior character of the civil servants, the distrust of municipal government, the lack of suitable organisation at the centre. The ministers were too overburdened with the details of administration to make provision for the future. ' There is need of a monarchical institution which, joining knowledge to experience, may prepare for the wisdom of the sovereign the materials for the study, discussion, and promulgation of the laws'.

The third obstacle to the successful exercise of government, according to the memorandum, was the existing form of the ' Economic Power'. ' It takes shadow for substance, it creates the danger by fearing it'. Its servants ' have a thousand ears to hear all the voices, even the most secret, of low passions, but they have not one ear to hear the language of intellect which meditates wise reforms, and of the heart which loves them'.

---

[1] *L. & D.*, 128, *et seq.* It must have been in its literary form the work of Salvagnoli, for it was published, with a few modifications, under his name. *Discorso sullo stato politico della Toscana nel Marzo del* 1847 (Lugano 1847). But Ricasoli wrote it out in his own hand. *Brolio MSS.*, M. 28.

What did Ricasoli hope to gain by this direct assault on the established order in Tuscany? He hoped for no party advantage, for he belonged to no party 'save that of honesty'. He was able to assure Cempini that his action was a secret between him and his two friends, that no one was waiting for him outside to learn the results of his interview. He had decided to leave Tuscany this very year, in order that he might complete his daughter's education abroad; he told his brother that the only Person to whom he was bound was his little daughter.[1]

If, on the other hand, he had hoped that the government would be convinced immediately of the truth of his principles, and set to work at once on the gigantic task of their application, a second interview with Cempini must have convinced him that this was an idle dream, for the minister answered him with the eternal argument of conservatism. The time was not ripe for great reforms; the government must wait till passions had calmed themselves. Yet Ricasoli did not feel himself defeated. He returned to his house, took up his pen, and wrote to the minister a letter[2] which he believed inspired.[3] Its theme was nothing more than the divinely-implanted reason which must infallibly guide society to a pre-ordained salvation, unless constrained by foolish men.

'Why fear the thought that comes from God, and leads to him, and is purified by him, every time that it breaks bounds, to return in just measure?'

Convinced that there was in society a higher force which impelled it inevitably to a predestined goal,[4] that 'Truth sought without passion inevitably leads men to the same conclusion',[5] he was content to narrow his negotiations to a plan[6] which would permit the natural leaders of Tuscany to appeal to the sound qualities of the people through a number of newspapers. The draft of a law which he prepared and presented to the government did not contemplate complete liberty of the press; for his

[1] L. & D., I, 191. [2] L. & D., I, 150. [3] L. & D., I, 182. [4] L. & D., I, 161 (to Lambruschini, March 24). [5] Interview of March 24 with Cempini. [6] L. & D., I, 167.

trust in 'the thought which comes from God' had its limits. The thought of Guerrazzi, for example, came from the devil. Then there were the Austrians. The spirit of the age held nothing good for them, but rather had marked them out for its victims; there was such a thing as wilful wickedness which set men against Truth, and then all the newspapers of the world would avail nothing. The first aim of Providence, which was to be expounded by men like himself, or Ridolfi, or Capponi, must be to fortify the people in its hatred of Austria, so that in time its anger would become a sword of righteousness, executing divine decrees against an Empire of evil.

'In all Italy, not excepting Tuscany', he told Cempini in his first interview, 'there is loosed a great anger against the Austrians, an anger which I will not judge in its methods of expression . . . but which springs from a fund of national susceptibility of which it is well to take account, so that the Italian princes may count themselves masters in their own houses, and more adequately do justice to the sentiments of the people'.

And, as Bismarck declared that the great questions of the day could only be settled by blood and iron, so Ricasoli declared, in his sententious fashion, that 'the shock of new facts with the consequences of old facts must lead to questions that can only be settled by war'.[1] Providence, he once said, knew how to break obsolete treaties.[2]

In the end, he had demanded nothing more than free expression for the ideal forces of the day, as he understood them; for nationalism, and for the institutions which could be the medium of nationalist agitation. It never occurred to him to doubt that his conscience had read aright all the questions of his age, or that his principles were infallible. Neither did he doubt that the men of his own class who agreed with him had a calling to expound those principles, and a right to the implicit trust of the people. The people, he had told Cempini again and again, would listen to the voice of reason and truth. As for the inflamed democrats, they were as guilty before God as were the Austrians, and

[1] *L. & D.*, I, 273, *et seq.* Interview with Charles Albert. [2] *L. & D.*, I, 219.

because of their guilt God and the people would not hearken to their clamour.

The government considered his project for a press law, and its modifications of the plan seemed to Ricasoli and his friends to show extreme distrust of 'the good' and 'the wise'.[1] Other patriots, like Guerrazzi, who were more passionate and less moral, denounced the law and violated it.[2] Ricasoli's initiative had as its chief result the outburst of a confused propaganda in which at times he found it difficult to recognise the benignant operation of a divine plan.

[1] *L. & D.*, I, 197, 198, 200.   [2] Guerrazzi, *Al Principe ed al Popolo* (Livorno, 1847). Baldasseroni, 218–9. Montanelli (*Memorie*, I, 275), describes liberal tactics as 'to consider virtually granted what was not in the intentions of the granter'. For a reasonable discussion of the law see Montanelli, *I scrittori e Rivisori* (Pisa, 1847).

APPENDIX I

Were the Food Riots of 1846–1847 Promoted by Austrian Intrigue?

The accusation was first made in Montanelli's secret press on January 22, 1847; and was generally believed, owing to a tendency which prevails among men in times of excitement, to credit their enemies with diabolical cunning, even if the evidence is of the slightest. It became a commonplace of patriotic oratory from 1847 till 1849 to ascribe all disorders to the treacherous machinations of Austrians and Jesuits. (See, for example, the declaration of Salvagnoli in the *Consiglio Generale* on July 15, 1848. *Le Assemblee del Risorgimento*, Vol. III, p. 153–4.)

The accusation must be dismissed as not proven. The liberal historians of these years base their case upon two pieces of evidence, both of which are inconclusive:

(1) The correspondence of Scarlett, British representative in Florence, of Abercromby, ambassador at Turin, of Ponsonby, ambassador at Vienna, and of Palmerston—which was printed in a Blue Book (*Correspondence respecting the affairs of Italy*, Part I, 1846–7), and which Gualterio quotes in part, omitting those letters which weaken his case. The relevant letters are the following: On March 9, 1847, Scarlett first reported to Palmerston the prevalent belief that the food riots in Tuscany were instigated by Austrian agents. On March 23 Palmerston wrote to Abercromby at Turin, asking

information with regard to secret Austrian activities. Abercromby wrote (March 30) dismissing the charge as unfounded; but on April 5 he in part retracted his opinion, reporting that the Austrian government had claimed a certain Giribildi, arrested by the Tuscan government for seditious propaganda, and had in addition paid his debts. He reported also that Austria had offered to the Tuscan government 5,000 men, to be stationed in or around Leghorn. On April 20 Palmerston wrote to Ponsonby at Vienna, enclosing these despatches, and asking the ambassador to make inquiries. Ponsonby reported on May 5 that the Austrian government had denied the charges, and strongly expressed his opinion that the denial was worthy of belief. In his opinion, Austria would not intervene in central Italy till a formal request for intervention should give to her a reasonable pretext.

Whether Ponsonby was right or wrong, the suspicions of Abercromby have little to do with the food riots, or with the alleged part which Austria is supposed to have played as *agent provocateur*. The offence of Giribildi had been to distribute a pamphlet vilifying Charles Albert, not to incite village riots in protest against the high price of corn.

(2) The liberal historians also base their case upon the reports of the local authorities in the Papal States, presented towards the end of 1847. (Gualterio, Part II, Volume I, Document 34.) These reports agreed that the food riots had been disproportionate to the cause, and had been fostered by interested persons who went from village to village stirring up discontent. But it was not suggested that the agitators were Austrian agents.

The evidence against Austria, therefore, is very flimsy. In addition, it should be noticed that persons of balanced judgment did not ascribe the disturbances, when they first broke out, to Austrian intrigue or Austrian gold. Giusti, who witnessed the first riot in Tuscany, gives a very natural explanation of its origin without dragging in this accusation (*Memorie*, p. 73 *et seq.*), and Lambruschini was content with denouncing the agitation as the work of the *canaille* (*L. & D.*, I, 122). It is possible that communist agitators had something to do with the affair: for there was a trial of communists at Pisa in 1847 (but here again the evidence was inconclusive: see note 17 to Giusti's *Memorie*, by Martini)—and Capponi declared in a letter of May 4, 1846, that he would not be frightened into gratitude to the government by the arrest of a few communists (*Lettere*, Vol. II, 286).

It is of course possible that the Vienna archives may contain evidence of the activities of *agents provocateurs*. But it is certain that Italian politicians and historians, in making their charges, could produce no evidence of any value whatsoever.

CHAPTER IV

'SONGS ABOUT FREEING ITALY' (MAY 1847–JULY 1848)

THE history of Tuscany,[1] from the publication of the Press
Law in May 1847, till the defeat of the Piedmontese
army at Custozza in July of the following year, illustrates
admirably the weaknesses which Cavour had in mind
when he exclaimed that the men of 1848 sang too many
songs about freeing Italy. Throughout this period there was
a dangerous predominance of enthusiasm over organisation, discipline, and co-operation. Towards the end of
1847 enthusiasm began to lose itself in the bitterness of
faction, for the democrats assailed the hesitations of a
government to which the moderates were half committed;
but in the first five months of 1848 enthusiasm revived
again with the outbreak of revolution in Sicily, in Paris,
in Vienna, with the proclamation of constitutions in one
Italian state after another, with the splendid risings of
Milan and Venice, and with the hopeful beginnings of
Charles Albert's campaign in Lombardy. In March and
April the Tuscan patriots were proclaiming that ' His
Majesty the People' had swept the chess-board, that
Civilisation had prevailed against Barbarism, that the
Austrians were already outlawed from Italy, and that
Italian frontiers would stretch to the crest of the Alps and
to Istria. The patriots, however, did little to transform
these boasts into realities. Even the volunteers who
departed for the front with high courage straggled back a
discontented rabble. The moderates who had control of
the government till October of 1848 proved utterly
incapable of organising it for the purposes of a war. The
democrats who were excluded from office attacked the
moderates bitterly for their inefficiency, and stirred up the
lower orders of the people, to help them clear a road to
power. They never doubted that they would be able to

1 This paragraph sketches the outlines of the narrative told in this chapter
and the following one.

transform enthusiasm into courageous action; but by the
time they had achieved power the state was weakened by
months of bitter faction-fighting, and they found that their
first duty was to discipline the mob whose passions they
had excited. For these reasons Guerrazzi was compelled,
from October 1848, till April 1849, to concentrate all
his energies in a struggle, not against Austria, but against
anarchy.

In addition to the weakness which sprang from too-
facile enthusiasm, from lack of resolution in government,
and from the bitterness of party struggle, a serious error
was made in Tuscany through distrust of Piedmont.
Ricasoli was the only leading character who looked to
Turin rather than to Rome, and this attitude of his was
doubtless one of the causes why he never attained to power.
All the other leaders, from the very moderate Ridolfi to
the passionate democrat, Guerrazzi, became involved in
negotiations which aimed, not only at creating a federation
of Italy to combat Austria, but at achieving through that
federation a balance of power in central Italy which would
hold in check the suspected ambitions of Piedmont. These
facts alone, apart from the military errors of Charles Albert,
the struggle of parties in Lombardy, and the repudiation
of the nationalist crusade by the Pope, are sufficient to
explain the failure of a revolution which had begun under
the most favourable auspices. It was only in the next ten
years that the nationalists learned that they must look for
their salvation to Piedmont, not to Rome. When they had
learnt that lesson Ricasoli was able to lead Tuscany successfully in a quieter, more patient revolution. For Ricasoli,
like Cavour, stored in his memory all that the failures of
1848 had to teach.

.   .   .   .   .   .

Never did anyone groan more deeply at the prospect
of new labours than did Ricasoli when he first crossed the
threshold of politics. He wished to serve his country, but
to tear himself from his retirement was hateful to him.
He felt the conflict of his sentiments as ' a veritable

martyrdom'.[1] Nevertheless, the prospect of new moral propaganda on a large scale soon attracted him. Before the dilatory government had published its press law (it was ready not till May), he was preparing with his friends the plans for their paper;[2] and in the privacy of his own room he was musing on the meaning of his new calling as journalist. When the first number of *The Patria* was ready, he sent out to the *gonfalonieri* of Tuscany a circular which proclaimed that a journal was a true ' civil institution ' by means of which the castle unites itself to the country districts, to the cities, to the provinces, to the Nation; the Nation unites itself to the Nations, and ' the Peoples are merged in the universal fraternity of the true human family'. With his friends he discussed the function of the journalist as educator, and concluded that, in order to direct public opinion, it was not necessary to lecture people as if they were children or students. ' To guide public opinion is nothing more than to associate oneself with what is noble and good in it, and to reveal it still more'.[3] The practical application of this maxim seemed to him to be simple, for the two noble ideas worthy of the time were already in the minds of men: ' To consolidate the state, to secure independence'.[4] The business of embodying these principles in the day-to-day criticism of events he left to his colleagues. After an article which he prepared for the first number of his paper on the Duties of Landowners, and in which he called his fellow-proprietors to rise above their pestiferous education, ' to know the people, and to make it better', he himself wrote very rarely.[5] His part once again was that of the directing conscience behind the genius of Salvagnoli, whom he urged, in each crisis of the state, to write an article which would recall the people to the principles of the *Risorgimento*, reminding them that ' Liberty was not a word nor a

---

[1] *L. & D.*, I, 191. [2] *Brolio MSS.*, I, 29. [3] *L. & D.*, I, 221. [4] *L. & D.*, I, 214. [5] Only three articles as a private person. *Patria* Nos. 23, 41, 48. He addressed seven messages to the people through the *Patria* as *gonfaloniere*.

pretext, but an idea, a passion; and Independence, Nationality, was an idea sublime and generous'.[1]

In the end, he found journalism the least satisfactory of all his educational ventures. Despite his insistence that *his* newspaper, the *Patria*, must stand for nothing but principle, it had its lapse. On one occasion a slander against the ex-governor of Genoa found its way into its columns, and the Marquis Torrigiani, son-in-law to the slandered man, went round the city in a fury looking for Ricasoli. The two men met under the Logge del Grano.

'I wished to justify the intentions of the Direction in inserting the notice', recorded Ricasoli, 'but Torrigiani was carried away by anger, and screamed out loudly: my words, calling him to be moderate and to remember where he was and who he was, increased his anger; and taking my sentiment of dignity and breeding for cowardice, he flung at me a *Pig of a Journalist*, and I retorted with a solemn *slap on the face;* he replied with a blow of the umbrella on the head, and knocked me on to the ground; then followed blows with the umbrella and the fists, and a rush of people to see us, and a crowd, and perhaps news for the *Popolano*'.[2]

The incident was the talk of the town for a few days, and so was the duel to which it gave rise. In this duel Ricasoli received a slight scratch on the arm, and his opponent, technically the victor, fell into convulsions. But in those months there were many things to give excitement, and Ricasoli remained the most dignified person in Tuscany. He took the lesson to heart, and vowed that in the future his journal would deal only with the great questions of reform and of independence.

Bitter disillusion came to him at last, for he discovered that the voice of the *Patria* had availed nothing against the passions and interests which swayed his fellow Tuscans.

'Friend, believe me', he wrote at last to Salvagnoli, 'the majority of those who took pleasure in the *Patria*, and read it, and praised you, did not do so for the sake of its principles and to educate themselves; it was because the principles helped to unchain their evil passions'.[3]

Even when he made this confession, he refused to repent of his efforts; but he stored up within his mind

[1] *L. & D.*, I, 338. [2] *L. & D.*, I, 336. Cf. Passerini's Diary (Martini), p. 23. [3] *L. & D.*, I, 422.

maxims on the function of newspapers in time of revolution very different from those which he had held in 1847. The next time that he was concerned in a nationalist enterprise he took care that he himself had a monopoly of propaganda.

The Tuscan press law of May had set all the potential journalists within the Grand-Duchy in competition with each other. The Ridolfi group made overtures to Ricasoli himself, knowing nothing of his interview with Cempini. When the baron refused to join in its schemes, Ridolfi himself wrote deploring the opening of a schism, and was not convinced when Ricasoli wrote back saying that they would be like the rays of the same circle, or again, that they would go to the same goal by different roads.[1] Then a member of Ridolfi's circle tried to secure the co-operation of Montanelli, whose secret press had suspended its activities;[2] but Salvagnoli wrote to the professor warning him not to accept the offer, for reasons which could not be mentioned in a letter, and some weeks later he definitely invited him to throw in his lot with the *Patria*.[3] Montanelli, however, did not wish to throw in his lot with anyone. He wished to keep his position as leader of the ardent youth and the spokesman of Pisa, and made his voice heard through a journal controlled by himself, the *Italia*. Another group of men, the Sicilian La Farina, E. Meyer, P. Thouar, Manzoni, and G. B. Niccolini himself, had banded together as collaborators in the *Alba*, the only paper in Tuscany which was consistently and openly hostile to the Giobertian propaganda. All these various groups protested that they wished to work in harmony one with the other, but nothing divides more than journalistic competition; and, since for many months the Tuscan liberals had no means of making themselves heard save through their newspapers, they never forged for themselves the discipline and harmony of a party.

The only prominent man of Tuscany, who in these

[1] *L. & D.*, I, 176, 178, 180, 187, 192, 194. *Ridolfi*, Allegato XI.
[2] *Gualterio*, IV, appendix XXV, No. 9.   [3] Montanelli, *Memorie*, Documents 358–70.

months had no friends and no journalistic foothold (the *Corriere Livornese* was at the beginning under other influences), was Guerrazzi. He had come out of prison in 1833 with a deep sense of the injustice and implacability of fate, resolving that he would cease for the time his struggle with the hateful powers that were too strong for him, and attend to his own interests. He would play the game which the world played, he would succeed, make himself independent of men. He resigned himself to that profession which was to him like ' the chain on the leg of the galley slave'.[1] His enemies said that his methods as an advocate were none of the cleanest, but he made money and boasted defiantly of his success. ' I am obliged to no man for anything; I owe all to my studies, to my industry, to myself'.[2] His love for Italy was still his great passion, but he hated men the more, and he despised himself because he had not proved himself a hero. In these years he lost almost every friend. The faithful Bini died as the result of a wound received in a brawl. The bitterness of Guerrazzi grew; he appeared to enjoy provoking enmities, he invented savage and contemptuous names for the leaders of respectable society, and they in return dubbed him ' an ogre, a parricide, a baby-eater'.[3] Giusti, when he came to Leghorn, found him almost isolated. He embarrassed the satirist by the savage onslaughts which he made on one individual after another. ' He who has bitterness in his heart', he declared, ' cannot spit sweetness'.[4] Yet, with all this self-inflicted torture of misanthropy, he had at bottom a longing to haul down his colours, to come to terms with the world, and enjoy the repose of friendship and cultivated society. If there had been in Leghorn anyone with charm enough to attract him and imagination to read the riddle of his passionate nature, to understand the battle of enthusiasm and despair which fought itself out in his strange, straining spirit, he might have broken down the barrier which Guerrazzi had

[1] Guerrazzi, *Lettere*, p. 63. [2] Guerrazzi, *Memorie*, p. 100. [3] Guerrazzi, *Lettere*, p. 70. Capponi, *Scritti*. [4] Giusti, *Memorie*, p. 110, *et seq.*

built between himself and an unsympathetic world. Two
men only knew something of the real Guerrazzi that was
hidden beneath all the bitterness and all the insincerity of
the posing Byronic novelist. The first was Niccolo Puccini,
the invalid *dilettante* of Pistoia, to whom he poured out
freely all the turbulent impulses of his nature and the
strained conceits of his fantasy. The second was Capponi,
with whom, throughout all these years, he carried on a
regular and affectionate correspondence. Though the two
men saw little of each other, Capponi understood better
than anyone else the contradictions of Guerrazzi's character. There were many things in it which he disliked, but
he continued the correspondence because the man himself
attracted him; he believed that he was capable of depth
and had a natural dignity, and that underneath he desired
always to take a place among 'the good'. One thing in
him was stronger than this desire, and prevented him from
using his powerful arts of fascination which at the best
could only secure him repose and pleasure in a circle led
by others. His greatest craving was for power; power he
pursued 'as the end of his being, and as his due'.[1] Since
he would not climb into respectable society, he must mix
with the dregs. He became a demagogue in his own
despite. A little later, with protests of loathing for those
who made a business and profit of philanthropy, he put
his lawyer's ability and his Byronic style at the service of
the Leghorn dock-labourers in a miserable quarrel which
they were waging with competitors from other parts of
Italy.[2] 'I do not hate or despise these persons', he wrote
in his typical demagogic vein. 'It is not right that I should
hate or despise them. After all, are they not Italians?'
And then he proceeded to do all that he could to stir up
hate against the 'foreign' labourers who had come to a
feast where they were not bidden, who lived apart in the
city, who seemed to think that their blood was better than
that of the men of Leghorn. It was poor use for his talents,

[1] Capponi, *Scritti*, II, 44, 128, 155.   [2] Guerrazzi, *Raccolta di Documenti relativi ai Facchini di Livorno* (Livorno, 1847).

but it served his end; and within him always was the
passion to do something for Italy, to rise to power so that
he might play the part of a hero from his own romances.
He used any means, however petty, to secure his end; in
these days one of his agents was enflaming the assistant-
bakers of Leghorn to agitate for no more night-work, no
more outside competition, and higher wages.[1] His influence was hard to trace, but the moderates of Florence
believed him omni-present, as the police had done before
them; and before long Farini was preaching to the Tuscans
that they should seize ' that damned soul, hateful to all
for his Pagan incredulity in God, in men, in virtue', and
send him on board a ship to make a tour of the world.[2]

From beginning to end, the tardiness of the government
made splendid opportunities for agitators, and even made
sober men agitators against their wills. The government
never moved till it was driven by some force from without
or from within, with the result that it received no gratitude
for what it conceded, and every concession was looked on
as the occasion for starting a new agitation. The press law
itself had followed a similar law of Pius the Ninth. Capponi
thought that this law was a poor prelude to a new era of
reform; it should have come after, not before, the concession of liberal institutions, and then the host of newspapers would have found something else to occupy them
than continuous agitation for what had been withheld.[3]
Giusti, in a series of poor puns, maintained that the right
course for the government was to act so that the extremists
would not have the right to declare that they were in the
right.[4] But the reforming plans sketched out by Ricasoli
remained in an official docket. At the end of May an
edict announced the appointment of a committee of
reform to draw up plans for a new municipal system, but
the committee did not meet till January of the next year,
when men were beginning to think of a constitution.

[1] P. Jona, *I moti politici di Livorno*, p. 45. [2] L. C. Farini, *Epistolario*
I, 797. [3] Capponi, *Lettere*, II, 148. Cf. Zobi, *Storia*, Vol. V, p. 55, *et seq.*
[4] A. D'Ancona, *Ricordi Storici del Risorgimento*, p. 218.

Another committee was appointed to draft codes of laws, but the eminent jurists who were chosen could not even agree on the desirability of this departure, and for the tenth time within the century the project of the codification of Tuscan law came to nothing. A third edict announced the project of a council of state for the discussion of policy (Rome had been granted one in April), but when the council was constituted in September, it was almost entirely an official body representing the old traditions of government.[1] It was not surprising that the more ardent minds, even those which claimed to be moderates, resented the conservatism preached by men like Digny,[2] and sought to hurry on the government by organising popular demonstrations. At Pisa the press law itself had been welcomed by a demonstration, and Montanelli pulled strings so that 'Leopold was a fiasco and Italy was the rage'.[3] Amid the riot of patriotism, however, voices were heard crying for cheap bread.[4] The government sought to restrain the agitation by a mixture of persuasion and firmness. On July 21, the prince issued a proclamation calling on his people to be good children of their father, who was planning still further measures for their well-being.[5] The proclamation had not the slightest effect; the demonstrators had taken a motto from Niccolini's *Arnaldo*—' The people is weary of being called a flock '—and agreed with Guerrazzi that ' the interminable father and son ' of benevolent despotism was played out. Sternness was as vain in its effects as benevolence. A law prohibiting public reunions and the posting of notices in the streets was completely disregarded; Ricasoli denounced as futile the mixture of wheedling and menacing to which the government was reduced;[6] and the English government reported that it had been seized by an entire paralysis, ' not even a policeman appearing in the streets'.[7]

---

[1] Among the few non-official members was Capponi. [2] Montanelli: *I moderati e gli esaltati*, in appendix to *Memorie*. [3] Montanelli, *Memorie*, II, 27. [4] Zobi, *Storia*, V, p. 58. [5] *Baldasseroni*, Allegato No. 12. [6] *L. & D.*, I, 206. [7] Hamilton to Palmerston, August 27.

The demonstrations aimed to conquer one very definite right—the right to carry arms. Pius IX had conceded a civic guard in July, and in August the Austrian occupation of Ferrara taught Italians that they were face to face with their great enemy. In the smaller towns men stole out secretly at night to paint on the walls ' We want the civic guard', and uncharitable persons of assured social position declared that these artists would be the very first persons whom a decent civic guard would arrest.[1] At Leghorn the wealthy brothers Bartolommei, and the perfectly respectable advocate G. Ricci, organised demonstrations and deputations to the powers of Florence. There were in the city nameless plotters of a different cast, who called themselves ' The People of Leghorn', and addressed to the soldiers quartered in the town messages like the following: ' If any try to make you believe that our popular reunions are directed against you, do not believe them. Thus they seek to stir up brother against brother. . . . Think that the arms directed by you against us might strike your father, your mother, your dearest kinsfolk.[2]' The general commanding the troops, De Laugier, had wished to make use of the soldiers against the rabble before it should be too late, but his advice was rejected; and so the *morale* of the miserable little force grew as bad as its equipment, and the foreign traders in Leghorn began to whisper to each other about the bloody intentions of the workmen.[3] At Florence, the ardent liberals who had co-operated in the campaign of the secret press formed a committee at the house of the Marchese Ferdinando Bartolommei,[4] and at every opportunity sent into the streets an army of demonstrators recruited chiefly from the medical students of Santa Maria Nuova, students on vacation from Pisa and Siena, youths without employment, and stray shopkeepers and artisans.[5] Rome already

---

[1] *L. & D.*, I, 206 (Lambruschini). [2] Zobi, *Storia*, Vol. V, Appendix XVI. [3] Hamilton to Palmerston, August 30. The Leghorn agitators later made a point of the middle-class character of the civic guard. [4] Gioli, *La Democrazia Toscana*, p. 13. [5] Hamilton to Palmerston, August 25.

had the civic guard, the Duke of Lucca yielded one to his subjects on September the first, and when a couple of days later a deputation set out to Florence from tumultuous Leghorn, the government could no longer resist. The liberals had won their arms.

The victory, of course, was the signal for new demonstrations, which, according to the best revolutionary precedent, took on a federal character. The first federation was at Pisa on September 6, where the inevitable professors of philosophy and commercial law cheered themselves and their audience with patriotic orations. On September 7 there appeared in Leghorn the Duke of Caiano, a portly person in the uniform of the civic guard of Rome. He aroused tremendous enthusiasm by swearing to the ' sacred cause', and threatening the vengeance of Italy against Austria on ' that day in which the first Austrian soldier shall dare to pass to the southward of Ferrara'.[1] This was a fitting prelude to the festival of September 8, when the respectable were scandalised by women who dressed like Amazons, ' forgetting the precepts of modesty and reserve laid down for their sex',[2] and the progressive governor of the city, Don Neri Corsini, shook his head over what he considered ' veritable revolutionary Bacchanalia'. It was at this demonstration that Guerrazzi made his first public appearance. He spoke to the people and was received with little favour, but somehow or other it happened that he walked back through the streets with Montanelli, and shared in the applause which greeted that popular idol.[3] . . . He had at last made his appearance as a leader, and from now on he began to overshadow the brothers Bartolommei, who were responsible for his appearance.

Florence had her federal demonstrations on September 8 and September 12.[4] The various contingents carried banners inscribed with legends demanding independence

[1] T. Trollope, *Tuscany in* 1849 *and* 1859, p. 70.   [2] Zobi, *Storia*, V, 121.   [3] Montanelli's account, *Memorie*, II, Ch. 28.   [4] See Ranalli, *Istorie Italiane*, I, 163. Zobi, *Storia*, V, 112.

from the foreigner, municipal reform, armaments, an Italian League, and the like; they acclaimed the press, the guard, Italy, Gioberti, Pius, and Greece; they acclaimed Prince Poniatowski because he was a Pole and his country had suffered at the hands of Austria. They applauded the Grand-Duke, and the *gonfaloniere* presented him with a pompous address; then they went to lay garlands on the busts of national heroes in the Loggia of the Uffizi. Enthusiasm passed all bounds. Ricasoli believed that the festival was ' the sublime frontispiece of the grand book which will comprise the political history of Italy in the future. Florence yesterday, before all Italy, constituted the Italian nationality, as well as her own'.[1] For several months the letters of Giusti had been full of a similar ecstasy. The succession of excellent measures, he told Poerio in June, had overwhelmed all with admiration and astonishment. The country was risen from death to life, he declared to D'Azeglio in August; one would think that the Po ran by his own town of Pescia! ' The People, eternal poet', he wrote again, ' has found its voice; I, poor interpreter of its life and dreams in the days of its dumbness, keep silence.' At the first of the Florentine festivals he was filled with joy and stupor to see the nation ' arise like this all at once'.[2]

There were some who did not share his confidence. Tuscany was cheating herself with the pretence of a unity which had no real existence.[3] Her peasants cared for none of these things, and the actors in her public life were divided into little groups who knew nothing at all of the inner motives and the inner knowledge which prompted each other to their separate policies. The Grand-Duke smiled forced approval of his subjects' extravagances, while his heart was sore within him, for on April 5 Metternich had warned him that concessions might force Austria to safeguard her ' interests and rights over Tuscany'. In the succeeding months Leopold watched simultaneously

[1] *L. & D*, I, 207.   [2] Giusti, *Epistolario* (Martini), II, 545 *et seq.*, 555, 558, 569.   [3] Bianchi, *Diplomazia*, V, 36.

and with equal anxiety both the agitations which were forcing him along a road which ran straight towards a rupture with Austria, and the steadfast obstinacy with which Metternich was defining and re-defining the intentions of Austria with regard to Italy. Italy, declared the Imperial minister[1] in a circular of August 2, was a 'geographical expression'. The peninsula was composed of sovereign and independent states whose existence was secured by public law and treaties. That law and those treaties, which Austria would defend to the last, were already menaced by the agitation in Italy—a continuation of the labours of the secret societies—which had no intention of being content with administrative reform. 'What these societies aim at is the fusion of these states into one body politic, or at least into a federation of States under the control of a supreme central power'. The Emperor, he concluded, sought no more possessions in Italy, but he was determined to keep what belonged to him. . . . . Palmerston replied to this effusion[2] with polite irony. He pointed to the existence of another right, which allowed the states to organise themselves internally just as they pleased; and he expressed the hope that Austria would employ her influence in Italy in support of the laudable reforms which the governments had initiated. After the occupation of Ferrara in August, he cautioned Metternich against any interference in the affairs of Sardinia or Rome, which would cause the most profound regret to Her Majesty's government.[3] Metternich clung to his point. In January of the following year he was still affirming that all the trouble sprang from a miserable minority which conspired against the traditions and the will of Italy, in open hostility to the political and national rights of all Europe, in the name of

---

[1] The following dispatches are in the *Correspondence* cited. [2] Palmerston to Ponsonby, August 12. [3] *Ibid.* August 13. For England's policy towards Italy see Palmerston's Instructions to Lord Minto (September 18). Palmerston authorised Lord Minto to encourage the governments in their reforms, and to make it clear that England recognised no right of Austria's to crush them by intervention.

an Utopian chimera which it called nationality, and which would mould all Italy into one wild revolutionary mass. Austria, he asserted, would know how ' to encounter this nationality in Italy and in the rest of her dominions'. He was not in the mood to listen to the lamentations of the unhappy Leopold, who bewailed that he was being forced on with the stream and asked the Chancellor what he was to do.[1] For a long time he kept silence, and then took means to let the Grand-Duke know that he was a simple tenant of an Imperial patrimony, and that he had no power to lessen any of the inalienable rights of sovereignty which, on the extinction of his family, would pass to Austria.[2]

Had Ricasoli known of this correspondence, he would perhaps have been less astounded at the folly of the government in refusing to come forward as leader of the liberal movement. Ridolfi, who knew Leopold intimately and perhaps guessed some of the difficulties of his position, sought in private to urge the government to trust itself to the paths of reform.[3] Another moderate of the same colour, alarmed at the excitement which grew feverish from July to September, appealed publicly for quiet and order. The advocate, Galeotti, had made himself on every occasion the spokesman of the reasonable liberals; early in 1847 he had written an excellent exposition of the political condition of the Roman states, and while Tuscany was awaiting a council of state he had produced a small book and a pamphlet analysing the weaknesses of the Tuscan state, and pointing out common-sense remedies.[4] After the events of September he published a fourth pamphlet,[5] which, while it referred again to the faults of the existing system, was chiefly preoccupied with warnings against undue energy in denouncing them. The writer tried to persuade himself and his readers that there was really nothing to fear, for the Tuscans were a ' people

---

[1] Ponsonby to Palmerston, October 26. [2] Bianchi, *Diplomazia*, V, 91. [3] *Ridolfi*, p. 150 *et seq.* [4] See bibliography under *Galeotti*. [5] *Osservazioni sullo stato politico della Toscana.*

already constituted', civil tolerance was to them a ' need
of the heart '; there were no real divisions of opinion, and
Utopia-mongerers were not likely to receive a following.
The prince ' had clasped the hand offered to him by the
great priest . . . and with a solemn pact united his
destinies to those of his people and to those of Italy'.
There was still, it was true, a lack of good institutions, but
luckily Tuscany possessed a band of moderates who
diffused among people political wisdom, ' not imposing
it with learned arrogance, but with the exquisite arts of
loving persuasion'. As for Austria, she had no power to
interfere with Tuscan progress till she was called by the
Tuscan prince, or till there was a disturbance of the *status
quo*. It must therefore be the aim of the Tuscans to avoid
all action which might lead to one of these eventualities;
they must condemn dangerous enthusiasm and patriotic
ambition; their rules of conduct must be moderation,
moderation, and again moderation. Liberals of Galeotti's
school were at this very time shaking their head over the
enthusiasm of Pisa, Leghorn, and Lucca, in raising and
saluting the tricolour banner which stood indeed for
Italy; but which staid people of that age regarded very
much in the same manner as later generations looked upon
the red flag.[1]

To the patriots who had organised the demonstrations,
with the express purpose of inflaming enthusiasm and
using it to force the hand of the government, all this talk
of moderation was anathema. To Guerrazzi, who saw the
chance of snatching at power, and who fought the cause
of Italy as he would have fought a private vendetta, it
was at the same time a personal challenge and national
treachery. In a long pamphlet[2] dedicated to Macchiavelli,
and impregnated with the teaching of that master, over-
loaded with quotations from classical authors, Italian
history, and the Bible, yet at the same time breathing with
passion, he took up the challenge. ' If the people rose in

[1] Farini, *Epistolario*, I, 694.   [2] Guerrazzi, *Al Principe ed al Popolo*.
It was written a little later, just after Ridolfi joined the ministry.

revolt', he said roundly, ' it is not its fault; waters deprived
of the necessary exit overflow the banks'. The necessary
exit which he demanded was a democratic parliament;
for, until the people had a share in the making of laws,
they would inevitably come into conflict with them, and
the civic guard, of which there had been so much talk,
would either be a tyrannous body sustaining the *status quo*,
or a revolutionary body overthrowing it. About the question of independence he would have no shuffling. ' Those
who cry, " Softly ", come to the pitch of denying the banner
of the three colours. Why this baseness ? . . . The banner
belongs to the independence of Italy'. Against the
moderates he quoted the condemnation of St. Paul to the
Church of Laodicea, ' I know thy works that they are
neither hot nor cold'. They feared enthusiasm because it
might drive the state into conflict with Austria; he welcomed enthusiasm because man was by nature egoistical,
and enthusiasm alone would make him work for a cause.
Why temporise in the work at hand for fear of Austria ?
' Austria looks to her interests, and she does well; if we
look to ours, we shall do better'. ' Called or not called,
whether Italy proceeds with her reforms or whether she
does not, we shall see Austria advance against Italy when
she is strong again'. Then let Tuscany set her own house
in order, and above all, let her look to the army. Did the
government shrink from expense ? ' Without many sacrifices', retorted Guerrazzi, ' Liberty is not won'.

Ricasoli and his journal, the *Patria*, occupied a middle
position between Galeotti and Guerrazzi. For the latter,
Ricasoli never had a good word to say; yet, strangely
enough, there is not one of Guerrazzi's central arguments
which he did not use himself, at this time or later. He, too,
welcomed the demonstrations and preached enthusiasm;
he bewailed, now and afterwards, the delays of the government; he preached the complete union of the government
with the ideal forces of the people; he came to see the
inevitability of war with Austria. He, himself, was to play

upon two occasions the same destructive part[1] which
Guerrazzi played later upon a larger scale. . . . In what,
then, consisted the unbridgeable gulf between the two
men ? A remark of Guerrazzi's, who, with all his passion,
possessed singular power of detached judgment, suggests
the answer. 'Usually the comfortable and educated
classes begin a movement', he said. 'The nature of these
is to stop soon; with small things they content themselves;
of the needs of life they do not have to think; their liberty
consists in this . . . to acquire part of authority by
winning larger institutions'. There were insinuations in
this sentence which were not true of the Tuscan moderates;
least of all were they true of Ricasoli. Nevertheless, the
opposition between the Livornese democrat and the
Florentine liberals was largely a matter of class. Ricasoli,
who had given laws to a community of peasants, hated to
see a man working through the passions of a mob. Leghorn
itself was an unpleasant, rough, uncultured place, and
Guerrazzi chose as his means to power the feud which it
was only too ready to wage with superior, aristocrat-
ridden Florence.

Ricasoli hated demagogy, but he was also weary of
paternal government. The *Patria* began a resolute attack
on the ministry. One day in September it made a revolution in Tuscan journalism by appearing 'with five or six
columns in print larger and blacker than the rest',[2] and
immediately afterwards the government fell. The article
of the *Patria* was not, as Montanelli seemed to think, the
real cause of the fall of the ministry, but the event appeared
to Ricasoli and his friends a veritable triumph. Two
among the most eminent of the liberal nobility took their
places with the old ministers, Cempini and Baldasseroni;
the first was Ridolfi, who became minister of the interior,
the second was Count Luigi Serristori, who went to the
department of foreign affairs and war. At last Tuscany

[1] The *Patria* helped to open the way for Ridolfi's accession, and also
to bring about his fall. For this it was blamed by Capponi. *Scritti*, II, 66.
[2] Montanelli, *Memorie*, II, 38.

was in the hands of its natural leaders, nobles from the *Georgofili;* and the *Patria* was so eulogistic of the new ministers that Ridolfi begged Ricasoli to moderate his praises.[1] Ricasoli, though he reminded his colleagues that their paper was still free, and constrained to enunciate its programme in clear propositions, did not believe that there was any fear of it diverging from that of the government; and Lambruschini believed that Salvagnoli would be able to direct official policy from behind the scene.[2]

The circumstances of Ridolfi's appointment made it inevitable that these hopes would be disappointed. At the end of August, Neri Corsini, Marquis of Laiatico, had been called to the ministry, but he had been kept at his post at Leghorn till a successor could be found. At Leghorn he had become more and more convinced[3] that justice must be done to those aspirations which Guerrazzi was to voice in *Al Principe ed al Popolo.* He wrote to Florence that public opinion demanded security on one essential fact: ' whether the government had, or had not, entered with good faith on the road of progress and wise reform'. He thought at the time that a widely representative council of state would be sufficient to satisfy the people on this score; but after the ' revolutionary Bacchanalia ' of September 8, he told the government that it could only satisfy popular demands by transforming itself from an absolute into a limited monarchy. ' To grant the constitution', replied the Grand-Duke, ' would be to provoke foreign intervention in Tuscany, in virtue of the right of " reversion " which the Austrian emperor claims over Tuscany'; and a convenient occasion was chosen for the dismissal of Corsini from the ministry. In choosing Ridolfi and Serristori, Leopold had avoided a change of system by a change of men.

Ridolfi, therefore, had inherited the quarrel with Leghorn; his programme had been condemned in advance by public opinion; the only elements of strength which he

[1] *L. & D.,* I, 212.   [2] *L. & D.,* I, 211.   [3] For what follows (Corsini's account) see Zobi, *Storia,* V, Appendix 21.

brought to the ministry were his own reputation, and
plans for a customs-league between the Italian states.
The preliminary articles of the accord were signed with
Piedmont and Rome on November 3rd, and Montanelli's
paper, the *Italia*, hailed them as the first step to a *Zollverein* which would be 'the base and the principle of
independence; the efficacious instrument of the union of
fraternal peoples'.[1] The venture was ruined in the end by
the obstinacy of Modena; but apart from this, events
were moving so fast that the plan became obsolete within
a month. The new ministry made the worst possible
preparation for the stormy days in front of it. Ridolfi,
almost at the moment of his accession to power, abolished
the department of the *Buon-Governo*. The 'low police',
however, was left untouched, so a Florentine mob took the
law into its own hands. On October 5 the *sbirri* were hunted
from house to house, the debtors were released from prison,
and the guillotine (which had not been used for eighteen
years) was publicly burnt. The government thereupon
suppressed the old police altogether, and for the future
trusted solely to a force of eight hundred *carabinieri*.
Liberals heaped praises upon Ridolfi for this enlightened
action; but Guerrazzi compared their panegyrics to the
applause of 'the fool who exulted while he watched the
burning of his own house'.[2] From now on the government had to rule by popularity alone.

Tuscany, too, was suddenly faced with an international
crisis in miniature, which stirred it as deeply as had the
Austrian occupation of Ferrara. The little principality of
Lucca[3] had, during the past year, presented a parody of
the agitations which had been shaking the larger states.
Its duke, Charles Louis, had returned after aberrations
of heresy and liberalism to orthodoxy of religion and
politics, and had managed to secure money sufficient to
satisfy his ideas on royal pomp by selling his pictures to

[1] *Ibid.*, Appendix 43.　[2] Guerrazzi, *Apologia*, p. 60.　[3] For an account
of what follows see *Esposizione dei fatti di Lucca dal 29 maggio al 28
luglio* 1847. Bastia, 1847 (liberal point of view).

Englishmen, and persuading Tuscany, which had the
reversion of his state, to recognise his debts.[1] But he had
the misfortune to have among his subjects a class of
enlightened middle-class persons who remembered that
the constitution of 1805 had been guaranteed in the Final
Act of the Vienna Congress, who read the mild nationalist
propaganda of Gioberti and Balbo, and who sometimes
caught the train to Pisa to listen to the lectures of Centofanti and Mcntanelli. So on May 29, Lucca, like the
other cities, had a demonstration of its own, and perhaps
the *carabinieri* were a little too rough in maintaining order
among the crowds gathered under the trees of its charming
ramparts. The duke issued an order forbidding people to
make a noise and to sing at night; the people obeyed for a
time, but saw in the edict an act of wicked despotism.
Early in July the city was excited by the marriage of a
spinster of seventy years or more with a young boy.
According to ancient custom crowds expressed their
derision by the ringing of bells and the beating of brass
vessels[2] outside the house of the happy pair; and indeed,
violated all precedent by performing the rite four nights
running. The authorities suspected dark political motives,
and the police took the first opportunity to charge the
people. Liberal voices thereupon rose angrily, denouncing
a massacre, and as the police continued their tactics of
hustling, a crowd defiantly assembled one Sunday to
shout: ' Down with the assassins', ' Long live Italy',
and ' We want a civic guard'. The duke thereupon
issued a proclamation to his beloved subjects, reminding
them that: ' There are in us the qualities of Sovereign and
Father, and We cannot tolerate that any of Our subjects
arrogate the right which belongs solely to Us, of guarding
the public tranquillity'. He proceeded to assert his right
by sending some of the popular leaders to Viareggio; but
on the first day of September the·people rose again, and
constrained Charles Louis to address his faithful subjects in
a different tone: 'To Our most loved subjects. We wish to

[1] Zobi, V, Appendices 6, 7, 8.   [2] The *scampanata*.

reign over you, not with fear, but with love, not with force, but with benefactions, and therefore We open to you Our Paternal Heart'.[1] The paternal heart prompted the duke not only to concede to his people a civic guard, but to accord them every other reform which would appease their just demands, and would satisfy his own most passionate desire to render them content once and for ever. After he had expressed his benevolence thus, his emotions did not suffer him to remain in his capital, and he went off with his family to Massa. Thither there followed him a commission elected by the people. He received it in the duchess's bedroom, where the duchess lay in bed, and read to it an act of abdication.[2] The commission then united its prayers to those of the royal family, begging him not to inflict so cruel a loss on his people. The royal heart relented. Charles Louis returned—escorted by six thousand Pisans and Livornesi, who had come by special train to see the show[3]—and was received in Lucca with 'extravagant joy'. Perhaps the publicity did not please him, for he waited till all were excited with the novelty of the guard, and then went off quietly to Modena to negotiate with the Florentine government the transfer of his patrimony to Tuscany.

Under the Vienna settlement[4] it was stipulated that Lucca should pass to Tuscany when Marie Louise or her son, Charles Louis, or their heirs, died or obtained another possession; and it was arranged that in the event of this occurring Tuscany should cede to Modena certain specified territories. Permission was however given in the treaty to modify the settlement, and this was done in a treaty of November 1844,[5] which rearranged the territorial adjustments to take place between Modena, Parma, and Tuscany, when the latter should receive Lucca. The result, from Tuscany's point of view, was that she would retain the valued vicariates of Barga and Pietrasanta, but

[1] Enclosed Hamilton to Palmerston, September 12.   [2] Hamilton to Palmerston, September 6.   [3] Ibid. September 16.   [4] Article 102.
[5] Zobi, Storia, IV, Appendix 68.

cede to the other two states the whole of the Lunigiana, Fivizzano and its surrounding districts going to Modena, Pontremoli and the surrounding country to Parma. The district, as a whole, is beautiful and prosperous; it has, moreover, a great strategic importance as one of the roads across the Apennines. Tuscany felt keenly a surrender which gave the 'Lieutenant of Austria' free entry to her territory. This surrender she was legally bound to make, when, on October 4, her representative and the minister of the Duke of Lucca signed a treaty which incorporated Lucca in Tuscany, anticipating the natural 'reversion' of the dukedom by three months only.

The incidents to which the cession gave rise, though not important in themselves, illustrate excellently the petty local jealousies and the larger egoisms which in 1848 broke the strong current of Italian nationalism. Lucca was aggrieved, Pisa jealous, the transferred populations despairing, and the Tuscans furious. A progress and a proclamation of Leopold's did not console the citizens of Lucca for the loss of their royal court and of their importance as the inhabitants of a capital city; neither did a distribution of money to the poor people who had goods in the pawnshops, nor a decree establishing in Lucca a court of appeal. That decree, nevertheless, provoked a riot in the streets of Pisa. It was monstrous that Lucca should have such importance, while Pisa, cultured Pisa, was passed by.[1] Meanwhile, there came from the Lunigiana loud complaints from the populations handed over to the rule of Parma and Modena.

Here was indeed a fine chance for patriotic enthusiasm. Even the moderate Centofanti maintained that the affair was monstrous, and called on the Grand-Duke to arrange an exchange with his Bohemian lands.[2] Lambruschini asserted[3] that it would be moral cowardice to surrender to a despot and a persecutor these loyal Tuscan subjects, and observed that the transfer of territory would bring

[1] Guerrazzi, *Lettere*, No. 261 (13-12-47 to Capponi). Marradi, *Montanelli*, Document 16. [2] Zobi, *Storia*, V, Appendix 35. [3] *L. & D.*, I, 221.

the enemy to the crest of the Apennines and give him a right of way into Tuscany. 'Take care that the *Patria* does not in an absolute manner sustain the treaties', he urged Ricasoli. Ricasoli had bewailed that unjust treaties were a 'hard thing', but became more cheerful when he reflected that God would know how to break them.[1] In the meantime, it was Francis of Modena who acted. He took a quick run to Vienna, and on November 4 the Tuscan government received a despatch informing it that the Modenese commissioner would on the following day take possession of the territories which belonged of right to his master. The Tuscan government, temporising, replied that the time was too short to allow its commissioners to be at hand; but the Modenese troops occupied the territory without waiting for any commissioners, and the duke, it was said, announced that he had behind him three hundred thousand men—the army of Austria.[2]

Passion blazed out in Tuscany with a new fierceness. In Florence, the flag of Austria was burnt outside the Imperial Legation, the Municipality publicly promised the government the support of all citizens in any steps which it took to safeguard the national honour, the citizens themselves burst into the Palazzo Vecchio clamouring for arms wherewith to succour their 'murdered brethren of Fivizzano'. The same clamour for arms filled the streets of Leghorn; in these days the city quivered for its first plunge into complete anarchy. Ricasoli went to the government to lecture it on artillery, and complained that the ministers laughed in his face.[3] He wanted the government to come to an understanding with the people, he wanted it to incite the population of the Lunigiana to revolution. All the civilised nations, he asserted, had munition factories,[4] whereas Tuscany's only munitions were an abundance of pens, of ink, and of blotting paper.[5] Like all the world, he ranted about 'natural frontiers'.[6] Suddenly he

---

[1] *L. & D.*, I, 219. [2] *L. & D.*, I, 244. Austria later disavowed this statement, *ibid*. 260. [3] *L. & D.*, I, 224. [4] *L. & D.*, I, 279. [5] *L. & D.*, I, 227. [6] *L. & D.*, I, 225. Cf. Giusti, *Epistolario*, III, 49.

was given a taste of the difference between declamation and diplomacy. On November 16 he received his credentials[1] as ambassador to the court of Charles Albert, where he was instructed to seek, on behalf of the Tuscan government, the mediation of Sardinia.

The details and delays of these negotiations are of no importance. After three weeks Ricasoli was able to report that a settlement had been reached through Papal and Sardinian mediation, and that, if Tuscany had to surrender her ' natural frontiers ' as the ' unjust ' treaties demanded, she would at least do so in an honourable manner. The Modenese authorities evacuated the occupied territory, and then received it back again with all due forms. It was a small success. But Ricasoli had treated of matters not mentioned in his official instructions; he had paid more attention to the letters of his friend Salvagnoli[2] than to those of the minister, Serristori, and in his interviews with the king and his foreign minister he had touched on the great questions of Italian independence. The gist of his arguments was that ' the supremacy in Italy, hitherto exercised by Austria to the loss of Italy', should in the future be exercised by Piedmont for her advantage. At first he had little hope in the resolution of Charles Albert or in that of his foreign minister, San Marzano; for both seemed to him to be afraid of Austria, and of the two, the king seemed to fear her the more. Ricasoli thought that the reforming princes would have to show extraordinary pertinacity in order to ' entice and compromise the King of Piedmont in an Italian policy'. But in his final interview with Charles Albert he strained every nerve to inflame his military spirit. He spoke of the inevitability of war, he pointed to the possibility of a partition of Parma, he described how ' men's eyes are turned towards the strong King of Italy, from whom we hope for common salvation, and the fortune of a new Italy'. Before he had finished this oratorical defiance of his instructions, the King had caught

[1] *L. & D.*, I, 218.   [2] *L. & D.*, I, 231. Salvagnoli sketched Ricasoli's argument for him.

something of his fire. 'What joy', exclaimed Charles
Albert, 'to be able to make a war of Independence and
of Religion!' and he bewailed the lost opportunity of the
occupation of Ferrara.

'The opportunity will come again', he added. 'I am
a man of the sword, and I shall not miss the chance'.

'Yes, sire', replied Ricasoli, 'the opportunity will
return, and Your Majesty may count on the Italian
people'.[1]

To this interview may perhaps be traced the beginnings
of that sympathy with Piedmont which, in the following
months, won for Ricasoli the sinister title of 'Albertist'.
He and his friends had risen above their pre-occupation
with the frontiers of Tuscany, and looked to Turin in the
days when it was heresy to look anywhere except to Rome.

Despite everything, Austria came nearer. In December
her troops occupied Parma and Modena. It seemed to the
Tuscans that they were already sweeping down through
the abandoned Lunigiana. It was too much for Leghorn.
For more than a month the advocate, Ricci, Ridolfi's
friend, had been urging that minister to come and see
the city for himself, to realise its special circumstances, to
meet its special problems.[2] But the Florentines persisted
in asserting that all the agitation there sprang from the
factiousness of a few individuals.[3] It was the same assertion
that Metternich had made of Italy, and which governments and interests threatened by popular movements will
make till the end of time. In the end Ridolfi came to the
city, but he came to punish. Guerrazzi was sent to his
fifth prison, protesting loudly that it was he and none
other than he who had saved the city in its days of revolution. Whether or not he had played the part of fireman to
extinguish a blaze which he himself had lighted,[4] he was

[1] *Brolio MSS.*, M. 48, for Ricasoli's account. Printed *L. & D.*, I, 273.
Cf. *Brolio MSS.*, O. 2.   [2] Jona, *op. cit.*, p. 25.   [3] Giusti, *Epistolario*, III,
39, 186, 221.   [4] For Guerrazzi's account see *Apologia*, 69 *et seq.* The
provocative pamphlet which provoked the rising would appear from internal
evidence to be written by Guerrazzi, and was generally ascribed to him.

disposed of for the time; but moderate Tuscans considered that the government had acted in panic,[1] and Leghorn itself nourished a new grievance against Florence. Guerrazzi went to prison an unpopular man; when he was released in March the citizens were ready to alter their opinion of him.

While the patriotism of Guerrazzi, working among the cosmopolitan democracy of Leghorn, had brought him a few days of the power which he craved and then condemned him to some months of prison, that of Ricasoli, expressing itself in respectable journalism and high diplomacy, had won for him a decoration and a high office, neither of which he wanted. He received the notice that he had been appointed *gonfaloniere* of Florence almost as a provocation;[2] the government should have remembered that he was a Father. He went to the Grand-Duke and declared that he must ponder over this conflict of duties;[3] he must ponder, too, over the nature of the office which was offered to him. After some days he returned to the Grand-Duke and to Ridolfi and submitted some ' reflections ' on the ' history of nations ' and the events of the last months. It was time, he said, for the government 'to cease playing a game with the nation', it was time ' to recognise the rights of the people'. Descending to particulars, he gave a list of necessary measures; there must be passed a new law on petitions, the *gonfaloniere* must be given a direct control of municipal police, he must be excused from assisting at public lotteries, he must be allowed to issue a manifesto on assuming office, the new municipal law must place local institutions on an elective basis. ' I could not to-day assume the task, unless I had permission to lay it down as soon as the new institutions are in force'.

Montanelli supported Ridolfi in his strong action (*Memorie*, II, 63). Guerrazzi protested his innocence to Capponi (*Lettere*, No. 261, 269, 274, 277) who chided him, but who later insisted on his release (*Scritti*, II, 44). Hamilton believed that he had been dragged into publicity against his will (to Palmerston, January 9).   [1] *L. & D.*, I, 300.   [2] *L. & D.*, I, 288. [3] For what follows, *Brolio MSS.*, O. 2 and O. 6.

Ridolfi was indignant that the offer of a post of honour and dignity should be answered with a lecture on history and politics and a list of conditions. Ricasoli, for his part, was overwhelmed by surprise and disdain when he was accused of imposing conditions. He protested that he had imposed none; he had only made certain *reflections*. . . . He was perfectly sincere. The fine distinction which no one else could see was firmly lodged in his mind, and he wrangled over it as eleven years later he wrangled over similar hair-splitting distinctions with Farini and with Cavour. And now, as later, his insistence on these small points did in despite of his logic win for him a victory. The ministry accepted him on his own interpretation, and accepted with him the obligation to listen to his insistent voice on every occasion that should arise. When Ricasoli issued the manifesto on which he had insisted, it was already the fateful year 1848.

.   .   .   .   .   .

Within three months the Austrian armies, which the Tuscans had already in imagination seen descending from the Apennines, were retreating to the fortresses of the Quadrilateral. Great events had succeeded each other with bewildering rapidity. On January 12, Palermo crashed out the wild overture to the revolutionary music of 1848; a few weeks later the King of Naples granted a constitution; on February 8 the King of Piedmont published the bases of a fundamental statute. The Grand-Duke of Tuscany, who had appointed a commission to treat of reform in a less dramatic matter,[1] was driven forward by a propaganda in which Ricasoli took a leading part.[2] As soon as the news from Turin came to Florence, Leopold, too, promised his subjects that liberty which Ricasoli declared to be the law of the Moral World, the prize of Humanity. Pius IX was

---

[1] Its leading figure was Capponi, who wished to develop according to old model institutions based on the municipalities. *Scritti*, II, 65, and Appendix I.
[2] *L. & D.*, I, 304 *et seq*. The *Patria* (An. I, No. 158), published the text of the French constitution. Cf. *Baldasseroni*, p. 272, and *Patria*, An. I, 164. To this agitation may be traced Ricasoli's break with Ridolfi.

swept forward by the same stream, and though the Roman constitution seemed to some to be a ' toy', it was hailed with enthusiasm throughout Italy. 'The restoration of man is complete', announced the *Gazetta* of Florence.[1] ' Ten centuries were required for his internal perfection, another nine for labours and struggles, till he could say with truth, "I belong only to myself and to God "'. ' The initiator of the Italian *Risorgimento*', announced Ricasoli to the Florentine citizens, ' has consolidated it. . . . Let us go to render thanks to God for this new boon to Italy, and together with this thanksgiving raise to him the prayer that the day of United Italy delay not'.[2] To Ricasoli, it seemed that the prayer was answered. God, who had given Italians constitutions as a means of struggle against Austria,[3] fought for them in ways still more marvellous. Vienna followed Paris into revolution, the citizens of Milan expelled the disciplined forces of Radetsky after five days of bitter and glorious battle, Venice freed herself with less sacrifice but with equal glory, and on March 24 ' the strong King of Italy ' kept his promise and crossed the Ticino to fight the battle of Independence and of Religion.

In the days of victory, as in those of fear, nationalist fervour expressed itself in a cry for arms. On March 21 Ricasoli carried to the Palazzo Vecchio the clamourous demands of a great throng of patriots, and brought back to them the glad news that regular and volunteer troops would descend, if need be, into Lombardy. Leopold forgot as best he could the threats and the power of Metternich, and proclaimed that the hour of the complete *Risorgimento* of Italy had come suddenly.[4] Ricasoli gathered the citizens in the Duomo to sing a *Te Deum* for the victory of Milan, and the municipality raised in the city the arms of its glorious Lombard sister. If *Te Deums* and demonstrations could have won the indepen-

---

[1] Zobi, *Storia*, V, 426–8. [2] *Patria*, Anno I, No. 205. [3] Cf. Montanelli, *Memorie*, II, 184; and Masi, *Memorie di F. Ranalli*, p. 36. [4] Hamilton to Palmerston, March 22.

dence of Italy, Florence alone would have conquered the
Austrians a hundred times; in those days manifestos and
proclamations rained from Grand-Duke and ministers,
gonfaloniere and generals. ' Brave Lombards! ' cried
Giusti, ' we at the most have freed ourselves: you have
freed Italy! . . . You have conquered, you have conquered for yourselves and for all! ' ' Now His Majesty
the People sweeps the chess-board, and cries: " It is my
turn. What avails skill against genius, a cabinet against a
nation . . . barbarism against civilisation ? " '[1] ' That
which is not, will be', exclaimed Ricasoli, ' that Italy
will again be ONE'.[2]

From Giusti's old university of Pisa there was in these
days an exodus of students and professors who, since
November, had been drilling in the University Battalion;
and the ardent young liberals who had fought absolutism
with the secret press set forth to fight it in the battlefield,
shoulder to shoulder with their brothers of Rome and
Naples. They enlisted after the manner of their class,
joining the army secretly so as to avoid painful arguments
with their mothers at home; and then, when they were in
the field, they wrote to their younger brothers solemn
admonitions that their duty lay in the family, and that
they were on no account to follow what had been a very
bad example.[3] And the younger brothers, of course, took
no notice. One of them, Giovanni Lotti, was a pacifist.
All day long at Montanara he stood under fire without
returning a single shot, while his brother, Francesco, was
killed beneath his eyes. To one who asked why he had
enlisted, he replied: ' For example'. ' I have taken
arms', wrote Enrico Meyer, ' as natural consequence of
the principles professed by me all my life. I am in this
army as a volunteer citizen, that is, as a free citizen, and
this liberty of action I intend to maintain'.[4] While the

[1] Giusti, *Epistolario*, III, 115–6.　[2] *L. & D.*, I, 322. But Salvagnoli
(April 14) prophesied a long war (*L. & D.*, I, 339).　[3] Gioli, *op. cit.*
Letters of L. Morelli.　[4] Oxilia, *La Campagna Toscana del 1848 in Lom-
bardia*, p. 44. Cf. F. Marazzi in *Vita Italiana nel Risorgimento*, Terza Serie,
II, 94 *et seq.*

young men fought, their little brothers played at soldiers,
and a *Battalion of Hope*, composed of *ragazzi* between the
ages of seven and twelve, drilled assiduously in the cloisters
of San Marco, and shouted to a tune that they were little
fellows, but that they would grow up to fight for the
fatherland.

'Blessed are those that have seen shot and shell', wrote
the Baron Bettino to his brother on May 16. 'You tell
me nothing, if indeed you were present at the affair of
Montanara. I hope that you were. Brave Tuscans!'
But the Tuscans so far had had nothing but skirmishes.
The real test came on March 29, when for seven hours
their little force held its own at Curtatone and Montanara
against an overwhelmingly superior body of Austrians.
Grief at the losses sustained was almost forgotten in the
exultation of the victory of Goito.[1] 'Now', exclaimed
Giusti, 'Italy is risen in all her greatness'.[2] Terenzio
Mamiani warned Minghetti that there was an intrigue
afoot to stop Italy at the Izonzo, and declared defiantly:
'Italy will extend beyond there, and all Istria is Italian'.[3]
Thus for a little while Italy continued to hope as she had
hoped in the glorious days of March. Even after Charles
Albert had been defeated at Custozza an English sea-
captain stationed at Leghorn noticed with amusement
that patriotic map-makers, with premature zeal, had given
Corsica and Malta to the new, mighty Italy.[4]

. . . .

In Tuscany, as in Lombardy, there had been throughout
these months undercurrents of faction and of disillusionment. Each set of patriots imagined that the country could
not be saved nor the war fought unless it had power itself;
every burst of national enthusiasm, therefore, became the

---

[1] For the battle and campaign see Oxilia, *op. cit.* [2] *Epistolario*, III, 168.
[3] Minghetti, *Ricordi*, II, 99. Montanelli (*Memorie*, II, 22) had attempted
an Italian propaganda in southern Tyrol. The Italians proclaimed fraternity
with the races of the Empire (Zobi, *Storia*, V, Document, 63), but all the
signs of racial conflict appeared in 1848. [4] Letters of Sir H. Codrington,
312.

occasion for petty agitation. A Florentine diarist and the newspapers record scores of incidents like the following: On March 21, when news came to Florence of the rising of Vienna, 'the people' collected and cried for arms. When Ricasoli returned from the ministers and announced that their demand would be granted, they cried Long Life to Leopold, to Lombardy, to the independence of Italy. But the radical, Mordini, and some others, tried to turn the demonstration to their own purposes by raising a cry against the ministry; and the crowd took up the shout till the 'good citizens' raised another against Mordini and 'the betrayers of the country'. In the end the fervid patriots narrowly escaped a ducking in the Arno.[1] Sometimes the 'good citizens' were not the victors in these vocal competitions, and sometimes, it must be confessed, they were the original provokers.[2] Songs about freeing Italy were all very well in their way, but the ministers often wished that they had a few policemen.[3]

Among the volunteers, too, enthusiasm had its drawbacks. Two hundred volunteers from Arezzo, discontented at the news that they would have to drill before they were allowed to succour their brethren in Lombardy, started a riot and almost came to blows with the Civic Guard.[4] A young soldier who had crossed the mountains of Pistoia by stealth in order to join the force as it marched to the front, and who wrote home that, if his clothes did not keep him warm and if there was not enough to eat, he had at any rate a big rifle with which to shoot Austrians, wrote also to his sister that, unless his 'imbecile' officers mended their manners, the first bullet which he fired would change its direction.[5] On the march towards the Po the regular corps of grenadiers had shown how easy it was to fire at a commanding officer . . . but the bullet missed. 'You ignorant cowards', cried their colonel, Giovanetti,

---

[1] Passerini, *Diario* for March 21 (Martini). [2] *Ibid.* for April 29 and May 2. 'The good' attacked the editor of the *Popolano* and a republican tobacconist. [3] *Assemblee del Risorg.*, III, 153–4 (police). [4] Passerini, *Diario* for March 26. [5] Gioli, *op. cit.* letters, pp. 19–13.

'you can't even shoot straight' . . . but their aim was
better on the way home. Every volunteer was an amateur
strategist, and ranted against the incapacity of his officers.
' If I could describe to you the kind and the greatness of
the dangers to which our officers have exposed us with
their ignorance', wrote one of them to the Marquis
Bartolommei, ' you would understand with what care
Providence watches over us'. A Piedmontese who published a little book[1] on the war of independence, said of the
Tuscan volunteers that ' discipline appeared to them
slavery unworthy of one who combats for liberty', a theory
which had been maintained with enthusiasm by Enrico
Meyer. A correspondent of Vieusseux described them as
' a crowd that refuses absolutely to obey, that pretends
absurd principles of liberty, does what it likes, as it likes,
and when it likes', and considered that a generous calculation would make one volunteer equal in value to a
quarter of a soldier.[2] They stood their ground worthily
at Curtatone and Montanara, but after that they degenerated
into a rabble. After all, they had been heroic once. The
best of them, like Vincenzo Ricasoli, took service with
the Piedmontese. Many of them deserted and straggled
home to boast of their military valour. Reflecting on the
apathy of the people as a whole, on the discontent of the
peasants, and the conduct of the volunteers, the English
ambassador concluded that ' Love of war is not a quality
of this amiable nation'.[3]

    At home and in the field there was everywhere a lack
of discipline, resolution, organisation. Serristori resigned
in March because the government would not adopt his
proposal for a special levy of 4,000 men, but Ricasoli
himself believed that such a measure would hopelessly
alienate the peasants,[4] and it is hard to imagine what the
government would have done with the new levies after
raising them. Patriots, who expected the comforts of

---

[1] *Memorie ed osservazioni di un ufficiale piemontese sulla guerra dell'*
indipendenza (Torino, 1848).   [2] G. Rondoni in *Archivio Storico*, Ser. V,
Vol. 22, 276–7.   [3] Hamilton to Palmerston, July 27.   [4] *Baldasseroni*, p. 289.

peace in time of war, grumbled at their minor hardships;
some of the soldiers were sleeping two in a bed; a whole
contingent slept on the floor in the Carmine, because
their quarters were 'populated by troublesome insects'.[1]
The cannon were without carriages, there were no reserves
of ammunition, and no supply of trained officers. It seemed
to impatient patriots that the government was doing
nothing at all to remedy this state of things. Ricasoli
reported that the Piedmontese officers, who had come to
help in the training of troops, were thinking of returning
home, in despair of accomplishing anything worth while.
He was convinced that Tuscany would always be last in
everything.[2] 'Disorder is at the height, and I am in
horrible anguish because things do not go as they should,
and because I have not the power to provide for them'.
For the first and the last time in his life he held a position
of high dignity and little power; he fretted himself almost
into a frenzy at the delays, the hesitations, the blunders of
the government. He begged his brother, Vincenzo, not
to confuse the *gonfaloniere* of Florence with the *gonfaloniere*
of Milan, who was the powerful head of a provisional
government. He complained to Salvagnoli:[3] 'Nobody
has given even a thought—*nobody*—of informing the
gonfaloniere'. He declared that he would have resigned if
it would not have appeared weakness. The reflections or
conditions which he had made before assuming office
meant nothing after the grant of the constitution. The
only hope of a change for the better lay in the meeting of
the new assembly. Long before it met he had lost all hope
in Ridolfi and was drifting into opposition; from April
on he had none but official relations with any of the
ministers,[4] and the *Patria* began to take its own line.

Guerrazzi, as usual, went further along the same road.
'When shall we finish conquering?' he demanded, as
the reports of little victories followed each other. Before
the Chambers met, his uncompromising hostility to all

[1] Passerini, *Diario* for June 15.   [2] *L. & D.*, I, 325.   [3] *L. & D.*, I,
354.   [4] *L. & D.*, I, 331.

the works of government, past and present, poured itself out in a reckless pamphlet[1] which raised the greater storm because so many of its questions were to the point. Why had not the treaty obligation resting on Tuscany before the war, to keep an army of ten thousand men, been observed ? Why had the army been allowed to fall into decay ? Was the country at war with Austria, or was it not ? If it was, when was the war declared ? Were the Tuscans fighting as auxiliaries of the Piedmontese, or on their own account ? Why had the government hindered the departure of volunteers ? If there was a shortage of arms, why did it not provide them ? Why did it not take the cannon from Portoferraio and Leghorn ? And, for the future, why could not Tuscany have an army as large in proportion to her population as that of Piedmont ? These questions, and many others in the same tone, were not a contribution to reasonable discussion, but rather a declaration of war to the knife. Guerrazzi, released from prison after the grant of the constitution, had no reason to be grateful to Ridolfi; the present ministry was the first obstacle which stood across his road to power; it was his policy to accept the Grand-Duke's protest that there had been no break with the old regime,[2] and to damn his present ministers for all the faults of their predecessors.

Ridolfi's one hope was to win a political success by negotiating successfully for an Italian League.[3] As a good Giobertian, he turned first and foremost to the Pope, and since there had been continual friction with the Papacy in regard to the ecclesiastical laws of the Grand-Duchy, he determined to encourage the Curia by pursuing simultaneous negotiations for a concordat. His ambassador found in Rome an eager readiness in the matter of the

[1] *Domande al Ministro intorno alla Guerra* in *Scritti Politici.*
[2] The *Patria* (Anno I, 164) had offended official minds by referring to the constitution as a ' new political pact'. Cf. Salvagnoli's address in reply and the discussion of July 19, in *Le Assemblee del Risorgimento*, III, 200–229; and Guerrazzi, *Scritti Politici*, p. 309. *Baldasseroni*, 298 *et seq.*
[3] For the following see Zobi, *Storia*, Book XIII, Ch. IV (Vol. V), and Documents 61 and 79.

concordat, and much reticence as regards the League.
Papal diplomacy insisted that the League must be
secret. 'No', wrote Ridolfi desperately to his representative. 'It must be explicit, solemn, immediate. Do not
weaken these words. We are ruined if, in a few days, nay,
in a few hours, we are not in a position to show ourselves
under the shadow of the cross'. This was in February,
when Austria still held the Duchies; but what Ridolfi
sought then he sought still more in the days of exultant
and disordered nationalism. His labours were in vain.
While Rome drew back before committing herself to a
nationalist programme, and preferred to pursue ecclesiastical advantages, Piedmont was suspicious of a league
which contemplated the Pope as its political head, and
Naples never conceded to her envoy full powers. Charles
Albert had declared his adhesion to the idea of the League,
but pretended that he could not enter into negotiations
because at the seat of war he was separated from his
ministers. Nevertheless, as late as April 26, Ridolfi urged
his envoy to use all his forces to break down the obstinacy
of Rome, hoping not only for a partnership of governments against the enemy, but for security against internal
disturbance and a guarantee against the ambitions of
Charles Albert. One by one the other governments dropped
the plan. In May the King of Naples deserted the
Italian cause; the troops that had gone to the Po
with so much acclamation from Italy were called back to
deal with Sicilian rebels, and in Florence a mob demanded
that the Neapolitan coat of arms, which had been prudently
taken down from the Legation, should be put up again so
that it could be pulled down with less ceremony and
burnt.[1] Towards the end of April Tuscan patriots had
been disturbed by rumours which came from Rome.
'My God!' wrote Minghetti to Farini on April 26,
'if His Holiness in this moment declares that he does
not will the war, what will happen to Italy ? '[2] His Holiness
declared it in the Allocution of April 29, and in Florence

[1] Passerini, *Diario*, May 19. Cf. May 26.   [2] Farini, *Epistolario*, II, 216.

people went about scratching off the walls all the legends
in honour of Pius, putting away the statuettes which
glorified in his person the union of religion and nationalism,
or else hanging on to them little pig-tails.[1] 'The fact is',
wrote Ricasoli, 'that from to-day Charles Albert is left
at the head of Italy'. Ridolfi did not see it. He persisted
in looking to Rome for Italy's salvation. On May 18,
nearly three weeks after the Allocution, he wrote to
Bargagli, the Tuscan ambassador at Rome: 'If the Pope
does not go to Bologna, if he does not proclaim the Italian
diet, if he does not undertake all that is necessary for the
security of the Peninsula, then all is lost. . . . Who can
be certain that the Legations will not proclaim Charles
Albert ?' On the 20th he wrote in the same strain.
'Piedmont seeks to aggrandise herself wherever she can,
and that government has everywhere agents at her disposal.
. . . Now, I repeat, the Pope must go to Bologna, and
place himself between the cross and the sword. . . .
Without this support Italy is lost'. And five days later he
wrote that the Papacy alone could satisfy the real need of
Italy, which he declared to be the expulsion of the foreigner
without the triumph of republican and democratic revolution, and without the destruction of any of the states
existing in lower Italy.[2]

These dispatches have been quoted as an illustration,
not only of the weakness of Ridolfi's statesmanship, but of
the error which pervaded all the policies of central Italy in
1848–9, the same error which Ricasoli fought without
truce in 1859–60. Ridolfi feared Piedmont as much as he
feared Austria. He sought in the League a counterpoise
to Piedmontese ambitions. All his successors approved his
aims, if they adopted different means. Capponi, who took
on the task of government after Ridolfi, was dominated
by the same fear.[3] Montanelli and Guerrazzi, who six
months later democratised the plan of Federation into the

---

[1] *L. & D.*, I, 346. The *codino* was a nickname for reactionaries, who
were supposed to cling to long perukes.   [2] Zobi, *loc. cit. Ibid.* V, 772, for
a similar letter as late as June 17.   [3] Capponi, *Scritti*, II, 89.

Constituent, sought equally in an *entente* with Rome
a counterpoise to the ambitions of Piedmont. Austrian
victory, says Guerrazzi in his *Apologia*, meant the ruin
of Tuscany; but a Piedmontese victory, if unchecked,
would also have meant her destruction. He told the Grand-
Duke, who was very doubtful of his sweeping democratic
venture, that it would bridle Piedmont; an Italian neighbour of ten million people was not an inviting prospect.[1]
Montanelli set forth the same considerations in his official
letters to the Tuscan envoy at Rome.[2] He was hostile
even to the Piedmontese annexation of Lombardy, and
considered that the proposed Kingdom of High Italy
would be too large in a federal Italy.[3] The great majority
of Tuscans were furious at the Piedmontese propaganda
for an enlarged kingdom. Government after government
wrangled with Turin over the Lunigiana, which Tuscan
troops had re-occupied, along with Massa and Carrara,
after the Austrian retreat in March.[4] Every patriot
ascribed to Piedmontese intrigue the reluctance of some
of the communes to throw in their lot with Tuscany, and
even the most ardent lovers of Italy hoped for territorial
gains for the state of Tuscany. Tuscany, declared Guerrazzi, must expand ' beyond the dimensions of an estate'.[5]

Ricasoli and his friends were almost alone in their
sympathy towards Piedmont. After the Papal Allocution,
Ricasoli had declared that Charles Albert was left alone
at the head of Italy; and his weariness at the bungling of
his own government had caused him to look longingly to
the efficiency of Turin. His brother, who had the instincts
of a soldier, had left the Tuscan service for the army of
Piedmont, and Ricasoli was influenced by him to form the
opinion that ' the army of Italy should be one'.[6] In the
end he had to counsel Vincenzo to write to him ' softly,

---

[1] Guerrazzi, *Apologia*, pp. 51 and 131.   [2] Letter of November
28, 1848. *Documenti del Processo*, p. 543.   [3] Montanelli, *Memorie*, II,
308. Cf. Guerrazzi, *Scritti Politici*, 205.   [4] *e.g.* Guerrazzi, *Apologia*,
pp. 454 *et seq.*, and *Zobi*, Appendix, No. 78.   [5] Guerrazzi, *Lettere*, No.
277, and *Condizioni Italiani* in *Scritti Politici*.   [6] *L. & D.*, I, 356, 358.

softly, when speaking of Charles Albert',[1] for the rumour had gone through Florence that he favoured a larger than military unity, and there was a threat to burn his newspaper, the *Patria*, in the piazza. Ricasoli himself, men whispered, was meditating flight, and not even a direct denial[2] from the *gonfaloniere* was sufficient to shut the mouth of slander. There is evidence enough to prove that he was not such an extreme partisan of Piedmont as men thought,[3] but he and Salvagnoli were damned with the names *Albertist* and *Parricide*[4] (did not they wish to take the life of their own fatherland, Tuscany?), and the taint which clung to them was no small factor in destroying their influence in the most critical time of the nationalist enterprise. The incident illustrates as well as any other the strength of the feeling for Tuscan autonomy, and makes it possible to estimate the extent of the revolution in opinion which was completed by Ricasoli himself in 1860.

When, therefore, the Assemblies at last met on June 26, they had before them the problem of a country divided by factions, led astray by erroneous theories, disorganised by governmental inefficiency, and threatened by mob passion. Ricasoli, who had refused nomination to the Senate in order that he might take his place as a deputy in the *Consiglio Generale*, felt his heart ' palpitate', at the thought of being able to serve his country in a real Parliament.[5] As ever, he went to his own room and took out pen and paper so that he could the better meditate on the qualifications which he, as a deputy, should possess. 'A deputy', he concluded, ' must be honourable, of independent condition; must possess an open mind and a frank character'.[6] Some of the practical questions of a deputy's conduct he passed by, and among them, the following: What should the deputy do when the hall where he is deliberating is invaded by an insane, violent mob, incited by individuals known to the police ?[7]

---

[1] *L. & D.*, I, 363.   [2] *Patria* of June 15.   [3] *L. & D.*, I, 359, 360.
[4] Capponi, *Scritti*, II, 66.   [5] *L. & D.*, I, 327.   [6] *L. & D.*, I, 322.
[7] Hamilton to Palmerston (August 1) reports that the mob was led by

This was what occurred in Florence on July 30, 1848, little more than a month after the much-longed-for Parliament had been opened by the reforming prince. On that day there had come to Florence the news that Charles Albert had been defeated by the Austrians at Custozza.

'three individuals known to the police as thieves and vagabonds'. One of them, F. Trucchi, of Nice, had a particularly unsavoury record. For the riot see Martini, *Il Quarantotto in Toscana*, 79–84, and Guerrazzi, *Scritti Politici*, 564. (Discourse of August 1 in *Circolo Politico*, which indicates Guerrazzi's influence on the movement.)

CHAPTER V

DEMOCRACY AND REACTION (AUGUST 1848–MAY 1849)

RICASOLI was not a voluble deputy. He spoke in the Tuscan Parliament only on seven or eight occasions, and always on some question of fact—on the relations existing between the municipal authorities and the government, on the poor physique of the Tuscan levies, or some similar question which enabled him to give his experience in a few dry sentences.[1] He watched with sympathy the oratorical efforts of his friends, especially Salvagnoli, who spoke on most occasions, and whose eloquence moved the baron to admiration, though he disapproved of it when it made people laugh or made them angry.[2] But his chief task as a deputy was to watch with anger and disdain the onslaughts by which the democrats cleared their way to power, and his chief conclusion with regard to parliamentary life was that it did not suit him. Parliaments, of course, would be necessary when Italy had won her freedom, and were indeed a means towards that conquest; but they should be kept within bounds. These conclusions, which he put into practice when the next great opportunity came, were a reasonable induction from the antics of Tuscan deputies in 1848–9.

As a body, they were a very respectable and reasonable collection of people. The franchise was a narrow one. 'Why', Guerrazzi had demanded[3] like a French democrat of 1792, ' should one who pays 8 lire of taxes be thought a helot, and one who pays 10 or 15 lire a Solon?' In many constituencies the number of those enrolled was less than five hundred, and the number of those who used their vote less than one hundred.[4] But events proved once again that a middle-class franchise is no guarantee of political ability nor even of a useful stolidness. Outside

---

[1] *Le Assemblee del Risorgimento*, III, 132, 322, 323, 349 *et seq.*; IV, 42.
[2] *L. & D.*, I, 372.   [3] *Scritti Politici*, 165 *et seq.*   [4] Examples in Martini, *Il Quarantotto in Toscana*, 51–2.

the Assembly the newspapers and the popular *circles* swayed the masses, and within it the same journalists and the same orators did what they wished with a bewildered, spineless majority.

Ricasoli and his friends stood at first with the attacking forces. While the *Corriere Livornese* was breathing out fire and slaughter against Ridolfi, the *Patria*, in its more august style, was equally uncompromising,[1] so that Guerrazzi demanded whether Saul also was among the prophets.[2] Before the riot of July 30, Ricasoli had risen to damn with a few short sentences Ridolfi's work as a nationalist apostle,[3] and after that day the *Patria* strained every nerve to prevent the stricken minister from rising again. Ricasoli himself received from the Grand-Duke a commission to form a ministry, and girded himself to the task with ' all zeal, saving, however, those principles '[4] which his own conscience and the times demanded. He could not find half a dozen adherents; the Austrians were marching back into the Duchies; something had to be done. So Ridolfi was given a short span of dictatorial power, whereupon Guerrazzi and his friends raised a howl of indignation and demanded the minister's impeachment.[5] The *Patria*, if it despised this agitation, was equally insistent in its call for new men,[6] and at last, on August 16, Ridolfi finally retired ' under the hiss of popular disapproval ',[7] an excellent man who had been too small for a gigantic task. His successor, Capponi, was universally loved and honoured, but it was an unkind fate which called him from his studies into the storm of revolutionary politics. Capponi was now totally blind; he was a gentle scholar, acute in judging the past but bewildered in facing the present; for years he had found his real life in the middle ages. He was so kindly that he had always a word of sympathy and understanding for the most abused of

---

[1] *e.g. Patria*, An. II, 14 and 19.   [2] *Apologia*, 31.   [3] *Le Assemblee del Risorgimento*, III, 322 (July 28).   [4] *L. & D.*, I, 377.   [5] Guerrazzi, *Scritti Politici*, 393 *et seq; Assemblee del Risorg.*, III, 488 *et seq.*   [6] *Patria*, An. II, 31–37.   [7] *Baldasseroni*, 310.

men, and the situation which he was called to rule demanded ruthlessness, resolute action, even cruelty. ' The time having come for action', he confessed, ' for me it had come too late, and God had already sealed his prohibition on my forehead '.[1] Guerrazzi, grateful for the friendship which the sage had given him, wrote with unconscious irony to wish him good luck in his labours.[2]

The English ambassador reported that he began his ministry with a declaration of principles which contained nothing very remarkable.[3] He would push negotiations for peace and foreign mediation; he would at the same time prepare for the eventuality of war; he would maintain the constitution and pursue the project of federation. The negotiations for mediation, in which Capponi placed at the service of his country his own unrivalled reputation throughout Europe, came to nothing. For the present, Tuscany, forgotten by the Piedmontese in the *Salasco Armistice*, which they signed in August with Austria, had by the grace of England a guarantee against immediate invasion through the Duchies; but neither France nor England was willing to press on Austria mediation on behalf of a state which had not known how to fight its own quarrel and which showed every sign of a speedy plunge into anarchy.[4] It seemed for a time that the project of federation, taken up again with new vigour by Capponi, had some chance of success; for the Piedmontese minister, Pinelli, had sent an envoy to Rome, and the envoy, Rosmini, put forward a plan of a federal diet to be chosen by the assemblies and governments of the associated states, and to control the higher diplomacy and the army.[5] The scheme failed for the same reasons which had prevented federation earlier in the year. The Piedmontese government still looked askance at such a political contrivance, presided

---

[1] Capponi, *Scritti*, II, 63. [2] Guerrazzi, *Lettere*, No. 310. [3] Hamilton to Palmerston, August 20, *Assemblee del Risorg.*, III, 541 and 573. [4] Hamilton to Palmerston, August 6 and 7., P. to H., August 21. Capponi, *Settanta Giorni del Ministro*, Ch. 5. [5] Rosmini, *Della missione a Roma di A. Rosmini* . . . 1848–9, *Commentario*, 1884. p. 33 *et seq.*

over by the Pope. Its jealousy was aroused by the attempt of Rossi to initiate co-operation between Rome and Naples[1] (whose king was hoping that the federal army, if created, would be used against Sicilian rebels), and it refused to sanction the plan which its own envoy had put forward. The efforts of Bargagli, the Tuscan envoy, were utterly in vain; in the end Capponi concluded that Piedmont was concerned only with her own supremacy, and was thinking of trying her fortunes in a new war.[2] His own hope was that Piedmont would be content with small gains— perhaps with Parma—and that Lombardy and Venetia should resign themselves to autonomy within the Hapsburg Empire. All such calculations were hopelessly beside the mark; for, if Austria continued her recovery, the question for all the states was one, not of aggrandisement, but of continued existence; and if, on the other hand, the scale turned again in favour of Italy, Charles Albert, the strongest Italian king, had no inducement to content himself with a federation of 'equals'. Nothing could be hoped for Italian organisation while the governments of the centre continued this struggle against political reality.

Ricasoli, who had imagined the bases of a similar plan,[3] clung to the Capponi ministry as the last hope of unity and liberalism; but almost in despite of the will of its directors, the praises of the *Patria* were soon punctuated with doubts.[4] On one side was a ministry which no more than its predecessor was able to grapple with the problems of order and of national aspiration; on the other side were the hated theories and passions of democracy. Ricasoli had exclaimed that Italy would find salvation only if the factions showed themselves ready to forget the past and to prove their repentance by according pardon to each other; but he himself would never pardon men like Guerrazzi. The *Patria* proclaimed that it was 'the duty of every citizen to disdain the bestial idol' of the radicals; it denounced them because they preached, 'not the

[1] Farini, *Lo Stato Romano*, I, 318.   [2] *Scritti*, II, 62 *et seq.*   [3] *L. & D.*, I, 379–380.   [4] *Patria*, An. II, 57–58.

balsam of love', but 'the poison of perverse doctrines
and savage passions'; it called 'eternal malediction on
the head of this foolish generation, which knew not how
to find one moment of concord in face of the common
enemy'.[1] In a moment of insight, Ricasoli had realised
that between him and the democrats there was a profound
gulf, not only of theory but of instinct. They believed that
society was an artificial construction which could be
moulded by human resolution, whereas to him it was a
growth whose tendencies could be hastened only by
discipline and care.[2] Perhaps he had read that sentence in
which Guerrazzi exulted that man truly is made in the
image of God, for when he is strong, 'he places his hand
on the shoulder of Time and constrains it to carry him—
Time with man, and not man with Time'.[3] Whither did
Guerrazzi and his friends imagine that they would carry
Time in these days, when the Piedmontese were back
across the Ticino, and the Austrians were in Milan and
Parma, and all the old parties had failed, and the indifference of the common people of Tuscany was turning to
hatred of the patriots and all their works ?[4] The *Patria*
saw well enough what the democrats aimed at.[5] 'Alleging
that the constitutional princes of Italy can no longer
sustain the cause of independence . . . they have
declared that there is nothing to be looked for but a war
of insurrection waged by the People'. This gospel the
Patria fought tooth and nail. Insurrection meant only
new hatred, new division . . . it meant, too, the end of
aristocratic leadership and aristocratic security. But why
should the democrats listen to their opponents? There
was still hope! France had conquered the world by insurrection. Venice held out, Rome and Florence were free.
'Up, peoples, up!' cried Guerrazzi. 'Perhaps there is
still time! Chase from you the new Jesuits who instead
of a heart have within them a serpent's tail. . . . Rise

---

[1] *Patria*, An. II, 82, 74, 66. [2] *L. & D.*, I, 422. [3] *Al Principe
ed al Popolo*, 30. [4] Guerrazzi half admitted this. *Scritti Politici*, 473.
Cf. Hamilton to Palmerston, July 27. [5] *Patria*, An. II, 66 (September 4).

and trust . . . in whom? IN GOD AND IN YOUR-SELVES'.[1]

As ever, Leghorn was the first convert to the new propaganda. 'Our blood', wrote a moderate Leghorn advocate to a still more moderate Florentine, 'compared to yours, is like boiling sulphur'.[2] The democratic nationalists, to hasten their rise to power, had taken up agitation on social questions. In days when capitalists were leaving the city and trade was stagnating,[3] orators of the *Circolo Nazionale* found a good hearing when they clamoured for progressive taxation, for public works to relieve unemployment, for reductions in rents and the price of salt.[4] And yet, strange to say, the greatest orator of all gradually came to be regarded by the middle classes of Leghorn as their hope of salvation. The same Guerrazzi, who had played the demagogue with the dock-labourers and assistant-bakers of Leghorn, came forward as an opponent of socialism and its works; all knew him for the Poor Man's Friend, and he had an eloquence, a prestige, a blasphemous assurance that kept for him working-class trust even when he slew working-class illusions.[5] It was vain, he maintained, to hope that the governments could give everyone work. The Redeemer had said: 'I am your bread and wine; but he said it mystically, and the disciples were twelve; the government has to say it materially, and there are millions of hungry and thirsty'.[6] This was very re-assuring propaganda for the Leghorn capitalists. So, too, in political matters; in his most violent periods Guerrazzi always kept his eyes open to the limits of the possible, and avoided committing himself to any gospel which might be embarrassing to him when he came to power. Throughout 1848, while he carried on his fierce

[1] *Scritti Politici*, 349.   [2] Ricci to Galeotti, Jona, *op. cit.* 52.   [3] G. Rondoni: in *Arch. Stor. It.*, V, 22, p. 78. Guerrazzi, *Scritti Politici*, 401. [4] Passamonti in *Rassegna Storia del Risorg. Ital*, 1919, I–II, and Jona, *op. cit. passim.*   [5] 'A man of the people I am, a man of the People I was born, so I need not flatter it to gain its favour', *Scritti Politici*, 149.   [6] *Ibid. Condizioni Italiani.* The gospel of the article is: no socialism, but practical reforms.

vendetta with the moderates, he took constant care that
the republicans should have no cause to claim him as their
own.[1] He prided himself on being no unworthy successor
to Macchiavelli, and he disposed of the republicans by
telling them that their theories were really excellent, but,
for the time being, quite out of the question. In this he
was perfectly sincere. Long before he had any prospect of
achieving power he stated his difference with Mazzini:
'You agreed to impose the good . . . on reluctant and
ignorant people; I, perhaps through excessive concern for
the free will of others, refused to compel them even to
that which was best'.[2] Slowly it penetrated into the minds
of the lawyers, the doctors, the bankers, the traders of
Leghorn, that the democracy of Guerrazzi was not such
a very terrible thing. He was a *safe* man—they realised it
almost with a shock of surprise. He loved Italy, too, and
he loved their city, while Florence seemed to understand
neither. And who else could discipline the working-men
and the unemployed?

Towards the end of August all the unruly elements
were again in full agitation. On the 23rd there had landed
in the port the Barnabite father, Gavazzi, a stormy petrel
of agitation throughout Italy; and the timorous government
decided that he must be chased out of Tuscany as soon as
possible. He left Leghorn in a gilded state carriage,
escorted by twelve members of the democratic *circle*;[3]
a day or two after his departure there came back rumours
that armed peasants had insulted him and burnt the
tricolour. The city thereupon rose in open rebellion against
Florence, and the government authorised L. Cipriani to
enter it with troops.[4] The people murmured for awhile, and
then attacked the Tuscan troops as the Milanese had

[1] *Scritti Politici*, 245, 276, 305, 336, 348, etc.   [2] *Memorie*, p. 12.
[3] Hamilton to Palmerston, August 26. Cf. Codrington, 291–2: 'It is very
amusing'.   [4] L. Cipriani, *La Breve Narrazione dei fatti che si riferiscono
alla mia missione come commissario*. Livorno, 1848. Cf. Letters of Sir H.
Codrington, 289 *et seq*. He said that his sailors could easily have held the
forts, if they had turned out 'all those wretched rabble they call soldiers,
officers and all'.

attacked the Austrians. Captain Codrington of the *Thetis*, who was a sturdy open-minded Englishman, described the rioters as ' blackguards ' and ' ragamuffins', and observed that in their spare time they shot (with fixed bayonets) at sparrows. After a few days all that was left of Cipriani's force was an undisciplined remnant of soldiers shut up with their commander in the fortress.

' The people called upon the soldiers to join them, and leaning ladders against the wall, passed them bread and wine, and the soldiers from the parapet exchanged their cartridges for the wine. An officer ordered that the ladders should be taken away, and another officer had them replaced; some of the soldiers openly climbed them; others fled by ways more secret. Meanwhile the mouths of the cannon, which pointed towards the city, were turned round, the sentinels left their posts, never was seen anything more shameful'.

Thus Capponi narrates the miserable end of his attempt to govern Tuscany.[1] With the army finally broken, there was nothing that he could do; he called the civic guard to Pisa, not to subdue Leghorn, but as ' a mark of solemn disapproval ' of what had occurred.[2] Even so, some of the contingents refused to march, and the Aretines, when they arrived, fraternised with their brethren of Leghorn. It seemed the end of government in Tuscany. Leghorn had led the way, and the state was breaking up into its component municipalities.

The situation was saved by the courage and resource of Guerrazzi. On August 25th he had written to Capponi as minister and friend, offering him his services if he should think them useful;[3] but Capponi, while he did not make the common mistake of attributing all the evils of Leghorn and Tuscany to the arts of this one plotter (governments believed too readily, he thought, that all their troubles sprang from individuals), could not bring himself to so frank a compromise with agitation. Meanwhile the middle classes of Leghorn were straining desperately to find some means which would rid them of their present master,

[1] *Scritti*, II, 113.   [2] Hamilton to Palmerston, September 9.
[3] Guerrazzi, *Lettere*, No. 312.

'General' Torres, and the mob which followed at his heels; they did not care how they were governed, so long as they were *governed*, and governed no longer from Florence.[1] The Chamber of Commerce decided to act, and sent a deputation which asked the ministry to send to Leghorn Guerrazzi and Neri Corsini. Capponi refused to have anything to do with the matter, so the deputation sought out the men on its own initiative. Corsini either could not be found, or refused to attempt so dangerous a task. Guerrazzi accepted. As he drove into Leghorn he put his head out of the carriage window and noticed that many of the armed men were marching without shoes. 'Truly, we had arrived at the dregs'.[2]

The achievement of Guerrazzi in the next month was an extraordinary one. He had no force of any kind, and no commission from the government, he was face to face with a nervous and infuriated populace that had by a mixture of corruption and terror vanquished the armed forces of the state, he was regarded by the worst elements of the population as one of themselves. Yet, within three days of his arrival, he was able to write to Capponi a triumphant letter announcing his success.[3] 'Now isn't it plain to you who is turbulent, who moderate ? I, so much slandered, little by little bring back peace to the city'. He got rid of the objectionable Torres. He quickly slew all idea of secession from Tuscany. He had, of course, to yield something in return. He was forced to reorganise a new municipal guard; but, since the old civic guard had gone over to the rebels and the city was in the hands of a motley collection of armed rioters, it was obviously sound policy to substitute partial discipline for indiscipline. It was doubtless an unfortunate precedent that free distributions of bread should be made to a disorderly proletariate; but the same proletariate, employed in public works of

[1] Jona, *op. cit.* 56. [2] Guerrazzi, *Lettere*, No. 313; *Apologia*, 85. Cf. *Codrington*, 313: 'A precious set of rascals'. He saw three patriots who had one shirt between them. His men searched an officer of the civic guard, and found his pockets full of spoons that had disappeared from an English ship (p. 320). [3] *Lettere*, No. 315.

doubtful economic value, was kept from the still more
uneconomic labour of building barricades, was forbidden
to sing seditious songs, was forbidden to indulge its
pastime of letting off firearms in the streets, was forbidden
even to waste its substance in public gambling.[1] All this
Guerrazzi achieved by the sheer force of his personality,
by his never-resting nervous energy, by the singular power
which his defiant boldness and his passionate, extravagant
oratory, his courage in moments of crisis, gave him over
the crowd. And throughout, the government remained
hostile to him. On September 9 he wrote a last friendly
letter to Capponi, but in that letter he complained that he
was left without support. A week later he wrote coldly;
he had learnt, he said, that Capponi was still planning
coercion, that he had given orders to fire on the people.
'Through me learn what is the people of Leghorn. I am
a piece of the people'.[2] In these days Capponi made his
fatal mistake; he could not bring himself to shake hands
with revolution, to accept the demands of Leghorn, and
recognise the man who had brought them to moderate
compass when he brought the city to order. He sent down
Tartini to Leghorn to take over its government; Guerrazzi
and the *gonfaloniere* met Tartini outside the city, and
Guerrazzi offered to stand by him to the death. He made
it clear that this death was the most probable eventuality.
. . . Tartini decided not to go inside the gates.[3] Capponi
could see no other plan than to break off all relations
with Leghorn, as if it were an independent state, and as if
the port and the capital really could afford to live without
each other.

From this folly the government and the assembly were
saved by Montanelli. When he returned from his mild
captivity in the Tyrol he was hailed by all men as the one
possible saviour; he had been the heart of the national
movement in its early days of struggle and hope; he had

1 *Apologia*, 103. See Documents in *Corsi and Menichetti*, pp. 17–62.
2 *Lettere*, No. 317.   3 *Documenti del processo*, 677. Hamilton to Palmerston, September 30.

fought for his country and had been mourned as dead; he was untainted by the miserable feuds and bitterness of the last six months. But on the way home, at Ferrara on September 5, he had written: 'We must finish once for all with these phantom governments which cannot govern and do not govern. . . . The republican standard is the only one under which we can fight anarchy'.[1] Tuscany knew nothing of this.

He had within his head a whole plan of government; but he regarded the question also as one of personalities. The exalted must be ruled by the exalted. Guerrazzi must come into the government; thus alone could Leghorn be kept within the state. But the government would have nothing to do with Guerrazzi, and by now Guerrazzi would have nothing to do with the government;[2] and, since Montanelli had forced it to take up the old hopeless work of treating with Leghorn,[3] it decided to send Montanelli thither to bear the brunt of the labour himself.[4] Guerrazzi generously made way, recommending his successor as a man worthy of obedience, and Montanelli, after some important conversations with Capponi, set out. No sooner had he arrived at Leghorn than he threw into the piazza a new war-cry. He called for a Constituent Assembly, representing the entire male population of the peninsula, and pledged to make for the peninsula one single government.

From his speech of October 8, even without his later comments on it, it is possible to comprehend that conception of the *Constituent* which was the last mirage of Montanelli, of Tuscany, and of Italy in these years of illusion. His programme, declared Montanelli,[5] was Christian; it appealed to equality and fraternity against the Pagan idea of conquest. It was, therefore, national. (Montanelli here skipped quickly over one or two uncertain

---

[1] Marradi, *Montanelli*, Appendix 18.   [2] Montanelli, *Schiarimenti*, p. 17.
[3] *Assemblee del Risorg.*, II, 171.   [4] *Ibid.* 184. Capponi, *Scritti*, II,
139.   [5] *Corriere Livornese*, No. 201 (October 9); Montanelli, *Schiarimenti*, 23 *et seq.; Memorie*, II, 403–5.

steps of his argument.) The various states of Italy were members of the same national mind and body; they must therefore be united politically through democracy. (Here again the reasoning was, at the least, rather vague.) The *Constituent* was to be ' the testing stone of the good faith or bad faith of the princes in sharing in the Italian enterprise'. When the people sent their representatives to Rome, elected by universal suffrage, they would be repairing the miserable errors of the last year with its unco-ordinated war and its unhappy pursuit of a federation of governments. The error of the past had been the search for independence first, and unity afterwards; the soldiers had fought as Tuscans, Romans, Piedmontese, in the hope of becoming Italians. That was folly, for it was ' impossible to chase Austria from Italy without uniting the arms of all Italy, impossible to unite the arms of all Italy without uniting her politically, impossible to unite all Italy politically without appealing to the people'.

These general ideas were very attractive. Montanelli might claim to be a prophet when he declared: ' The idea which brought the Italian states to communion of political life being national, the government which arose from it could not avoid being national equally'. It was, indeed, as a prophet or as a preacher that Montanelli had won a strong claim to the gratitude of Italians. But Italy at this time had no present need of prophets. There was nothing in Montanelli's speech which could help her to solve her immediate problems: how to secure co-operation between her conflicting states, and how to expel the Austrians. Austria was not prepared to be a passive observer of her own expulsion from Italy. The existing governments were not ready quietly to stand aside. The nationalist politicians had shown no inclination to forego the luxury of oratory. It was, therefore, unreasonable to hope that an assembly at Rome could make a brand-new Italian organisation, with a civil and military machine at its disposal, before the Austrians decided that it was time to send an army corps across the Apennines. Capponi was aghast at the idea to which he was committed.[1] It had appeared to him a 'toy', a theory like those which were being discussed at this very time in a rather academic congress at Turin; but Montanelli had made it into a war-cry. In Lucca, in Arrezzo, in Pisa, in Florence herself, the cry was caught up. At last men could be enthusiastic again! But Capponi, although he had unshaken support in the Assembly, ended the long agony of government by resigning. 'Our lot', he wrote later,[2] 'I may almost say our task, was not to govern, but to see the government break up in our hands, piece by piece, from one day to another'. Who could mend the ruin ? Capponi saw too late that it could only be mended by the grace of Piedmont. And in all Tuscany there was only one man, Ricasoli, who might possess the will and the power to gain that grace, and then to save the state in the strength of it, and by his own power.[3]

Ricasoli was ready to 'stand beneath the ruins', provided that he was given the power to fight democracy and reaction in his own way. 'What did the three of the *Patria* hope to make if a wind had carried them to power ? ' demanded Giusti contemptuously, and answered, 'Eclogues and ideals as usual'.[4] But Ricasoli had for his Louis XVI a plan[5] like that of Mirabeau. Leopold must leave his capital and go to Siena, which was conservative and defensible; from there he must appeal to his people in a proclamation; there he must govern, and there, if

---

[1] The accusation brought against Montanelli that he committed the ministry without its authorisation, is false. See Capponi, *Scritti*, II, 140–2; Montanelli, *Schiarimenti*, p. 26, *Documenti del processo*, 899, *Assemblee del Risorgimento*, IV, 719. Capponi and Leopold were weak and bewildered, and left Montanelli 'to his own conscience' without knowing what this implied. Still, he was not a very loyal servant of the ministry. Marradi, *op. cit.* Appendix XXIII. [2] *Scritti*, II, 147. [3] *Ibid.* II, 152. Capponi judged it a fatal mistake that he had taken office without Ricasoli, *ibid.* 67. [4] Giusti, *Epistolario*, III, 218. [5] For the following see *Ricordi Politici del Barone B.R.*, 15–21, October 1849 (edited by G. Biagi, Firenze, 1908), also *Brolio MSS.*, A. 4 (record of a conversation with Poniatowski, October 10, 1851). Cf. *L. & D.*, I, 382 *et seq.*

necessary he must defend his throne. One more attempt must be made to secure an *entente* with the Pope and with Charles Albert; with D'Azeglio in his ministry Ricasoli had hopes of winning Piedmont. But D'Azeglio was too wily to be caught, and the negotiations dwindled into an attempt to stiffen the old ministry with the energy of the *Patria* group. With such half-measures Ricasoli would have nothing to do. The Grand-Duke assured him that he would not allow the democratic faction to impose itself upon him; he would descend into the Piazza to defend the laws; if he fell, he would be happy to die at his post. ' Never can it be that I surrender to a party my Tuscany, which I have loved as a bride'. He wept, and stretched out a hand which Ricasoli took reverently. ' This is the language worthy of one who rules a people', declared the baron. A few days later the prince declared again, bravely and affectionately: ' Yes, Bettino, we shall avoid this storm too ' . . . but as Ricasoli descended the stairs he passed a deputation from Leghorn on its way up, and that afternoon he heard rumours that Montanelli and Guerrazzi had been commissioned to form a ministry.[1]

Ricasoli took this issue of the crisis almost as a personal affront. Confidence had been refused to him; ' men risen from anarchy', a ' party without principle', had prevailed by a mixture of terror and corruption; they had abused the best citizens. There seemed something wrong with the moral order of the world. He, at any rate, would not countenance evil. He hoped that the successful democrats would forget their origin and work for the good of the country. But whether they did or did not, he would have nothing more to do with government. He resigned his position as *gonfaloniere*. ' I could not make myself their instrument even for good . . . because the methods they have adopted hitherto . . . cannot have the sanction of an honourable citizen, who looks above all to the morality

---

[1] Guerrazzi had ordered in Leghorn ' a clamourous demonstration of the Piazza' to hasten on events. La Cecilia, *Memorie*, V, 231.

of his actions'.[1] So the baron nursed his outraged pride
and virtue. He did not realise that the dictates of his
sensitive conscience were enjoining on him a course of
action which was at the time of positive harm to the
country. Guerrazzi, after all, was not quite a devil. The
English ambassador and Capponi himself[2] had urged the
sovereign to seek his aid; men like Giusti were willing to
forget the past and wish him God-speed.[3] If he sincerely
wished the good of the country he had a right to claim
support, or at least toleration, even from those who disliked
his political theories and his political methods. It was punishment enough for Guerrazzi that he should have won his
way to power too late to realise any of his dreams of
patriotic triumph, perhaps just in time to save a country
which Ricasoli had described thus: ' Public spirit none;
the multitudes standing by as indolent spectators. The
militia corrupt and unfaithful. The other instruments of
government ignorant and infected'.[4] Guerrazzi himself
asserted that he received the state as a burning house given
over to the firemen, or as ' a corpse given into the hands
of the priests, to bury it, and chant its requiem'.[5] No one
could contradict him.

·   ·   ·   ·   ·   ·

In the five months during which Guerrazzi held power,
first as minister of the Interior in Montanelli's cabinet,
later as a Triumvir, and finally as sole head of the state,
there was apparent a subtle change in all his political
utterances—not in their style, which rose in a crescendo
of flamboyance till it was as vivid as the most flaming
passages of his romances—but in their content. In the old

[1] L. & D., I, 383–4.   [2] Capponi, Scritti, 45–6, 154–5. M. Tabarrini
was the envoy of Capponi, and probably of the Grand-Duke, in these negotiations. Cf. Montanelli, Schiarimenti, 31, and Brolio MSS., A. 4. Poniatowski
told Ricasoli in 1851 that he and Hamilton had urged Leopold to accept
the democrats. Cf. Hamilton to Palmerston, October 27 and November 1.
[3] Giusti, Epistolario, III, 227–9.   [4] Ricordi Politici, October 1849
(Bragi).   [5] Le Assemblee del Risorgimento, IV, 686 (January 29, 1849).
Cf. Corsi and Menichetti, pp. 109–122.

days of opposition he had heaped anathema on the moderates
for raising the ' scarecrow of order ' as a means of damping
the enthusiasm of the people. Now he began to rhapsodise
of an order which was 'the order of life, of power, of
liberty'.¹ The terrors which the moderates believed him
to have loosed against order when it was in their custody,
paled into insignificance beside the terrors which he
threatened against those who violated order when it was
under his protection. When the rabble of the little town
of Castagnetto committed some serious violence, Guerrazzi
the minister wrote threatening to destroy their town.
The citizens wrote back protesting; they desired from
the government protection for property against the
oppressions of the aristocrats; they had a right to expect
more affectionate treatment from a democratic minister.
. . . Guerrazzi answered that many knaves attached
themselves to the cause of liberty, and added: ' When a
people burns, attacks life and property, breaks open the
prisons and frees criminals, this people is not worthy to
belong to the Tuscan family, and is destroyed'.²

Even patriotic enthusiasm seemed to have lost for him
some of its glamour and fascination. He charged the
prefect of Florence to put an end to the gibes against
Austria with which non-combatant citizens gave vent to
their warlike fury at the theatre, declaring: ' Enemies
are to be vanquished, not insulted; since before victory
insult is foolish arrogance, and after victory, base cowardice'.³ Suddenly, it seemed, the country had ceased to
need even oratory; why else should the minister have
warned the new governor of Leghorn, that undoubted
patriot, Professor Pigli, that he must not make any
speeches?⁴ The governor himself thought the prohibition
rather a hard one. As vice-president of the popular *circle*
of Florence he had often applauded and seconded the

¹ *Scritti Politici*, 434, and letter to commander of Civic Guard at Lucca,
10/1/1849. ² *Lettere*, No. 351. ³ *Lettere*, No. 350. ⁴ *Apologia*, 44-5;
Pigli, *Risposta*, 87. P. Orsi in *Nuova Antologia*, October 1, 1923 (new
letters).

oratory of President Guerrazzi. Not even six thousand lire for his expenses consoled him. The fall of the Roman minister, Rossi, under the knife of an assassin, was an occasion which he could not pass by; he announced to the citizens how ' God, in his hidden counsels, had willed that he should fall by the hand of a child of the ancient republic'. For this Guerrazzi severely blamed him; and blamed him again, when, instead of allying himself with the solid order-loving bourgeoisie of Leghorn, he actually supported employees of the government in their demands for higher wages. This was more than Pigli could endure; justifying himself at length for ' governing with affection', he complained that the attitude of his chief was ' not very democratic', and probably would have resigned if stirring events had not made him forget for a time his grievances.

Guerrazzi, in fact, was seeking to break free from his old friends of the *circles*. He complained later to Mazzini that he was pestered by ' a mob of people which boasts of having raised me, and says that it is free, and that seeks to put greedy hands into the public chest'.[1] Against such persons he appealed in an election proclamation (one of the first acts of the new government had been to dissolve the old Assembly) for ' men who fear God and love the country, men who have less on their lips and more in their hearts the sacred name of liberty, men straightforward, simple, of antique virtue',[2] men just like the heroes of American independence, whom he mentioned in large numbers. Unfortunately, the men who approached most closely to this ideal were the very men who were most hostile to Guerrazzi; because they were straightforward, they suspected the arts by which he had attained power; because they were loyal, they disapproved the *Constituent*, which might vote away the rights of their sovereign; because they were simple, they could not understand his subtlety. And the more antique their virtue was, the more certain were they that Guerrazzi was a very wicked man. Ricasoli, for example, saw in the government

[1] *Lettere*, No. 378. Cf. 358 and 359.   [2] In *Scritti Politici*, p. 575.

nothing more than a negation of the principles for which
he himself stood. In an address to his electors[1] he reaffirmed
his belief in liberty, declaring that the plant had not come
to flower because it had not been watered by education
and fostered by leadership, and that he saw no hope save
in a return to the early months of 1848, 'a time of true
concord'. But he did not believe that Guerrazzi could
lead the people back along that road, and, even if he had
believed it, he would not have made himself an instrument
of such a man 'even for good'. The moderates left
Guerrazzi to fight his battle alone.

The man fought it with real courage and patriotism.
'My country! My country!' he wrote to his closest
friend, Puccini, 'how light a sacrifice it is to consecrate
to you this remnant of days redeemed from doubt—from
doubt, which is the death of the soul'.[2] He realised now
that he was the 'last barrier before the abyss', that the
passions which he had stirred up against other governments threatened his own, and that after him there was
nothing but anarchy. He could not sleep,[3] he felt over-
come 'by fatigue and the growing difficulties', but he
struggled on. Capponi realised that the disease of the
state was planted deeply in the hearts of the people; at
the root of all their turmoil was *fear*,[4] fear of victorious
Austria, fear of revolution, fear of each other. The middle
classes feared the workers and unemployed of the towns,
and the cottagers of the country; these classes feared
starvation. Unemployment led to rioting; there were
sturdy and threatening beggars in Florence, country
people came into the capital to clamour for work, there
were disturbances at Empoli, at Prato, at Borgo San
Sepolcro; round Lucca the people refused to pay taxes.[4]
Guerrazzi found difficulty in securing obedience from the
small force of *carabinieri*, from the local agents of the

[1] *L. & D.*, I, 389.   [2] *Lettere*, No. 338.   [3] *Lettere*, No. 341 (to
Puccini).   [4] Capponi, *Scritti*, II, 118.   [5] Corsi e Menichetti, *Documenti*:
Nos. 225, 237, 244, 249, 254, 261, 264, 267, etc.

government, from the magistrates.[1] His own tireless activity, his courage, even his melodrama, warred with their timidity and disobedience. 'Energy, governor, energy', he telegraphed to Pigli, 'or within a month Tuscany will be a heap of ashes'.[2] He protested that the ministry would save even those who hated it. When the *Patria*, which fought him with a bitterness that Giusti and other moderates thought excessive, was burnt by a mob in the Piazza at Leghorn, he wrote to the director of the Pisan post-office: 'The *Patria* is hostile to us . . . another reason for respecting it. . . . This despatch comes from Guerrazzi, not from the minister Guerrazzi'.[3] Perhaps he was not above using means known to governments for hastening that sensational fall in the subscriptions to Ricasoli's paper which forced it to come to an untimely end on November 30.[4] Now and again he gave signs of the old spirit of vendetta; he drove from Florence the poet Giovanni Prati, whom he believed the author of certain caricatures which had appeared in the *Vespa;* and denounced him in the *Monitore* as a 'Seller and poisoner of women, a scandalous person, a reputed foreign agent, an insulter of the people'.[5] There was in these days a scattering abroad of the moderates. D'Azeglio was burnt in effigy, the windows of Salvagnoli's and of Ridolfi's houses were broken, and Salvagnoli fled, perhaps with exaggerated caution, to Brolio. With all this violence Guerrazzi had nothing to do; he fought the passions of his former followers, and in the end made Florence safe for his opponents. He turned to them expecting at the least 'a word of comfort'. In his strained egoistical way he described how he had given to the state indefatigable

---

[1] *Ibid.* Nos. 140, 161, 199, 232, 260. [2] *Ibid.* p. 110. [3] *Ibid.* p. 139 and *Scritti Politici*, 372; Giusti, *Epistolario*, III, 215, 216. [4] See Passamonti, *loc. cit.*, and *L. & D.*, 400 *et seq.* The effects were sold to Celstino Bianchi (*Brolio MSS.*, I, 29). Ricasoli denied publicly that the *Nazionale*, Bianchi's paper, was a continuation of the *Patria*. Bianchi in fact took a less intransigent line, to the grief of Ricasoli. See *L. & D.* Letters of December 1848. [5] A. D'Ancona, *Ricordi ed Affetti*, 308 *et seq.* Ricasoli urged Bianchi to protest.

care, how he had stolen time from the hours of sleep, how—supreme punishment for one 'educated in gentle disciplines'—he had been unable to give attention to his beloved studies, unable even to 'smell their fragrance'.[1] . . . Ricasoli, at any rate, had nothing but contempt for this appeal to sympathy. Guerrazzi was to him, at the best, a repentant demagogue; he remained damned for ever as a man 'risen from anarchy'.

Yet Ricasoli himself had born testimony to the success of the demagogue's efforts. On November 29 he admitted to Salvagnoli that the people was less cruel than it had been a month ago; he wrote later that he had been informed that honest citizens were again safe from the ill-disposed, and that the cause of the Republic had suffered great losses within the last month. Throughout the country there reigned 'profound quiet'.[2] Such private testimony gives greater authority to the statements returned by the prefects to the government in January;[3] these were un-animous in declaring that the country folk were indifferent to the reforms and disliked the civic guard, but that they were passive; that the people of the towns, with one or two isolated exceptions, had not been guilty of serious disturbance, and that the majority of the politically-minded were content with the existing constitution and not desirous of a republic. There had been some disturbance in Florence on the occasion of the elections, but order had been kept by the intervention of Guerrazzi himself.[4] The English ambassador, who had a distinct appreciation of Guerrazzi's qualities, had reported as early as November 24 that the crisis was past, and that the government had restored order.

All this labour and achievement of Guerrazzi was ruined by the vague idealism of his nominal chief, Monta-nelli, and by the impossible project to which that idealism had committed the ministry. The disciple of Macchiavelli must have wondered at the fortune which gave him such

[1] *Assemblee del Risorg.*, IV, 687 (January 28, 1849). [2] *L. & D.*, I, 404-7. [3] Printed in *Marradi, op. cit.*, Doc. 26. [4] *Apologia*, 45.

a colleague when he heard Montanelli expound his programme in words like these: ' Now every day clear proof is made manifest that God in his counsel has decreed that Italy is, and shall be, one. We, seized with reverence, should religiously set ourselves to second with spirit and labour the decrees of God'.[1] This! when the state was trembling on the verge of anarchy, when the government could only hope to pay its way by alienating the public demesnes,[2] when the brave Tuscan volunteers of six months ago had come back a rabble, when the masses of the people were weary of the patriots, when Austria was ready for the first pretext to cross the Apennines! A conversation between Montanelli and the envoy, Hamilton, gives some idea of what a cool observer with an eye for facts thought of such rhapsodies. Hamilton, after some difficulty, succeeded in making it clear to the minister that France and England would not drive Austria out for him. ' He then replied: " Nothing remains, I fear, but the Italian sword, which must never be sheathed while an Austrian soldier remains in Italy". I said that I did not believe that the Italian sword alone would be able to achieve that object'.[3] . . . Guerrazzi looked on Montanelli's plan of the *Constituent* as a cross which he was called upon to bear;[4] a humbler Tuscan, either in ignorance or in jest, explained to a friend that the *Constituent* was nothing else than Montanelli's wife.

All that Guerrazzi could do was to whittle down the most dangerous elements in the plan. He even hoped that, despite everything, it might be made the instrument of securing special gains for Tuscany and her prince.[5] By a modification of Montanelli's original scheme, the government saved itself from the obligation to promote through the *Constituent* a complete democratic union of the entire

[1] *Assemblee del Risorg.*, IV, 382–3 (October 28). [2] *Ibid.* IV, 344, and IV, 473, where the minister, Adami, explains the scheme. IV, 555–646 for the debate. [3] Hamilton to Palmerston, November 19. [4] *Apologia*, 159. [5] His programme was ' *Principe salvato e ingrandito*'. *Lettere*, 272; *Apologia*, p. 126 *et seq.*

peninsula.[1] Another modification which occurred in Montanelli's circular of November 7 cut right across the original conception; the *Constituent* was now conceived as having two stages, of which the first would be given solely to an elaboration of a common war organisation, while the second would lay down the future organisation of the peninsula after the war had been fought and won.[2] Then there came from Piedmont the claim that the various states must be allowed to limit the mandates given to their representatives, and Guerrazzi, after an obstinate struggle with his chief, forced him to accept this modification also. On the surface, it would have seemed that Montanelli had at last a real chance of winning a practical success. On December 16 Gioberti himself, Montanelli's spiritual father, had achieved power in Piedmont. He had been carried by the same stream which had swept forward the Tuscan democrats, for, after the Salasco Armistice, he had dismayed the moderates by swinging sharply to the left.[3] In October he had been president of a conference which at Turin discussed that same problem of a national Italian Constituent Assembly which Montanelli was to crystallise in his speech at Leghorn. Arrived at office, Gioberti, like Guerrazzi, sought to discipline the forces which had carried him there, not because the problem of order was as acute in Piedmont as in Tuscany, but because political parties were indifferent to him, and he used them in turns as a means to the realisation of his national end. His attitude to the Montanellian initiative was clear and consistent. He wanted to renew the war with Austria, he wanted the states of Italy to aid him in that war, and he wanted a central organisation for those states. But he was not willing to renounce the special position which belonged to Piedmont, and he was not willing to defy Europe and deny his own gospel by accepting as part and parcel of

[1] *Assemblee del Risorg.*, IV, 382–3; Montanelli, *Schiarimenti*, p. 41.
[2] Montanelli, *Schiarimenti*, 27. [3] Minghetti, *Ricordi* (Torino, 1889), II, 387, 418.

the *Constituent* a democratic feud with the Papacy.[1] So at Rome his policy clashed with that of Montanelli. The latter had accorded very cavalier treatment to the head of the Roman state. He had intrigued to secure the dismissal of Rossi, he had sent the radical, La Cecilia, to make combinations with democrats like Sterbini, and in the end he had instructed him to work for the expulsion of the Pope and the proclamation of a provisional government.[2] Gioberti, on the other hand, from the time of the Pope's flight to Gaeta (November 24) had supported the efforts of Mamiani to achieve reconciliation, and as the failure of these efforts became apparent, he began to consider a Piedmontese intervention in favour of a liberal Papacy. This clash of policies was alone sufficient to ruin Montanelli's plan, but more serious still was his insistence on the error which had ruined every attempt at combination for the last twelve months, the error of seeking in central Italy a counterpoise to the power of Piedmont. In instructions to his official envoy and to his unofficial agent, Montanelli repeated that the *Constituent* must serve this purpose.[3] It was no wonder that Gioberti put an end to the negotiations on January 17, offering to Tuscany alliance on the condition that she had no relations with the existing government of Rome, and none with the existing government of Sicily.

Montanelli, like everyone of his predecessors, chose to ruin himself with Rome rather than to save himself with Piedmont. The decision did indeed mean his ruin, and with him the ruin of Guerrazzi, and the ruin of that order which Guerrazzi had painfully re-established and whose maintenance alone could save the state from Austria. On the first day of the new year the Pope had declared war to the knife against rebellious democracy by launching excommunication against all who accepted the *Constituent*

---

[1] See A. Anzilotti, *Gioberti* (Firenze, 1922), Ch. 6–7. A. D'Ancona, *Ricordi Storici del Risorg.*, 263–8. [2] *Documenti del Processo*, 543–546. *Schiarimenti*, 41 *et seq.* La Farina, Lo Stato Romano, V, II, 654. [3] *Documenti del Processo*, 543, 547 (Letters of November 28 and 30).

or took part in the election of its deputies. On the 16th of
January it was proclaimed at Rome that the Roman
Constituent would also make the new constitution for Italy;
and the peoples of the other parts of Italy were called
upon to send their deputies to the Eternal City. When
the news came to Florence, the *circles* held tumultuous
meetings[1] and demanded that the government should take
action in accordance with the expressed will of Rome and
Italy. Guerrazzi, if he had the will, had not the power to
struggle against the prestige of Montanelli and the claims
of the democracy. There was nothing for it but to draft a
bill to put before the newly-assembled chamber, to secure
the consent of the sovereign, and to introduce the bill in
his name. Guerrazzi brought all his persuasive eloquence
to bear; he declared to Leopold that the *Constituent* would
check the ambitions of Piedmont and chasten the furies
of the republicans; he swore that the prince would be a
gainer, not a loser, by his generosity; and he declared in
the Assembly that Leopold, in signing the draft bill, had
won a title to the gratitude of Italy which the Italians
would know how to honour.[2]

The day on which the Senate passed the law, Leopold
withdrew quietly to Siena. His minister at Rome had
warned him that he must choose between Revolution and
Religion, his confessor had urged him to flee from Florence,
his assistant private secretary had been inspired by St.
Catherine of Siena to warn him against the *Constituent*,
and His Holiness the Pope had explained to him with
gentle firmness the will of the Lord.[3] The Papal excommunication had done its work. This Tuscan Louis XVI
was faced by a question of conscience. Florence, ignorant
of the struggle which had fought itself out in the breast
of its mild prince, knew only that his absence was very

---

[1] Hamilton to Palmerston, January 23. [2] *Apologia*, 130–6. *Assemblee
del Risorg.*, V, 539–40. Guerrazzi sincerely hoped that the introduction
of the bill would 'calm passions'. See *Nuova Antologia*, October 1, 1923,
p. 195. Hamilton to Palmerston, January 23, reports Leopold's reluctance
to sign project. [3] Letters printed in Gennarelli, *Le Sventure d'Italia*.

alarming. The *gonfaloniere* and the general of the civic guard went after him to Siena, and returned to Florence without him; but he had asked to see one of his ministers, and Montanelli set out for Siena on February 6. The Grand-Duke had betaken himself to bed, the never-failing refuge of princes besieged by disturbing visitors. Montanelli talked to him at length, and perhaps not wisely, about politics. When he called next morning he found that Leopold had fled secretly to an unknown destination, leaving behind him a letter which explained to his ministers and to the people the inner workings of his troubled conscience.[1]

.   .   .   .   .   .

'The state fell like a corpse into the public road'. For the next two months Guerrazzi had drama enough to satisfy all his passion as an artist. He posed, acted, de-claimed with the fury of any of his own romantic creations. But it must be admitted, even by his critics, that he played his part with courage. The question of the *Constituent* dropped into the background. The only issue that remained was whether the country would still keep some sort of government, or whether the rabble of the *circles*, clamour-ing for a republic and union with Rome, would be strong enough to drag it into anarchy. Guerrazzi considered now that he had only one task, to keep some vestiges of law and order. The history of Tuscany throughout February and March is nothing more than the story of the ceaseless fight which he waged with his assailants, at one time openly opposing them, at another seeming to yield to

[1] Montanelli, *Memorie*, II, 459 *et seq. Schiarimenti*, 63–7. *Assemblee del Risorg.*, V, 829–30. On the state of Siena, where Leopold alleged that his own presence was the cause of disorder, see *Apologia*, 256, and *Appendice all' Apologia;* also *Documenti del Processo*, 206, and Hamilton to Palmerston, 6/2/1849. Leopold fled to Porto Santo Stefano, where Captain Codrington came to look after him. The captain disliked his task. 'Oh dear me, I'm not made for chamberlain to grand dukes and duchesses and six children and seventeen attendants'. *Letters*, 326.

their demands, at another time evading them, always
speaking their language, but always standing between
them and their goal, till at last the attack spent itself, and
its dying fury provoked reaction.

The famous trial which Guerrazzi underwent after the
restoration, has distracted attention from the political and
social significance of his struggle, by raising the question
of the legal aspect of his actions. Guerrazzi made this
issue the central theme of his *Apologia*, and the falsifica-
tions of history which he sometimes introduced into his
defence tend to blind critical readers to the real merit of
the labours which he chronicles. It must be admitted that
he committed treason for which a government less mild
and weak than that of Tuscany would most reasonably
have hanged him. After struggling with undaunted passion
against the mob which burst into the chamber on February
8, and insisting that the government which it demanded
(a Triumvirate of Montanelli, Manzoni, and himself)
must hold its title from the duly-elected representatives
of Tuscany,[1] he signed a proclamation which announced
to the Tuscans: 'The prince, on whom you spent
treasures and affection, has abandoned you. . . . The
princes pass, the peoples remain'.[2] 'Leopold of Austria
is fallen', he telegraphed to the governor of Leghorn,
'worthy punishment of a man without faith'. Then, that
evening, news came to Guerrazzi that the fallen prince
was still on Tuscan soil, probably at Portoferraio. 'Since
he has abandoned Tuscany', the minister telegraphed
rather quaintly on the following day, 'the provisional
government cannot permit him to remain in any part of
it'.[3] There was more treason in the next few days; expeditions to chase the prince from Elba and from the island

---

[1] *Assemblee del Risorg.*, V, 829–41. Capponi justified the action of
Guerrazzi and the Senate, *Scritti*, II, 47. [2] *Ibid.* 458. [3] *Documenti
del Processo*, 568. In addition to these documents, to the collection of
Corsi and Menichetti, and the narratives of Guerrazzi and Pigli (*Risposta
all' Apologia*), see the correspondence published by P. Orsi in the *Nuova
Antologia, loc. cit.*

of Giglio;[1] then the discovery that he was in neither place, but in the little southern port of Santo Stefano; wires from Guerrazzi calling Pigli to send troops to deal with 'reaction' in Florence, more wires to say that the troops were not needed, and still more wires to say that they were needed, after all; then a marching of troops backwards and forwards to Empoli to deal with reactionary movements which had interrupted the communications between the two cities. There was an expedition to expel the Grand-Duke from Porto Santo Stefano, and Guerrazzi bombarded the governor of Leghorn with telegraphic instructions. He was in particular to prepare a proclamation 'written with the greatest simplicity, suitable for a simple people', explaining how Leopold of Austria had broken his sworn word, how he was 'a deserter of the people who loved him', how he had run away with 'the people's blood', the money that was in the mint, how he had kept vast quantities of wine in his cellars, and spent the people's treasure in paying pensions to the numerous women whom he had seduced.[2] Even Guerrazzi's lawyer, Corsi, might have had difficulty in explaining that such simple fiction for simple folk was not really treasonable, if the Governor Pigli, who with all his vanity was a loyal, honest person, had surrendered this document to the prosecution. There was still more treason, when general De Laugier, acting in accordance with instructions received but perhaps misinterpreted, advanced in the name of Leopold and with the vain hope of Piedmontese support.[3] Guerrazzi issued hysterical proclamations calling the people to arms,[4] and marched out himself at the head of an 'army', which by his order fixed olive branches to its rifles . . . not in imitation of the stratagem of Macbeth's enemies. . . . It

---

[1] Captain Codrington met the Tuscan navy—*i.e.* his 'old acquaintance the *Giglio*'—with two large boats in tow, full of patriots and large tricolour flags, on one of these expeditions. Codrington, *Letters*, 325. [2] *Nuova Antologia, loc. cit.* 212–213. [3] See Anzilotti, *op. cit.* 352 *et seq.* There was dissension in the Piedmontese cabinet, and shortly afterwards Gioberti fell. Cf. Gennarelli, *Le Sventure d'Italia*, 15–23. [4] *Atti del Governo Provisorio Toscano*. Proclamations of February 18, 19, 20.

was not exactly treason, but it was Guerrazzi in his best style, when he appealed to the Tuscans that ' no insult be shown to the aged mother of the perjured De Laugier. Is she not', he demanded, 'wretched enough, in having carried in her womb the traitor of her country?'

Yet this strange disciple of Byron and Macchiavelli soon forgot his anger against the Grand-Duke, and was able later to argue truly that much of his treasonable ranting had been forced upon him by the needs of his situation. On the very day when there came to Florence the news of De Laugier's proclamation, he had a violent quarrel with Mazzini, who had landed in Leghorn the day Montanelli returned from Siena. Guerrazzi evaded the republicans whom he could not withstand by promising to proclaim the republic ' on the condition that the Florentine people give on the morrow two thousand men to defend it'[3]—a condition which he well knew would be distasteful to the champions of Liberty. He wrote later to Montanelli, who had gone with the tide, that immediate union with Rome would only bring discord and weakness, and that ' the most efficacious formula to bring a better order is defence of the country'.[2] To this end he issued proclamation after proclamation, and the young Tuscans, by now a little indifferent, passed on their several occasions beneath flaming posters which shouted to them from the walls that even the brutes defended their lairs, and demanded whether they wished to be lower than the brutes; which enumerated the great men of Tuscany and her great monuments, describing the emotions of Guerrazzi when he thought about them, and the emotions which Tuscan Youth should feel; which drew stirring but improbable pictures of thousands of courageous young heroes rushing to the frontier, blessed by the priests and worshipped by their mothers, to unchain the thunder of cannon among

[1] *Documenti del Processo*, 420. Mrs. Browning wrote:
' . . . If we did not fight
Exactly, we fired muskets in the air
To show that victory was ours of right '.
[2] Guerrazzi, *Lettere*, No. 381

the Apennines and listen to the wild blast which, like the Archangels' Trump, would call Italy to new birth.[1]

The patriots preferred to stay in Florence and fight Guerrazzi. Even before the flight of Leopold, the Florentine *circle* had been in permanence. It organised tumults on February 8, and continued to organise them. It attracted to itself a number of ' soldiers', and was fortified with the support of various Lombard fugitives of various degrees of virtue. In the tumult of February 8 it had been led by a Roman called Niccolini, whom Guerrazzi described as a man ' without faith and without past, except the most shameful one', and who invited the Triumvir to make good use of the coin and the jewels left behind by the Grand-Duke.[2] Another leader was the journalist, Montazio, whose impudence was disconcerted on one occasion only. ' See the power of words! ' he boasted. ' With a writing of mine I drove out the Archbishop from Florence; with two articles I drove out the Pope from Rome; with a letter I drove out the Grand-Duke from San Stefano'. . . . ' Then why don't you send a word to Radetsky? ' shouted someone, and for once the orator was a little nonplussed[3] . . . But opposition to the demagogues of the piazza was dangerous, and impartial observers in Florence reported that the *circles* maintained a genuine, though bloodless, reign of terror.[4] They organised festivals of ' republican joy', in which they manifested to the government 'the will of the people'. They desired no longer that it should be declared in a democratically elected assembly, for they claimed that ' the popular instinct, with its exquisite good sense, has already anticipated your judgment and demands this union'.[5] ' The Tuscans wish to be united in one sole state with the Romans. Say the solemn word; do not dare to usurp the People's sovereignty! . . . Dare ! Dare ! ' And if Guerrazzi refused to see in

---

[1] *e.g. Atti del Governo Provvisorio*, dates cited, and *Assemblee del Risorg.*, V, 320, 553.   [2] A. D'Ancona, *Ricordi Storici del Risorg*, 269.   [3] *Ibid*. 320. On Montazio, see F. Martini in appendix to Giusti, *Epistolario*.   [4] Hamilton to Palmerston, February 19 and 27.   [5] *Apologia*, 335.

the ravings of Niccolini's jackals the expression of the
people's will, if he refused to 'dare' as they demanded,
they threatened to throw him from his own window into
the street.[1] It was hard that one who had dreamt and
written of Victory or Death in a nobler struggle should
be threatened with mere vulgar defenestration by a mob
whose mean violence he himself, alas! had once chosen
as an instrument.

The battle which Guerrazzi fought with the *circles*,
with his colleagues in government, and with Mazzini
himself, had its theoretical side. Eight months before, in a
private letter, he had expressed the opinion that Mazzini
would never be a statesman. 'He wishes too much at a
time. And between him and me there is this very great
difference: he wishes to impose his opinions on the people,
while I, on the contrary, declare myself ready to renounce
my opinions before the will of the people consulted with
peace and legality'.[2] He had his quarrel with the great
agitator on February 18, and after it Mazzini went off
to Rome with his work in Tuscany unaccomplished.
Guerrazzi, writing him a letter in which he generously
asked pardon for the hard words which he had used,
advised him 'not to look at things with the eyes of desire
and hope, but in the manner of our Niccolo'.[3] Perhaps
this was the only time when anyone suggested to Mazzini
that he should become a new Macchiavelli!

In the end, Guerrazzi triumphed, though he ruined
himself. He saved Tuscany from the immediate proclamation of the republic and of union with Rome. He
secured at last for a *Tuscan* Assembly the right to
decide the question of union with Rome.[4] When this last
of the revolutionary assembles met on March 25, Montanelli called on the deputies to answer the false prophets
who foretold Italian failure with 'an embrace of love';

1 *Documenti del Processo*, 530; cf. *Apologia*, 241.   2 Guerrazzi, *Lettere*,
p. 246. To Puccini, 3/6/1848.   3 *Ibid*. No. 377.   4 The different proclamations concerning the Tuscan and Italian constituents register the
phases of the struggle. *Assemblee del Risorg.*, V, 459, 466-7, 470.

and some days later G. Modena read an essay which proved that the unity of Italy was ' the law of God, of truth, of justice'.[1] But already there had come to Tuscany the news that Charles Albert had lost his last throw at Novara, and the Assembly, while intransigent republicans murmured, at last conferred upon Guerrazzi the powers of a dictator.[2] He had already seen that the only hope for Tuscany lay in a restoration of the legitimate government; but the moderate leaders had rejected his secret advances.[3] For more than a week he struggled on, scattering to the last flamboyant proclamations, acting his drama of patriotic tragedy. Montanelli went off to Paris. ' The break begins', Guerrazzi wrote to him, ' I feel death. . . . But Christian martyrdom does not please me; in this I am a little Pagan; I would rather cast myself into the gulf like Curtius'.[4] In these last days one who lived to second the sounder patriotism of Ricasoli, and to combat, years later, the legend of Guerrazzi the Democrat, saw him ride by. ' He was alone, but he sat firm in the saddle'.[5]

It would be fruitless to multiply evidence of the rising disgust with which the great masses of the population had witnessed the last convulsions of degenerate democracy and nationalism. Those same peasants who, fifty years before, had heaped together the trees of liberty into a pyre with which to burn Jacobins and Jews, meditated dark things when once again venal Jacobins collected from door to door on the plea that they must be paid for planting the hated emblems of democracy.[6] The people of the provincial towns murmured when undisciplined levies,

[1] *Ibid.* 482, 536.   [2] On March 28 he was invested with the executive power; on April 2 he demanded dictatorial powers, insisting on the adjournment of the Assembly and the postponement of constitutional discussion. Granted on April 3. *Ibid.* 596.   [3] *Assemblee del Risorg.*, V, 528, 596, for his denials. But see Capponi, *Scritti*, II, 49, and *Lettere*, II, 475; Giusti, *Memorie*, 146; Guerrazzi, *Apologia*, 650, *Lettere*, 382; Gennarelli, *Epistolario*, 93.   [4] *Lettere*, No. 379.   [5] A. D'Ancona, *op. cit.* 277.   [6] Trollope, *op. cit.* 204. The same workmen, it was said, after April 12 made similar collections to pay them for removing the trees. Martini, *Ricordi ed Affetti*, 12.

composed largely of mere boys, descended upon them,
took counsel with the local agitators, and then sought out
all who were reputed to be *codini* and forced them to kiss
the symbolic trees.[1] 'Plant them in your hearts', cried
Guerrazzi, ' and then all will be well.'[2] The factions would
not listen to him. The moderates would not help him to
control the factions. In the valley of the Upper Arno
fights began to break out between the organised rabble
and the unorganised conservative masses. The people
would shout for Leopold, and hiss the democrats as they
came back from their festivals.[3] Early in February the
English ambassador had reported that the great majority
of the people would welcome intervention—even Austrian
intervention.[4] The end came in another way. The citizens
of Florence rose furiously against an undisciplined body
of the municipal guard of Leghorn. Guerrazzi in vain
risked his life in trying to still the combat. From that
evening of April began in effect his long captivity. The
municipality of Florence took control, and added to its
number five men, among them Ricasoli and Capponi.
People believed, erroneously, that this governing commission would decide the destinies of Tuscany. They
were decided at Gaeta, whither the Grand-Duke had fled
from Porto Santo Stefano,[5] and at Vienna.

The commission did what it could.[6] Throughout April
it worked unceasingly in the hope that, by the restoration
of order and moderate government, it might take away
all pretext for a reaction based on Austrian intervention.
It refused all co-operation with the men of February, it
secured the adhesion of all the municipalities (save Leghorn)
to the constitutional monarchy, it fought the reactionaries
who hoped now to glut their vengeance against the fallen
tyrants, and who in various parts of the country pursued

[1] *L. & D.*, I, 440–443.   [2] *Lettere*, No. 374.   [3] *L. & D.*, I, 432.
[4] Hamilton to Palmerston, February 15.   [5] Observers realised that the
flight to Gaeta was decisive, *e.g.* Codrington *Letters*, 333, *et seq.*   [6] See
in general G. Cambray-Digny. *Ricordi sulla commissione governativa Toscana*
(with documents).

vendettas or private aims in the name of Leopold II.[1]
After little more than a week it had brought back relative
order; only Leghorn remained unsubdued.[2] Here indeed
was the great problem; the commission was forced to seek
foreign intervention. France and England refused, Piedmont feared to give a pretext for Austrian invasion. At
last the government of Turin decided to send ships on the
pretext of punishing insults to the Piedmontese flag, but
it acted too late.[3] The Austrians had already come.

The commission had sent to Gaeta first a courier, then
a deputation, to inform Leopold that it had set up a government in his name, that it had established order, that the
country looked to him to return as a constitutional prince
and to save it the humiliation of an Austrian occupation.
The deputation, after various delays, had arrived at Gaeta
and had found the Grand-Duke as Montanelli had last
seen him, in bed. It was introduced into the presence of
'all their feminine Highnesses and the princes and
princesses'. Yet it was not charmed with this reception;
somehow or other the atmosphere seemed a little strained.[4]
Florence waited long for news. The first message from
the sovereign was dated April 24, and announced simply
that he would return as a Father; the next message, dated
April 28, brought comfort by referring explicitly to the
constitution, and announced that the Count Serristori had
been sent to take over the government. When Serristori
arrived, the commission asked him formally whether he
knew anything of the intentions of the Austrians, and, as
a result of his reply, issued a proclamation—its last act—
announcing that the Grand-Duke had declared explicitly
that he had not requested Austrian intervention.[5]

The very next day the Austrian general D'Aspré

[1] *Ibid.* 118–124, and Documents 119, 120, 121, 125. Capponi,
Scritti, II, 52. Guerrazzi, *Apologia*, 749. Vanucci, *Niccolini*, I, 78.
[2] Cambray-Digny, *op. cit.* 89 *et seq.* Docs. 92–8. Also 155 *et seq.* [3] *Ibid.*
Ch. XVI and documents cited. Gennarelli, *Le Sventure d'Italia*, 34–45,
and 74. Cf. Ricasoli's letters of April 20, 22, 27 (*L. & D.*). [4] Capponi,
Scritti, II, 160. [5] Cambray-Digny, Doc. 160. Ricasoli was suspicious.
L. & D., I, 465.

crossed the Tuscan frontier with eighteen thousand men, announcing that he had come to safeguard the rights of the legitimate sovereign, and that he would co-operate with the sovereign's representative in pursuit of this 'common end'. Was there a plot? Serristori announced in the *Monitore* that the arrival of the Austrians was 'unexpected'; he reported that he had sent an emissary to the Austrian camp to point out that order had already been restored, and to demand that the occupation should limit itself to Leghorn alone. Public opinion waited for an official protest against the 'arbitrary' action of Austria. It did not come. The Austrians captured Leghorn, after a merciful bombardment. Then, on May 25, they entered Florence. D'Aspré proclaimed that 'the bonds of blood and many treaties' had imposed on his sovereign the duty of protecting Tuscany and her Grand-Duke, and that he himself had come at the calling of Leopold.[1] Leopold's representative still kept silence.

It was not till more than ten years later, when a professor-journalist had the opportunity of rummaging among the papers which the fallen prince had left behind him,[2] that the Tuscans learnt the inner history of that surrender which Leopold had at last made to the system expounded in 1847 by Metternich. Driven from Tuscany by the too-exacting claims which the democrats made upon his conscience, he became that bane and godsend of diplomacy, a sovereign to be restored by intervention. After his flight to Porto Santo Stefano he had been willing to accept Piedmontese intervention, but news which came from Gaeta made him realise that this was impossible; he frankly told Charles Albert that the powers would not consent to it, and that Austria in particular would consider it a provocation.[3] This was decisive. If Piedmont was impossible, Austria was inevitable. Leopold at Porto Santo Stefano had

---

[1] *Chiamato da lui.*   [2] Gennarelli, *Le Sventure d'Italia, Epistolario Politico Toscano*, and *Atti Diversi*. Discussion in A. D'Ancona, *Ricordi Storici*, 351 *et seq.* All the following is taken from the above sources.   [3] *Le Sventure d'Italia*, 22.

written to the Emperor a letter of true dignity, asking nothing, recounting his services to his subjects, asserting that he had at last broken with them only to save them from the excommunication of the Holy Father.[1] But the atmosphere of Gaeta was different, and he wrote in a new strain on February 26: 'I can only recommend my country, myself, and my family to the fraternal interest of Your Majesty, and nourishing full faith in the benevolence of your sentiments, I believe I can refrain from mentioning the political considerations which join the interest of Tuscany and Austria'.[2] The dilemma which he had to face was a hopeless one, and his choice had been forced upon him. He was received back into the bosom of the Imperial family with some hard words from its young head, who told him that he had had no business to forget that his right of sovereignty was founded solely on his quality as a member of the Family.[3] Throughout April secret envoys came and went between Gaeta and Lombardy, where the details of intervention were arranged at the camp of Radetsky. It was no wonder that Leopold had been a little cold in his reception of the deputation from Florence, and no wonder that the Tuscans put the worst interpretation upon the silence of the government in face of the proclamation of the Austrian general.

When the Austrians entered Florence, Capponi blessed the affliction which made it impossible for him to see them.[4] Ricasoli, however, had gone to Leghorn with a new notebook, and recorded every phase of the struggle in which the turbulent city protested for the last time that it was Italian rather than Tuscan.[5]

. . . . . .

In a note written in his copy of Dall' Ongaro's *Ricasoli*,

[1] *Ibid.* 13. [2] *Ibid.* Letter of 26/2/1849. [3] *Ibid.* 55. [4] Tabarrini, *Capponi*, 278. [5] *Brolio MSS.*, A. 13. Ricasoli noted that the Austrians were careful to do the least possible harm to the city, and he rated low the courage of the democrats. All the shooting they did, he wrote, was from windows or from behind.

the subject of that short biography thus summarises his conduct in the months succeeding the accession to power of the democrats. 'Ricasoli, after resigning the office of *gonfaloniere*, did not abandon Florence. He kept himself a careful observer, and nothing more'.[1] Lambruschini decided not to place himself in any position where he would provoke violence or run unnecessary risk, and retiring to his estates at San Cerbone, set himself to write a book on silk-worms, taught the children of his *contadini* reading, writing, and arithmetic, led the devotions of his household, and contemplated 'that moral order which does not fail, because the Eternal reigns there'.[2] Salvagnoli, who had twice before been chided by his friend for excessive caution,[3] drew upon himself a third reproof when he fled from Tuscany to Turin. 'They wished to make me flee too', declared the baron, 'to make an *émigré* of me. . . . I am in my own house, convinced that I have kept my independence and dignity towards all . . . I have not bent before anyone . . .'[4] So Ricasoli was at hand to join in the conservative government of April 12. 'Send all those talkers to the devil', his brother urged him. 'You *alone*, make no mistake, you *alone, alone*, have heart. Gird yourself to the task with all your courage'.[5] Vincenzo Ricasoli imagined that his brother's energy would create a Tuscan army and 'make the uniform respected'; but Bettino suspected early that his efforts and those of his friends would end only in Austrian occupation.[6] Later, when uncompromising nationalists were wont to blame the moderates for the part which they had played after the fall of Guerrazzi, he refused to judge his own work by its apparent unhappy results. 'It was necessity', he wrote, 'and it was providential'. And again: 'Why repent? . . . No. It was well'.[7]

He stored in his heart the bitter lessons of these years of enthusiasm and failure. He did not see the whole truth;

[1] *Op. cit.* 26. [2] *L. & D.*, I, 434, 436, 439, 440, 444. [3] *L. & D.*, 422 and 431. [4] *L. & D.*, I, 446. [5] *L. & D.*, I, 454. [6] *L. & D.*, I, 465. [7] Autograph notes to Dall' Ongaro, pp. 27 and 31.

did not realise, for example, that the moderates should share with Guerrazzi the blame of that miserable feud which wasted the energies of Tuscany throughout 1848; did not realise the full force of Hamilton's serene but cutting criticism: ' Love of war is not a quality of this amiable nation'. But he was right in insisting that the initial cause of all the disasters lay in the weakness of the government. It had not known how to discipline, and had refused to lead.[1] Ricasoli, like Guerrazzi, believed that the exalted must rule the exalted. Men who presumed to call the people to the new life of a free Italy must have faith in their ideal and courage in pursuing it. It was characteristic of this man who, before he had a political faith, had worked out in detail a complete moral code,[2] that he should in the end summarise the whole history of this abortive revolution in one moral generalisation. In a memorandum[3] on ' the duty of those who seek to work for the people', on which he laboured from time to time, he wrote: ' How can men ever hope that they will win pardon, if, after accepting such obligations, they depart for a single instant from the religion of duty? ' In those months in which ' he kept himself an observer and nothing more', and in the long years of disillusionment which followed, he reflected on his religion of duty, judged all the leaders and all the parties by this single standard, and as a result furnished himself with a small stock of maxims by means of which the conscientious man might guide himself and others, if such decisive days should ever return again.

The people, first of all, must be educated. He had always believed in education. But in 1848 he had broadened his efforts, turning from the moral and agricultural apostolate of Brolio to a moral and political apostolate in Tuscany. He had hoped much from newspapers, from festivals, from Assemblies. Now he realised dimly that in a multitude of voices the message had been distorted and

[1] *L. & D.*, 389 *et seq*. Address to electors of Radda, November 1848.
[2] *L. & D.*, I, 413.   [3] *Brolio MSS.*, C. 17.

lost. The rival preachers of nationalism had shouted each other down. Within his mind there shaped itself the plan of a single, unending propaganda, directed by a single, all-powerful leader. It was inevitable that he should confuse propaganda with education. He believed that it was written in the decrees of God that the Tuscans should become free Italians; and Providence demanded apostles of nationality to enlighten the people, as it had demanded apostles of agriculture to raise them.

In the second place, he half understood that the Italians were fighting a battle in which liberty, so often on their lips, so often on his own, was a matter of secondary importance. Few of the nationalists had thought seriously about liberty. There was in Florence in 1848 one man who quite deliberately put liberty before everything else;[1] but nobody understood him, and he was claimed by the Republicans as their own, whereas the Republic in which he believed had passed away for ever with the passing of Greece. To the others, liberty meant, at the time, freedom to fight and to expel the Austrians, whom they hated. They assumed that, once their national existence had been conquered, freedom would belong to them as a matter of course; but they knew little of freedom except that it seemed to mean Parliaments, like those which Frenchmen and Englishmen possessed. Ricasoli had perhaps more precise ideas of liberty, for he believed free trade to spring inevitably from a natural law,[2] and reasoned from the individual character of his own religious life to a complete theory of religious toleration.[3] Political toleration did not come to him so easily. That Liberty which to him was a faith, was nothing more than the expression of the predestined plan of God for Man, unfolding itself so that Man should live a full and free life—within the national state. Those who opposed this plan, whether they were Austrians or Tuscans,

---

[1] Ferdinando Ranalli. See Masi, *Memorie di F. Ranalli*, p. 39 and *passim*.
[2] *e.g. L. & D.* X, 361. He thought it mischievous for a government to do anything that private persons could do, even if the government did it better. [3] See *infra*.

were enemies of Liberty. One should try to persuade them; but if they refused to be persuaded, they must be fought. There could be no liberties for the enemies of Liberty. Liberty was nothing more nor less than Nationality. ' With the national idea', he wrote in one of his note-books, ' there can be no compromise. Face to face with this the other liberties must yield place '—and he reflected that, if a new Napoleon should arise to destroy the little kingdoms of Italy and to make in their place one great Italian kingdom, the people would have no right to make terms with him. If he ruled as a despot, they must not sigh for Parliaments and a free press, but be content with that one incomparable blessing he had brought to them— their organisation as a Nation. 'They should await that form of government which it might please him to impose on the new Kingdom'.[1]

Ten years after he had written this sentence, he was able to look back upon two revolutions, the first, a failure in which he had played a small and unavailing part, the second, a great success which had been won by his own faith and resolution. He recorded all his experience in one short sentence:

' Revolutions are not made without Captains'.[2]

---

[1] *Brolio MSS.*, A.B. A notebook of reflections, 1849–50. The passage quoted shows that Ricasoli was converted from the principle of federation to that of union earlier than has hitherto been believed. [2] Autograph note to Dall' Ongaro, p. 31.

CHAPTER VI

YEARS OF PREPARATION (1849–1859)

L'Italia non fa più da se in nessuna cosa.[1] The full measure of Ricasoli's disappointment appears in this weary turning of the vain boast which the Italians had made again and again only a year before—the boast that Italy would manage her own business. Italy now could do nothing by herself or for herself; could not even find tasks for her devoted sons. Ricasoli remembered that he was a Father, and turned to the work that had met with such splendid interruption in 1847 and 1848. ' My heart has become empty to the hopes of the earth; but God be blessed for the force which he gives to the man who trusts in him, force perennial, force efficacious. And God be blessed that in the education of my daughter is opened to me a way of occupation, which can largely fill the void of my heart'.[2] He told himself that he had lost two years, all to no purpose. He told himself that he would be able to help his country in some small degree, by giving to it a woman of noble character.[3] Having decided long before that his daughter must see the world and learn languages, he had sought abroad a place suitable for an education that was to be ' moral and domestic'.[4] When he arrived at Zurich in 1849, his only regret was that he had not kept his resolution and brought Bettina there in 1847, resisting the deceitful attractions of public service.

He remained in Switzerland with his daughter for two years, making pleasant friends, supervising her instruction in the French and German languages, occasionally taking with her long expeditions in which he and she scorned the high road and wheeled traffic except as a means of bringing them to the remote mountains among which they loved to tramp.[5] He discussed with Lambruschini her intellectual and moral progress; and when

[1] *L. & D.*, I, 473. [2] *L. & D.*, II, 10. [3] *L. & D.*, II, 60. [4] *L. & D.*, I, 465. [5] *L. & D.*, II, 117.

she was nineteen years old, realising that he might die before this work was completed, he took Bettina herself into his confidence,[1] unfolding to her his ideas on the religion of his country. ' Italy to-day', he warned her, ' needs something different from a new schism'. At Geneva she would find all that was necessary to the formation of mind and spirit, but she was not to attribute the qualities of the Genevan people to their Protestant faith.

' Let no hasty resolution sink your spirit in the desolating sea of scepticism. Distinguish the errors of Catholicism from the essence. . . . Feed yourself always and without satiety on the book of Salvation, the Bible, especially the New Testament. Satisfy the precepts of your Church so long as they do not conflict with the sublime and solemn maxims of the Faith of Christ. Flee Theology and the theologians of every sect. The doctrine of Jesus has no need of interpreters'.

This was a more intimate expression of the same essentially Puritan gospel which he had preached to his peasants at Brolio. Yet Ricasoli believed that the Church, when it was reformed, would attract to itself even the cultivated Protestants of Switzerland.[2] The part which he took long afterwards in negotiations between the Italian state and the Papacy, and rumours which spread as to his own unorthodoxy on matters of authority, caused in later years a good deal of discussion as to whether he was or was not a sincere member of the Church of Rome.[3] He believed that he was, though an Inquisition would have convicted him of a hundred heresies, though he once debated within himself whether there should or should not be a Pope, though he was ready to believe that the Papacy might go to perdition through the will of Providence,[4] though he denounced the materialism of the Church, and saw in many of its forms and ceremonies an arid human organisation which choked the Divine spirit. Like Lambruschini, his faith was in a Church which lived as an ideal within his own mind, a Church which one day would turn back again to the primitive purity of the Evangelists. He had

[1] L. & D., I, 113. [2] L. & D., II, 49. [3] See Finali, op. cit. 44, 49-50; Gotti, op. cit. 142-3; and studies by A. Valle and G. Gentile.
[4] L. & D., VI, 211. Cf. VII, 145, 211; IX, 77, 116, 177; X, 305.

learnt, too, and not only from Gioberti, that the Church of Rome was a creation of Italian genius and a custodian of Italian civilisation. It was therefore the duty of good Italians to reconcile their personal religion—a possession beyond all price whose sanctity was decreed by God and must in the end inevitably be respected by man[1]—with loyalty to that ideal order which had its centre in Italy's spiritual capital. He explained to Lambruschini that his daughter might remain Catholic in form without harm to that development of spirit towards which all her education had been directed. In teaching her to remain a Catholic, he was teaching her to be a good Italian. ' I have sought to educate Betta for her country, Italy'.[2]

In his pursuit of this task which had occupied the first place in his thoughts for nearly twenty years, in his delight in the Alps and his studies of Swiss civilisation, he could not forget his regrets for Italy, nor avoid the irritating intrusion of distracting memories. The civic life of Switzerland awakened in him unbounded enthusiasm. ' Here the individual, taking upon himself the true qualities of a citizen, becomes a real man'. He saw ' true and indigenous nationality incarnate in a government that is national in law and in fact'.[3] He explained in his letters the historical causes of this happy state of affairs, and dwelt at length upon the moral qualities of the people which alone had made it possible. But, whenever he wrote about the blessings of Switzerland, he saw in contrast the curses and afflictions of Italy. Whatever was good in Switzerland suggested Italy by contrast: whatever was bad in Switzerland suggested Italy by comparison. The sight of a popular demonstration in Geneva excited him to fury. ' You can believe how it stirred my blood. I boiled with rage, and thought to what these demonstrations had brought us Italians'. [4] He mused with vain regrets on his own share in the shameful past, reminding

---

[1] *L. & D.*, III, 138, and *Carteggio Vieusseux, Cassetta*, A., 90, 8. He declares religious toleration a *sacred principle*, which must prevail ' through the fatal decrees of Providence'. [2] *L. & D.*, II, 115. [3] *L. & D.*, II, 84. [4] *L. & D.*, II, 34.

himself how power had passed him by, until it was too late. Every time that he took up the Tuscan *Monitore*, it cost him an hour of agitation before he could recover his serenity.[1] Politics nauseated him. He told his brother that he would refrain from speaking of them, though he could not refrain from thinking of them; but he was unable to keep even this partial resolution. Within two months he was pouring out to the same brother his utter disgust. ' The country has not the shadow of national government. . . . The people is nerveless, ruined'. How could the country ever find a good government that would hammer it into shape ? A good government demanded *men*, but Tuscany possessed only ' chattering children, incapable of deep sentiments, incapable of any virtue, without character and without convictions. . . . Children, children, children'.[2] Or, if they were not children, they were weak old men, who had of late years tasted too much wine, and now felt weaker and older than ever before.[3] His thoughts began to turn longingly to the idea of the strong man, the Hero sent to earth by Providence as a benefactor of the human race,[4] one of those ' rare heads, thinking courageously, which are a light in the general darkness',[5] a leader who would know how to teach and how to discipline that ' people ' which spoke much and did little, which spoke well and acted ill. But, he lamented to Salvagnoli, ' at this time generous and right-thinking minds are few, while the ignorant, delirious crowds increase ever more, and they are not disposed to hear reason'. He himself had the will and the principle to be such a leader; but he put aside the thought that he might be reserved by Providence for the great task, for it called for one who had made ' profound studies in Philosophy'.[6]

The letters which he received from his most intimate friend were not calculated to lessen his depression. Lambruschini was even more persistent in melancholy than

[1] *L. & D.*, II, 32. [2] *L. & D.*, II, 61. [3] *Carteggio Vieusseux*, A., 90, 6 (5/9/'50). [4] *L. & D.*, II, 155. [5] *Carteggio Vieusseux*, A., 90, 7 (30/9/'50). [6] *L. & D.*, I, 20.

was Ricasoli. He thought that he might be dead before his friend returned, and said that he would die without even the comfort of having done a little good.[1] 'All the world', he lamented, ' is sick'.[2] He reported every misfortune that befell the country, the failure of the crops, the errors of the government, the growing numbers of ' the reds'.[3] ' Poor country !' he wrote, ' Wretched times'.[4] Amid all his gloom he professed a sort of optimism that was more dreary than pessimism for a disappointed man. If all the world was sick, the remedy was plain. It lay simply in a return to the principles of Christianity, and then without doubt society would be saved by a strong moral authority, ' benignant without being weak, basing its claim to obedience on the order of God and not of man'.[5] Here was food enough for an optimism that would content itself with looking a few centuries ahead. Sometimes the idealistic abbé turned away even from this optimism to find relief in fatalistic resignation. 'All in this world', he wrote to Ricasoli, ' is bad or mutilated or imperfect. We must adapt ourselves to the order which God himself tolerates'.[6] Against this pious resignation even Ricasoli rebelled. He sketched out for himself a reasonable attitude towards present conditions, and tried to live up to it. He admitted to Salvagnoli[7] that things could not be worse than they were. A rational faith in God, however, suggested that he could bring good even out of the blackest evil. The peoples were now wax in the hands of their governments, and perhaps one of the governments would seize the unique chance of rising to ' proclaim some of the great moral laws of the world, destined ever more and more to embody themselves in the public law of peoples'. The moral law of which the baron was thinking was the law of Nationality, and the government which proclaimed it would lead the world back to ' lasting and life-bringing tranquillity'. But what

---

[1] *L. & D.*, II, 11. [2] *L. & D.*, II, 57. [3] *L. & D.*, II, 67. [4] *L. & D.*, II, 95. [5] *L. & D.*, II, 2. [6] *L. & D.*, II, 130. [7] *L. & D.*, II, 20—22.

if no single government arose to announce the new gospel,
or what if the other governments did not listen to the
gospel ? ' Then men's spirits will always remain disturbed
and discontented, and after an interval . . . the struggle
will be renewed, with an issue that admits few doubts'.
As for Ricasoli himself, he hoped that, although he was
not a ' world-historical ' individual, he might nevertheless
have a humble part to play in the great design of Providence.
He decided to stand upon the watch. ' I limit myself
to study, to strengthen my spirit. I cultivate and
prepare myself, while I keep myself in touch with events
from day to day'. It was a wise resolution, and in the end
it bore fruit. But at the time it did not free him from the
daily torment which his own brooding temperament and
present circumstances inflicted upon him—the torment of
continually affirming a problem without being able to find
any immediate solution. At last his constant despair drew
a gentle reproof from the most serene, the most practical
of his Florentine friends. ' It seems to me', wrote Vieusseux, 'that you trust a little too much to the ancient virtues
of the Swiss, and despair too much of the poor Italians'.[1]

Throughout the years in which his melancholy lay most
heavily upon him, he continued his old diligent habits,
jotting down in little books notes on viticulture, on the
rearing of silk-worms, on the new bridge at Terranuova,
on the affairs of his estate, on the books of history and
politics which he was reading.[2] In the autumn of 1851 he
made a short expedition to England, and the details of
prices, cooking, service, and the conveniences, which he
recorded of the different hotels where he stayed on his
way thither, have the same incisive charm as a page from
Baedeker.[3] At London he visited the docks, the markets,
the ragged-boys' schools, Richard Cobden, and a score of
similar English institutions. He compared the Thames to
a street; he numbered the public omnibuses of the city

[1] *L. & D.*, I, 92. [2] *e.g. Brolio MSS.*, A. 16 (April 1852, till February 1854). [3] *Brolio MSS.*, A. 4. Diary of September 10 till October
10, 1851.

at three thousand, and considered that the astonishing
infrequency of accidents was due partly to the skill of the
drivers, partly to the cries of the conductors, (of whose
honesty he had a poor opinion), and partly to the dexterity
of the pedestrians. He left England determined to return
again, and at Paris, on his way home, had interviews
with Gioberti and with Prince Poniatowski. The latter
asked him what could be done to bring the Grand-Duke and
his people into harmony again. Ricasoli answered that, as
a beginning, Leopold would have to dismiss the Austrian
troops and to change his government; but, since neither
event was likely, he must in effect answer—Nothing.
Poniatowski asked whether there existed in Tuscany an
'Albertist' party. 'I told him that I did not believe that
there existed a *party*. There did exist, however, people who
saw how events were proceeding, and saw in Piedmont
the future hope of Italy'.

Of these people Ricasoli himself was one. He had
already dreamed of a strong king who would cast down
all the little states of Italy and fuse them into one great
kingdom under his sceptre,[1] and from the early days of
the restoration he began gradually to turn his eyes to 'the
gentleman king' of Piedmont as the man who was, perhaps,
marked out for this work by Providence. His brother,
Vincenzo, had realised early in 1848 that salvation would
come from Piedmont and from nowhere else, and at the
end of the war he had remained in service under the
Piedmontese flag—the *Italian* flag. 'Come and stay with
me some months in Italy, that is to say in Piedmont', he
wrote to Bettino, 'for Piedmont to-day is all of Italy,
where the tricolour flag of Italy remains'.[2] Vincenzo
Ricasoli was only too ready to admit the follies and iniquities of the Tuscan government, for they did not distress
him one whit. The more they multiplied, the sooner would
the Tuscans come to realise that their future lay with
Piedmont, and Piedmont alone. 'The worthy Tuscans',
he declared, 'lose their time in asking for the constitution,

[1] See the end of Chapter V. [2] *L. & D.*, II, 3.

not seeing that from now on Tuscany has ceased to have
an existence, and that she will be nothing more than a
province of another state'.[1] Ricasoli began to hope; but
he laboured slowly towards each new article of faith, and
he was not ready as yet to follow his brother and work for
the new cause.

The old enterprises which had so absorbed his energies
were beginning to lose their attraction. ' I have need of
action', he complained to Vincenzo after his return to
Brolio, ' and here I can find it no more'.[2] A series of
calamities in successive years seemed to have undone
much of his work in the Chianti, and he did not feel
enthusiastic enough to make a fresh start. He saw too many
years of life stretching out before him. He was unable to
write, and too old to choose a new career. He felt that the
great task of his life had come to an end. His daughter
was getting married. He would still be her Father, but
someone else would become her Educator. His life,
which had been centred for so long round this one passion,
suddenly felt very empty. A brief hope flashed through his
mind when he thought that he might make a new beginning
in the wilds of America; but he soon reflected that he was
too old, and that America was very far away. He could have
wished that there was an American wilderness somewhere
in the middle of Italy, if possible, in Tuscany.[3]

Within two months of this gloomy letter to Vincenzo,
his wife was taken ill. The doctors reported that she had
cancer in the stomach, and told him that she was going to
die. He broke the news to her, and she expressed a wish
to see her daughter married before her end came. No
moment in all his life so impressed Ricasoli as that in
which he stood ' with his heart in pieces', while his wife
gave her dying blessing to the young girl and her husband,
brought from the little chapel of the castle to her bed-side.
In the midst of his grief he could not help thinking of the
dramatic intensity of the scene; he resolved to seek a
painter who would interpret on canvas this struggle of the

[1] *L. & D.*, II, 65.   [2] *L. & D.*, II, 164.   [3] *L. & D.*, II, 166.

elemental forces of love, anguish, and death.[1] A few days
later his wife died. He brooded over his own sorrow, as
he brooded over the afflictions of his country. ' Je me
familiarise avec l'affliction', he wrote to one of his Swiss
friends, ' si je ne finis pas par m'y complaire . . . la
douleur a ses voluptés'.[2] In the diary[3] which he kept
throughout these days he recorded every phase of the
crisis through which he was passing. Mingling itself with
the abysmal grief of the present, with the comfort sought
in his faith in immortality, there was always the terrifying
realisation of the long empty years before him. One after
another, all the duties and all the affections which had made
life supportable had become barren or had been taken
away. ' The base of my life is broken. I must find another'.
But where ? 'Agriculture pleased me; now it is insuf-
ferable'. He thought of taking up the study of chemistry
and natural history where he had left it twenty years
before, but it was too late. ' There is nothing that I would
not accept, so long as it was really a profession, an art, a
task'. He longed for something difficult into which he
might throw himself, and struggle, and conquer. He
thought of turning missionary. If only there had been
dusky savages awaiting him in Italy! Politics for the time
were unthinkable; and, while his spirit cried out for action
as its one outlet, he swore that he would accept only
' action joined to authority'. He was afflicted by a *noia*
as black and enveloping as that which had weighed upon
Leopardi, but he was not a Leopardi that it should inspire
him to create beauty. Nothing but ' extraordinary events'[4]
could save him from himself. If they came, he would be
ready. It was clear that they could only come as a result
of the initiative of Piedmont. He began to look to Piedmont for his own salvation, as for Italy's.

For nearly three years, indeed, he remained in the most
painful moral state; not idle, but occupying himself by

---

[1] The painting, by an indifferent Sienese artist, hangs now in the *Archivio*
at Brolio.   [2] *L. & D.*, II, 227.   [3] Extract in *L. & D.*, II, 184–92;
Brolio MSS., A. 7. Cf. *L. & D.*, II, 178–184.   [4] *L. & D.*, II, 224.

force of will, managing his estates, reading Cicero, Macchiavelli, Gioberti, the Bible; ' knocking at all the doors '
of his inclinations, living ' a life without life', ' a life
which has no tastes, nor aim, nor object'.[1] Just when his
friends began to despair of his recovery, the cloud began
to lift. Piedmont joined the western powers in the war
with Russia, and then, once again, he had hope for his
country. He would have liked to see the other states take
their stand beside Piedmont, and send a contingent of
fifty thousand Italians to the war;[2] but he rejoiced that
Piedmont had bought for herself a strong position in Italy
and in Europe. This might in the future have notable results.
Perhaps Providence would work its inevitable will sooner
than men believed, for, if the movement of 1848 had
failed because of its extravagances, the ideas underlying
that movement were making progress ' through the logic
of fact'.[3] His brother, Vincenzo, had gone to the war,
and he felt pride that one of his family was doing something for Italy. It seemed that he had recovered some of
his zest for life as Italy recovered hope for the future, for
he now threw himself into a plan suggested before by
Vincenzo and hitherto spurned by himself, a plan of new
agricultural experiment in the Maremma. The area was
unhealthy,[4] but he had no objection to risking his life and
health. Labour, owing to the lack of a settled population,
was migratory, expensive, and unreliable; but this gave
him an opportunity to be a pioneer of the industrialisation
of Tuscan agriculture. He explained seriously to a Swiss
friend that his lonely holding in the Maremma would
suit him better than the cloister for which he had sometimes longed, for cloisters had lost their prestige and were
not held in high esteem by the world.[5] He took a second

---

[1] *L. & D.*, II, 249, 30/5/'53, to Salvagnoli; II, 26/1/'54, to V.
Ricasoli. [2] *Trentacinque Lettere* [Zanichelli], p. 8. Cf. *L. & D.*, II, 316.
[3] *L. & D.*, II, 309. [4] He was, as a result of this venture, liable to attacks
of fever. *Brolio MSS.*, A.C. For accounts of his work in the Maremma see
writings collected at the end of *L. & D.*, Vol. II, 502–514. He did
not care for his ' insolent ' neighbours. See *XII Lettere di B.R. a Sansone
D'Ancona*, No. 5. [5] *L. & D.*, II, 323.

journey into England to examine agricultural machinery;
attended the exhibition, sought to recapture history in
the Tower of London, judged the tunnel under the Thames
a 'useless marvel', and considered England the land of
true liberty. He made pleasant friends, and cursed the
new property in the Maremma which prevented him from
staying longer to study 'the first country in the world'.[1]
Almost in his own despite, his own vigorous nature was
asserting itself against his melancholy. He had already
written to his brother urging him to return from the
Crimea, because he could serve his country better in the
Maremma. Events were maturing, he declared, which the
eye could not see but for which the will might prepare
itself.

'Seeing things in this aspect I believe that we should prepare ourselves
for the great events in which our country may be involved, without abandon-
ing our ordinary occupations, but rather performing them with greater
assiduity, so as to have them in good order, if the good of our country calls
upon us to abandon them for it'.[2]

Before the end of 1856, at the very latest, his political
convictions had finally settled themselves. Throughout
that year he had pursued his work in the Maremma and
followed the events of Europe with something of the old
enthusiasm. He had collected signatures for a petition to
the government on Tuscan agriculture, and had frightened
Vieusseux and Ridolfi by the daring with which he
organised a subscription list to buy cannon for Alessandria,
'an Italian fortress'.[3] Collecting cannon for Alessandria
was more to his taste than the address of congratulation
which other Tuscans were preparing to present to Cavour.
He thought the address childish;[4] and affected a superiority
towards the Italian liberals who were working honestly
in the only ways open to them.

'What a liberal is', he wrote to Vieusseux, 'I find it every day harder

[1] *Brolio MSS.*, A. 10. *L. & D.*, II, 337–345, 347–350.   [2] *L. & D.*,
II, 344.   [3] For the two ventures see his letters in *Carteggio Vieusseux*,
A. 90, Nos. 20, 21, 22, 24, 25, 27, 28, 29, 30. *L. & D.*, II., 374 *et seq.*
[4] *Lettere Politiche*, p. 9 *et seq.*

to define . . . I do not wish this label of liberal to be attached to me.
I would rather be a Jesuit than an Italian liberal'. [1]

He would not share the enthusiasm of the liberals for
Count Cavour, and seems to have disapproved that statesman's excursions into diplomacy. The work of recon-
quering Nationality demanded 'great, solemn, terrible
acts'.

'Woe to this people, all my life I shall say it, woe to it a hundred times
if it becomes a people through the work and will of others, not through its
own work and will. Woe to it, because it would then be for ever Nothing'.

Italians, he declared, must not be treated as children
unable to stand upon their own legs.[2] He hoped that the
Congress in which Cavour was speaking for Italy would
have an issue 'which men do not expect and would not
wish. . . .' But, if he had not yet placed faith in Cavour,
he had subscribed to the same cause for which Cavour was
working.

'I abhor eunuch projects', he wrote to his brother in October of 1856,
'and I consider eunuch all those which more or less leave Italy divided
into parts'.

He declared that there had been enough of partial revolution. Italians should postpone action until they could
make that final and decisive revolution which would
destroy for ever 'narrow and proud municipalism'.[3]

Ricasoli was now ready for the labour to which his own
self-preparation, the dreams and ambitions of Napoleon,
the genius of Cavour, and the energy of those liberals whom
he despised, were combining to call him.

.   .   .   .   .   .

The Grand-Duke and his government, ignoring the
invitations of moderates like Ridolfi[4] and Galeotti[5] to find
their salvation in the constitution, and in the counsel of
those prosperous and not too-excitable patriots who had
overthrown Guerrazzi and left him in prison—thrown
him to the judges as Nero threw the Christians to the beasts,

[1] *Carteggio Vieusseux*, A. 90, 34.   [2] *Ibid.* A. 90, 21.   [3] *L. & D.*, II,
376–379.   [4] *Ridolfi, op. cit.* p. 183 *et seq.*   [5] *Considerazioni Politiche
sulla Toscana di L. Galeotti*, Firenze, 1850.

Guerrazzi said[1]—sought with simplicity and benevolence to lead Tuscany back once more to the Earthly Paradise. The erring children of the prince, they reasoned, had returned after their prodigal dissipations to loyal obedience within their father's house. They would realise now that excitement was very bad for them. The Father, on his side, was glad to forget and to forgive the past; and the fatted calf would be made ready. All sorts of plans were made in the next ten years whereby the people might have tangible and pleasant testimony to the sovereign's benevolence. There was, first of all, an amnesty for all save the most prominent traitors. There were medals for the most distinguished loyalists.[2] There were new public works at Leghorn, a treaty of commerce with France, prizes for 'Industrial Merit', a reform of the banking system, new provisions for education. In the end, the minister Baldasseroni was able to look back with some reasonable satisfaction on the results achieved[3]; and in later days, when taxes were rising and the Tuscan cigar, like a good patriot, increased in price as Italy increased in size, many Tuscans looked back with regret to the good old days, and told each other that 'they were better off when they were worse off'.—*Si stava meglio quando si stava peggio.*—At the time, however, the people of the towns refused to be bribed into tranquillity. There are none so deaf as those who will not hear, and the persuasive voice of Baldasseroni was answered by the angry cries of liberal economists who accused him of ruining the country, blamed him for his best measures, and damned him for his worst.[4]

There were a number of reasons that made hopeless the

---

[1] A. D'Ancona, *op. cit.* p. 317. Through a mixture of mismanagement and nervousness the Governing Commission had kept Guerrazzi in prison till the Austrians arrived. Guerrazzi accused it of breaking faith. See *Apologia*, 746–765; Cambray-Digny, *op. cit.* Ch. VI; Documents XI, XII, XIII (Ricasoli's evidence); *The Times*, 10/7/1852; Capponi, *Lettere*, II, 489; and F. Martini in Appendix to Giusti, *Memorie.* [2] Among them Ricasoli, much to his disgust, *L. & D.*, II, 45–49. [3] Baldasseroni, *op. cit.* Part III *passim*, espec. Ch. 42. [4] *e.g.* Zobi, *Manuale*, Appendix, *passim*.

attempt of Leopold and his minister to create again in
people's minds that pleasing image of the benevolent
prince. In economic affairs they were dogged by persistent
misfortune. Starting with the inheritance of financial
confusion handed down to him from the days of the
revolution,[1] Baldasseroni set before himself—as so many
Italian governments have done in later days—the ideal of
a balanced budget. The government had the courage to
lay new burdens upon the people, and the ministers had
the generosity to forego substantial portions of their
incomes. A deficit of 2,500,000 lire had become by 1852
a surplus of 619,774. Then the tide turned. The burden
of increased taxation appeared to be too heavy for the
country, and a series of calamities forced the government
to throw away all hope of a balanced budget and shoulder
a number of extraordinary expenses. Ever since 1846 bad
seasons had been recurring intermittently, and in 1853 the
appearance of the fungus *crittogama* among the vines overturned disastrously the basis of the Tuscan economy.[2]
In the following year late frosts ruined a variety of crops,
and the towns were invaded by the cholera. Cholera
returned with greater malignity in 1855. In that same
year disastrous floods devastated the valleys of the Arno
and the Upper Tiber. While the government had to
resign all hope of fiscal recovery, and confess in 1856 to a
deficit of a million lire, the social effects of the past disorders and the present calamities were appearing in an
unpleasant form throughout the country. The vagabonds
who, in 1850, had been 'besieging' landowners with
demands for charity,[3] had by 1852 organised themselves
into troops of fifteen or twenty strong which went from
village to village terrorising the peasants with demands
for food or money.[4] If the demands were not granted, the
recalcitrant peasant was menaced with destruction in his

---

[1] *Ibid.* 492 *et seq.*   [2] Ricasoli saved himself and his peasants by his
success in applying Lambruschini's methods to the rearing of silk-worms.
For his accounts see *L. & D.*, II, 497–501, 515–517.   [3] *L. & D.*, II,
68.   [4] *L. & D.*, II, 214.

fields and vineyards. The menace grew so serious that
Ricasoli thought it unsafe to leave his estates.[1] The evil
was too deeply rooted to be cured by a book from the
facile pen of Lambruschini in praise of the virtue of self-
help,[2] and the proprietors of the *Georgofili* argued among
themselves on the advisibility, or unwisdom, of uprooting
the whole social system of the Tuscan countryside.[3] 'At
Corniola', wrote Salvagnoli in 1858, 'the grapes are
dead in flower; little grain; no potatoes; no beans; hay a
failure. Hunger advances—and war? I do not believe so
—for the time'.[4] It was unfortunate for a government
assailed on grounds of idealism that its most staunch
supporters, the conservative peasants, should have been
shaken by a series of calamities for which its own policy
was in no sense at all responsible.

The economic discontent merged itself into that idealistic
nationalist opposition which was the root cause of the
government's failure. In the budget of extraordinary
expenses which is the refuge of hard-pressed finance
ministers, there appeared year after year large sums for
the Austrian troops—'the auxiliaries', as they were
called in polite official language—who, according to the
liberals, had come to destroy Tuscan liberties. The Tuscan
economists reckoned the total expenses under this heading
at a sum exceeding thirty-six million lire,[5] and one wonders
whether they were more alarmed at the size of the bill, or
more delighted at the opportunity given them for political
propaganda. With the Austrians in Florence, the most
efficient and fortunate of governments could not have
won the support of any who really cared for Italy. A cook
with a salary of 12,000 lire was sufficient inducement to
entice a portion of the Florentine aristocracy to meet
Austrian officers at the palace of Prince Demidoff.[6] At a

---

[1] *L. & D.* II, 278. [2] R. Lambruschini, *Della necessità di soccorere
i poveri, e dei modi*, Firenze, 1855. [3] See Ch. 1, on *mezzadria*. [4] *L.&
D*, II, 448. [5] B. Cini, *Sui danni recati dall' Austria alla Toscana*,
Firenze, 1859. [6] F. Martini, *Ricordi ed Affetti*, Ch. 9; *Brolio MSS.*, A.12
(Ricasoli in his diary notes a dinner). Cf. Gennarelli, *Epistolario Toscano*, 250.

great ball given in the Pitti to honour Radetsky, ladies of distinction collected plumes from the old Field-Marshal's hat. But ' the poet of Italy ' in stilted verses compared them to the city harlots, much to the advantage of the latter;[1] and when Valerio's paper in Turin announced that ' the Ricasoli exposed to the Austrians the volup-tuousness of their wives and daughters', Vincenzo Rica-soli needed no prompting from his brother to challenge the editor to a duel.[2] The great majority of the indepen-dent Florentine aristocracy held severely aloof from the Austrians, and in the end succeeded in establishing some-thing that approached social boycott. Young officers of the Tuscan army who had fought in Lombardy could not conceal their hatred of these late enemies who posed as the guardians of their country, and within the first year of occupation the constantly recurring duels were a source of anxiety to the Austrian commander, Liechtenstein, who used the utmost tact to make the occupation as little offensive as might be. Many of the Austrian officers were generous enough. One of them, wounded in an affair with an officer named Enrico Lawley, sought to save his opponent from punishment by swearing stoutly that he had been hurt accidently by his own weapon.[3] But charming manners and generosity could not reconcile the uncom-promising liberals, and the Austrians were blamed as a matter of course for every unfortunate incident. ' Perhaps they are not always responsible', wrote Leopoldo Cempini, ' but so much the better. The more things that are said against them, the nearer comes that far-off blessed day'.[4] Sometimes, too, a subordinate laid bare the mailed fist. One officer punished with the *bastinado* a citizen who collided, perhaps accidentally, perhaps deliberately, with an Austrian soldier. Liechtenstein removed the offending officer, but he could not undo the harm of the act. At Leghorn, which was under martial law, there was no attempt to veil the character of the occupation; and

[1] G. B. Niccolini, *Poesie Nazionali*, Firenze, 1859, p. 45. [2] *L. & D.*, II, 12 *et seq.* [3] M. Gioli, *op. cit.* 177. [4] *Ibid.* 178.

Leghorn victims figured largely in the martyrology which was compiled in 1859 as a stimulus to the national spirit.[1]

The Grand-Duke could not hide from his subjects the full significance of the presence of the Austrians in his capital. His appearance in the hated uniform was hailed as an admission that he ruled as the lieutenant of Franz Josef. The liberals suspected dark things when, in 1850, he and Baldasseroni made a visit to Vienna;[2] and, when five years later the Emperor returned the visit, they told each other how the Baron von Hügel, asked whether his master would go to Rome, answered: 'Oh, no! His Majesty is only going into his own states'. They had good cause for offence when the government took down from the churches the memorials to the Tuscans who had fallen in Lombardy, and prohibited services of commemoration; better cause still, when in 1851, the *carabinieri* fired upon the crowds who had risked official displeasure to honour in Santa Croce the dead of Curtatone and Montanara. Ricasoli, who had disapproved of what he considered a too-formal display of grief and defiance, was nevertheless shocked at this 'cowardly crime'.[3] The shooting on that May morning sealed with blood the quarrel between the well-meaning prince and his subjects.

Every unpopular act of the government, whether it was large or small, was invested with vast anti-national significance. The restoration of the death-penalty to the penal code,[4] and the appearance in Florence of a brand-new guillotine given over to the care of an efficient butcher, aroused in liberal breasts an ecstasy of horror. It mattered not one whit that this least bloody of all absolutisms never on one occasion claimed the full penalty of the law, that the butcher allowed the knife of his instrument to rust, and pocketed 176 lire a year for doing exactly nothing.

---

[1] 300 *vittime Toscane dell' I. e R. casa Austro-Lorenese*, Firenze, 1859.
[2] See Gennarelli, *Epistolario Toscano*, p. 130 *et seq.*   [3] *Brolio MSS.*, A. 4 (Interview with Poniatowski) cf. *L. & D.*, II, 145; and Tabarrini, *Capponi*, 288; Gioli, *op. cit.*, Ch. 4 and 5; and A. D'Ancona, *Lettere di illustri Italiani*, Pisa, 1895.   [4] Decreto of 16/11/1852.

The affair was grave enough to inspire an indignant nationalist pamphlet.[1] Even the demagogues of 1849 began to win sympathy from some who had violently opposed them. 'For 32 months', wrote Guerrazzi[2] in November 1851, 'I have been buried alive, confused with thieves, assassins, parricides'. His trial dragged on month after month, and though it ended in his condemnation, 'the novelist prisoner of state appeared before Europe as the accuser of his judges'.[3] The English ambassador, Hamilton, asked Prince Liechtenstein whether he had been present at the trial of Guerrazzi. 'You mean the trial of the Grand-Duke?' answered the Austrian. 'No, I was not'.

There was good reason why even many who had opposed Guerrazzi should welcome his trial as a demonstration against the government. The constitution, to which the sovereign had sworn in his first proclamation after the restoration of 1849, had, till 1852, been suspended; and in that year was definitely abolished. The condition of the country remained the same, no worse and no better; but Leopold took his place beside King *Bomba* as a breaker of faith. Tuscans spoke with a new emphasis of *Il Re Galantuomo*. Pius IX had turned his back on liberalism, but the Piedmontese king stood firm, and in these years every Tuscan patriot began to look to Victor Emmanuel and his army as the one hope of Italy.[4]

When at last the Austrians left Florence, the city settled down to await the future which the restlessness of Europe and the brain of Cavour was preparing for Italy. Open opposition was difficult, but no population could hope to emulate sceptical Florence in expressing its opinions by pin-pricks of impudence and wit. Many of the epigrams

---

[1] *La Ghigliottina in Toscana. Chi la vuole?* etc. [2] A. D'Ancona, *Ricordi Storici del Risorg*, 319. [3] Carducci's preface to his edition of Guerrazzi's *Lettere*. [4] *L. & D.*, II, 92. Vieusseux to Ricasoli, 14/5/1850: 'Piedmont is considered with reason as the last anchor of Italy's salvation, and it is a notable thing how the Piedmontese party keeps growing even among those who were most averse to Charles Albert'. It would be possible to multiply *ad infinitum* evidence of this decisive change in opinion.

which were passed round the city from mouth to mouth
were born in the bawdy atmosphere of the café Michelangiolo,[1] a haunt of the Florentine caricaturists, or in the
café Elvetico, where journalists, lawyers, minor poets and
players were wont to pass final sentence on the new plays,
operas and ballets that came to the city. A favourite target
for irreverent wit was *Babbo* himself. All those peculiarities
of his, the bent head, the protruding upper lip, the peering
short-sighted eyes, the lisp—which once had rather endeared
him to his subjects—were now pounced on with a savage
and rather petty glee. It was reported that the doctors
had prescribed for his health a cure of mother's milk, and
rumour went so far as to point out a buxom *contadina* as
the regular royal nurse. It was said that his Neapolitan
wife, whom the citizens cordially hated, rated him for
coming to dinner with inky fingers. In 1859, mild middle-
aged English ladies of liberal sympathies[2] hugged themselves over an alleged address with which Leopold, they
told each other, had tried to win back the wavering loyalty
of his troops in the last days of his reign. ' The duty of a
good soldier and a good Christian is to be in any case
faithful to his sovereign, and . . . and . . . (he stam-
mered, his eyes sought the ground until at last they gave
him an inspiration) . . . 'to keep his boots clean'.
Salvagnoli, in 1857, sent flying through the city an
epigram whose only point was that Leopold was an ass.
The poor prince realised the hostility and irreverence of
the people who had once acclaimed him, the people whom
he had really loved to think of as his children. He held
himself as far as he could aloof, for otherwise he might
be forced to shut his eyes to some insolent smirk which
greeted the latest whispered anecdote of *Broncio*. There
came a day when Ricasoli stood on a street corner near
the Duomo, and stared at him through and through, cold

---

[1] Telemaco Signorini, *Caricaturisti e caricaturati al caffe Michelangiolo.
Ricordi*. Firenze, 1893. (with many reproductions of caricatures).
[2] Theodosia Trollope, *Social Aspects of the Italian Revolution*, London,
1859.

and rigid, as he drove back from the Easter service.[1]
The stern disapproval of the iron baron was kinder than
the obsceneties and flippancies of pettier people, but it
overshot the mark. The prince was too kindly, too pathetic
a figure to inspire a sincere wrath, and Ricasoli's gaze
looked beyond him to the armies of Austria.

In the years which followed the withdrawal of the
Austrians, the Tuscan government began to sink back
into its old inertia. The newspapers were able to talk a good
deal of politics under the cloak of allegory, and the *Spet-
tatore* of Celestino Bianchi, who gathered the aid of De
Sanctis, Tommasèo, Gualterio, Reumont, and others, did
for Tuscany what the *Crepuscolo* did for Lombardy. Ferdinando Martini has recorded[2] in his old age how he once
saw Cesare Tellini sell through the streets portraits of
Felice Orsini, and how he was present at a reunion in the
café *La Fenice* where Cempini, Puccioni, Bartolommei
and a crowd of others talked sedition without the least
interruption from the police. But the theatre was the chosen
medium for liberal demonstrations. The stupendous
popularity of Verdi was due in part to his initials, which
to patriots signified *Viva Vittorio Emmanuele Re d'Italia.*
In 1858, Niccolini's *Medea* was interpreted by an actress
whom all good Italians venerated as a mistress of the
gentleman king himself. Some enthusiasts dragged
Niccolini from his retirement, and when he appeared at
the theatre the voices of the actors were drowned by a
crowd which called: *Viva Niccolini, Viva il poeta Italiano,
Viva la gloria d'Italia,* and finally, *Viva Italia.* The poet
of Italy, meanwhile, was assailed in his box by enthusiasts
who shook his hand, kissed it, kissed his peruke, jostled
him and acclaimed him, while all the time he sought to
protect himself and exclaimed gasping: ' Thank you,
Stop it; Thank you, Go away; Thank you, Stop it; Thank
you'.[3] Perhaps that night the spectators thought it wise
to forego their usual after-theatre gossip in the cafés of

---

[1] Rubieri, *Storia Intima della Toscana*, p. 56.   [2] Martini, *op. cit.* p. 240.
[3] *Ibid.* Ch. VI and in *Da Palo in Frasca*, pp. 8–9.

Gigi Porco or *Beppe Sudicio*,[1] but the police took no blood-thirsty vengeance.

After the meeting between Cavour and Napoleon III at Plombières in July of 1858, there appeared signs that the time for more serious demonstrations was approaching. On the first day of the new year the French Emperor, at an official reception of diplomatists at Paris, publicly expressed his regret to the Austrian ambassador that his relations with the Austrian government were not so happy as he would have wished. Piedmont made the next move on January 10, when the king declared at the opening of Parliament, that he was not insensible to the cry of woe that reached his ears from many parts of Italy. On February 7 the Emperor opened the *Corps Législatif*, and asserted that the marriage of Prince Jérôme with the Princess Clotilde[2] was not an isolated event, but that France and Piedmont stood together. Then La Guerronière published his inspired pamphlet on Napoleon III and Italy, announcing to the world the federalist programme that the Emperor had unfolded to Cavour at Plombières.[3] 'Italy in history', said La Guerronière, 'represents something more than nationality; it represents civilisation'. The Emperor had declared on February 7: 'The interest of France . . . is there, above all, where there appears a cause of justice and civilisation'. It was easy enough for the world and for Italy to draw the right conclusions.

The time had obviously come when the nationalists of central Italy must be prepared to second the work of Cavour. In Tuscany, there existed several groups which had within them the possibility of expanding into parties

[1] The name may be translated *Dirty Joe*. Only three cafés were kept open in Florence late at night, and from the nicknames given to the proprietors it would appear that they were not of the cleanest. There is an unpleasant caricature of Gigi Porco's daughter in Signorini, *op. cit.* [2] The marriage of *Plon Plon* and the princess was arranged at Plombières, and took place on January 31. [3] Nothing was fixed as regards Tuscany at Plombières, but Napoleon made clear his idea of a central Italy, composed of Tuscany and part of the Papal States. Bianchi, *Cavour*, 68 *et seq.* Chiala, *Lettere*, III, clxxxiv.

and claiming the leadership of the country. The most active of the Tuscan nationalists was the *marchese* Ferdinando Bartolommei, who represented in Florence the National Society which had been founded in Piedmont by Manin and Pallavicino, and of whose Italian propaganda La Farina, as secretary, held all the threads. The *marchese* belonged to the little band of conscientious agriculturalists, but his colleagues of the *Georgofili* sympathised more strongly with his ideas on cheese than with his ideas on politics, which they found a good deal too ardent. They were ready to concede, however, in days when all danger had passed, that his agitation, if it might make a politician smile, would never cause a moralist to blush.[1] Bartolommei found his friends and accomplices among the younger and more ardent men. His eager nature attracted all the enthusiastic, and his purse was as open as his heart. 'The resolution of every difficulty was always: " Let us go to Ferdinando"'. He got into trouble with the government for his share in the Santa Croce episode of 1851, and later for the distribution of clandestine pamphlets. The government punished him with a year's exile, which he spent in the company of persons like Manfredini and La Farina. La Farina marked down his man, one who was equally impatient of the timidity of the moderates and of the extravagant plotters who thought 'to liberate Italy with a miserable parody of the Sicilian Vespers'. The group of men which gathered round Bartolommei[2] called themselves the National Party, but the name is too exclusive, for there were no hard and fast frontiers between the various liberal groups. The *nazionalisti* were, however, ahead of all others in organisation, and Bartolommei's house early in 1859 was the centre of a feverish activity which collected and despatched the Tuscan volunteers who were flooding into Piedmont.[3]

[1] Tabarrini, *Vite*, 164 *et seq.* Gioli, *op. cit. passim.*   [2] The most important were E. Rubieri and V. Malenchini.   [3] At Genoa they were received by Guerrazzi, who was spending his exile in Piedmont. See G. Cecconi, *Il 27 Aprile*, 1859, p. 21. Ricasoli supported the volunteer movement. See G. Baccini, *Lettere inedite di uomini illustri*, Firenze, 1905, p. 19.

But there was larger work on hand. On February 8 Cavour confessed to the Sardinian representative at Florence, Boncompagni, that he had in things political a conscience rather more expansive than that of the envoy.[1] Boncompagni was called to a conference at Turin, and returned to Florence convinced that Cavour, whatever might be his ultimate plans, did not expect him to pursue any plot against the existence of Tuscany. From now till April Cavour's official diplomacy aimed to secure the co-operation of the Tuscan government in the inevitable war with Austria. Whether or not Cavour really hoped that Leopold would yield to his pressure,[2] he asked La Farina to secure the union of the Tuscan liberals and the Tuscan troops that they might force the government to break the treaty with Austria and to form an alliance with Piedmont.[3] La Farina passed the word to the *nazionalisti* of Florence, and these decided to approach the other patriotic groups.

Of great importance were the radical democrats. These, composed in the main of poorer people, had on the whole been unfortunate in their leaders in 1848 and 1849. Men like Pigli and Montazio, helped by the mistakes of the government and the moderates, had roused them to a pitch of factiousness which made them a hindrance rather than a help in the struggle for independence. The Florentine democrats had now found a leader who had come to the fore in days of adversity, after keeping silence in the days of triumph, a Mazzinian who was ready to set aside matters of secondary importance for the sake of the great national end. Giuseppe Dolfi[4] was of the people by birth and upbringing, a baker, who by his fine appearance, his humour and shrewdness, his commonsense and eloquence, had made himself the idol of the politically minded working-

---

[1]Chiala, *Lettere di Cavour*, II, 23. [2] See below. [3]Chiala, *op. cit.* III, 22.
[4] I. W. Mario, *Giuseppe Dolfi;* G. Mazzoni, *Biografia di G. D.;* G. Valeggio, *G. D. e la Democrazia in Firenze* (with documents). Dolfi, following Garibaldi, joined the National Society in 1857. On these radicals see also L. Aspring, *Vita di Piero Cironi.* Piero Cironi and Manzoni stood with Dolfi.

men and small shop-keepers. His pride as a *popolano* was equal to that of Ricasoli as a baron. He was a democrat of antique stamp who was able to mix with all classes without denying his own, and later knew how to refuse a decoration offered him in person by Victor Emmanuel without creating any embarrassment either for the king or for himself. Witn no thought of personal ambition, he threw in his lot with the *nazionalisti* who made the revolution of April 27; and later, advancing no pretensions for himself, he used his unrivalled influence to champion and maintain the dictator who guarded that revolution and gathered its fruits.

The third important group of liberals was composed of those nobles, lawyers, and professors who, despite their internal divisions, had been known as the moderates in 1848 and 1849. The other parties came to speak of them as the conservatives, and thought them then and later to be too cautious, too circumscribed by their former record and class.[1] After all, these were the men who had fought anarchy and restored the monarchy in April 1849, and it was natural that they should distrust popular initiative and cling to the dynasty as long as it was possible. That the radicals had measured them aright is in the main true; but this party was no more homogeneous than that which grouped itself round Bartolommei and Rubieri. The banker Fenzi or the professor Giorgini were equally at home in the *palazzo* Bartolommei and in the *palazzo* Ricasoli; and if Ridolfi, who had been tutor to the hereditary prince, clung to the dynasty, and to Tuscan autonomy as long as he was able, Ricasoli had long ago turned his back upon 'eunuch projects'. The more ardent nationalists might show impatience with aristocratic caution, but they realised that these men held by right of birth and wealth and character an authority in the country without which no revolution could succeed. The very fact that they would not as a class lightly commit

[1] For an expression of this attitude see Rubieri, *Storia Intima,* esp. Chs. 1 and 3.

themselves to an attack on the house of Lorraine was the best asset which Tuscany possessed in the days to come. Europe was not allowed to forget that the men at the head of revolutionary Tuscany in 1859–60 were the same men who had restored the Grand-Duke in 1849.

At the end of 1857, Ricasoli, Ridolfi and Peruzzi, who, with the exception of Capponi, were the three most prominent of the liberal nobility, had decided to take the one avenue open to them of respectable propaganda— that of publishing. They added to their number Celestino Bianchi, Galeotti, and T. Corsi (who had been one of the defenders of Guerrazzi) and formed a publishing society which they called the *Biblioteca Civile dell' Italiano*. Their first publication, a short book[1] by Corsi, dealing chiefly with the Leopoldine ecclesiastical legislation, led imme- diately to a protest from the Papal government and an admonition from the minister of the interior.[2] Social equals of the publishers began to think of them as ' reds '. ' People want to sleep', wrote Emilia Peruzzi to Ricasoli,[3] ' suddenly a noise is heard: oh! what a nuisance! The sky was so calm! They were sleeping so sweetly! Rash fellows! Be silent, it is not the opportune moment. . . . Poor folk, let them sleep. They have forgotten that they have a spirit'. The venture that seemed so rash to the bulk of the *Georgofili* and so important to its authors, must have appeared a poor thing to the intrepid Bartolommei; but each group judged its own conduct by that of its immediate neighbour, and Bartolommei and Rubieri themselves appeared to the republicans to blow very hot and cold.[4]

It must be remembered, too, that between the Pied- montese and Tuscan liberals there were relations that did not pass through the organisation which linked La Farina and Bartolommei. Bartolommei was the representative of

---

[1] *Apologia delle Leggi di Giurisprudenza, Amministrazione, e Polizia Ecclesiastica pubblicate . . . sotto . . . Leopoldo I*, Firenze, 1858. [2] See *L. & D.*, II, 417. [3] *L. & D.*, II, 429. [4] *e.g.* Manzoni, *op. cit.* Cironi's followers called the La Farinians *malve*—mallows, a term for luke-warm persons.

the national society in Florence, but Cavour had warned
the secretary of the society that he was ready, if necessary,
to deny him like Peter; and side by side with the more
revolutionary counsels which La Farina, obeying or
interpreting the will of Cavour, sent to the Florentine
members of the society, there were discussions of a different
sort between the Tuscan conservatives and Cavour or his
friends. In June of 1858 Ricasoli himself had serious
conversations in Turin, especially with Cavour and with
Massari.[1] The latter stood very close to the Piedmontese
minister, and throughout the succeeding months he and
Ricasoli kept constant touch. It was understood between
the two men that Ricasoli, who had warned Cavour that
the Grand-Duke himself was more dangerous than any of
his ministers,[2] would be ready for any crisis. In October
1858, Cavour was definitely planning with the National
Society a Tuscan rising for the following May,[3] but his
plans changed, possibly as a result of the growing activity
of the Conservatives. Gentlemen from Piedmont began
to make visits to Brolio to look at the baron's silkworms,[4]
and among the visitors was D'Azeglio, whom Cavour had
sent to make him a report on Tuscany.[5] Then, in November and December, Ricasoli was in Turin again. It
was assumed as a matter of course that he would see
Cavour;[6] but after his return to Tuscany events moved so
rapidly that any general conclusions arrived at in Piedmont
became suddenly obsolete. On January 15, 1859, he
wrote to Massari asking for further instructions.

'Marching orders are most necessary here. The eyes of all are turned
to Piedmont, but now all ask: " What is expected from the Tuscans ? " In
colloquies we held there the intention was at the time clear. Therefore I
must know if the intention is in anything modified. I understood then, that

---

[1] *Brolio MSS.*, A. 11. Ricasoli's diary. Ricasoli was in Turin à propos of
silk-worms. Cf. *L. & D.*, II, 443, 447–8.   [2] *L. & D.*, II, 30/9/1858.
[3] Chiala, *Lettere di Lavour*. II, 442–4.   [4] *Brolio MSS.*, A. 11. Diary.
L. & D., II, 445 (July 2).   [5] Chiala, *op. cit.* III, 17–18.   [6] *L. & D.*,
II, 460–1. Salvagnoli was in Turin in November, after an interview
with Napoleon. Bianchi, *Cavour*, 300–4.

Tuscany would stand firm, except assisting in the war. And by firm I mean the conservation of the actual political state of the country'.[1]

There is every reason to believe that Cavour hoped to gain by encouraging the conservatives to act in accordance with their natural tendencies.[2] He even wished them to demand a constitution, as a means of bringing the full power of nationalist pressure to bear against the government. Ricasoli wrote to Massari expressing his strong disapproval of the plan, which he feared as a possible cause of faction. Far better was it, he maintained, to await the opportunity for one great demonstration, a demonstration for 'the great principle of nationality and independence'.[3] The words in which he couched his repudiation of half measures recall irresistibly his declaration of political faith almost three years before. He still believed that it was vain to have two revolutions. Every prince who stood for Austria must be swept away by one resolute effort.

Cavour had sent a special messenger to urge his point of view, and almost three weeks later he wrote to Ridolfi asking that a representative should be sent to interview him. Ricasoli was away, so T. Corsi and Ridolfi set out for Turin together. Ridolfi kept a record of his interview with Cavour,[4] and the record shows that now, as earlier, Cavour realised the advantage of moderate action. Ridolfi demanded flatly what was expected of him and his friends. 'Nothing else', he was told, 'than to induce the dynasty to make an alliance with Piedmont and to put the constitution once more in force'. To this Ridolfi replied that no man, who respected himself, could again sit in the councils of the perjured Grand-Duke. Cavour suggested that Leopold might abdicate in favour of his son, and did not doubt that the *marchese* Ridolfi would add to his other patriotic services that of consenting to be the new sovereign's

---

[1] L.D., II, 465.   [2] Cf. Bianchi, *Cavour*, p. 300.   [3] *L. & D.*, II, 468. Ricasoli feared that the government mig it *grant* the request. Gualterio came to Florence as Cavour's emissary.   [4] Ridolfi, *op. cit.* 231, and Appendix XVII. Cf. article of F. Carega, who accompanied Ridolfi and T. Corsi, in *Fanfulla della Domenica*, 31/1/1892. ('*Del Conte Cavour nel Feb.* 1859.')

minister. The Tuscans, however, would have nothing to do with a constitution. And if they were right in this refusal, Cavour was right in vetoing an alternative plan of theirs, the plan of beginning as they had begun in 1847, with journalism.[1] Cavour's confidant, Michelangelo Castelli, wrote to Corsi,[2] that a journal would have been a 'mystification for all'. 'Now it is time to show yourselves, and no more talking: act then, in God's name'. The *Biblioteca Civile* planned now to launch a manifesto, which in the form of a small book would set forth the whole case of Tuscany against Austria. Celestino Bianchi was set to work at it in a fury,[3] and at the beginning of the fourth week of March it appeared under the title: *Toscana e Austria*. The book exactly suited the times, and an ill-judged attempt of the government to prevent its appearance gave it a special advertisement.[4] The publisher, Barbèra, succeeded in having it ready just one day before a new press law would have made its publication illegal, and within a short period over a hundred thousand people had subscribed to it as a nationalist manifesto.[5]

Meanwhile, others beside the conservatives had been receiving orders from Turin. Cavour himself had on February 19 written to Bartolommei asking for a demonstration in favour of alliance with Piedmont;[6] but in March he warned La Farina against promoting demonstrations of the piazza,[7] and sought from the conservatives permission to print as a manifesto the letter with which they had sent him a copy of *Toscana e Austria*.[8] La Farina, however, had already shown his weariness with temporising, and early in March had sent to Bartolommei official instructions from the National Society for the promotion of a

---

[1] *L. & D.*, II, 469. *Trentacinque Lettere*, di B.R., p. 14. [2] *L. & D.*, II, 471. [3] Salvagnoli, who was engaged on a similar book of his own (*Dell' Indipendenza d'Italia*), criticised the draft severely. [4] See Barbèra, *Memorie*, 152–6. Despite a sequestration, Barbèra hurried the work through. Cf. *Parere per la Verità*, a defence of Barbèra and the editors, Firenze, 1859. [5] Rubieri, *op. cit.* 21. [6] Letter in Gioli, *op. cit.* 239. [7] Chiala, *op. cit.* III, 48. [8] *L. & D.*, III, 485–8.

revolution.[1] Meanwhile, Cavour's diplomacy limited itself
to securing the adhesion of the Tuscan government to
Piedmont in the approaching war. In April he approached
the Tuscan envoy at Turin on the matter; but, in the
opinion of Chiala, 'with no confidence, and let us say
too, no desire that he would be hearkened to'.[2] On April
24, the day on which the Austrian ultimatum was delivered
to the government of Victor Emmanuel, the Sardinian
envoy, Boncompagni, formally requested the alliance of
Tuscany. Leopold and Baldasseroni clung to a policy of
neutrality, notifying Austria that Tuscany could not
fulfil the military treaty of 1815, and refusing an offer of
troops; but at the same time rejecting firmly the invitation
of Piedmont.[3] This stiffness of attitude decided the fate
of the dynasty. Both the conservatives and the more radical
groups had received from Piedmont definite instructions
to bring pressure to bear upon the government in one way
or in another. From April 24 till April 27 they were both
acting feverishly according to their different plans.

On April 21, 23, 24, and 25, Ricasoli noted briefly in
his diary that he had attended a 'meeting'. On the 25th
his memorandum reads: 'Meeting in the evening: perhaps
the last'. These meetings to which he refers[4] had been
held for the most part in his own palace in the Via Cocomero (now the Via Ricasoli), and had been attended by
the conservatives who had co-operated in the *Biblioteca
Civile*,[5] the chief representatives of the Florentine branch
of the National Society, and representatives of the more
radical group led by Dolfi and Cironi, which had decided

---

[1] *Epistolario di La Farina Giuseppe* (Milano, 1869), 127–8, 137–9.
[2] Chiala, *Lettere di Cavour*, III, clxvii. Cavour's good faith is maintained
in the documented histories of N. Bianchi (*Cavour* and *Diplomazia*). Cf.
Castelli, *Ricordi*, 84; and Cambray-Digny, *Carteggio*, 147–9. Tuscan loyalists
doubted it (*Baldasseroni*, and *I casi della Toscana*. Cf. *Della Torre*, p. 27,
18, 33). So did the English ambassador.   [3] Bianchi, *Diplomazia*, VIII,
77–90.   [4] *Brolio MSS.*, A. 11 (Diary). For the various conferences see
especially early chapters in Rubieri, *Storia Intima*. Cf. Gioli, *op. cit.* 245.
The conservatives were not willing to make a piazza revolution.   [5] With
some others, *e.g.* Giorgini, who was in Ricasoli's confidence.

RICASOLI

to co-operate with the *nazionalisti*. All three groups agreed
on the necessity of leading or forcing their country to
stand side by side with Piedmont in the approaching war.
The conservatives, however, in accordance with their
tendencies and with their interpretation of the intentions
of Cavour, were working feverishly to win the Grand-Duke
and his ministers by persuasion and menace. From the
middle of March, Corsini, Landrini, Galeotti, the manu-
facturer Ginori, G. B. Fossi, president of the chamber of
commerce, the banker Fenzi, Peruzzi, Cambray-Digny,
had one after the other spent their eloquence in the *palazzo*
Pitti or the *palazzo* Vecchio.[1] On April 25 Ricasoli himself
tried in vain to see Baldasseroni; on the following day he
saw him, but failed to secure his submission.[2] That evening
there was one more meeting, in which the radicals, weary
of conservative negotiations, sketched out a programme of
revolution for the morning. It was not Ricasoli's nature
to descend into the piazza with common shouting patriots,
and he refused to make part of a proposed revolutionary
junta. Early next morning he set out for Piedmont to
take counsel with Cavour.[3] Before he left Florence, however, some of the nationalists asked him if he would head
the revolution when it had been begun. He answered:

'If it is a question of the usual *little Tuscany*,[4] make it your business,
for I will have nothing to do with it. But if it is a question of making a
great Italy, I am ready, you may count on me'.

When he arrived at Leghorn, he found awaiting him a
telegram which called him back to Florence. He demanded
an explanation. Another telegram followed:

'Grand-Duke does not abdicate. Leaves under escort: country in its own
hands: return immediately'.[5]

[1] See Zobi, *Cronaca*, Document XVI, and I, 109 *et seq.* Galeotti, *L'Assemblea Toscana.*, p. 90. [2] Zobi, *Cronaca*, I, 120, and Ricasoli's Diary. [3] *Brolio MSS.*, A. 11 (Diary). For the final meeting of the nationa-list committees see L. Assing, *Vita di P. Cironi*, 166–7. Rubieri, *op. cit.* 69. G. Cecconi, *op. cit.* 41. [4] *Toscanina. L. & D.*, III, (viii). [5] *Brolio MSS.*, A. 11. Diary, April 27. Cf. *L. & D.*, II, 494. Wire sent by Cempini, Bianchi, Fenzi.

The next entry in his diary runs:

'Nevertheless, I decided to continue my journey. We set out in the evening for Genoa'.

And on the following day:

'April 28. Fine weather. Turin. Massari, Cavour, Minghetti, Torelli. In the evening I go to Cavour. Tuscan affairs'.

On the following day he left Piedmont for Florence, carrying with him a rough memorandum[1] of the things to be done in Tuscany.

. . . . . .

Just ten years had passed since Ricasoli had helped to snatch the state from the control of the extreme democrats and nationalists, and to prepare the restoration of Leopold II. He had never repented his action in April 1849, for he believed that there had been no other possible course. Nevertheless, the years that followed were weary years of disappointment and regret. It seemed to him that he could no longer serve Italy, for his country had become little less than an Austrian province; his old activities had begun to pall upon him; his domestic life, which had absorbed so much of his energies for twenty years, suddenly collapsed. He envied his brother, Vincenzo, who was able to satisfy his patriotism and his longing for action by serving in the Piedmontese army. At last he became convinced that the one hope for Tuscany and for Italy lay in the creation of a great kingdom under the 'constitutional sceptre' of the Piedmontese king. The Tuscan state seemed to him to be a mischievous anachronism, doomed to destruction by the Spirit of the Age; he declared to his brother in 1856 that Tuscany must disappear, along with the other little states of Italy. Throughout 1858 his activities were directed to hasten its destruction.

[1] *Brolio MSS.*, Q. 4. Among the things agreed with Cavour were: Troops to take oath to Victor Emmanuel—nomination of a civil and military governor of Tuscany—circular to diplomatic agents—agitation in Roman states—increase of Tuscan police. The other points affected the armies, volunteers, etc.

Many of his friends did not share his advanced opinions, and desired no more than that Tuscany should fight side by side with Piedmont in the approaching war against Austria. This was all that Cavour demanded, and the interview which took place between Cavour and Ridolfi, the correspondence which passed between Ricasoli and Massari, prove that Cavour thought it essential to work hand in hand with the Tuscan 'conservatives'. A bolder policy, however, was directed by the National Society of which La Farina was secretary, and the ideas of Ricasoli were more akin to those of La Farina's followers in Florence than they were to those of Ridolfi or Peruzzi. On the eve of the revolution he pledged himself to stand with them, provided that they were planning a new future, not for 'little Tuscany', but for Italy.

Then he hurried north to consult with Cavour. Cavour, while taking care that the official diplomacy of Piedmont should be 'correct', had made use of those patriots who were not bound to justify their actions before Europe; and, while openly he demanded comparatively little, it is certain that he hoped for much. Ricasoli brought back with him from Turin a list of practical recommendations for the organisation of the Tuscan revolution. Before long, the control of that revolution fell into his hands. He proved that he knew how to master and to guide it, and when a premature peace and the fall of Cavour seemed to have cut short the work of Piedmont, Ricasoli took on the task at Florence, and held his own against Europe till Cavour returned to complete the work which he had begun. Ricasoli had found at last the enterprise for which he was most fitted—that of a Dictator.

CHAPTER VII

RICASOLI AND TUSCANY (APRIL 27–JULY 12, 1859)

THE Tuscan government, in seeking to withstand the strong demand of the liberals for alliance with Piedmont, had taken risks against which the reports of its own agents should have served as a warning.[1] The prefect of Florence had reported in January that the city, led by the aristocracy and the professional classes, was strong for Italian independence. From Lucca it was reported on March 27 that the masses of the population were ever more imbued with the ideas of Italy and ' Out with the Austrians'. The people, reported the prefect on April 12, wanted the French alliance and war: ' if it were not granted! . . .' he did not finish the sentence. From the province of Pisa the government was warned that the ideas of so-called civil progress, propagated by the cultivated classes, were spreading also in the smaller country centres. The prefect lamented that the younger generation, which was enthusiastic for ' the so-called national idea made concrete in the policy of Piedmont ' should be unfortunately so much more excitable and so much more numerous than the declining generation of sagacious grey-beards. From Arezzo, from Grosseto, from Leghorn, there came similar warnings. Leghorn, characteristically enough, was nursing at the same time its old grievance for the enlargement of the city walls, and its nationalist fervour, offended so bitterly in 1849 and the succeeding years. The governor of the city reported that the people was quiet, because its leaders kept it so, but asked what would happen if liberal tactics should change character? Could the troops be relied upon? From Leghorn, from Lucca, from Pisa, from Siena, the authorities wrote that they could not.

The followers of Bartolommei and Dolfi, fearing that

---

[1] An extract from these reports was enclosed by Ridolfi in his letter of May 15, 1859, to Cambray-Digny, accredited as envoy to London. See Cambray-Digny, *Carteggio*, p. 11 *et seq.*

the conservatives might cheat them of their revolution, had set themselves the important task of winning over the soldiers. There was no question of corruption on a large scale, nor has there ever been forthcoming one scrap of evidence to support the accusation that the army was bought with Piedmontese gold.[1] Enrico Lawley, who was influential with the artillery officers, came and went between Bartolommei and La Farina at his own cost. A few years of discipline after the Austrian fashion had not succeeded in turning the officers into a caste with a purely professional code of honour, and many of them still remembered the battles of 1848 or the duels of 1849.[2] They had pride enough to resist any attempt to disintegrate the little army, but they wished it intact to fight for the Italian cause. Therefore, while they closed their eyes to the obvious fraternising which went on over glasses of red wine between the soldiers and the civilian patriots, they urged the nationalist leaders to refrain from any extravagant incitement, which might lead either to desertion or to discord.[3] Were they ready to turn against Leopold II? The question had not yet arisen, and the officers for the most part devoutly hoped that a little judicious pressure applied by them and their civilian accomplices would save them from any unpleasant conflict of loyalties.

On the evening of April 26 a long procession of soldiers and civilians, arm in arm, had trooped through the streets, heckled the unpopular general, Ferrari da Grado, and given clear enough signs that it was ready for a word of command. The plan was sketched out in Dolfi's house. At ten that morning, one of the plotters has written,[4] the idea of provoking a demonstration was not yet born. At ten that evening the day of the demonstration had not yet been fixed. At ten the next morning the streets of Florence

---

[1] The British representative at Florence made this assertion. *Correspondence, Italy*, No. 516 (Parl. Papers, 1859). [2] For the attitude of the officers see Col. G. Cecconi, *Il 27 Aprile*, 1859. [3] Cf. G. Rondoni, *Foglietti della Clandestina alla viglia del 27 Aprile*, in *Il Risorg. Italiano*, I, 308 *et seq.* (1908). [4] *Rubieri*, 69.

were packed with a crowd 'gathered as if at the touch of a magician's wand to attest and sustain a common will'. That evening, Tuscany remained 'what it had been on April 26, except one family the less'.[1]

The events of the day centred round the *palazzo* Pitti, the Piazza di Barbano (now dell' Indipendenza) and the palace of the Sardinian ambassador, Carlo Boncompagni.[2] Cavour had reflected with some displeasure that Boncompagni's conscience was less elastic in political matters than his own, but had decided to leave him at Florence with instructions to press only for Tuscany's alliance in the war. This the envoy had done in good faith, but it must be confessed that on April 27 there was something hardly conventional in the manner in which the embassy became the headquarters of nationalist revolution.[3] While ordinary-looking persons in the Piazza di Barbano handed out a manifesto calling for war, and the crowd waited good-temperedly to see the tricolour hoisted from Fortezza da Basso, the liberals of various parties were gathered with Boncompagni. Thither came Neri Corsini, from the Pitti, where he had been called by Leopold. Leopold had realised too late the strength of the movement, and, after sending in vain for Ricasoli, had bethought himself of this other nationalist noble. Corsini reported that the Grand-Duke had given way, and that he had been commissioned to form a ministry; but Ridolfi now spoke up and announced that he had already written to Leopold, informing him that abdication in favour of the hereditary prince would alone save the dynasty. So Corsini went back to demand abdication, a long list of reforms, and a ministry whose names had been decided on by compromise between the rival

[1] A. D'Ancona, *op. cit.* 409. [2] On April 27, in addition to general accounts by Rubieri, Zobi, etc., see N. Corsini, *Storia di Quattro Ore;* C. Ridolfi, *Breve Nota a una Storia di Quattro Ore;* G. Cecconi, *op. cit.;* V. Soldani, *Pasqua di Liberazione* (Firenze, 1909); *XXVII Aprile, MDCCCLIX, a cura del comitato Toscano* (Firenze, 1909). There are many scattered writings on the subject, of which the best is by F. Martini in *Confessioni e Ricordi.* [3] *Further Correspondence, Italy,* (Parl. Papers, 1859), No. 31 (Scarlett, May 6).

leaders at the Piedmontese embassy. By now the army officers had carried through their mutiny in the most gentlemanly way, and the Italian flag was flying from both the fortresses. Leopold refused the demands of the conspirators, which seemed to him dishonouring. He preferred to reserve his rights, to leave Tuscany to his disobedient subjects, and to trust to the fortunes of war and to Tuscan fickleness to bring about his return, as they had done ten years before. At sunset a long procession of carriages passed out the Porta San Gallo and along the Via Bolognese. The demonstrators, who had throughout the day been splendidly disciplined by Dolfi and his friends, stood silent while the Grand-Duke and his family passed, attended by the court staff and by the foreign diplomats accredited to the fallen government. The nationalists never wearied in praising the moderation of their ' rose-water revolution '; but perhaps in the silent crowd which watched the departure of the prince there was a tinge of regret for one who for more than thirty years had tried to live as the first servant of his people.

Leopold's fault as a sovereign had sprung from his position as a member of the house of Austria. He embodied in himself the conflict between the dynastic principle, protected by the sanctity of treaties, and revolutionary nationalism. Because he had chosen the former, nationalism, the most unforgiving of passions, denied him all praise for the things which he had done well. Before long, ' the slanderous accusation of a liar '[1] pointed him out to popular hate as one who had planned to destroy with ruthless

[1] Martini, *op. cit.* 259. For this accusation, which was accepted by all the liberal chroniclers (Zobi, Rubieri, Trollope, etc.), see Zobi *Cronaca* Documents 53–55, and *Atti ufficiali concernenti il bombardamento di Firenze,* which contains all the evidence. The facts are: (1) sealed orders of date 14/4/1858, existed. These set out the measures to be taken in case of revolution. (2) These were opened on April 27 on receipt of a written order from the general. (3) The Archduke Charles demanded information on preparations made. Major Mori said that he did so *per atto puramente academico,* but a lieutenant and a doctor deposed that their own patriotic speeches thwarted his bloodthirsty intentions. In either case, Leopold was not concerned. Cf. Martini, *op. cit.* 155–156.

cruelty the city which he had loved so well. Common
people love their country the more if they have something
very definite to hate, and it did not suit the Tuscan patriots
to permit any regretful tolerance for *Babbo*. While the
sovereign was meditating, on the long road to Vienna,
proclamations[1] which would recall his services to the
Tuscans and protest against the violation of his rights,
active pamphleteers were teaching the people that Leopold
had been a willing agent of all the brutalities of the
Austrians,[2] and were spreading little poems of patriotism
which recounted how only *Babbi* could break their oaths,
how one *Babbo* in particular had joyfully plotted to lay
his capital in ruins, and how tyrants in general lay awake
at night planning miseries for their subjects. Before long
the wife and the son of the ' mild ' prince were included
in a little collection of these pleasant songs.[3]

But before this, the liberals had secured their hold
upon the country. The ardent patriots who had made the
revolution had the generosity to make place for the
moderates, who alone possessed the necessary prestige to
safeguard the victory throughout Tuscany. As a result, it
was decided on April 27 to call together the sole surviving
authority in Florence, the municipal council, and to
procure from it some legitimisation of revolutionary
power. The municipality showed no eagerness to perform
a disagreeable task, and very soon the *gonfaloniere* decided
that he felt ill; but that evening there was installed a
triumvirate in which Peruzzi represented the moderates,
Malenchini the ardent nationalists, and Dandrini the
insurgent army. No sooner were the three installed than
they issued a proclamation informing the citizens that
their power was merely provisional, and that it would be
resigned as soon as Victor Emmanuel was able to make
some arrangement for the government of the country
during the war.

[1] Zobi, I, 162.   [2] *Testamento dell' I. e R. Casa di Lorena* and *300
Vittime dell' I. e R. Casa Austro-Lorenese.*   [3] *Voci del Popolo* (approved
by government).

'THE ROSE-WATER REVOLUTION'

From a picture by Enrico Fanfani

One or two examples will serve to show by what means the liberal revolution spread from Florence into the provinces. In the Val d'Arno, telegrams[1] were flying for two days between Arezzo, San Giovanni, Pontassieve, and the capital. On April 27 Peruzzi wired from Florence ordering the prefect of Arezzo to fly the tricolour, to tear down the Grand-Ducal arms, and to maintain order. The prefect transmitted these instructions to San Giovanni and Pontassieve, but without enthusiasm. At 6.30 a.m. on the following morning the *gonfaloniere* of Arezzo wired to Florence that the prefect must be changed, and three hours later the prefect himself telegraphed that he was retiring owing to serious, sudden ill-health. Then there arrived on the scene Count Fossombroni, who had been appointed special commissioner to secure the adhesion of the district to the revolutionary government. At 10.45 a.m. he wired to Peruzzi that there was perfect quiet in Arezzo, and at 3.20 p.m. he announced that the former prefect (the 'sick' man) and his chief assistant were retiring under an escort of gendarmes. Meanwhile, at San Giovanni, which was in the department of Arezzo, the chief of police had telegraphed to Florence at 7.20 on the evening of April 27 that carriages full of tricolour flags were arriving in the city. At 7.30 he wired to the prefect of Arezzo that the tricolours had been hoisted, he himself being unable to prevent it. At half past nine he reported that the people up and down the valley were demonstrating without permission. Early the next morning the delegate of San Giovanni, more subtle than his chief at Arezzo, telegraphed proudly to Peruzzi that everything was in order. He was modest enough to claim no special credit.

It appears from this collection of dispatches that the revolution consolidated itself easily enough, owing to the resolute action of the provincial patriots, and the prompt measures of the special commissioners sent from Florence. But another example will show a slower and less definite

[1] A copy of these is kept in the Brolio *Archivio*, Q. 4.

response to the impulse of Florence, in a district which is very typical of much of the remote country of Tuscany.[1] The little town of Firenzuola lies in a deep valley on the Adriatic side of the Apennine water-shed. Under the Grand-Ducal régime it was the *capo-luogo* of a commune widely scattered over the high plain, a country not very rich, with poor communications, save for the old highway which ran from Florence to Bologna, given over in large degree to the chestnut woods where the peasants pastured their animals. Of the 8,000 inhabitants very few were able to read, all the education and experience of the outer world being concentrated in the little town of 800 inhabitants, which indeed was specially favoured by the presence of an archiepiscopal seminary. Society had that patriarchal basis which was general throughout Tuscany; and since there was no landowner predominating greatly in wealth, the peasant proprietors (who were relatively numerous), the *mezzadri*, the cottagers, the agricultural officials, and the small shopkeepers of the towns, formed a clientele which attached itself to one or other of the more important families. The commune was tranquilly aloof from the ideas which prevailed in the less isolated centres; and with the exception of a score of persons, including two doctors of medicine, one family of proprietors which had a young hopeful trained at the University, a few of the teaching priests, and a number of youths, the population was staunchly loyalist when the revolution of April broke out. Some of the proprietors were fanatical supporters of the old order, but the majority had given it unreflecting loyalty, and was ready to go with the stream of political and social orthodoxy. But it must first be convinced which way the tide was flowing. It is not surprising, therefore, that the *gonfaloniere* delayed ten days before sending to Florence the adhesion of his municipality. This tardy submission by no means implied the commune's approval of extreme policies, least of all of any move to sink the destiny of Tuscany in that of Piedmont. When

[1] A. Savelli in *Rassegna Storica del Risorg. Ital.*, 1908, Vol. I, 480–93.

later Ricasoli authorised Dolfi to send round to the communes a manifesto in favour of union with Piedmont,
Firenzuola delayed reply for week after week, was unmoved by a reprimand from the prefect of Florence, and
in the end only adhered when forced by the intervention
of thirty-two nationalists, of whom only eight resided in
the commune, and only two were born there. Then the
council, three of the five priors being absent, and a substitute being called in to make up the legal number,
declared that, ' making itself faithful interpreter of the
wishes of the *communisti*', it adhered to ' the union of
Tuscany to the other states of Italy, under the constitutional government of the magnanimous King Victor
Emmanuel II, and his dynasty'.

Investigations similar to that which has produced these
facts about Firenzuola would have to be multiplied, before
it would be possible to realise exactly the meaning of
that ' national will ' to which the Tuscans appealed
throughout 1859. As it is, the story of the little town and
its surrounding country throws into relief that extraordinary work of propaganda and discipline by which
Ricasoli overcame the hesitations of his own colleagues,
chastened the vulgarities and extravagances which would
have alienated slow-moving people, awoke faith in those
who doubted, and in the end forced an incredulous Europe
to confess that his will did appear to be the will of Tuscany.
At the beginning of his enterprise, the suspicions of
Firenzuola were shared by almost every peasant community throughout Tuscany. From the Val d'Arno, where
the revolution had won such immediate and clamorous
success, Lambruschini wrote to Ricasoli[1] that the country
would be thrown into violent disturbance by any attempt
to impose a conscription. If the Austrians invaded their
fields, the peasants would come out to fight. If they were
not dragged away from their vines and olives, if they were
not expected to pay for the glory of the new Italy, they
would work contentedly enough under any government,

[1] *L. & D.*, III, 2.

and might even absorb some of the gospel that came to them from the towns or from their masters. But, wrote Lambruschini: 'If this resolution (that of a military levy) is taken or suggested, by anyone who does not know Tuscany and wishes to compare it to Piedmont, I can only say that it would do everything to make the return of the Grand-Duke desired, Piedmont hated, the cause of Italy abhorred'. Here was a bitter pill for the more ardent nationalists to swallow. They had made their revolution in the name of military co-operation with Piedmont, but they were forced to realise the truth which Hamilton had noted in 1848, that love of war was not a quality of their amiable nation. In the end, Napoleon and Victor Emmanuel won their victories without any aid from Tuscan regiments.

In addition to the conservatism of the country-folk, the new rulers of the state had to reckon with the powerful influence which the clergy exercised upon the simple population. On the whole, the clergy was less hostile to the new order than the recent history of the Church would have led the liberals to expect. At Firenzuola, various priests of the seminary figured among the minority which imposed its will upon the commune, and priests of similar tendencies were scattered throughout the country. Some of them, too, were among the most useful of the popular propagandists who in the next eleven months set themselves to make a 'general will' in Tuscany. Among the higher Clergy, the Bishop of Lucca[1] and the Vicar-General of Grosseto were avowed patriots. The Archbishop of Florence himself was willing to take up a conciliatory attitude towards the new powers.[2] The bulk of the clergy, however, sympathised with the old order, and any lack of tact on either side could kindle the old controversy between Church and State, and awaken the conflict between two ideal systems equally unyielding in their refusal to accept a mere partial loyalty.

---

[1] His clergy, as a body, published a manifesto of adhesion to the revolution. *Monitore Toscano*, No. 108. [2] E. Poggi, *Memorie Storiche*, I, 56 *et seq.*

On the whole, the nationalists could look with satisfaction on the reception of their revolution. Giorgini
thought[1] it a case of the toothache ending when the tooth
was drawn, and considered that the operation itself had
been less painful than he had anticipated. But the work
had only been begun. What was to be done with Tuscany
now that the Grand-Duke had been expelled? Most of
Ricasoli's friends would have been shocked at any suggestion that she should give herself to Piedmont. Others,
who would have taken the suggestion calmly, would still
have maintained that merely to think of such a thing was
folly. Europe would never consent to it; the Emperor had
other plans for Tuscany. Ricasoli, convinced that God
and the spirit of the age had already decided the question,
cared nothing for the mistaken scruples of his friends, or
the displeasure of the diplomatists, or the schemes of
Napoleon. He knew nothing of the conversations that
had passed between Cavour and Napoleon at Plombières,
and cared less.[2] A few months later, when the God, not of
Battles, but of Peace, seemed to have turned against his
cause, he wrote with ardent faith to his brother that a
great and strong Italy was necessary for Napoleon, necessary
for France, necessary for Europe, necessary for Humanity,
necessary for Christianity.[3] Faith in predestination was not
fashionable among the diplomatists and politicians of the
age, and perhaps that was why they found the baron such
an extraordinarily difficult person to deal with.

For the first week after his return from Turin, Ricasoli
had no opportunity to carry out by his own energy the
proposals which he had brought back from Cavour, and
the maxims which he had garnered in years of meditation.
The appointment of a triumvirate in Florence was a
disappointment for Cavour,[4] who had desired a military
and civil governor for Tuscany, and perhaps had wished

[1] *L. & D.*, III, 8. [2] His note to Dall' Ongaro, p. 36, runs: ' Non
ne sapeva niente, e fu bene. Ricasoli operò da sè, e con s'è. [3] *L. & D.*,
II, 142. [4] A. Commandini, *Il Principe Napoleone*, 143–5. *Brolio MSS.*,
Q. 4.

Ricasoli to be the man. The actual government was not satisfactory. In addition to organising provisionally the revolution by making necessary changes in the public service (Corsi, for example, was appointed prefect of Florence and Bartolommei *gonfaloniere*) the triumvirate embarked on a feverish career of incidental legislation. At last the stalwart butcher who had lovingly fondled his unused guillotine was sent about his business, and the death penalty was summarily removed from the penal code.[1] Commissions for the reform of the penal and military codes were established. The bronze tablets were put back again in Santa Croce, and the two Universities of Pisa and Siena were once more given a separate existence.[2] Funds were voted for the erection of a bronze copy of Michelangelo's marble David. An amnesty was published, but its terms compelled political offenders to plead their cause in the courts, and Guerrazzi, at any rate, refused this humiliation.[3] Such activity upon the part of a two-weeks' government lent itself to ridicule, and Vincenzo Ricasoli told his brother that Turin was displeased at this ' vomit of decrees'.[4] In the all-important matter of the war, the triumvirate failed badly. It resigned the army to General Ulloa, the hero of the defence of Venice in 1849; but the general, instead of drilling his men for battle, immediately threw everything into confusion by attempting an ill-timed reorganisation. The *morale* of the soldiers did not improve under this treatment, and a little later Ricasoli was very curious as to their conversations in the wine shops.[5] 'A revolution has been made', he imagined them saying, ' we can make another'.

The triumvirate's merry course came to an end on

---

[1] *Atti e Documenti* . . . *del Governo della Toscana*, I, 26.   [2] *Ibid.* I, 16, 25.   [3] *Ibid.* I, 32. Della Torre (*op. cit.* 70) says that Cavour gave this counsel to Ricasoli, but it does not appear in Ricasoli's memorandum. Similarly (p. 80) he says that Cavour favoured a civic guard rather than an increase of the police. Ricasoli's memorandum says nothing of the guard, and definitely notes the necessity of an increase of police. *Brolio MSS.*, Q. 4.   [4] *L. & D.*, II, 8.   [5] G. Baccini, *Lettere inedite*, Vol. V, Firenze, 1905, p. 21 *et seq.*

May 9. On April 28 it had written to offer Victor Emmanuel the dictatorship of Tuscany as long as the war should last, with the understanding that even in this period the state should keep effective autonomy, and that the final political settlement should be postponed till the peace.[1] Cavour, forced against his will to whittle down a proposal whose acceptance would have been distasteful to Napoleon,[2] replied that for reasons of high policy His Majesty could not accept the offered dictatorship; but that he was ready to assume command over the troops, and the protectorate of the Tuscan government during the war, delegating the necessary powers to his plenipotentiary, Boncompagni, with the title of ' Extraordinary Commissioner of the King for the war of independence'.[3] There was some dispute as to the real powers which should go with this title. In the end Boncompagni was recognised as the legatee of the powers of the provisional government, as well as the appointed commissiary of the king.[4] He announced that he would exercise all the powers which belonged to a head of a state, but in such a way that the administration of Tuscany would be kept separate from that of Piedmont. Those who favoured a close union with Piedmont, including Ricasoli, hoped that he would act as a governor, choosing solely non-political persons to manage the affairs of state.[5] Such an arrangement would in all probability have been the mask for a dictatorship exercised by Ricasoli himself. It was defeated by the moderates whose first pre-occupation was for the autonomy of Tuscany, and Boncompagni was forced to adopt the rôle of a constitutional president advised by a council of ministers.[6] Among the ministers designated, the autonomists were in the majority, and the most important of them, Ridolfi, had control of the department of foreign affairs.[7] The only resolute supporter of annexation to

---

[1] *Atti*, I, 16. [2] Commandini, *loc. cit.* Chiala, *Lettere di Cavour*, III, clxx. [3] *Atti*, I, 36. [4] Poggi, I, 11–12. [5] *Ibid.* 3–8. *L. & D.*, III, 14–16. [6] *L. & D.*, III, 17–19. *Poggi*, I, p. 3 *et seq.* [7] Less important than his other department of education. Piedmont did not favour a separate diplomatic service for Tuscany. See Cambray-Digny, *Carteggio*, p. VIII.

Piedmont was Ricasoli himself, who had taken charge of the department of the Interior.

He entered upon his new labours with the usual protestations of reluctance.

'I love the life of Cincinnatus', he wrote to Giorgini, 'and am loath to give it up. Unless the country is in peril, I shall return to the fields within sixty days'.[1]

He made it a condition of his acceptance, that he should be permitted to resign his office within two months. He thought that the war would have a speedy and victorious conclusion, and he did not intend to become involved in post-war politics. But a premature peace upset all his calculations, and he found before him the opportunity of an apostolate whose immensity surpassed his wildest dreams. The very limitations of his narrow intellect were the best equipment for the task which unfolded itself before him. His evangelical gospel of duty had turned to a wearisome lament on the decadence of the age, when he had preached it, month after month, year after year, to a small circle of sympathetic friends. Ideas had lost their charm, even to Ricasoli, when they were eternally twisted to furnish some moral lesson. But concentration on one central purpose was the one thing which Tuscany needed throughout the ten months which followed, and preaching became the most efficient form of propaganda. As for Ricasoli, he had never known such complete mental and spiritual satisfaction. There was a great difference between setting forth his faith for the hundredth time in a letter to Lambruschini, and expounding it as master to the prefects, his deputy-missionaries throughout the country. Their one duty, he told the prefects in his first circular,[2] was to raise the moral level of the people. And this at the time meant nothing else than to awaken enthusiasm for 'the enterprise, founded on reason and justice, and visibly blessed by Divine Providence'. Ricasoli's

[1] *L. & D.*, III, 16. [2] *Atti*, I, 96 (May 12); *Brolio MSS.*, Q. 13, contains two drafts of the circular, one annotated by Galeotti, the other by Salvagnoli.

religion was one with his political faith, and both were now
bound together in a work of a hundred daily details, a
work that made constant demands upon his energies, his
endurance, his firmness. In the months that followed he
never gave the Tuscans one instant in which to doubt the
cause he preached, to lose sight of that single goal to
which he was leading them. The idea of the unity of Italy,
he said later, was inborn within him. He cultivated it in
others until it prevailed. The pride of action, the passion
of management, which had spurred him to mould the daily
lives of his peasants at Brolio, now forced him to fight for
his will even against those allies who saw matters a little
differently and at times a little more clearly—against Farini,
Garibaldi, Cavour himself.

At the end of the two months which he had believed
would confine his period of power, he was able to look
back with pride on things achieved. He declared to his
brother that his government was the first which had really
governed in Tuscany for the last thirty years. He claimed
that he had not compromised with his principles, that he
had made no bargain with anyone, that, without any
force from without and with a poor enough force of his
own, he had made the law respected towards all and against
all.[1] His work is illustrated by the records of his department.

'To physical force', he told the prefect of Florence, 'must be added
moral force, and to-day the authorities of the government must show themselves resolute to the point of rashness'.[2]

Audacity was good, but he added to the numbers of the
police.[3]

No revolution can be successfully carried out unless
there is something of a purge of the officials who are
bound in sympathy to the fallen order. Ricasoli was
not ruthless enough to satisfy the extreme nationalists.[4]
He explained that all the officers, from the highest to the
lowest, must be animated by the same political principle;

[1] *L. & D.*, III, 140. [2] *L. & D.*, III, 106. [3] *Atti*, I, 131–6.
[4] *Rubieri*, 186.

but added that it would be a mistake to hurry on an offensive against those in subordinate positions. What he did
he did thoroughly, and among his papers there remains
a list which he compiled throughout the months of May
and June, containing the names of the most important
civil servants and his own reflections on their fitness for
the task in hand.[1] He treated the misbehaving with the
rigour of an old-time schoolmaster. A wretched delegate,
who was too slow in taking action against the posting of
secretly printed notices, was given a whole decree to
himself, which, after a series of *considering thats*, suspended
him for a month without pay. The penalty was mild, but
the moral lecture was such a new thing that it had a strange
efficacy.[2]

He was determined that there should be no repetition
of the follies of 1848. The first rumour of disorderly
conduct among undisciplined young vagabonds in a little
town of the Val d'Arno moved him almost to ferocity.
' I desire nothing better than to put the dregs of the people
in their place', he fumed, ' and I should like my name
to become their terror'.[3] The disorderly elements, who
had hoped that the revolution would bring them happy
days, were terrified into compulsory virtue, and petty
thieves were admonished by a circular which announced
to them that the country had risen to a new life.[4] Gambling,
even lotteries in aid of patriotic objects, was sternly prohibited.[5] Undisciplined enthusiasm provoked the same
moral disapproval as petty theft. Musical instruments and
church bells could not testify to nationalist exultation
unless Ricasoli had authorised the bell-ringers to ring and
the trumpeters to blow.[6] He prohibited demonstrations
even when they were organised by the supporters of
his policy.[7] He would permit the expression of public
opinion only through the channels which he could control.
In notifying the prefects of his intention to maintain the

1 *Brolio MSS.*, S. 46. Cf. Q. 19.   2 *Atti*, I, 235.   3 *L. & D.*, III,
139.   4 *Atti*, I, 128.   5 *Atti*, I, 175.   6 *Atti*, I, 271.   7 *L. & D.*,
III, 99.

existing press laws, he declared: 'The time for free discussions will come. Now is the time for manly effort'.[1] The scanty notices that appeared in the *Monitore* did not satisfy many of his old friends, among them Vieusseux, who, with the publisher's instinct, wrote to Ricasoli a number of suggestions. At least there might be daily war-bulletins posted up in the piazza.[2] Ricasoli did not like to think of people discussing politics in the piazza. 'Immoderate curiosity', he answered, 'must restrain itself'.[3] What was the use of having a newspaper? he asked Peruzzi. A newspaper existed to discuss ideas, but now there were no ideas to discuss. There was but 'one sole idea, one sole thought, unity in everything and for everything'.[4] He decided, however, to expand the *Monitore*, and from time to time called upon Salvagnoli and Tabarrini to write special articles.[5] With the *Monitore* he could do the same work that he had done with the *Patria* in 1848, with this great difference, that now there was no other journal to answer back. Thus, to the discontent of some of his colleagues,[6] he gathered to himself the whole task of giving Tuscany news and telling the people their duty. He declared publicly that the people must come to recognise in the government 'a salutary tutelage, an educative force, a true expression of its sentiments and its interests'.[7] Woe to the people if they did not! He ordered the prefects to post up his circulars on the doors of the parish churches, and later, on the walls of public buildings.[8] All the public officials must co-operate in the task. Thus his voice reached to the most remote of the little cities that blazed behind their walls under the summer sun. Once or twice a week the peasants would climb the hill on which their market-town seemed to sleep, and they, too, would be told by those who could read that the country had risen to new life, and that it expected something even from them. Perhaps they found it all rather perplexing.

[1] *Atti*, I, 124.   [2] *L. & D.*, III, 46.   [3] *L. & D.*, III, 50. But see *Atti*, I, 153.   [4] *L. & D.*, III, 94.   [5] *e.g. L. & D.*, III, 74, 87.   [6] *Poggi*, I, 184 and *passim*.   [7] *Atti*, I, 187.   [8] *Atti*, I, 167.

But Ricasoli had fellow-workers who could make things very clear, even to the peasants. One of them brought out a little book which he called: ' Leopold II and Tuscany. Words of a priest to the People'.[1] The preface explained that the author, ' though nourished upòn select, vast, and profound studies, thought it his duty to adopt a style, for him most difficult, that would be intelligible to the most vulgar intellects'. In this style he announced to the vulgar intellects that God had given the Italians their house, but that the Austrians had come to rob them in it, with the sanction of the Kings. The rule of Austria, he told them, ' means that the People should never count for anything; that it should work like donkeys, be beaten like donkeys, have little and nothing good to eat, like donkeys'. In Tuscany, Austrian supremacy had meant ' oppressing us, and drying us up, and deceiving us, and depopulating us, and gnawing us right to the bone, to reduce us to the most extreme misery'. He counted up the fabulous sums of money which the Austrians had taken from the country, and told the vulgar intellects that, if they had that money now, everybody would be a gentleman. Then he began to speak of Leopold II. It was he who had called the Austrians into their land. He, therefore, was responsible for all the assassinations and barbarities that they had committed. Then he began to speak of the royal family, one by one. They were a bad, blood-thirsty lot. He told the glorious story of April 27, when the wicked despot and his brood had been expelled once and for all. Now that they were gone, nothing remained but to vote for the union of Tuscany to all Italy.

An educational reformer, some months later, set himself to enlighten vulgar intellects in similar fashion.[2] The preface to his first little book explained how the author,

[1] *Leopoldo II e la Toscana. Parole di un sacerdote al popolo.* Compare *Lettura popolare. Le conversazioni del villagio,* etc.   [2] *La Pianeta dei Morti. Veglie del Prior Luca, raccolte e commentate da Renzo.* This pamphlet, though mentioned here, was published after the Villafranca preliminaries. The author, Prof. S. Bianciardi, became later a correspondent of Ricasoli's.

left a widower at forty-five with four children, became an exemplary priest who divided his time between the duties of his parish and a school for twelve young ladies. In the evenings he gathered his flock around him and taught them the things which they ought to know. He was writing an account of these conversations, so that the poor people, who laboured all day and had no time to read the papers and often no money to buy them, might understand the great things which were happening in the world. The first talk which he recorded showed him explaining to his pious listeners how he, who had been a *codino* and an ignorant person, had all of a sudden become a liberal. He had gone down to Florence, and heard the tender children of the poor toilers singing every day in the streets: ' Tories, go to bed. Daddy won't come back any more'. He had spoken to respectable people like doctors and lawyers, and they had told him about the wickedness of the Austrians and of the Grand-Duke, and what a pious thing the revolution had been, and what a noble king was Victor Emmanuel. One family after another was becoming liberal. What did it mean? ' It means that the world progresses, it means that the kittens have opened their eyes, that people to-day won't let the flies rest upon their noses. It means that it is the will of Our Lord'. In another conversation he explained the meaning of the old flag and the new. The red and yellow of Austria meant the Land of the Dead, it meant ' tyranny, buying and selling of people, a few with enough money for bread and all the rest starving, slaving and paying . . .' and so on for a page or two. The tricolour flag, on the other hand, stood for the three theological virtues. It meant also the rule of law, a free press, religion in the hearts of men, upright judges, a real nation like England or France, and a reduction in the price of salt. The peasant had a duty to think about all this. He must work and live as before, but remember what the good priest told him: ' You are not only Christians and fathers. . . . You are also Italians, children of a great *mamma* which is Italy, our country'.

Pamphlets such as these had the approval of Ricasoli, and on occasion he was ready to pay the local authorities to distribute them.[1] The more vulgar work of propaganda, however, was left to private patriotic initiative, and it stands to Ricasoli's credit that he was always ready to check its most offensive manifestations. His position was particularly fortunate in that the radical nationalists, though at times impatient, recognised the force of his faith and trusted him; while his intimates among his own class were ever ready to point out the mistakes that might be made through excessive haste or through alienating the feelings of scrupulous people.[2] Usually, he found the latter too undecided for his taste. Within a few weeks of his accession to office he was engaged in a struggle with the moderates in general and those of his own colleagues in particular who thought it their business to defend Tuscan autonomy against Piedmont.

The crisis arose from an unfortunate mistake made by Salvagnoli, who at the time was in Piedmont. Ricasoli, confident though he claimed to be in the good order of Tuscany, did not hanker for the vainglory of meeting every emergency without a reliable force.[3] The Tuscan army under Ulloa was not yet in a fit state for war, and the Minister of the Interior, angry at his helplessness in a matter beyond his province, expected no good from it. Even the disinterested patriotism of Ulloa was doubted in some quarters, and Piedmontese officers were very displeased with the colour scheme of the new Tuscan uniform.[4] Ricasoli spoke of the volunteers as cannon-fodder, and thought that mischief might come from them.[5] Unde-

---

[1] *L. & D.*, IV, 371.   [2] In contrast to the usual propaganda it is refreshing to note a prayer of Capponi's: ' Let us pray God to save and prosper this city and Tuscany and Italy, which is our land; and that he give us peace and concord among ourselves, and love even for our enemies, who have come upon us for our sins; and that he keep us in the observance of His divine precepts and His holy religion'. (*Lettere* of Capponi, III, 270). [3] *L. & D.*, III, 51.   [4] *L. & D.*, III, 11 and 13. Some thought the colours too like the Austrian ones; others, too like those of Napoleon. [5] *L. & D.*, III, 29.

sirable persons were flocking in from the Romagnas and the Marches to join the colours, and it was rumoured that the Pope had let loose all the Roman criminals in the hope that they might throw the Tuscan forces into confusion.[1] There was, in addition, the usual uneasiness with regard to the Mazzinians. Ricasoli, therefore, asked the Piedmontese government to call away the Tuscan troops at the earliest possible moment to incorporate them in the Piedmontese army, and to send in their stead a few thousand Piedmontese soldiers, as well as the officer for whom the ministry of war was being kept vacant. Cavour did not take very seriously Ricasoli's admonitions, and only a few hundred soldiers were sent to Leghorn. Ricasoli was angry. Cavour should have done what he had been told to do.[2]

Salvagnoli made the serious mistake of declaring immediate the dangers which Ricasoli had thought possible, and the still greater mistake of painting his gloomy picture to the Emperor, instead of to Cavour. He won a success which caused consternation to Ricasoli and deeply vexed Cavour.[3] On May 18, the Emperor called Salvagnoli to him. He announced his attention of securing order in Tuscany, and at the same time fulfilling undefined military purposes, by sending to Tuscany a whole army corps, under the command of the Prince Imperial. The Emperor suggested to Salvagnoli that he himself should enter the Tuscan ministry, and sent him off to Cavour to tell him what had been decided.

There were many reasons why Ricasoli and Cavour should be annoyed with Salvagnoli and alarmed at the result of his interference. Ricasoli wrote to the Tuscan envoy at army headquarters that the decision could not seriously have been taken because of fear for Tuscan order. He hoped that the Emperor's reasons would be found to be of an urgent military character.[4] But there did not seem to be any Austrians to fight on the Tuscan frontiers.

[1] *L. & D.*, III, 52.   [2] *L. & D.*, III, 29.   [3] Cambray-Digny, *Carteggio*, 31. Poggi, I, 76; *L. & D.*, III, 30.   [4] *L. & D.*, III, 51.

. . . Ricasoli evidently suspected then, as historians have
suspected since, that Jérôme was sent to Florence to spy
out the possibility of a crown. It was well-enough known
that Napoleon had put forward at Plombières plans for
a central kingdom of Italy. The same federal idea had
appeared in La Guerronière's pamphlet. Ricasoli knew,
and Cavour probably knew, that Salvagnoli had flattered
the Emperor on his pet scheme only six months before.
At an interview with Napoleon III at Compiègne, in
November, 1858, he had presented a memorial which
favoured a federation of four states as the sufficient guarantee of Italian independence, and definitely advocated a
French prince for the kingdom of central Italy.[1] It was a
curious coincidence, at the very least, that a French prince
should now be sent to Tuscany with an army corps behind
him, as the result of an interview between the same Emperor
and the same politician.[2]

Cavour kept his fears in the background. He did not
hide from Napoleon that he considered the move an
unfortunate one, but pretended that his only concern was
for the scandal and suspicion which the move would
inevitably occasion in Europe.[3] In none of his despatches
did he even suggest that Piedmont's ally was seeking to
prejudice the future of the peninsula. But Piedmont
must save the ally from the consequences of his own hasty
action, must give an open and peremptory refutation of
'the malevolent insinuations directed against France'.[4]
One of the Tuscan envoys in Piedmont wrote to Ridolfi
that Cavour would act to save the face of France before
Europe.[5] Cavour had summoned the two envoys and had
told them that, as a result of Napoleon's action, only three
alternatives remained for Tuscany—a Mazzinian republic,

[1] Bianchi, *Diplomazia*, VIII, 11–16. Salvagnoli had undertaken a sort of
Napoleonic propaganda in Italy. See *Sul Monumento a Vittorio Alfieri in
Santa Croce* (Firenze, 1857).   [2] The question is discussed in Appendix II.
[3] Chiala, *Lettere di Cavour*, III, clxx—v.   [4] Bianchi, *Diplomazia* VIII,
497 *et seq.* Despatch to Villamarina, and Circular of May 24.   [5] Cambray-
Digny, *Carteggio. Ibid.* 40, 45, 48, 49.

the restoration of the Grand-Duke, or annexation to Piedmont. In reality, Cavour was determined not to let the Emperor steal a march on him, and had chosen the occasion to steal a march upon the Emperor. It was a breach of the implied bargain between the allies, the opening of the rift which led towards Villafranca.

The new move of Piedmont for the time overshadowed the mission of the Prince Imperial. It awakened all the self-conscious pride which the nobility and upper middle classes felt in Tuscan autonomy. Ridolfi complained indignantly that Piedmont wanted to swallow Tuscany little by little, as the snake sucked and devoured the frog.[1] Ricasoli himself was furious, though for a different reason. He saw to it that Cavour's agent, Nigra, was bundled unceremoniously back to Turin. He told Corsini that he, who put the national idea before everything else, deplored Nigra's mission as a folly devoid of all political sense.[2] Corsini could show his letter to Cavour, or to anyone he liked. Then, when the Piedmontese journals took up the tale and accused Tuscany of indifference to the cause, he became more emphatic still. He had not expected that the seeds of discord would be blown from Turin. The Tuscan government and Italian victories would make the issue certain enough in Tuscany, if there was no foolish meddling.

' Is it not real stupidity to accuse Tuscany of municipalism and egoism? I do not see in all this either the mind, or the acuteness, of Cavour'.[3]

There was good reason for his complaints. Much work was to be done before Tuscany would be converted to fusion with Piedmont. Dall' Ongaro, in his biography of Ricasoli, wrote that to many it might well seem an insensate abdication, the sacrifice of Athens to Macedonia, for Tuscany to throw all her memories, all her glories, all her hopes, at the feet of the roughest and newest province of Italy. ' Wrong! ' wrote Ricasoli in the margin of his

[1] *Ibid.* 37. [2] *L. & D.*, III, 53. [3] *L. & D.*, III, 76.

copy,[1] 'it is to Italy, and not to rough provinces!' In
June and July of 1859, the most cultured of the Tuscans
would not have agreed with him. Vieusseux, who had
been at the centre of every literary movement of note for
the last forty years, denied that the sentiment for Tuscan
autonomy was narrow municipalism. ' It can go excellently
in accord with the most lively desire for national independence. It is founded in Tuscany, more than in other parts
of Italy, on history, language, affections, geographical
conditions'.[2] Gino Capponi, renowned through Europe
as a sage and the friend of sages, was afraid lest union with
Piedmont would take from Tuscany her personality and
make her ' mere commercial stuff'. He was willing that
there should be military and diplomatic union during the
war, ' but when it comes to the negotiations, it is a different
matter. Here Tuscany should take again her person and
have the right to it, and she cannot be absorbed. Among
other things, Europe would never consent to it'.[3] A
correspondent of Cambray-Digny,[4] who himself would
have preferred, at this time, a separate Tuscany under a
prince of the house of Savoy, wrote that nearly everyone
of note favoured a separate kingdom. Annexation to
Piedmont was supported only by the brothers Ricasoli,
by Corsi, Peruzzi, and the hot-heads of the piazza. Of the
men mentioned, Peruzzi, at any rate, had a very uncertain
faith. Ridolfi told Neri Corsini that he did not wish his
name to pass down to history as that of a traitor to his
country.[5] Lambruschini wrote to Ricasoli that Tuscany, if
she passed to Piedmont, ' would cease to be what she has
been, and what she is, would cease to be of service to
Italy'.[6] In letters of increasing alarm he protested against
the policy to which Ricasoli was lending himself, till at
last his friend told him that he argued just like the Austrians,
saying that the nationalists were only an aggressive
minority. Ricasoli, on his part, declared, that fusion with

[1] Dall' Ongaro, *op. cit.* p. 60.   [2] A. Linaker, *Enrico Meyer*, I, 270.
[3] Capponi, *Lettere*, III, 262.   [4] Cambray-Digny, *Carteggio*, 26 *et seq.*
[5] *Ibid.* 52.   [6] *L. & D.*, III, 58, 107.

Piedmont was 'the sentiment of the majority, and the most lively'.[1] It was certainly the sentiment of the most lively, partly because it was the sentiment of Ricasoli himself. His own lively activity had as its chief aim the creation of an echo to his own voice which he could welcome and reverence (for he was a good liberal) as the voice of the majority.

No sooner, therefore, were the autonomists reassured by the recall of Nigra, and by a radical modification in Cavour's plans,[2] than they were scandalised to find Ricasoli himself taking the lead in that very propaganda for which he had rated Cavour. Ridolfi discovered in circulation an address to Victor Emmanuel, hailing him without equivocation as ' King of United Italy'.[3] The address, he knew, could not have been published without the sanction of the Minister of the Interior, since it was displayed for signature in public places. Then he discovered that the minister himself, and his colleague for ecclesiastical affairs, were among the signatories. He at once made a scene, and threatened resignation. The two ministers were forced to withdraw their signatures, not by the caution and petulance of Ridolfi, but by a threat from no less a person than the French ambassador.[4]

The new minister of ecclesiastical affairs was Salvagnoli himself, who, according to the Emperor's wish, had entered the cabinet. If Napoleon had hoped that he would have from Salvagnoli continued support for a central Italian kingdom under a French sovereign, he must have been roughly disillusioned. Ricasoli and Salvagnoli entered again into their old partnership, the former supplying moral force and an unwavering will, the latter spurring on his friend with fertile suggestions and expedients. The

---

[1] *L. & D.*, III, 122.   [2] His points were (1) separate administration for Tuscany; (2) Tuscan war management and diplomatic service under Piedmontese control; (3) Soldiers to take oath to Victor Emmanuel. Bianchi, *op. cit.* VIII, 500, 502   [3] *Poggi*, I, 82 *et seq.* A copy of this address, signed by Ricasoli and Salvagnoli, is in *Brolio MSS.*, Q. 26.   [4] *L. & D.*, III, 92. Cambray-Digny, *Carteggio*, 65.

two friends occupied adjacent rooms in the *palazzo*
Vecchio, they dined together whenever occasion offered,[1]
and even so, they found opportunity for exchanging
frequent letters. The other ministers showed signs of
resenting this cabinet within a cabinet. Ridolfi, in particular, was vexed to see his two colleagues come to council
meetings with cut and dried policies and plans, to mark
how they forced a quick discussion, and then retired again
to their own work without paying much attention to the
labours and proposals of others.[2] The finance minister,
Busacca, took his lead from Ricasoli, and since the war
ministry was being kept vacant for a Piedmontese officer,
it was plain that the party of movement would have an
unquestioned majority in the government. The most
faithful supporter of Ridolfi was the Minister of Justice,
Enrico Poggi, a little round man. He was a capable lawyer,
and later wrote excellent memoirs dealing with his year
of power. All his instincts were for moderation and con-
ciliation, and his own memoirs show him as one disposed
to govern by a series of pleasant chats. He went with the
times, and became an annexationist before Ridolfi, but
from time to time the placid surface of his character was
ruffled with resentment at the high-handedness of Ricasoli.
He, Enrico Poggi, had risked his fortunes and those of
his faithful wife and numerous family to serve his country!
The middle classes had their virtues as well as the haughty
aristocracy! Ricasoli should not have forgotten it!

A day or two after his forced retreat in the matter of the
address to Victor Emmanuel, Ricasoli sought an interview
with Boncompagni, and made the head of the state understand exactly what his principles were, and therefore what
policies he was compelled to follow.

'I am firm in the policy of Italian unity, and I wish that Tuscany should
have the merit of casting away the policies of circumstance, such as fusion
with Piedmont, protectorate, etc., to put in their place the formula of
Victor Emmanuel, King of Italy, with the hereditary title in his dynasty.
The autonomy that Tuscany should desire is that of grandeur of ideas. . . .
Tuscany's task is to make the new Kingdom of Italy'.[3]

[1] *L. & D.*, III, 124.   [2] *Poggi*, I, 81.   [3] *L. & D.*, III, 96 (to Salvagnoli).

Such a programme was more revolutionary than any that had been put forward. Annexation to Piedmont seemed radical enough, but it could be kept within the old formula, a little stretched, of the Kingdom of *High Italy*. That was the very extreme which Napoleon and European diplomacy was prepared even to consider. Even so, Napoleon was resolved, High Italy must not cross the Apennines. But Ricasoli, no more than Capponi, would consider Tuscany as a province of Piedmont. Her destiny was to be a member of *Italy*, of Italy and nothing less. His words were not empty. Magenta had been fought six days before, the Austrians were back to the Mincio, the Duchies and Legations were ready to acclaim Victor Emmanuel. 'Italy', exclaimed Ricasoli, 'will be one to the Garigliano. But a little, and she will be one to the Pharos'.[1]

That very day, June 12, he brought into the cabinet a plan which threw his colleagues into confusion, and once again threatened a dissolution of the government.[2] The government, he said, must immediately vote the union of Tuscany and Piedmont. Otherwise there would be a rising of the Piazza. There may have been some truth in what he said, but those who knew him well did not doubt that he himself had let the restless Genius out of the bottle.[3] The autonomists in the cabinet maintained strongly that a government which held no mandate from the people could not by mere decree settle the destinies of the country; but in the end the cabinet unanimously approved an edict which, reciting the successes achieved by allied arms, the gathering of the trans-Apennine peoples round the throne of Victor Emmanuel, and the desire of Tuscany to co-operate in the formation of a strong and united Italy, called together the *Consulta* (a body which hitherto had existed only on paper[4]) 'to pronounce an opinion on the proclamation of the national sovereignty of Victor Emmanuel II'. Thus the government had at last pro-

---

[1] *L. & D.*, III, 97. [2] *Poggi*, I, 91 *et seq.* [3] Cambray-Digny, *Carteggio*, 82. [4] The chief business of its members had been to attend *feste*. See *Carteggio. Lambruschini, Cassetta* 14. 1, 2, 4.

nounced, perhaps with some indecision, the creed of unity. This time it was Cavour who held back. Some suspected that he was piqued by the reception which his own move had received at the hands of the Tuscans; others called to mind that the decree of the Tuscan government had too close a resemblance to a recent resolution of the National Society, which by demanding a union of all Italy raised the questions of Rome and Naples. At Turin, it was insisted in political circles that the Tuscan ministers, whether they liked it or not, held their powers only by delegation from Victor Emmanuel himself, and that therefore they had no right to any initiative in deciding the lot of the country.[1] In fact, the real reason of Cavour's veto sprang from the impossibility of sanctioning a step which ran counter to every plan of Napoleon III.[2]

But Ricasoli was determined that Tuscany should make a profession of faith before Europe. He and Salvagnoli called in the aid of Dolfi, and sticklers for legality were aggravated and alarmed when the Florentine baker sent round to the *gonfalonieri* an address which expressed the desire of the Tuscans for union to an Italy under the sceptre of Victor Emmanuel.[3] The *gonfalonieri* were invited to call together the municipal councils, and, after these had voted adhesion to the address, to send it back, with signatures, to Dolfi himself. The thin pretence that the Minister of the Interior was a passive spectator in the affair, deceived nobody. An article in the *Monitore* explained the true position to all who cared to read. Ricasoli, indeed, notified the prefects that they must leave the municipal bodies free in their voting, and protested that the government had no part nor lot in the address. He added, however, that they were to 'illuminate' the voters, so that the municipalities might refute the calumny directed against Tuscany, that she wished to oppose the will of the nation, 'maintaining those divisions of territory by which

[1] Cambray-Digny, *Carteggio*, 72–82, 89, for these speculations. [2] *Ibid.* 84. Cf. 153 *et seq.* Piedmont would have rather had soldiers than votes. [3] See *Della Torre*, 156–7.

Italy was prevented from taking her place among the independent nations, or minimising the homage to King Victor Emmanuel, whose name symbolises the independence, union, liberty of the Italian peoples'.[1] The prefects, quite certain that they understood the master, 'illuminated' opinion with vigour. Bossini, the prefect of Florence, whom Ricasoli had learnt to know in the Maremma and had marked down as a useful man,[2] may be seen at work in the little commune of Firenzuola. The council would not adhere to Dolfi's address, and as a result received a very direct reminder from the prefect, acting under Ricasoli's orders. A miscellaneous crowd of local patriots did the rest.[3]

The voices of the autonomists were raised in alarm and anger. There was another cabinet crisis. The quarrel was taken up outside the *palazzo* Vecchio, and pamphleteers, one of them a volunteer of '48, warned the people that they must respect the will of Napoleon III.[4] Other pamphleteers gave answer.[5] Cavour, prompted by the Emperor, planned to recall Boncompagni and to send D'Azeglio with a proclamation calling on the Tuscans to suspend their discussion till the end of the war.[6] Lambruschini wrote to his friend,[7] the minister responsible for all the trouble, rebuking him for allowing himself to be dragged at the heels of a noisy chattering faction of the cities. Still more, he warned Ricasoli not to be led on by ' an abstract idea'. An abstract idea! Was *Il Re Galantuomo* an abstract idea? Ricasoli exulted as the reports came in that one

---

[1] *Atti*, I, 236. [2] *Rassegna Nazionale*, 1905, October 1, p. 414.
[3] *Rassegna Storica del Risorg. Ital.*, 1908, I, 407. The final result of the voting throughout Tuscany was given as 225 *pro*, 1 *contra*, 20 abstained. *Atti*, II, 175. Ricasoli was in touch with radical patriots in the various districts. *e.g. Brolio MSS.*, 31, 11. (Orlandini reports on Pisa, Livorno, Lucca.) For a very critical analysis of the figures see Della Torre, *op. cit.* 234. [4] E. Alberì, *La Toscana durante la guerra dell' indipendenza*. A. Conti, *Napoleono III, o la norma degli Italiani*. [5] *La Toscana dopo il 27 Aprile*, M. Carletti, *La Fusione*, and others. [6] Cambray-Digny, *Carteggio*, 191-2. [7] *L. & D.*, III, 115. Cf. Capponi, *Lettere*, 113-116; Digny, *Carteggio*, 137 *et seq.*

municipality after another had adhered to the address.
He had told his friends of Piedmont, he declared, that
they had only to wait and Tuscany would prove herself.
'I kept saying to all . . . "Be good, for Tuscany is
more Italian than you believe, and the day will come when
she will show it to you worthily". The day has come, and
she shows it!'[1] Napoleon might like it or he might not,
but he would have to learn that a People was not a 'flock
of sheep'. There must be no more talk of Piedmont, nor
of Florence, nor of Tuscany, nor of fusions, nor of annexa-
tions, but only of Italy, and Victor Emmanuel.

Then, very suddenly, there came the news that Napoleon,
whose education the baron had been willing to undertake,
had asserted himself in an unexpected manner by signing
an armistice with the enemy while victory was only half
won. Consternation filled Florence, as it filled Turin.
Ricasoli took a decision. It would be as well to have a
newspaper, 'apart from the government . . . but in
accord with the government'. Some of his supporters had
been urging this course upon him, but he had turned a
deaf ear. They saw him now, calm and erect, amid an
agitated crowd in the *palazzo* Vecchio. He called them
to him, and said: 'I want the newspaper for to-morrow'.[2]
He was not shaken by the disaster which shook the temper
and resolution of Cavour. He had known nothing of the
conversations of Plombières, and cared nothing; he understood little of the confused threads of European politics,
and cared little. Other men's motives were as a rule beyond
his understanding. He held lodged in his mind one single
idea, the product of every belief, every thought, every
experience of his toilsome life. 'The formation of a great
kingdom of Italy under the constitutional sceptre of Victor
Emmanuel', he wrote that evening, 'is demanded by
good sense, morality, and civilisation'. He added that it
was demanded by the European equilibrium, by Reason,

[1] *L. & D.*, III, 136. [2] A. D'Ancona, *Ricordi ed Affetti*, 335–6. Cf.
G. Barbèra, *Memorie*, 162.

by Humanity, by Christianity.[1] What was Napoleon, and what was diplomacy, that they should prevail against such a combination?

Convinced that Providence would know how to break wicked treaties and overthrow absurd policies, Ricasoli went steadily upon his way.

[1] *L. & D.*, III, 142 (July 8 to V. Ricasoli).

APPENDIX II

PRINCE JEROME IN TUSCANY

CAVOUR officially denied that the Emperor had designs on Tuscany. (Bianchi, *Diplomazia*, Vol. VIII, 497, 499.) Kossuth (*Souvenirs et écrits de mon exil, période de la guerre d'Italie*, Paris, 1880, pp. 166–8) also denies it. These denials were not believed in government circles (Cambray-Digny, *Carteggio*, p. 27). Corsini, in despatches of May 17 and 20 (Poggi, *Memorie*, Vol. III, Appendix 5) maintained that the Emperor had hopes which, because of circumstances, he could not turn into projects. This seems the most likely interpretation of his conduct. The emperor's despatches to the prince are printed in Alfredo Commandini, *Il principe Napoleone nel Risorgimento Italiano* (Milano, 1922), pp. 126 *et seq.* In giving his cousin his marching orders, the Emperor spoke of the danger of socialism (May 17). In the instructions of May 18, he ordered him to await orders and reinforcements in Florence, and to send on the Tuscans as an advanced guard. He was not to enter the Papal States unless the Austrians violated their neutrality. In a letter of May 20 he enclosed the draft of a proclamation and his own corrections to it. (The proclamation, which announced that the mission was solely military, had been obtained by Cavour's pressure.) The first definite mention of politics is in a letter of May 24, when the Emperor suggested that his cousin might have a part to play in calling back the hereditary prince. He sent 20,000 lire for secret service funds. On June 1 Napoleon instructed the prince that he must limit himself to alarming the Austrians, and must try to put them in the wrong by making them violate the neutrality of the Papal States. The one thing that appears clearly from this series of orders is that the dispatch of the fifth army corps to Tuscany had not even the slightest military justification.

From the Prince's answers, it is equally apparent that he was not a party to any of the Emperor's vague political schemes. Cecconi (*Il Principe Napoleone in Toscana*, Roma, 1891) records that the French officers used aggressive language. Baron du Casse (in *Revue historique*, 1898, Vol. 66, 301–23; Vol. 67, 36–58) accuses the prince of having designs on Tuscany. This article is severely handled by J. Bicchierai (*Archivio Storico Italiano*, 5 *serie*, Vol. 22, 417–427). The prince's letters to the Emperor show that he disliked his task in Tuscany, and that he continually demanded his marching orders. He abused the Tuscan officers, quarrelled with Boncompagni, and described the Tuscans as a nation of eunuchs led by women. He rejected with scorn the suggestion that he might possibly work for the return of the hereditary prince (Commandini, *loc. cit.*). He was overjoyed when, on June 16, he was able to depart, the reluctant Emperor having at last given permission. His public behaviour in Tuscany was exemplary (*Rubieri*, 144 and 171). In private, he stoutly championed annexation to Piedmont (A. Linaker, *Enrico Meyer*, Vol. 1, 270 *et seq.*). Peruzzi was able to remind him later that he himself had combatted most effectively any idea of his own candidature. (Letter of August 24 to Galeotti, in *Lettere Politiche*, Zanichelli.) Evidence of similar import could be multiplied to prove that the prince himself did not share in any dreams of his Emperor's.

After the preliminaries of Villafranca, conditions changed. The Tuscan diplomatists, while they knew clearly enough the mind of official French diplomacy, were able to understand through Conneau and others in the Emperor's immediate circle that his plans did not correspond with those of Walewski. Their judgment of the situation may be summed up in one of Peruzzi's despatches. Napoleon had, Peruzzi reported, no *plan* for the candidature of the prince imperial, but he was not extraneous to the intrigues that favoured it, was divided between hopes and fears, and would be glad if the matter could be resolved by a successful *coup*. (For Peruzzi's despatches, and others, see *Poggi*, Vol. 3, Documents 21–25, 44, 55, 69, 83. Cf. Zanichelli, *Lettere Politiche*.) This time the prince himself was not extraneous to the intrigues. In August his aide-de-camp approached Peruzzi, who maintained that the candidature was dead, but was induced to play with the idea of a regency for the prince, as a scarecrow to the dynasty of Lorraine (*Lettere Politiche*, Sec. 2, No. 4, August 24). In October, the prince set this idea aside, and counselled a regency of Cavour, the Prince of Carignano, or D'Azeglio (*L. & D.*, 432; Bianchi, *Diplomazia*, Vol. 8, 608). It is difficult to say whether or not he was acting in good faith. All the diplomatists, even Corsini, got entangled in the various intrigues, but Ricasoli serenely disregarded them.

CHAPTER VIII

THE DICTATOR (JULY 13–DECEMBER 3, 1859)

On July 13 there came to Florence the news that the two Emperors had signed, on the previous day, preliminaries of peace at Villafranca. The fears aroused by the news of the armistice now became certainties. Italy was to be a confederation under the presidency of the Pope, Venetia was to be left to Austria, the expelled princes of central Italy were to return. A mob invaded the office of the *Monitore*, and destroyed the type which was diffusing this gloomy news. There was an attempt to insult the French embassy;[1] and in the shops, the portraits of Napoleon III gave place to those of his attempted assassin. The nationalists were desperate, for their ally had deserted them, and their great leader, Cavour, had resigned, after exchanging bitter words with his King.

Yet neither Cavour nor the King had failed Italy in the crisis. Victor Emmanuel had signed the preliminaries only ' as far as they concerned him'. A few days later he told a Tuscan emissary that he expected all Italians to have faith in him, that he hoped much from the expected Congress, that he hoped more from a renewal of the war. Central Italy must remain tranquil, and refuse to receive back her old dynasties.[2] Cavour, while he threatened to make himself a conspirator and a revolutionary, while he vowed to place himself under the orders of D'Azeglio as a simple soldier seeking death for Italy,[3] had not left his post without giving marching orders to the people of Central Italy. Farini, whom he had officially recalled from Modena, returned thither as a simple citizen and became dictator, and Cavour telegraphed to him 'Arms and money'. To the Tuscans his instructions were precise: ' No terms with the fallen dynasty. No disorder. A vote

---

[1] *Rubieri. Brolio MSS.*, 33–51. Cf. 31, 136; 31, 141, 142, 148, 149.
[2] *L. & D.*, III, 160. Notes of C. Bianchi. [3] Chiala, *op. cit.* III, ccxxiii.

for union with Piedmont, on the earliest possible occasion.
Ricasoli, dictator'.[1]

Less than a year later he wrote: 'How many times
. . . have I not exclaimed: Blessed be the peace of Villafranca'.[2] The two men whom he had marked down to
continue his work in central Italy had achieved more in
peace than his own policy and the Piedmontese soldiers
could have won in war. The first of these men, Farini,
displayed a resolution and a resourcefulness equal to
those of Cavour himself. Farini had all the passion of the
conspirator, but also the elasticity of the politician and the
acuteness of the political student. He was a Romagnol,
of the middle classes, luxurious, cultivated, a man of
expedients in whom the reasoning faculty was predominant,
a man after Cavour's own heart. The second leader,
Ricasoli, was moved by a religious and political mysticism
which contrasted strongly with Cavour's practical and
positive temperament. In the months that followed,
Ricasoli's obstinacy more than once awoke in Cavour the
most profound irritation, till at last he burst out in petulant
anger against his ' pig-headedness and asinine stupidity'.[3]
Yet Ricasoli never wavered nor lost faith when Cavour
himself doubted and was ready to compromise.[4]

The news of Villafranca had awakened in Ricasoli one
very profound conviction. He felt, as if by revelation, that
his own life mattered nothing. He declared that a great
faith had come to him, and that because of it he had
' spat upon his own life', with its old affections and its
old duties. He would have killed himself, he would have
killed his daughter, rather than fail the cause which
Providence had raised him up to serve.[5] The instrument
would be true, though God might cast it away. When the
work was almost finished and triumph was in sight, he
challenged the world to point to one single word, one
single act which would show that he had compromised or

[1] L. & D., III, 160. [2] Chiala, op. cit. III, 187. [3] Michelangelo
Castelli, Ricordi, 216. [4] See next page. [5] Note to Dall' Ongaro, p.4. L. &
D., IV, 311; X, 385.

hesitated even for twenty-four hours.[1] He called to his aid the twelve centuries of his proud ancestry. ' Go and tell those gentlemen', he said to one who left him on a private mission to Paris, ' that I have twelve centuries of existence. I am the last of my line, and I will give the last drop of my blood to maintain the integrity of my political programme'.[2] The programme, which to many was an affair of passions and interests, ordinary enough, was to Ricasoli a struggle of Light against Darkness.

' If we succeed in completing this work', he wrote, ' it will be such a monument of civilisation as has not been dreamed of in the past'.[3]

And he said again,

' The Italian question, let us not deceive ourselves, is not a question of miserable interests. It is a solution of those principles without which there can be no more peace in the world. Once these are settled, once humanity is organised on this basis, there will be no more war in the world'.[4]

Mazzini might have claimed him as a convert. The faith of the two men was the same, and each of them, in his different sphere, fought for it with the same passionate, uncompromising devotion. In July of 1859 victory seemed almost impossible. Piedmont seemed to have given up the struggle. The new ministry, which had La Marmora for president and Rattazzi as its leading spirit, felt that it could do no more than wait for the final signing of peace at Zurich, and hope that the firmness of central Italy and the continued benevolence of Napoleon might make possible the partial realisation of Italian hopes. La Marmora counselled Ricasoli to bow to the inevitable, and to receive back the old dynasty on the best terms that he could get.

' Tell General La Marmora', the baron wrote to his brother, ' that I have torn his letter into a thousand pieces'.[5]

In the past months the Piedmontese had complained of the pettiness of the Tuscans, and of the poor aid which they gave to Italy in her struggle for independence.[6]

[1] L. & D., IV, 228.   [2] Dall' Ongaro, 50.   [3] L. & D., IV, 307.
[4] L. & D., IV, 135.   [5] L. & D., III, 181.   [6] Cambray-Digny, Carteggio, passim.

Ricasoli now proved that Tuscany, if she had not the trained army of Piedmont, could stand fire in another way; and lamented the cowardice and irresolution of Turin. 'In brief', he declared, 'it is our lot to receive from Piedmont all that can give us trouble, and nothing that can be of any use'.[1] The Piedmontese minister for war, Dabormida, reminded him that he was not in constant relations with the great Powers, and therefore free to declaim against the realities of politics.[2] Ricasoli cared nothing for the realities of politics, but only for his principle. Had he been a good politician, he would not have won the battle.

The key to the situation was the policy of France. Within two days the Tuscans knew through Corsini, and through Bianchi, who had been despatched post-haste to Turin on a special mission, that there need be no fear of a restoration carried out with battalions of Croats, like that of 1849. The preliminaries of Villafranca laid it down that the expelled princes should re-enter their states, but they did not stipulate that they should be restored by force of arms. The Emperor was too much concerned with the balance of power and with his own prestige to stand idly by while the enemy whom he had defeated at Magenta and Solferino marched back unhindered to the lordship of central Italy. The envoys told their government,[3] and Ricasoli at once told the country,[4] that if the Tuscans remained tranquil they would still be able to decide their own destinies. Yet in the months that followed it became clear that, though Napoleon III was willing to disavow plainly enough his minister's threats of a restoration of the dynasty, he was resolved to struggle to the last against the union of Tuscany and Piedmont. His reasons were definite and plain. Parma and Modena did not matter so much, and in a sense Farini had an easier battle than Ricasoli. But Tuscany was the political pivot of the peninsula.

'If annexation crossed the Apennines', Napoleon declared to Pepoli

[1] *L. & D.*, III, 197.   [2] *L. & D.*, III, 351.   [3] *L. & D.*, III, 151, 156.   [4] *Atti*, I, 300.

on July 15, ' Unity would be made, and I do not wish unity. I want only independence. Unity would bring danger to me in France herself, because of the Roman question, and France would not with pleasure see arise on her flank a great nation which might diminish her preponderance'.[1]

These were sound reasons of policy, and there was not a prominent man in Tuscany, save Ricasoli, who did not at one time or another believe that the little state would have to come to terms with her great protector. Cavour himself, early in August, counselled Tuscany to work for union, but to accept in the end a compromise which would establish a government of Italian temper in Florence.[2] Ricasoli, wholly inexperienced as he was in international politics, saw the situation more clearly. One day in his room at the *palazzo* Vecchio—it might have been any day in July, August, or September—he wrote down on a little sheet of rough paper:[3]

'Emperor does not believe himself sufficiently loosed from the obligations of Villafranca to give any other counsel than restoration with ample guarantees for independence and liberty. Emperor is always most decided not to permit any intervention . . . says that his obligations have no other limits than those of the possible, recommending as essential order. Hence we hold our fate always in our hands'.

Ricasoli did not appreciate the reasons of state which made Napoleon's opposition to union a matter of prime political importance. He probably knew little of the nice balance between the Catholic and nationalist parties in France, which made the weak joint in the Imperial armour. But he did know that the Emperor would not and could not permit an Austrian invasion of central Italy. This was why the bold spokesman of a small, weak state, was able to force his will on the absolute monarch of a great nation. By refusing every alternative, save one, to intervention, he forced Napoleon in the end to choose the lesser of two evils and to seek compensation elsewhere.

The curious diplomatic struggle may be illustrated by the story which the *Comte* de Reiset tells of his mission to

[1] Chiala, *Lettere di Cavour*, III, ccxxxviii.   [2] *Ibid.* III, 121. Cavour to Massari, 10/8/1859.   [3] *Brolio MSS.*, Q. 55.

Italy in August of this year.[1] Walewski, the French foreign
minister, who fought without truce for the execution of
the preliminaries of Villafranca, introduced de Reiset into
the presence of the Emperor, who opened the interview
by asserting the necessity of carrying out the Treaty of
Villafranca. ' It is important', the envoy answered, ' that
the Italians should not have the shadow of doubt as to
what is the will of the Emperor'. But when he arrived in
Italy, he found that all the Italians claimed to know much
more about the intentions of the Emperor than he did
himself—to know, in particular, that Napoleon had not
the least intention of executing the treaty, or demanding
its execution. The record of his conversations with Farini,
with Pepoli, with Minghetti, with Cipriani, suggests the
remark of Massari, that all Italy had become Macchiavelli.
But at Florence de Reiset found a temper still more disturbing than that of Macchiavelli. He had never seen
people so insolent, so obstinate, as the Florentines. Ricasoli,
with little care for the diplomatic conventions, told him
that the Emperor, in taking up the cause of Italy, had put
his feet in a machine which would swallow up all his body.
—' L'Italie', osa-t-il dire, ' est une machine à vapeur
dans l'engrénage de laquelle l'Empereur a mis le pied,
tout son corps y passera'.—De Reiset replied that a gulf
of disaster was opening for Tuscany and its dictator; but
Ricasoli was ready to turn Mazzinian, and answered that
if he was engulfed, he was at least certain of being engulfed
and destroyed with the envoy's sovereign. De Reiset was
scandalised and furious, and reminded Ricasoli that the
French troops remained in Italy, and that a word of
command would suffice to bring them, with flags flying
and drums beating, to chastise Tuscan insolence. But
Ricasoli knew that the Emperor must keep his troops
where they were, to prevent the Austrians from doing
this very thing.

Ricasoli had not been made dictator, as Cavour would
have wished. Even before Bianchi had reported the advice

[1] Comte de Reiset. *Mes Souvenirs* (Paris, 1903), Vol. III, pp. 1–45.

of the fallen statesman, Ricasoli and Salvagnoli had tried
to force through this very plan, by presenting their resig-
nations in a meeting of the ministers.[1] Their colleagues,
Ridolfi and Poggi, refused to follow suit, being determined not to open the way of dictatorship to a man who
had combated at every turn their attempts to safeguard
Tuscan autonomy. This resistance was strengthened by
the attitude of Boncompagni, who was eager to play a
part of his own. Cambray-Digny, who had been one of
the Tuscan envoys in Piedmont, came to Florence bearing
Cavour's recommendation that the commissary should
retire at once to make place for Ricasoli (a similar course
had been followed in the Duchies); but Boncompagni
lingered, and tried to persuade the King to let him remain,
at least until Tuscany was ready to declare her own will.[2]
Thus it was that he did not transfer his powers to the
Tuscan government till August 1, and that he then transferred them, not to Ricasoli as dictator, but to the whole
ministry, of which Ricasoli was merely president.[3] The
minister Poggi, who together with Ridolfi had achieved
this success, was wont to reflect indignantly that the
minister who overshadowed him was, after all, only a
colleague with titular supremacy, and a department of his
own to look after. In fact, Ricasoli made himself a dictator
with authority as real as Farini's, by the sheer force of his
will.

Cambray-Digny, who had on occasion been an unfriendly
critic of Ricasoli's policy and methods, saw now that he
was the only man for the task.[4] ' Bettino is admirable.
He goes unruffled and undoubting on his way'. ' Remember that the country, in general, trusts in Bettino,
and trusts little in the others'. Even his adversaries,
reported Digny, believed in him. The same perfect confidence in Ricasoli is apparent in the letters of Capponi;
and the old liberal, whose criticisms and judgments on
the persons and events of his day were as acute as his

[1] *Poggi*, I, 114–7. See *Della Torre*, 184.   [2] Cambray-Digny, *Carteggio*,
183–186, 188.   [3] *Ridolfi*, 273.   [4] Cambray-Digny, *op. cit.* 181, 182, 185.

reflections on history, was ready at times to distrust even his own opinions because of his trust in Ricasoli.[1] The best of the Tuscan diplomatists, all of whom were under Ridolfi's authority, carried on a double correspondence: with Ricasoli, as well as with their immediate chief. Peruzzi decided to write, in matters of importance, not to the minister of Foreign Affairs, whom he did not trust, but to the Minister of the Interior.[2] A typical illustration of Ricasoli's unchallenged authority is to be found in a single phrase from a letter of Salvagnoli's. Ricasoli had sent him to Turin, without mentioning the matter to his colleagues; and Salvagnoli, finding that Tuscan diplomacy in Piedmont was being managed in a rather slipshod fashion, wrote back: ' You must discipline the diplomatic side'.[3] Ricasoli disciplined it, and Ridolfi came more and more to seek compensation in an unfortunate but well-meaning attempt to make Florence once again a city of creative art.

The same calm assumption of authority is apparent in Ricasoli's relations with his other colleagues. The Minister of Justice and Grace nursed his vexation as he saw the President of the Council interfere, time and time again, with matters which did not concern his department. One day, when Ricasoli, discontented with the action of a magistrate at Grosseto, sent to Poggi a memorandum which made a sweeping attack on the whole magistracy, the little man's pent-up irritation burst out in a fit of temper. He swept out of the room, he resigned—and next day he withdrew his resignation. Ricasoli continued to act in exactly the same masterful manner. He worked hand in glove with Salvagnoli, and it was often the more ready mind of the latter which suggested the things which needed to be done and the way in which they should be done. Both men had the habit of sending to their colleagues short memoranda which had the appearance of the curtest

[1] Capponi, *Lettere*, III, 313 (September 27).   [2] *Lettere Politiche*, No. 2. Peruzzi to Galeotti, 24/8/1859.   [3] *L. & D.*, III, 419, 456.
[4] *Poggi*, I, 282 *et seq.*; II, 153–4. *L. & D.*, III, 311.

orders; and to Poggi, who felt very much that he too was saving his country (as, indeed he was, by the most praiseworthy industry and efficiency) this was very galling. But Ricasoli had too much to do, and was too accustomed to authority, to sweeten command with forms and ceremonies.

Despite his reliance upon Salvagnoli, it never occurred to anyone to suggest that the latter was the power behind the throne. One letter alone from Ricasoli to his friend would suffice to lay any doubts upon this score. In a moment of crisis, when Salvagnoli showed signs of losing his head, Ricasoli wrote sharply: 'Take care you obey me, and keep quiet. Send away all those who come to chatter of conspiracies. Go to bed. Good night'.[1] The Tuscan nationalists knew who was their real leader, and the municipalities, to the disgust of some of Ricasoli's colleagues, began to send messages of congratulation and encouragement, not to the government, but to the president alone.[2] People began to acclaim him in the streets, but it was part of his pride to distrust small vanities, and he let it be known that the practice displeased him. Yet even iron barons have their little weaknesses, and it pleased him to think that the applause continued despite his disapproval, and that the Florentines began to speak of him as *Bettino*.[3] . . . As for the world outside Tuscany, it believed that the will of Tuscany was nothing more nor less than the will of Ricasoli.

'All the diplomatists', wrote Salvagnoli to his chief, ' good or bad, believe that all the force against the restoration lies in Tuscany, and principally in you. Hence they believe that if you were taken out of the way, and Tuscany thrown into disorder, all would be finished'. [4]

Ricasoli won this unchallenged control by the energy and faith which he showed from the first minute when

---

[1] *L. & D.*, IV, 241.   [2] *Poggi*, II, 49. *Brolio MSS.*, T. 8. Ricasoli disapproved this action.   [3] An autograph note to *Dall' Ongaro*, p. 44. [4] *L. & D.*, III, 442 and 444.   Cf. *Revue des Deux Mondes*, January 15, 1860. Ricasoli, said the article, had been a unionist since 1848, and it was he alone who was forcing the country along the path it was taking.

the news of Villafranca came to Florence. He revealed his policy in a phrase. ' We must put ourselves at the head of the agitation',[1] he wrote to Salvagnoli. This meant, first of all, the most rigorous measures against suspected plotters for the old dynasty. Very precise were Ricasoli's orders to the prefect of Florence. At the least sign of disturbance the police was to make arrests. It was to disperse immediately even the most casual groups which the chatter-loving citizens might form in the streets, ' for such groups ' (Ricasoli did not forget 1848) ' are the origin and the nucleus of demonstrations'. ' I am averse to every sort of turbulence', he wrote again, ' and above all to that which comes from priests and peasants'. (He did not forget 1849.) ' I wish the first at the altar, and the second in the fields'.[2] Perhaps it was a mere coincidence, but a few days later the government brought joy to the peasants by removing an unpopular tax upon their dogs.[3] . . . In the capital, Dolfi payed a call upon the minister, and was given three hundred rifles to distribute among the faithful, for the maintenance of order.[4] A little later, Ricasoli decided to establish a national guard, and once again made use of the invaluable Dolfi in its organisation. It was a middle-class institution; so the minister hastened to calm democratic touchiness by announcing that he did not wish to make invidious distinctions, but only to lay the burden on those who were able to bear it. A reserve would be shortly formed, and all citizens who could give proof of their ' probity ' would be eligible as volunteers.[5] ' Probity', of course, would be judged by the nationalists with whom the minister was co-operating. He was arming the patriots against the reactionaries.

He had, in fact, sealed that *entente* with the radical nationalists, which, before the armistice, had caused so much dismay among the moderate champions of autonomy. The propaganda for union with Piedmont broke

[1] *L. & D.*, III, 149. [2] *L. & D.*, III, 152, 154-5. [3] Also the unpopular *tassa dei macelli*, which had been abolished in 1824 and reimposed after the restoration. Decree of July 17. [4] *Rubieri*, 192. [5] *Atti*, I, 360.

out with new passion,[1] and this time the opposition was weak. The armistice and the preliminaries of peace had sapped the autonomist position, for none who believed in the independence of Italy would care to enter the confederation sketched out at Villafranca, and all—Ridolfi, Poggi, Vieusseux, Lambruschini, as well as Ricasoli or Bartolommei—were bound together in opposition to a restoration.[2] From that they could be saved only by France and Piedmont; but their nearest protector was Piedmont, and they could only approach France effectively through the government of Victor Emmanuel. The autonomists, therefore, were ready to keep silence while the enthusiastic cried for annexation, or even to join in the cry, for they did not share Ricasoli's faith that Providence would hearken to it, and would also incline the ear of the Emperor. Many believed that it was good policy to demand a maximum in the hope of maintaining a minimum. The pamphleteers who advocated confederation and a central Italian state now set aside the question of principle, and fell back upon reasons of expediency, admitting implicitly or explicitly that confederation was only a second best.[3] These reasons explain why the *Consulta*, which had been a stronghold of the autonomists and which Ricasoli, therefore, had carefully kept upon one side, did not hesitate to follow Ricasoli's lead by calling on the government to take every means whereby it might secure respect for the free vote of the Tuscans, and to call together an Assembly through which this vote might legally manifest itself.

This resolution was passed[4] on July 14, and the government immediately began its preparations for the elections. The *Consulta* had called on the government to re-establish the electoral law of 1848, its real fear being that a wider

---

[1] Annexationist pamphlets published at this time were: R. Volpi. *La Toscana abbandonata da Leopoldo II, ha trovato un padrone migliore. La neutralita degli stati italiani e l'indipendenza* (anonymous). Niccolini's *Poesie Nazionali* were also published as propaganda.   [2] *e.g.* Capponi, *Lettere*, III, 276–277.   [3] *e.g.* A. Gori, *Interesse della Toscana.*   [4] *Atti*, I, 313–314.

franchise might open the way of influence to the priests
and the peasants, and thereby provoke undesired results.[1]
From the Emperor[2] and from Guerrazzi,[3] who was at
Genoa, there came counsels to the government to trust to
universal suffrage; but it is noteworthy that this suggestion, whatever form it took, always awakened the most
profound disquiet in the Tuscan leaders.[4] There were
modifications of the law of 1848, but in a restrictive and
partisan sense. Special measures were taken to minimise
the influence of the priests and of noble reactionaries.
The army officers, who were discontented and good
material either for Mazzinian or for reactionary propaganda, were not allowed to vote. The supporters of the
old order were harassed by constant pressure exercised
by the government agents; and for the most part they
abstained from voting.[5] The action of the government
was, as ever, supplemented by the voluntary efforts of the
nationalists. There were local committees which demanded
' professions of faith ' from candidates, or imposed upon
them ' imperative mandates'.[6] The inner working of the
elections may be illustrated from three letters which Ricasoli wrote to his brother Vincenzo. On the fourth of
August he wrote: ' I should like you to be elected a
deputy'. On the fifth of August: ' I believe that you will
be elected a deputy'. On the sixth of August: ' I am
assured that you will be deputy of Grosseto'.[7] The government and its defenders maintained stoutly that the elections
had been free.[8] They pointed to the total lack of government candidates, and to the instructions sent to the prefects
that they must respect the liberty of voting. All this was

---

[1] Capponi *Lettere*, III, 276. This is definitely stated.   [2] *L. & D.*,
III, 158.   [3] Guerrazzi, *Scritti Politici*, 620 *et seq.*   [4] See *Lettere Politiche*
(ed., Zanichelli), pp. 106 and 166. Peruzzi lost his balance in combating
Walewski at Paris, and in a moment of impulsiveness suggested the trial
of a plebiscite. Corsini, at London, suggested ways of retracing this false
step.   [5] The whole matter is carefully treated by *Della Torre*, 263–279.
See *L. & D.*, III, 173–4.   [6] Cf. *Rubieri*, 200.   [7] *L. & D.*, III, 198,
200, 206.   [8] *e.g.* L. Galeotti, *L'Assemblea Toscana*, *passim*. M. Carletti,
Quattro Mesi di Storia Toscana, 109 *et seq.*

true, because Ricasoli was the ideal nationalist dictator. It would have been poor policy to shock Europe with elections that were obviously a farce, and such a course of action would have shocked still more the sturdy liberal conscience of the baron himself. As ever, he did not bludgeon opinion, but he 'illuminated' it, which was much more effective. In his manifesto to the electors he announced to them that they were perfectly free, but added that they were morally free to choose the cause of duty only.[1] The limitations which morality opposed to anarchical freedom were brought home to Tuscans in the manner which has been indicated. One side possessed a monopoly of organisation, a monopoly of government support, exercised through the prefects, and a monopoly of propaganda. Pamphlet after pamphlet drove home the arguments which were being dinned into the ears of the people by articles in the *Monitore* and the *Nazione*.[2] Not a word could be said on the other side, for, as Ricasoli expressed it in one of his circulars, 'the government, faithful executor of the wisdom of the country, has left to the press in these difficult times liberty to help, and not to harm, the national cause'.[3] Ricasoli, the sincerest and most moral of dictators, saw no reason to conceal the assumption which lies behind every idealistic nationalist revolution. There is a 'real will' of the people, it is assumed, which is something very different from those whims and egoisms which might be reflected in an assembly elected without discipline and without 'illumination'. The real will is conceived of as some great destiny necessary for the grandeur and the morality of the nation, and as the struggle to achieve this destiny. The protagonists in that struggle never doubt that they have interpreted the destiny aright. If they did, their efforts would be devoid of those

---

[1] *Atti*, II, 46.   [2] Among pamphlets published at this time were: *Come finirà—Leopoldo II e la Toscana. Parole di un sacerdote al popolo.—Non più Austriaci in Toscana.—Delenda Carthago.* The last two dragged up the old story of the alleged attempt of Leopold II to bombard Florence. [3] *Atti*, II, 369.

qualities of idealism and self-sacrifice which so often lend grandeur and romance to movements of this kind.

The elections were held from August 4 to August 7. Ricasoli, trusting to the careful work of preparation, had sent to the prefects a circular calling on them to secure a heavy poll.[1] The result was hailed as a success, or the reverse, according to the opinions of those who discussed it.[2] Of 68,311 electors on the rolls, a little more than a half (35,240) exercised their right of voting. The elections, at any rate, produced an assembly which the nationalists could justly claim to be representative of the leading classes in Tuscany. The majority of the hundred and eighty deputies were new to politics. Among their number were two princes and a baron (Ricasoli himself), 25 marquises and counts, 12 cavalieri, 6 militari, 10 professors and men of letters, 45 doctors of law and science, 31 lawyers, with numerous others of similar class. It was an assembly whose vote must carry considerable weight in the country and in Europe.

Ricasoli was quite clear as to what he expected of it.[3] It must first of all decree that the dynasty of Lorraine had fallen and would never be received back again by Tuscany. It must, after that, vote the union of Tuscany to Piedmont. When this work was over, it must be adjourned. Ricasoli saw no advantage in long parliamentary debates.

The opinion of the country, in so far as it was articulate, was wholly with the minister on the first point.[4] Leopold II had been persuaded to abdicate in favour of his son; but this sacrifice, which might have saved the dynasty early on April 27, came too late. One fact was sufficient to ruin the hopes of Ferdinand. He had fought in the Austrian army against the Italians. The government, and free-lance

[1] *Atti,* I, 338 and 376. [2] *e.g.* see Galeotti, *op. cit.* Zobi, *Cronaca,* II 552, *I casi della Toscana,* Chs. XVII and XVIII. [3] *L. & D.,* III, 206. Ricasoli consulted with Salvagnoli, Tabarrini, and Bianchi as to the programme. [4] Pamphlet propaganda continued. *e.g. La Toscana e i suoi Granduchi Austriaci della casa di Lorena* (by Peruzzi); *Pensieri ai rappresentanti del popolo toscano convocati per l'undici agosto* 1859 (G. Toscanelli).

pamphleteers, maintained a disdainful propaganda against
'the defeated of Solferino'. No liberal, not even the most
moderate, would raise his voice in favour of the hereditary
prince. On the second point, however, there was more
diversity of opinion. All the deputies, indeed, with the
exception of Montanelli and one or two followers, were
ready to vote for annexation; but many of them hoped
that the vote would have value only as a bargaining factor,
and few of them believed that it would be accepted by
Napoleon and by Europe. Cambray-Digny, who on July
16, had believed that Tuscany should ask only what she
was likely to obtain,[1] was now convinced that she should
ask for more. Yet he did not consider that her demands
would find serious attention, and suggested that, as a
separate state, she might do well enough under a German
sovereign.[2] Massari believed that Tuscany should proclaim
Victor Emmanuel, because Europe might then give her
the Duchess of Parma.[3] Cavour had expressed the opinion
that the government should work for union, but in the
end accept a compromise.[4] Ridolfi, in his official instructions to one of the Tuscan envoys, had ordered him not
to exclude in his negotiations the possibility of a separate
Tuscany, in which case the throne might be offered to a
branch of the house of Savoy, or to Prince Napoleon. And
the envoy had written back that Tuscany would be happier
under the house of Parma.[5]

It is worth while to examine briefly the activities of the
diplomatists—very amateur diplomatists—whom the
government had sent to maintain its cause in Europe;
and it is interesting to note the counsels which they sent
back to Florence. Peruzzi, who had been sent to Paris,
found himself, as has been seen, at the very centre of
diplomatic intrigue.[6] On the one hand he received from
Walewski nothing but threats of an imminent restoration;

[1] Cambray-Digny, *Carteggio*, 185. [2] *Ibid.* July 26. He suggested the
Duke of Leuchtenberg. [3] *Ibid.* 200 (August 10). [4] Chiala, *Lettere di
Cavour*, III, 121 (August 10). [5] N. Bianchi, *Matteucci*, 276–277. [6] See
Appendix to Chapter VIII.

on the other hand he was faced with the hopeless task of
divining the real intentions of the Emperor, and was
surrounded by intrigues which indicated persistently that
Napoleon and Prince Jérôme had taken up the scheme of
a French dynasty for central Italy. Perplexed and uncertain, he wrote later that he was among a den of robbers.
Although he was the author of a long pamphlet which
stoutly maintained annexation,[1] he wrote to his colleague
in London that he advised a vote in this sense only because
it would gather the greatest number of adherents in the
Assembly. The Assembly and the government, he maintained, must demand annexation, 'but not without
leaving the door open to compromises'.[2] The ambassador
was terrified lest Napoleon might decide to give real
support to his foreign minister; and he was so worked
upon that he telegraphed to Florence that Tuscany must
save herself by choosing Prince Napoleon as regent.
Corsini, at London, immediately wired that the government must do no such thing.[3]

The ambassador at London had a much easier task than
his colleague of Paris. He had to deal with Russell and
Palmerston, who reminded him that the position of Tuscany
was very similar to that of England after the flight of
James II, and with Gladstone, whom he found ' Italian
as we are, frank and positive'.[4] Even so, he had written
to Galeotti, whom Ricasoli found very useful for purposes
of the higher propaganda, that the government must on
no account call the Assembly, which would mean intrigue
and discord and in the end its own destruction. God knew
what would take the government's place when it fell, as
fall it must.[5] This was on July 17, when uncertainty was
natural; and before the end of the month Corsini was
counselling a vote for annexation. But he counselled it as
a manœuvre in the diplomatic battle, as a ' maximum

1 La Toscana e i suoi Granduci Austriaci.   2 Lettere Politiche (Zanichelli), p. 95 (August 7). Cf. Poggi, Doc. 23 and 25.   3 Poggi, II, 342.
4 Lettere Politiche, p. 129 et seq. Cf. The Later Correspondence of Lord John
Russell (Longmans, 1925) p. 254. 5 Ibid. 121.

to obtain a minimum'.[1] His judgment coincided with
that of Capponi, who wrote: 'Let us demand union as
a profession of principles, though union we shall not
obtain', and who saw salvation for Tuscany only if she
accepted the Duchess of Parma.[2]

It might have been expected that the envoy at Turin
would have given more optimistic counsels. The envoy
was the scientist, Matteucci,[3] who had sought Capponi's
influence on his behalf, believing that his intellect could
render signal service to the country, and who had been
originally accredited to the government of Berlin. Matteucci brought into politics the methods of the laboratory,
and his projects were the result of an ingrained hostility
to pre-conceived ideas and absolute formulas which did not
correspond with his day-to-day observations of fact. The
observation of fact at Turin convinced him that to vote
annexation would be the maddest folly. La Marmora's
cabinet was basing its foreign policy on intuition or knowledge of the Emperor's will, which it sought to divine and
to modify by the intervention of his friend, Arese. It knew
well enough that Napoleon would not welcome a vote of
annexation from Tuscany, and that he would not permit
Piedmont to accept it, if it was proclaimed at Florence.
Matteucci, influenced by the caution and the pessimism
around him, felt himself called upon to save his country
from disaster. Let Tuscany put herself in the hands of the
Emperor, let her choose the Prince Napoleon, let her
accept the Duchess of Parma, or place herself under the
regency of the Prince of Carignano—anything rather
than face the peril of declaring for union under the sceptre
of Victor Emmanuel.[4]

Ricasoli serenely ignored the pessimism of others. He
was determined that the Assembly should vote the union
of Tuscany with ' a strong kingdom under the sceptre of

[1] *Ibid.* 122. [2] Capponi, *Lettere*, 285. Cf. 283. Capponi maintained that
it would be good policy to offer Tuscany to Napoleon 'in deposit for
six weeks' (August 5). [3] Bianchi, *Matteucci*, Ch. 7. [4] *Poggi*, III, Docs.
26, 27, 28, 30, 31.

Victor Emmanuel', and he was determined to die rather
than yield one inch after the vote had been taken. For
bargains and compromises he had nothing but contempt.
He called in the aid of Salvagnoli, of Tabarrini, and of
Bianchi, to help him compose an address which would
rally the country to his own faith.[1] He read it in the Sala
dei Cinquecento in the *palazzo* Vecchio, on August 11.

'Gentlemen', he concluded, 'let us not be dismayed by the smallness
of our state, because there are moments in which even the little states can
do the work of great ones. Let us remember that while in this hall, dumb
for three centuries to the voice of liberty, we treat of Tuscan affairs, our
thought should aim at Italy. The Municipality without the Nation would
be a contradiction. Without clamour and without effrontery let us proclaim
what we, as Italians, wish to be. Then Tuscany will give a great example,
and we shall congratulate ourselves that we have been born in this part of
Italy. Nor, come what may, shall we despair of our beloved Country'.[2]

Perhaps Ricasoli laid stress on the words 'without
clamour'. In the published debates of the assemblies which
met in Tuscany in the period of the *Risorgimento*, the
best part of three ponderous volumes is taken up with
the debates of 1848–9; but all the parliamentary pro-
ceedings of 1859–6 are comprised within sixty-eight pages.
In this first, and most important session, there was practically no debate at all, but merely a series of motions
referred for report to committee, and then voted. The
first resolution recited the iniquities of the House of
Lorraine, declared that it had 'rendered itself absolutely
incompatible with the order and happiness of Tuscany',
and finally asserted that the country could never receive
it back as the ruling house. It was voted on August 16,
with unanimity. The second resolution, which asserted
'the firm intention of Tuscany to make part of a strong
Italian kingdom under the constitutional sceptre of Victor
Emmanuel', was voted on August 20. Two of the deputies
were absent on public business, three were ill, and three—
Manzoni the republican, Montanelli, who maintained the
cause of a central Italian kingdom, and his follower Parra
—stayed away so that they might not dim the bright

[1] *L. & D.*, III, 206. [2] *Atti*, II, 65–70.

spectacle of an unanimous declaration of faith. Among the deputies present there was not a dissentient voice. Only one thing remained to be done by the Assembly. By a last unanimous vote it legalised for the future the powers of the government. Then it was prorogued.[1]

Ricasoli had obtained all that he wanted. Just a month previously, his attempt to obtain from the country a declaration in favour of union had awakened dissension and scandal. Now the country's representatives had endorsed his faith and echoed his voice. He had created a divinity in his own image, and called on the world to worship ' the sacred principle of popular sovereignty'.

Six months were to pass before Europe was ready to resign itself to being converted by this nationalist apostle. The declaration of the Tuscan Assembly had, in the eyes of Europe, no force of law. It could have no force of law until the vote of Tuscany was accepted by the sovereign of Piedmont and recognised by the great Powers. The preliminaries of Villafranca had, after all, laid down the principle of legitimacy as regards central Italy; and Tuscany stood committed to a struggle against the fears of Piedmont, the policy of the Emperor, the will of Austria, and the prevailing assumptions of international law. It was a struggle devoid of striking events, monotonous in its endless revolution round the same fixed points. On the one side, that of European diplomacy, there was a wearisome series of intrigues, rumours, suggested compromises, which spread outwards from their centre at Paris and marked the efforts of Napoleon to escape from the dilemma which the states of central Italy, and above all Tuscany, had placed before him. On the other side there was nothing but an obstinate reiteration of the will of central Italy, which, as Farini had declared, would not be bound by the pact

---

[1] *Assemblee del Risorg.*, V, 672–710. Garibaldi called on Montanelli, ' in the name of Italy', to vote for union. A. D'Ancona, *Ricordi Storici*, 314. The deliberations of the Assembly were published in order to encourage the country. *Atti dell'Assemblea Toscana ed altri Documenti Relativi alle sue deliberazioni del 16 e 20 Agosto*. Firenze, 1859.

of Villafranca. Ricasoli directed all his efforts to secure from Victor Emmanuel a frank declaration which would announce to the world that he accepted the vote of Tuscany, and that he was ready to defend the revolution before the law and against the law. The Piedmontese ministry, and Cavour himself, knew that such an act was impossible, so long as Napoleon III imposed his veto. Time after time Ricasoli attempted to force forward the question of principle, and time after time the government at Turin took counsel with the Emperor and evaded the issue.

The first struggle was fought round the King's answer to the vote of the Assembly. Ricasoli tried to keep at arm's length the doubts which would assail the armour of his confidence and loyalty.

'The King cannot refuse'. 'He must accept'. 'Refusal! That would be discouragement, great loss of heart among the liberal and national forces of the country, renewed audacities, new designs, new revolutionary enterprises on the part of the extremists'.[1]

His optimism was artificial and desperate. The Tuscan envoy had wired from Turin imploring the government to delay in sending the deputation which was to present the votes of the Assembly to Tuscany's chosen king. Ricasoli answered by announcing the date of its departure. Then the envoy rained upon the government telegrams of protest, supplementing them by letters of the deepest gloom.[2] Rattazzi, he said, had sent Arese to consult the oracle at Paris; a hopeful reply could not be hoped for; the deputation would not even be received. 'For pity's sake', wailed Matteucci, 'confine yourself to reasonable schemes. Let us escape from this dangerous position, which will end as in 1849'. In the end even Ridolfi, to whom these dispatches were addressed, reproved the hysterical ambassador for his 'scandalous behaviour'. Corsini described him to Galeotti as 'the Austrian minister at Turin',[3] and thought that Tuscany would be better served in Piedmont without a representative at all. Ricasoli,

[1] *L. & D.*, III, 248 and 267.   [2] *Poggi*, III, Doc. 47. A series of dispatches.   [3] *Lettere Politiche*, 153, 162.

if he read the dispatches, ignored them. The deputation
was dispatched and given audience. The King told the
Tuscans that he received the votes which they carried to
him as the solemn manifestation of the will of their country,
and that he would avail himself of the rights conferred
upon him by these votes to maintain their cause before the
great Powers. Europe, he trusted, would recognise the
justice of their cause, as it had done justice to Belgium,
to Greece, to the Danubian provinces.[1] Cavour thought
that this was the best answer which could have been given
in the circumstances;[2] but it was obviously not the frank,
unqualified acceptance of honour and responsibility for
which Ricasoli had hoped. The deputation itself believed
that the reply would not satisfy Tuscany.[3]

Ricasoli pretended that Victor Emmanuel had accepted
the sovereignty of Tuscany without qualification. Capponi
thought his conduct rather immoral, and feared that no
good could come from this barefaced deceiving of the
people.[4] The nationalists, however, ' willingly closed one
eye'.[5] So, when Ricasoli announced that Tuscany and
Piedmont were now one state, and that Tuscany's act
had meant ' not vassalage of provinces, but constitution
of the nation':[6] when the Te Deum was sung in the
church of the Santissima Annunziata: when the city was
illuminated, and ' a transparency of Victor Emmanuel's
bold frank features, in the midst of a cloud of banners'[7]
smiled out upon a crowd gathered before the Riccardi
palace: when the government redeemed all the blankets
that the needy had pawned[8]—the city good-temperedly
allowed itself to be deceived. Ricasoli, before long, was
completely deceived himself. He spoke of an ' accomplished
fact'. He waxed morally indignant when the government
of Turin refused to accept the implications of what, in his
wilful blindness, he imagined that it had done. ' Willingly
or unwillingly, the King, in accepting the vote of the

---

[1] *Poggi*, I, 235.   [2] Chiala, *Lettere di Cavour*, III, ccxxxv. (note).
[3] *L. & D.*, III, 269.   [4] Capponi, *Lettere*, III, 306.   [5] *Rubieri, op.
cit.* 247.   [6] *Atti*, II, 208.   [7] Trollope, *op. cit.*   [8] *Atti*, II, 220.

Assembly, accepted the sovereignty of Tuscany'.[1] Tuscany's part had been played; it was now the turn of Piedmont.

'I marvel when I hear voices which come to me from there, telling me to *move*, to *act*, etc. What is there to move, what is there to do, when action to-day belongs to him who accepted the sovereignty of Tuscany?'

Ricasoli had been aided in his self-deception by a useful verbal vagueness in Victor Emmanuel's answer. The King had used the word *accogliere*, to which the baron gave all the implications of full acceptance. He pounced upon this verbal ambiguity and built up from it a great construction of principle; just as in 1847 he had refined with apparent subtlety and yet with ingenuous simplicity, on the difference between 'reflections' and 'conditions'.

Something, however, had to be done to prove to the people and to Europe that Tuscany had in very truth entered upon a new life as part of a strong Italian kingdom under the constitutional sceptre of Victor Emmanuel. The problem was much talked about in Piedmont as well as in Tuscany; and various shades of opinion became apparent. According to the first, and most cautious, it would be sufficient if Tuscany proclaimed Victor Emmanuel, and then introduced the Piedmontese system of weights and measures and the Piedmontese tariff; being content, that is to say, with a *Zollverein*. The second, which had the support of Cavour, maintained that Tuscany should add the arms of Savoy to the tricolour banner, print the image of Victor Emmanuel upon her coinage, and call together the Assembly to deliberate on further measures of union. Others went into further detail, maintaining in particular that the Assembly should decree for Tuscany the fundamental statute of Piedmont, and should nominate a regent to govern in the name of the King.[2]

This last was the course most favoured at Parma, Modena and Bologna; and it was the hope of Farini that Tuscany would co-operate closely with the other governments in the work of unification. The question of co-

[1] *L. & D.*, III, 291. [2] *L. & D.*, III, 274.

operation in central Italy had already come to the fore.
The Tuscan army, which Ricasoli distrusted and which
the peoples to the east of the Apennines were glad to have
as a guarantee against a raid from hostile powers, had
not returned home. An unauthorised intervention on the
part of Malenchini,[1] shortly after the armistice, had
awakened in Garibaldi the belief that he would be chosen
as its general; but such a step seemed too rash both to
Piedmont and to Ricasoli, and the governments solved the
problem as best they could by choosing Fanti to command
the forces of central Italy, with Garibaldi as his lieutenant.
This solution, and the unavoidable necessity of military
co-operation, led the various governments of central Italy
to conclude with each other a defensive league. During
the negotiations, Farini made it clear that he would have
liked to obtain also a political union of the governments
of central Italy;[2] but Ricasoli unceremoniously waved the
plan aside. On August 10, before the Tuscan Assembly
had decreed the future of the country, the articles of the
League were agreed upon between Florence and Modena.[3]
There was one other problem, however, which was of
special importance to Italy. The Romagnas, which were
governed by Cipriani from Bologna, had most to fear from
military action ordered by the Papal government. Ricasoli,
determined as he was to accept responsibility for Tuscany
and to fight the battle on his own ground, was unwilling
to become involved in a quarrel with the Papal government
which might give a real pretext for intervention in central
Italy as a whole. The problem was solved for the time by
allowing the Romagnas to ' adhere ' to the league, in a
manner which gave them the realities of protection without
giving offence to a very sensitive European ' Diplomacy '.[4]

The trans-Apennine states, for the very reason that
they were geographically in the vanguard of revolution
and would be the first to face the peril of a raid or ot

---

[1] *L. & D.*, III, 167. *Scritti Politici e militari di Giuseppe Garibaldi.*
Roma, 1907. 107. [2] *Poggi*, I, 136. *L. & D.*, III, 220, 241. Minghetti
negotiated for Bologna and Modena. [3] *Atti*, III, 318. [4] *Poggi*, I, 137-9

intervention, persisted in their efforts to balance their own instability by a closer union with compact and orderly Tuscany. Minghetti had urged this point of view prior to the meeting of the Tuscan Assembly, and Farini, as Ricasoli thought, sought to introduce the thin end of the wedge by calling for a supreme war council to act in control of General Fanti.[1] Ricasoli did not need Massari's warning to reject what he considered a dangerous alliance with the Romagnas, and a possible cause of antagonism to Piedmont. Then, when Farini asked him to delay the Tuscan deputation which was entrusted with carrying to Turin the vote of annexation, so that it might act with the deputations of the Duchies and the Romagnas, he refused to wait,[2] and proclaimed the formula: 'Acts identical, but distinct'. His attitude was the same after the King had given his answer to the deputations of central Italy. Throughout, it was determined by the fear that any organisation of central Italy as a whole, even if it were provisional, would play into the hands of Napoleon III, and of the opponents of union, by giving them a pretext for fastening a monarch on to the embryo state and hurrying the peninsula into federation. The *comte* de Reiset, in his journeyings to and fro, had found a resolute faith in union nowhere save in Florence. Farini himself[3] had not spoken of annexation to Piedmont. If this reticence may be ascribed to the mental agility of the Modenese dictator, the fact remains that he was associated with persons whose chief aim was to escape from the dangers of a provisional arrangement, and who neither planned nor hoped for anything beyond a central Italian kingdom. This was the general attitude in the Romagnas, and it was revealed plainly enough by Marliani, who twice came to Florence to try and break the obstinacy of the Tuscans.[4] After Marliani came Pasolini, whose memoirs, gathered together

---

[1] Bianchi, *Diplomazia*, VIII, 575–585. [2] *L. & D.*, III, 243. [3] De Reiset, *Mes Souvenirs*, III, 22. Cf. III, 46, on Cipriani, Governor of Bologna. [4] *Poggi*, I, 207, 274–278. Cf. Bianchi, *Diplomazia*, VIII, 183.

by his son, show clearly that he did not then possess a unionist faith.[1] They contain, too, a letter which the envoy wrote in September to Minghetti, and which recounts that Cavour himself had told him that Italy must content herself with something like the plan of 1856.[2] It must be remembered, too, that all through these weeks, the best of the Tuscan diplomatists made it clear that they had only limited faith in the final success of Ricasoli's battle. Peruzzi lost his head and wired urging the government to appoint ' Plon Plon ' regent; and Corsini, though he telegraphed to Florence a caution against Peruzzi's pessimistic counsel, gave a list of the possible princes who might be presented with the crown and sceptre of central Italy.[3]

Against all these intrigues and compromises Ricasoli fortified himself in his own obstinacy. His policy, compared with that of Farini, appears at times pettifogging, unresourceful, lacking in flexibility. Yet flexibility was at the time the one gift which it would have been dangerous to possess, and a rigidity which showed itself in the re-iteration of a single idea was the best means of forcing Napoleon to raise the veto which he had imposed upon the Piedmontese government. Ricasoli waged a double war, against the government of Turin, and against the proposals of the trans-Apennine states, which called on him to join them in taking measures which would assimilate the laws of the states both to those of Piedmont, and to those of each other. Apart from questions of policy, Ricasoli was too much the proud Tuscan baron to listen to these proposals. He would surrender Tuscany to Victor Emmanuel, and to no one else.[4] He would surrender her to Italy, but he would not allow her to be merged in an indistinguishable, characterless mass of central Italy.

[1] G. Pasolini, *Memorie Raccolte da suo figlio*. See Ch. XII, esp. pp. 232–33. [2] *Ibid*. 236. [3] *Lettere Politiche*, 180. [4] He was very emphatic in maintaining that he was giving Tuscany to Italy, not merely to Piedmont. He asserted that Piedmont, like Tuscany, should modify some of her institutions in order to make the new Italy. *L. & D.*, III, 245.

The centralists awoke in him the same sort of repugnance that the Button-moulder inspired in Peer Ghynt. There was, moreover, a question of principle. In Ricasoli, as in Mazzini, the habit of erecting every political question into a matter of principle sometimes bred intolerance and perversity, and sometimes was nothing more than a habit of making mountains out of molehills. He started now from the erroneous assumption that the King had really accepted full sovereignty over Tuscany, bowed before this assumption as a great political fact, and proceeded to deduce from it the most topsy-turvy consequences. He maintained the paradox that every act of union carried through by the Tuscan government or the Tuscan assembly would really be a potent instrument of disunion. Tuscany might adopt the Piedmontese statute and the whole Piedmontese code of laws, she might place the cross of Savoy on her banner, she might stamp the bold frank features of Victor Emmanuel upon her coins. But, unless these acts emanated from a government which received its credentials directly from the King, they were nothing more than usurpations of his authority, a testimony by which Europe might prove that the King's sovereignty over Tuscany meant nothing, and that the authority of the government was really derived from another source.

'If the King does not move after having accepted the vote', declared Ricasoli, 'we cannot act for him. . . . To-day the sovereignty of Tuscany is in his hands. To him it belongs to put it into force'. 'Assimilating our laws to those of Piedmont', he affirmed again, 'is the very opposite from fulfilling the union. It is the efficacious method of constituting ourselves in a possible federation of independent states'.[1]

This was the idea underlying his opposition, not only to those in Piedmont who expected to see him prepare the union of Italy by 'Piedmontising' Tuscany (a course of action that he would have abhorred, for he valued Tuscan tradition and considered that Piedmont as well as Tuscany would have to make sacrifices for the common fatherland) but also to those who called upon him, in the name of

[1] *L. & D.*, III, 292.

Italy, to co-operate with the trans-Apennine peoples in a simultaneous approach to the economic and political order of Piedmont. His formula was still, 'Acts identical but distinct'. He was indeed ready to do his part in preparing a *Zollverein* with Piedmont, but he was not ready to take the same steps towards Modena and Parma. He maintained instead that the result would be the same if all the states negotiated separately, but loyally, with the Piedmontese government. In political matters he preferred to keep the country in its present provisional position, rather than take a step upon the slippery road which might lead to diplomatic bargaining and compromise. He was asked to join the other states in proclaiming the Sardinian constitution and in electing a regent from the House of Savoy.

'This act', he said of the first proposal, 'if consented to by the King, may be efficacious: not consented to by him, it is an act of sovereignty which runs ahead of his august will, and can only be justified by the gravest reasons'.[1] Of the second proposal he said: 'Crying to us, " Make the regent", is a singular thing, when we made for ourselves a King, and the King accepted our vote'.[2]

His only alternative plan was that the King should publicly confirm the powers of the existing government, so that it should rule the country as his recognised lieutenant.[3] Beneath all his rather sophistical arguments was an ardent desire to force the Piedmontese government to have done with Napoleon and to face the question of principle. La Marmora's ministry, not being concerned with the unjustifiable interpretation which Ricasoli had chosen to place upon the words of Victor Emmanuel, refused point-blank to fly in the face of Napoleon and of Europe by performing what would have been ' a true and proper exercise of sovereignty'.[4] The foreboding of Capponi seemed to have been justified, for the Tuscan dictator had run his head against a brick wall. In reality, it mattered little; for none of the arguments which awoke

[1] *L. & D.*, III, 302–307 (cf. Bianchi, *Diplomazia*, VIII, 588 *et seq.*).
[2] *L. & D.*, III, 294. [3] *L. & D.*, III, 285–293. [4] *L. & D.*, III, 294.

his enthusiasm were more than a cloak, assumed unconsciously, for his inflexible resolution. He cast away the
cloak without realising his own inconsistency, and his
will expressed itself in other policies. For a time, indeed,
he allowed himself the luxury of abusing the cowardice of
Turin. This cowardice had ruined a Heaven-sent chance
of presenting 'Diplomacy' with an accomplished fact such
as History had never known. Was it not plain that 'Diplomacy' could not prevail against the will of twelve million
Italians ? Unless 'Diplomacy' surrendered, he, for one,
would become a Mazzinian.[1] . . . But while he vented
his chagrin in exclamations such as these, he forgot the
policy which a few days before had been such a vital
matter, and reflected that union could be made, not only
by the *head*, but by the *feet*.

'Every day', he wrote with a new enthusiasm, 'I confirm my belief
in the necessity for *unification*. This can be done in *fact*, or in *law*. If the
language of law is not believed by that cabinet to be possible to-day, then
speak with the language of fact'.[2]

That language, he observed, was most efficacious in
speaking to the multitude. Through economic facts
(which, of course, had their moral side), he would create
such a state of mind that the pretenders themselves would
fear to return to a country which had tasted the joys of
freedom. And so, on September 17, the *Monitore*
announced a whole sheaf of unifying decrees—decrees
affecting passports, money, customs, the post-office—
economic 'facts' which the baron valued for their moral
content.[3] Three days later there were issued from the department of the minister Poggi decrees on extradition, the
execution of sentences, University degrees, and the like,
so 'that this country under the sceptre of Victor
Emmanuel might profit without delay from the advantages
of national union'.[4] On the twenty-ninth of September,

[1] *L. & D.*, III, 335, 343, 351. The Tuscans were always ready to
threaten that they would ' go Mazzinian ' if they did not get what they
wanted. *e.g.* de Reiset, *Souvenirs*, III, 39. *Lettere Politiche*, 109.   [2] *L.
& D.*, III, 335.   [3] *Atti*, II, 237.   [4] *Ibid.* 243.

the government proclaimed that it exercised power in the name of Victor Emmanuel, the Elected King.[1] 'If the present government must rule for His Majesty', the proclamation announced, ' it should also pride itself and find its glory in his August Name'. The cross of Savoy appeared upon the tricolour banner, the arms of the House of Savoy were set up in public places, and from now on all public documents were headed, *Regnando S.M. Vittorio Emmanuele*. Similar decrees followed in the succeeding weeks, and patriotism was given a pleasant seasoning for tender palates by a reduction in the price of salt.[2]

Ricasoli even took up the idea of a regency to be exercised by the Prince of Carignano, which Farini had urged since September 5. On this matter, and on the important questions of the forms to be established in the decrees of September 29, he had had a conference with Farini at Scaricalasino, half way between Bologna and Florence, on September 28. He yielded a good deal of ground to the Modenese dictator (who had now become the dictator of Parma also, and was soon to take over the government of Bologna); for only six days before he had insisted to Fabrizi that Carignano could indeed be sent by the King with or without an invitation from the Tuscans, but that he could not be appointed by the Tuscans themselves.[3] He now consented that the regent should be elected by the assemblies, though he insisted that Florence, Bologna, Modena and Parma must take separate action for this end. Minghetti was sent to Turin to arrange the affair with the government there. Ricasoli was suspicious of the method with which the envoy conducted the negotiations[4] but he was saved from his preoccupations by an indiscretion on Minghetti's part which allowed news of the

---

[1] *Ibid.* 277. [2] *Ibid.* 307 (October 8). For decrees affecting a customs union, *Ibid.* 302, 327, 332, 335. Other decrees came later, *e.g.* February 4, 1860, the Sardinian military code was introduced (*Atti*, IV, 7 *et seq.*). Then came the Sardinian system of weights and measures (*Ibid.* IV, 61), etc. [3] *L. & D.*, III, 338–40. [4] *L. & D.*, III, 375.

negotiations to leak through to Paris.[1] Once again the Emperor opposed his veto—an act which suggested to Ricasoli that there was more promise in the scheme than he had at first believed, and that it was worth his while to take it up again. An encouraging interview which a Tuscan deputation had with the Emperor on October 16,[2] when Napoleon admitted that time and good order might enable Tuscany to acquire new claims to the consideration of Europe, encouraged him to press for a new step forward. The negotiations at Zurich, also, made it clear that many questions would be postponed in the treaty of peace, soon to be signed. From now on all the talk was of a Congress, and Ricasoli hoped to be able to present the Congress with an accomplished fact.

The regency question, moreover, was forced to the front by the peril of anarchy and dissension in central Italy. The agitation of the Mazzinians, the unreliability of the army, the impetuosity of Garibaldi, and the bad faith of Farini, placed before Ricasoli the alternatives of dissolving the league, or strengthening it. The root cause of the crisis was that constant struggle between two theories of revolution and two brands of revolutionaries which persisted in Italy throughout the century. Before and after the vote of the Tuscan Assembly, the question had been debated to the bottom between Ricasoli and Mazzini. Among the papers at Brolio there is kept, together with various letters, an official circular in which Ricasoli set forth his conception of the revolution, and which he sent to Mazzini for comment.[3] The annotations of the latter reveal a real respect for the sincerity and the achievements of the Tuscan dictator; but they show also how the similar mentality of the two men, twisted in different directions by their widely different traditions and experience and

[1] *L. & D.*, III, 418, 429.   [2] *Poggi*, III, Docs. 57, 58.   [3] *Brolio MSS.*, Q. 15. Circular of September 1. Cf. Q. 54 (*b*) and *L. & D.*, III, 257. Ricasoli's attitude towards Mazzini (though at a later date) is well described by C. Bianchi, *Il Barone Ricasoli, Mazzini, Garibaldi,* etc. Torino, 1862.

class, made them uncompromising champions of opposed policies. Just as Ricasoli pressed with fervour and obstinacy to achieve the accomplished fact of union through a courageous and revolutionary declaration which would announce to the world that Piedmont had accepted the sacrifice made by Tuscany, and that this sacrifice had constituted Italy: so Mazzini preached with similar enthusiasm that the same end could only be achieved by a revolutionary crusade in Papal territory. It seemed to Mazzini to be cowardice for Tuscany to save herself, while she left her neighbours to languish under Papal tyranny. He called on Ricasoli to force the hand of Europe by loosing a people's war in the Papal States, by rousing all Italy to revenge the Papal 'terror' in Perugia. 'One splendid act, the reconquest of Perugia, would be the signal of insurrection for the Marches and Umbria.' ' Internal order', he admitted, ' has wonderfully helped to win sympathy in Europe from a side hitherto hostile'; but he added that ' external energy would have raised, not blame, but enthusiasm among all'. Ricasoli lent no ear to such arguments. His policy was one of daring with regard to Tuscany, which was in his own hands, but of resolute non-interference with the rest of Italy. If the votes of the central populations were made to prevail, he argued with justice, the questions of Rome, of Naples, of Venetia, would be solved as the Mazzinians wished by ' a logical deduction'.

For a time Ricasoli allowed Mazzini to remain in Florence, on the condition that he kept himself hidden. It was Dolfi who saw to the business, and an inscription on the democrat's house in the Borgo San Lorenzo records to-day his hospitality to the exile of Genoa. Then Mazzini complained to Ricasoli of the treatment meted out to the radical exiles, and Ricasoli informed him through Dolfi that he would have to leave Tuscany, ' because his presence was more troublesome to the population than to (Ricasoli) himself'.[1] The baron would have given him asylum in

[1] Autograph note to *Dall' Ongaro*, p. 92.

Brolio, had he wanted it;[1] and perhaps he was surprised
that Mazzini did not agree with him that he would best
serve Italy hidden away, comfortably enough, in the wilds
of the Chianti. It was part of Ricasoli's policy to ship out
of the country everyone who shared Mazzini's faith in
an aggressive war, and the police was as vigilant against
extreme patriots as against plotting reactionaries. The
dictator would not admit that his precautions amounted
to persecution. He was, he claimed, 'without fear and
without hate'. When La Cecilia and De Boni found their
way to Tuscany, he shook hands with both, and then
moved them on, telling them that they brought him
only embarrassment. He asserted that he would have
preferred to keep Tuscany free for all patriots, but that he
had to give to the country a proof of his strength, and to
bear in mind that neither the people nor 'Diplomacy'
thought as he did.[2] It may be doubted whether Ricasoli,
despite these perfectly sincere assertions, would have
acted differently even if there had been no suspicious
'Diplomacy' and no timorous moderates. He did not
encourage people who sang a tune different from his own.
He felt very much that the Tuscan revolution was his
revolution, and he wanted no meddling.[3]

The Mazzinians, driven out of Tuscany, found more
favourable ground for propaganda in the Tuscan army,
which was under the charge of Garibaldi. Mazzini attempted to win over Garibaldi himself,[4] and though the general
kept aloof from any pact with the former, he absorbed the
ideas which Mazzini had expounded to Ricasoli and even
to Victor Emmanuel.[5] A vacancy in the war ministry at

[1] The same, p. 88.   [2] The same, pp. 46–47.
[3] Cf. His attitude to Guerrazzi. Guerrazzi could have returned
if he had applied for an amnesty, but he was too proud to do so.
He maintained that he should be welcomed back as a patriot who
had suffered for his country (see F. Martini, *Due dell' Estrema, Carteggi
inediti*, 17–48. Also *Il Risorg. Ital.* Nuova, Serie IX, 159 *et seq.*). Ricasoli
was probably wise in refusing to smooth Guerrazzi's path.   [4] La Farina,
Epistolario, II, 209–211.   [5] *Ricordi e Scritti di Aurelio Saffi*. Firenze,
1900. p. 55.

Florence seriously weakened the civil control over the army, especially as Farini was willing to give to the military chiefs a good deal of rope. Thus it was that Garibaldi concentrated his forces on the borders of the Romagnas, and Fanti, his commander, whose business it should have been to restrain the provocative action of his second-in-command, actually gave him instructions which authorised an invàsion of the Marches and Umbria, in the event of a serious nationalist movement taking place there. These orders were all the more alarming in that the National Society, of which Garibaldi was now president, was at this very time organising such a rising through its local committees.[1] It was against the cardinal point of Ricasoli's policy to let Tuscany become involved in such an adventure. He tried to spur Farini to act with him in calling the two generals to order;[2] but Farini himself was in the plot.[3] So he arranged a meeting with Cipriani, the governor of Bologna, and proposed nothing less than a dissolution of the league, the dismissal of half the troops, and with them, of Fanti and Garibaldi.[4] But he was told that Garibaldi would not be got rid of so easily. ' In the Romagnas the true master of the situation is Garibaldi. The government which set itself against his power would fall within twenty-four hours'.[5] Since Ricasoli and Cipriani could not restore the situation, and since Farini would not, nothing remained but to call in the aid of Victor Emmanuel and the liberal leaders of Turin. Even so, it was no easy matter, for the King himself had had ambiguous dealings with Garibaldi, and among the liberals there were divided counsels and expedients. The incident dragged on into the middle of November, when it ended with the disdainful resignation of Garibaldi.[6]

Since the trouble had arisen from insufficient co-operation

[1] F. Carandini, *Manfredo Fanti*, 286. [2] *L. & D.*, III, 455–461, 465–468. [3] F. Carandini, *Manfredo Fanti*, 286–287. G. Finali, *Ricordi della Vita di L. G. Farini*, 35. [4] See especially G. Finali, *op. cit.* 78–80. Finali was present at the conference. [5] *L. & D.*, III, 470. [6] See Garibaldi, *Memorie* (Torino, 1907), 292 *et seq. L. & D.*, III, 472–5, 472–501; IV, 360. C. Tivaroni, *L'Italia degli Italiani*, 141 *et seq.*

between the governments, it seemed logical to tighten the
bonds between them, rather than to dissolve them altogether, as Ricasoli had threatened. As Fabrizi said, the
breach of concord between Ricasoli and Farini had thrown
into relief the need of entrusting the direction of common
interests in central Italy to one who by his wisdom or his
high authority would be able in future to dominate the
situation.[1] It happened also that on October 27, a day
before Ricasoli and Cipriani had had their meeting at
Pratolino, Corsini wired from London urging the government to act promptly and appoint the Prince of Carignano
regent. It appeared from his wire that the Emperor was
throwing himself on the support of England, and that
England wished Piedmont to act with resolution and secure
an accomplished fact.[2] On October 30 Fabrizi telegraphed
in the same sense from Turin, urging the government to
convoke the Assembly and obtain the nomination of the
regent without delay. Victor Emmanuel, it appeared, was
' resolute and benevolent'.

On November 2, a government decree convoked the
Assembly for the 7th of the month. But on this very day
a despatch from Fabrizi announced that the whole scheme
had fallen through. Corsini's optimistic message had
been unjustified, and the Piedmontese ministry was not
ready to run risks. Ricasoli wired back immediately:
' Your despatch received, I consider it unwritten, keep
it secret'.[3] The next day (November 3) Corsini wired that
Palmerston himself did not consider the scheme practi-
cable till peace had finally been signed at Zurich. Minghetti wrote from Paris, warning Ricasoli that none could
know better than he that there was little likelihood of
obtaining the prince. Ricasoli took no notice. This time,
he was determined, the government of Turin must face
the question of principle. He concerted plans of joint
action with Farini,[4] he opened the Tuscan Assembly

---

[1] *L. & D.*, III, 478. Fabrizi had succeeded Matteucci as Tuscan
envoy at Turin.   [2] *L. & D.*, III, 468.   [3] *L. & D.*, III, 481–3, for the
various telegrams concerning this affair.   [4] *L. & D.*, III, 483–488.

according to programme, and the Assembly voted unanimously a resolution which nominated Prince Carignano
as regent of Tuscany, ' to govern in the name of His
Majesty the Elected King'.[1]

Then there came the usual wires from Turin, begging
Ricasoli not to send any deputation.[2] The oracle of Paris
had again been consulted, and had imposed his veto.

' If you permit the Prince Carignano to accept', Napoleon had telegraphed, ' the Congress will not take place, and the fault being on your
side, I shall not be able to save you'.[3]

Michelangelo Castelli was sent post-haste to Florence to
expound the message of the Emperor, and to induce
Ricasoli to bow once again to his decree.

The envoy, after an interview with Ricasoli, wired to
his government that he had found him ' unshakeable'.[4]

' I shall only say that the new move of the Emperor has renewed my
forces', he had declared, ' and I *swear* that I will not fall short of my
task. . . . I shall let myself be crushed rather than yield'.[5]

The deputation set off for Turin. If the government
had been foolish enough to refer this Italian business to a
French sovereign, Ricasoli said to Castelli, well and good.
Tuscany would get on happily enough without the regent.
But Piedmont must shoulder the results of her weakness,
and atone for it. Justice must be done to Tuscany, which
had manifested her will through her chosen representatives.
The King might refuse what the deputation asked; but
that which was important, that which was cardinal, was
that he should speak officially, proudly, solemnly, wisely,
to Europe. He must declare that he refused for the time,
because he respected the freedom of the approaching
Congress. But he must declare also that he expected from
this great tribunal of Humanity a sentence which the very
rights of humanity demanded. He must proclaim that his
sole care was the interest of the Italian peoples who

---

[1] *Le Assemblee del Risorg.*, V, 715 *et seq.* Cf. *Poggi*, 353 *et seq.*, 390 *et
seq.* Poggi claims that his resolution saved the situation.   [2] *L. & D.*, IV,
5.   [3] Bianchi, *Diplomazia*, VIII, 230.   [4] *L. & D.*, IV, 14.   [5] *L. &
D.*, IV, 8.

appealed to him, that he made their cause his own, that he was sworn to consecrate to it in every event his sword, his life.[1]

Instead of such a proclamation, which would have satisfied Ricasoli and at the same time left matters very much as they were, the next move was, in Ricasoli's opinion, 'an indecorous and puerile intrigue', 'an expedient without value and without utility', 'an ignoble farce', 'the most puerile intrigue that can be imagined'.[2] The Piedmontese government had decided to satisfy the Emperor and central Italy simultaneously by calling on the Prince of Carignano to 'indicate' Boncompagni as a suitable substitute for himself. Even Cavour, though he was disgusted at the manner in which the government slavishly turned to Napoleon, had approved this scheme as the only one possible after the Emperor's opinion had been sought and obtained.[3] It happened that Peruzzi was in Turin on his way back from Paris, and the government asked him to act for Ricasoli. Peruzzi wired to Florence in cipher, but the cipher had been changed and his message could not be understood. He took silence for consent, and the baron, who had counted on presenting Europe with a startling act of union, found that he had been bound behind his back to surrender power to a person who, though 'eminently respectable', was, like himself, a mere servant of the King. Boncompagni, assuming that everything was arranged, wired that he was coming immediately to establish himself in Florence to assume 'la haute direction politique et militaire'.[4]

Ricasoli thought differently. He wired immediately:

'Peruzzi had no mandate. . . . His action is arbitrary and blameworthy. All his acts are null and cannot be recognised by the government of Tuscany'.[4] To Minghetti he telegraphed: 'It must be the prince or nothing. We intend to save the King and Italy'.[5] 'Won't they understand', he wrote to Fabrizi, 'that the cause of Italy must be sustained openly, solemnly, on its own merits, before Europe ?'[6]

[1] L. & D., IV, 15. [2] L. & D., IV, 76, 22, 57. [3] Chiala, *Lettere di Cavour*, III, 149. [4] L. & D., IV, 34. Cf. *Brolio MSS.*, R. 50, 52, 53, 57. [5] L. & D., IV, 20. [6] L. & D., IV, 23.

He yielded only to this extent: that he professed himself willing to accept Boncompagni if he came with a letter from the prince expressly constituting him vice-regent, and that he took no measures to confound Tuscany with the other states. Cavour, in a mixture of despair and irritation, denounced his conduct as ' pigheadedness and asininity '[1]—but he took care that the denunciation remained extremely private. Minghetti, who had accepted the compromise on behalf of the three governments of ' Emilia ' (now united under Farini), begged him to be reasonable. Farini telegraphed a plea urging him to do all he could to maintain harmony with the government of the King. From that government came dispatch after dispatch imploring him to give way. Ricasoli called the dispatches ' evil fruit of a base seed'.[2] Some of the more ardent spirits in Florence began to mutter against the obstinacy of the baron. ' These gentlemen', he declared disdainfully, 'with their chattering and inaction, lose what sense they have. Unfortunately they do not lose their presumption'.[3] Salvagnoli became worried and excited, and Ricasoli told him to go to bed.[4] Boncompagni and Farini signed jointly a dispatch which enclosed a letter from the Emperor explicitly approving their conduct. Ricasoli saw only one reason the more for disapproving it. ' I shall not lend myself to any other course than that which I have followed in the past', he wired to Fabrizi. In particular, he would not join the others in ' wandering from our *Italian* course, and taking that of central Italy'.[5] Dabormida announced that the whole question had arisen from the unstable order in central Italy. Ricasoli publicly denied this statement as a calumny, and suggested that, if Farini was afraid that he could not keep order, he had better retire, and let Boncompagni rule in his stead. The quarrel went on for weeks, and the wags of Florence went

---

[1] Michelangelo Castelli, *Ricordi*, 216.   [2] *L. & D.*, IV, 58.   [3] *L. & D.*, IV, 100. The complaint was that Parliament should have been consulted. Gioli, *op. cit.* 293. Guerrazzi, *Lettere* (Carducci), 483, 486–7.   [4] *L. & D.*, IV, 41.   [5] *L. & D.*, IV, 66. Cf. *Poggi*, I, 417 *et seq.*

about declaring that Tuscany was ready to fight Piedmont, in order to unite with her.

Finally the peacemakers bethought themselves of the weak joint in the baron's armour of obstinacy—his loyalty to the King. Early in December he consented to make a journey to Turin, had an 'admirable welcome'[1] and came back with a compromise in his pocket and the praises of Victor Emmanuel upon his lips. ' Who has not seen this magnanimous King', he proclaimed to his Tuscans, ' this King who turns every act and thought of his to Italy, cannot realise how he is a great idea personified in the highest expression of warlike and civil power, loyally devoted to the service of a great cause'.[2] Any occasion served for a profession of loyalty to the King and to Italy. Boncompagni came to Florence, ostensibly as the head of a very shadowy league. He had a high salary, no work, and an obscure palace in a back street as his official residence.[3]

The great demonstration for which Ricasoli hoped had come to nothing; but the struggle had at least given proof once more of the inflexible opposition which Tuscany, personified in Ricasoli, opposed to compromises. Napoleon himself was almost convinced, and thought of turning to England to pull his chestnuts out of the fire for him.[4] The struggle was almost over, and before long the vexation of patriots at Ricasoli's obstinacy turned to admiring wonder at his firmness. One of the moderates of the Ramagnas, who had implored him to keep harmony with his brethren,[5] admitted a few months later that, without his constancy, the separate kingdom of central Italy would have been an accomplished fact. Ricasoli, in conversation with the same person, expressed in a phrase the rule by which he had guided his policy.

---

[1] L. & D., IV, 78. [2] Atti, III, 140 et seq. [3] Ibid. III, 131, for the terms of the settlement. [4] Chiala, op. cit. cccx.–et seq. [5] Pasolini, Memorie, 242 et seq. Cf. Cambray-Digny, Carteggio, 211.

'He who walks on the blade of a knife', he said, 'should not let himself be distracted to the right hand or to the left'.[1]

In the midst of his troublesome quarrel with the other leaders of Italy, Ricasoli inaugurated a cherished plan of teaching the Tuscans to shoot. Thus, he told them, would they return to the 'austere virtue of ancient days'. He followed Macchiavelli in tracing the misfortunes of the Italians to the decay of citizen valour.

'The prostration of their bodies was followed by a debasement of their spirits, and all manner of moral decadence. The writer who was no more soldier and citizen wandered from virility of thought, and the hand of the artist, which could no longer grasp a sword in defence of the down-trodden fatherland, had no skill to carve and to paint the true forms of beauty'. [2]

Ricasoli, in his simplicity, believed that by strengthening the Tuscans in their struggle for independence, and by teaching them to shoot straight, he would restore to his country the creative spirit of her warrior republics.[3]

[1] *Ibid.* 256–7. That Ricasoli was not fighting a phantom is shown by the attack made on his policy at this time by an avowed centralist, E. Alberi: *La Politica Napoleonica e il Governo Toscano.* Alberi was answered by 'Collodi' in *Il signor Alberi ha ragione.* [2] *Atti*, III, 98. [3] Pasolini (*op. cit.* 245) wrote of the Tuscan National Guard: 'Very good; but all this will not last long. As arms are not put in hands where for malice or lack of skill they become dangerous, so they cannot be given to those who become ridiculous carrying them'.

CHAPTER IX

'TUSCANY', Ricasoli claimed proudly, early in November, 'is in my arms'.[1] He proved his claim in the month which followed, and as soon as the tiresome quarrel about the regency was settled, he began to reap the reward of his obstinate perseverance. A change in French policy made it possible for the Italians to settle their affairs in their own way.

Napoleon's foreign secretary, Walewski, had made it the cardinal point of his policy to prevent Piedmont from expanding into central Italy. That policy failed, first, because France was not in a position to permit a renewal of the war by Austria, and secondly, because the Emperor kept balancing one possibility against another, and denied frank support to his foreign minister. The first open check to Walewski was the signature on November 10 of the Peace of Zurich, which, while it upheld still the principle of a federation of Italian states, removed the stipulation of the preliminaries of Villafranca that the expelled princes should return, and merely reserved their rights till the future of Italy was settled at a congress. The Tuscans were well content with the terms of peace,[2] for they did not doubt that Ricasoli would be able to keep the country orderly and disciplined till he forced Europe to accept the one solution which he himself admitted.[3] It was reported from Paris that Napoleon was still insisting on a kingdom of central Italy,[4] but the Italians believed that his resistance to their wishes would crumble when they reiterated their intentions in the European Congress. Cavour himself, sacrificing his own inclinations, had consented to represent at the Congress 'a government which can inspire neither

[1] *L. & D.*, IV, 9.   [2] *L. & D.*, III, 457 (Salvagnoli).   [3] Capponi, *Lettere*, III, 313. 'We can go ahead for some months to come as we are, because . . . the strong government inspires us with confidence. . . .'
[4] *Poggi*, III, Doc. 83. Dispatch Incontri, 24/12/1859.

esteem nor confidence'.[1] D'Azeglio had been chosen to speak for the governments of Tuscany and Emilia.[2] Then Ricasoli, who kept 'immovable' his resolution to maintain the autonomy of Tuscany until he finally broke down the opposition to her union with Piedmont, insisted upon sending a special envoy of his own.[3] 'Since the end is one, there will be three voices, loud, distinct, which will solemnly tell Europe that to leave Italy to her own destinies is to proclaim and to apply the eternal principles of law and justice'.[4] One of the three voices, he was determined, should be his own. He sent a short memorandum to his colleagues of the government informing them that the affair of the Congress must be in the hands, not of the Minister of Foreign Affairs, but of the head of the government himself.[5]

'If we succeed in completing this work', he exclaimed, 'it will be such a monument of human civilisation as has not even been dreamed of in the past'.[6]

The cause for which he stood had become to him a religion, and it rather grieved him that Italy had to go, hat in hand, before a Congress of godless diplomatists. When, therefore, there came to him rumours that the Congress, after all, was unlikely to take place, he exclaimed, 'So much the better'.[7] In December the Emperor decided that it would be better for him to escape from the predicament in which central Italy had put him by yielding to its demands, and by seeking compensation in co-operation with England and the acquisition of Savoy and Nice. He could only do this by ruining the Congress, and to ruin the Congress he called in the aid of the pamphleteer, La Guerronière. His brochure on 'the Pope and the Congress' was hailed by Cavour and by the Italians as 'a great event';[8]

[1] Chiala, *Lettere di Cavour*, III, 149. Cavour's appointment had been suggested by Napoleon himself. Bianchi, *Diplomazia*, VIII, 230. [2] *L. & D.*, IV, 105–6, 115, 120, 136. *Poggi*, II, 15. [3] *L. & D.*, IV, 151.
[4] *L. & D.*, IV, 143. [5] *L. & D.*, IV, 125. [6] *L. & D.*, IV, 307.
[7] *L. & D.*, IV, 135–6. Final notice of the adjournment came to Florence on January 4. [8] It was translated into Italian, published in Florence by Barbèra, and had large sales.

this Napoleon had intended. Walewski's attempts to discount the pamphlet as unrepresentative of the official policy of France came to nothing, for on December 31 the Emperor wrote to the Pope a letter which put his intentions beyond all doubt.[1] Rome was asked to make concessions which it certainly would not yield; as a result neither Rome nor Austria would accept the Congress, and France recovered her liberty of action. On January 4 Thouvenel succeeded Walewski. On the following day there were announced at Paris certain economic reforms, based largely on the principle of free-trade agreements, and hailed by the *Morning Post* as ' a phase of the Anglo-French alliance which will begin a new era in Italy'. ' There will be no Congress', wrote Ricasoli in delight, ' we shall finish our work by ourselves'.[2] He still considered that the deputation should go to Paris, but he told it very clearly what its business was.

' You will not interrogate Napoleon; but instead . . . you will tell him what our will is, and what we intend to do, never turning aside from our road'.[3]

But what would Piedmont do? The old cabinet had shown few signs of possessing the courage to take a forward move. Even Rattazzi, who had been converted to annexation,[4] could not hope easily to escape from the precedents which had accumulated in the last six months. On January 14, D'Azeglio wrote to Ricasoli that the cabinet must be overturned;[5] and overturned it was, a few days later. On January 17 Cavour was back in power. ' The rigid Ricasoli was beside himself with delight'.[6] The Tuscans did not know who was in the new cabinet, wrote Ricasoli to Massari, but they knew one name, and that was enough for them. They waited for Cavour to act. 'Annexation or the *status quo*. If you want us, take us'[7]—that was the policy of Tuscany. Ricasoli made up his mind that Tuscany

---

[1] The letter did not reach the Pope till January 9, and was summarised in the Tuscan *Monitore* on January 12.   [2] *L. & D.*, IV, 158 (January 13). [3] *L. & D.*, IV, 162 (January 16).   [4] *Poggi*, II, 126.   [5] *L. & D.*, IV, 161.   [6] *L. & D.*, IV, 174. Cugia to Cavour.   [7] *L. & D.*, IV, 172.

would have her deputies ready for the next Piedmontese
parliament—the first *Italian* parliament—and published
the constitution and the electoral law of the northern
kingdom.[1] It remained for Turin to give marching orders.
'Let the King speak!' exclaimed Ricasoli. It was his
constant refrain. 'Let the King speak forth!' The
time for subterfuges and hesitations was past; Tuscany
had a right to look to Piedmont for leadership, and Piedmont had a duty to give it. It was 'the last step'.[2] It
would be a beautiful Assembly, mused Ricasoli, but it
must not waste time in vain chatterings. There was a
Kingdom to be organised, an old and civilised 'municipal'
life to be reconciled with the wider life of a great nation.
For himself, he dreamed of retirement.

'The Parliamentary life does not attract me. I love strong and decisive
action, especially if it be accompanied by risks for a great end. I hate the
life of chattering, of jealousies and miserable passions'.[3]

He sighed for peace, for the country, for expeditions in
the Alps; yet it was with regret that he saw the months
of great endeavour drawing to a close.

By the end of January it seemed that the end would
come within a few weeks. Cavour's circular of January 27
set forth without equivocation the programme of union.[4]
It was seconded, on January 31, by a dispatch of Thouvenel
to the French envoy at Vienna, in which France cut herself
away, once and for all, from the principles of Villafranca.[5]
On February 1, Cavour communicated to Ricasoli the
four points set forward by England and accepted, with
one academic reservation, by France.[6] As regards central
Italy, their burden was to permit a Sardinian occupation
of the territory governed by Ricasoli and Farini, on the
one condition that the populations were again consulted
as to their wishes, through the medium of new assemblies,
elected for this special purpose. Cavour could congratulate
himself that victory was within his grasp.

[1] *Atti*, IV, 127 and 172.   [2] *L. & D.*, IV, 188.   [3] *L. & D.*, IV,
199 *et seq.* Cf. IV, 312; *Poggi*, II, 43.   [4] Cavour's points were (1) no
restorations, (2) union, (3) union to be carried out by the Italians themselves.   [5] *Poggi*, III, Doc. 91 (II).   [6] Chiala, *Lettere di Cavour*, III, 192.

But for the last time, and most inopportunely, Ricasoli saw a question of principle. Why should Tuscany be called upon to register a new vote? Had she not manifested her will in one solemn act, and repeated the manifestation in every possible way? If the resurrection of Italy was decreed by Providence, if it was a European necessity, if it was a guarantee of peace, if it was a monument of civilisation, then it must be sealed in a noble and dignified manner.

'This Italy which has shown herself so noble, so high, must not be forced to undergo humiliations of any kind. . . . For six months I have laboured to raise the minds of the Tuscans. Who will dare constrain me to offer them a new humiliation?'[1]

He went down to Leghorn to present the national guard of that city with its colours, and the festival of patriotism at which he presided increased his disdain for those who would make him stoop and bargain.

'Italy cannot enter the family of nations humiliated, dishonoured. And for this reason I insist that Cavour keeps himself well informed about us; let him take account of us. We shall not budge a hair's breadth from this way'.[2]

Cavour asked Ricasoli to come and discuss the matter with him at Turin. Ricasoli refused to budge.[3] Cavour must have sighed; but he bethought himself of Massari, a friend of them both, and sent him to Florence bearing a letter of patient, reasonable persuasiveness. After all, he suggested, they were faced with only a question of means. Was it so humiliating that the will of Tuscany should receive a second popular baptism? The Emperor had been wrong in committing himself to the policy of Villafranca; but now that he had seen the light, it was surely good policy to aid him in his effort to make honourable amends. Whatever the Italians thought about it, they were not in the position to argue about forms with the head of an armed and benevolent nation of thirty-six million people. All this wisdom made no impression on Ricasoli's obstinacy. Cavour, however, had another card

[1] *L. & D.*, IV, 219.   [2] *L. & D.*, IV, 221.   [3] *L. & D.*, IV, 243.

to play. The King, he said, had accepted the new necessity: would Tuscany desert the King?[1] Massari came to Florence to drive the argument home, and Ricasoli's pride was vanquished by his loyalty. ' You will understand', he said, ' that I cannot deny my confidence to the King whom I have chosen'.

'You cannot conceive', wrote Massari to Cavour, ' what an impression that man's words, full of faith, made upon me, as I listened. "My reign is finished", he said to me, "I consign to the King a pearl which will be a great jewel in his crown. I should have preferred that the great principle had triumphed in a great manner, but I sacrifice my personal conviction to the common good ".'[2]

He yielded to the extent of permitting the Tuscan deputies, who were to be elected to the Italian Assembly, to assemble in Florence before they took their departure for Turin, in order that they might repeat the vote already given for union. But he was forced to yield still further; for on February 7, his ambassador had telegraphed from Paris[3] that the Emperor demanded that the peoples concerned should reiterate their will by means of plebiscites. Ricasoli found all these negotiations a ' great mystification'.[4] He was restless, too, at the delays which dragged on through February into March; the news of the pact between Cavour and Napoleon for the surrender of Savoy and Nice had leaked out to England, and the Anglo-French *entente*, which alone made it possible for the Italians to act, was in consequence almost wrecked. Napoleon was distrustful of the road on which he had set his feet, and supporters of a central Italian kingdom again raised their heads in Paris.[5] Cavour thought it necessary to assure Ricasoli of his resolution; he telegraphed that the Tuscans might count upon his devotion, even upon his audacity;[6] and Massari wrote that he was standing firm in face of a threat that the French would withdraw their troops from

[1] *L. & D.*, IV, 261. [2] *L. & D.*, IV, 279. [3] *L. & D.*, IV, 258-9.
[4] *L. & D.*, IV, 346. [5] *L. & D.*, IV, 304 (Fabrizi to Ricasoli, February 17). Cf. *Poggi*, III., Doc. 94 (Incontri's dispatches). [6] *L. & D.*, III, 313 (February 20).

Italy.[1] Ricasoli, meanwhile, was making more difficulties with regard to the form of the plebiscite, which, he claimed, must not admit the possibility of a central Kingdom, but should simply put the question: ' Union to the constitutional throne of Victor Emmanuel: yes or no'.[2] In the end, he gave way upon this point as upon the others. Cavour communicated to him a French dispatch which urged upon Sardinia the advisability of encouraging a central Kingdom, and informed her that, if Sardinia rejected this advice, France, while accepting Savoy and Nice, would yet act in the whole matter in accordance with her own interests.[3] The dispatch seemed almost to conceal a threat, and Ricasoli liked being threatened. He was now ready to vent his disdain upon the French representative in Florence,[4] and to push on his preparations for the plebiscite.

The Tuscans had from the beginning disliked the idea of appealing to a vote of their whole people. The newspaper *La Patrie* had first put forward the suggestion at Paris; and the ambassador Peruzzi, perplexed by the intrigues with which he was surrounded, had in a moment of impulsiveness challenged Walewski to abide by the issue of a plebiscite.[5] He tried to reassure himself and his colleague in London by asserting that his move had been purely ' strategic', and that it had been nothing more than a personal expression of opinion which could not bind the government. Even if this were not the case, he reasoned, the battle of opinion would be fought out between the country and the towns, and there were ' more town proletarians than peasants'. But Neri Corsini, the ambassador in London, shook his head over the ' arduous proof' which had been suggested, and wrote urging his friends

[1] *Ibid.* [2] *L. & D.*, IV, 320, 327. [3] *L. & D.*, IV, 362. Thouvenel's dispatch is dated February 24. Cavour communicated it to Ricasoli on February 29. [4] *L. & D.*, IV, 391. On March 3 Baron de Mesbourg protested that France did not approve Tuscan conduct, and was answered in strong terms by Ricasoli. The French protest was a feint. [5] *Lettere Politiche*, p. 106. Cf. *Poggi*, III, 145 (September 3) cf. Arguments against universal suffrage in Galeotti, *L'Assemblea Toscana*, 6–7.

in Florence to placard the walls in the towns and country
of Tuscany with little poems of patriotism.[1] There was
indeed no fear that the opponents of the revolution would
be able to organise a 'reactionary' vote, but the nationalists were with good reason nervous that the opposition
or indifference of the countryside would be revealed by
abstention on a large scale. This was exactly what had
occurred in the case of the municipal elections which
Ricasoli organised in October. He took every reasonable
precaution to secure a heavy poll, even calling on the
landed proprietors to send their dependants to vote;[2] but
his friends admitted that these elections had been a distinct
failure.[3]

In March of 1860, however, neither Ricasoli nor his
supporters doubted that they would win a great triumph.
' I have no doubts', declared Pasolini, ' for the simple
reason that I have faith in Ricasoli'.[3] Was Pasolini's faith
so freely given because of his admiration for the Tuscan's
enthusiasm and constancy, or did he trust in some more
concrete manifestation of Ricasoli's will ? One of Ricasoli's
biographers, Dall' Ongaro, speaks of the issue of the
plebiscite as a ' spontaneous lyric song ' of the Tuscans:
' the spontaneous outburst of a need long suppressed,
the manifestation of a latent principle sown by the words
of patriots, and confirmed with the exiles, with the sufferings, with the blood of the most generous'. Ricasoli
scribbled opposite this passage a marginal note which
ignored his biographer's mixed metaphor, but rather dryly
questioned his poetical explanation of what had happened.
' Ricasoli', he wrote, ' believes it possible to doubt this
assertion as too absolute'.[5]

The letters of Capponi, one of the most trustworthy of

---

[1] *Lettere Politiche*, p. 164 *et seq.*   [2] *Atti*, II, 358. Cf. M. Carletti,
Le Elezioni comunali spiegate al popolo, and *XXXV Lettere Politiche di
Bettino Ricasoli a L. Galeotti*, p. 15. Ricasoli made use of Galeotti's propaganda in the *Nazione*. [3] *Lettere Politiche*, 201–2. Corsini made the best
of a disappointment by asserting that the poor result proved that the government left the people free to do as they liked.   [4] Pasolini, *Memorie*, 256.
[5] *Dall' Ongaro*, 38 (autograph note).

witnesses, give further reason for doubting Dall' Ongaro's theory of 'a spontaneous lyric song'. Ricasoli, wrote Capponi, found support in ' the live part' of the people, who were the only people worth considering. ' This idea dominates all, that is, the live part of the country, and you abroad '—he was writing to Matteucci, who was at Paris—' know how they impose it, if I may say so: you know the *feste*, the tears of joy, the embraces, the kisses. . . .'[1] The quiet timid section of the people—' which at bottom would not be discontented with the old order '[2]—was, says Capponi, carried away by the enthusiasm and energy of the ' dynamic majority'. A ' scruple for truth ' forced Capponi to admit that the ' numerical majority ' was perhaps not ranged upon the side of Ricasoli.[3] Whether or no this was the case, it is important to consider the activities of this ' live part ' of the people, and to examine Ricasoli's relations towards it.

Before beginning this examination, however, it is necessary to give some attention to what Capponi calls by inference the ' dead part ' of the country—especially to those who remained loyal to Leopold. In the language of the time these may be called the ' reactionaries'. A glance at the correspondence which passed between Ricasoli and any one of his prefects—the prefect of Florence may be taken as an example—makes it clear that the government, in addition to preventing them from exercising any sort of propaganda (it allowed ' in these difficult times ' ' liberty to help, and not to harm, the national cause ')[4] kept them under the closest police supervision.[5] Individual patriots, including women, also offered their services as spies.[6] The reactionaries, therefore, deprived of all opportunity to champion their interests and opinions openly, were reduced to leaving large numbers of visiting cards at the house of one of Walewski's emissaries,[7] or of sending to

[1] Capponi, *Lettere*, III, 310.   [2] *Ibid.* III, 313.   [3] *Ibid.* III, 325.
[4] *Atti*, II, 369.   [5] *Brolio MSS.*, 34; 102, 105, 124. 35; 124. 35; 16. 37; 17, etc.   [6] *Ibid.* 39, 25. A certain Maddalena Lori reports reactionary gossip.   [7] *Poggi*, III, Doc. 41. *I casi della Toscana*, 412-3. Prince Poniatowski.

the members of the government portraits of certain famous criminals of Lucca, with the names of Ricasoli and his colleagues written underneath.[1] In January of 1860 they were still more desperate, and made an attempt to remove Ricasoli from their path by bombing his house. Ricasoli wished to know who would pay for his broken windows.[2] The reactionaries, in fact, completely lost heart, and in March they could do no more than prophesy that ' the French troops will come as vanguard of the dear white-coats', or that Russia would put ' the pretender ' (Victor Emmanuel) in his place. Their only method of protesting against what they claimed was an unfree plebiscite was to abstain from voting, and to influence others to abstain.[3]

The ' live part of the country', therefore, was free to carry on its propaganda unimpeded and almost unanswered. That propaganda had many aspects. It was, to a certain extent, social. A certain Cugia, who was an emissary of Cavour's in Florence, reported that almost all Florentine ' society ' had been won over to the cause of union, and that well-bred women spoke with passion of Italy.[4] Massari confirmed these reports, and added that the Prince Strozzi was turning his social activities into veritable manifestos for annexation.[5] Ricasoli made use of Florentine society, and encouraged the municipality to spend from forty to fifty thousand lire on a patriotic ball.[6] Patriotism became something of a fashion; and fashion, if one can judge from Giusti's satires, counted for a good deal in nineteenth-century Tuscany. It even gave to many a means of liveli-hood. Throughout these months the hackney coaches which plied the streets had huge and hideous woodcuts of Victor Emmanuel under their splash-boards, while social pressure encouraged the citizens to paint ' Vittorio Emanuele Nostro Re ' upon their shutters.[7] The hawkers sold slices of Victor Emmanuel watermelons, or stamped

[1] *Poggi*, I, 453. [2] *L. & D.*, IV, 180, note. Bombs were thrown on two occasions, and Salvagnoli's house also received attention (see *Brolio MSS.*, 33, *passim*). [3] *Poggi, loc. cit.* [4] *L. & D.*, IV, 174. [5] *L. & D.*, IV, 278. [6] Trollope *op. cit.* 170. [7] *Ibid.* 87.

on their wafer-biscuits[1] crude representations of the King's
features. A body of resolute singers can easily popularise
an air, and one of the most popular songs in Florence
called upon the Austrians to get them gone from Italy.[2]
Carducci's star was in the ascendant, for his ' Cross of
Savoy ' had been set to music, and was in high favour
with the bands of the National Guard. The theatre, as
ever, was in close partnership with the nationalists.[3] It
had been useful to them in the days of opposition, and
now that they were in the ascendant, it was organised as
a medium of patriotic education. Ricasoli established a
board of censors, and laid down the principle that the
theatre must ' aid the work of the national *Risorgimento*
of Italy'.[4]

This is an example of what may be called the ' higher '
propaganda. Ricasoli was just as much the moral schoolmaster as he had been during the early days at Brolio.
He believed sincerely that he was achieving the regenera-
tion of his fellow countrymen; and in effect he told them,
as he had told his peasants, years ago, in one of his Sunday
sermons: ' My will ought to be your will, for what I will
is to do you good'.[5] He tried to make the Tuscans feel,
as he felt, that the Italian question was ' not a question of
miserable interests',[6] but a struggle between good and
evil, liberty and tyranny, civilisation and barbarism. When
he addressed the National Guard of Florence, or of Leghorn,
or of Pisa,[7] he left no doubt in the minds of his audience
that he and his cause, they and their cause, were in the
special care of Providence. He multiplied the volume of
his voice by means of his circulars to the prefects; and he
called in the aid of educated persons like Galeotti, Bianchi,
or Tabarrini, who could appeal through the *Nazione* or

[1] *brigidini (ibid.)*. [2] *Va fuori d'Italia*. It was the song of the *Cacciatori
delle Alpi.* [3] Niccolini was still the literary fashion, and his *Arnaldo*
was performed at the *Cocomero*, amid scenes which did not please Ricasoli
(*Brolio MSS.*, 38, 31). All sorts of patriotic songs and poems were popu-
larised. See bibliography. [4] *Atti*, II, 348 and 350. [5] See Chapter III.
[6] *L. & D.*, IV, 135. [7] *L. & D.*, IV, 45, 212, 282, 335. Salvagnoli
helped Ricasoli to compose these discourses. *Poggi, op. cit.*

through their pamphlets to the better classes of the population.[1] He realised that the battle must be fought in the schools, and he invaded the sphere of the minister Ridolfi in order to give an extra propagandist twist to education.

Ridolfi, as has been seen, had gradually been dislodged from the control of the department of Foreign Affairs. He consoled himself with the congenial task of carrying out those measures which he had so often urged when his activities were limited to the Academy of the *Georgofili*. As a good beginning, he increased the government subsidy to that Academy.[2] Then he established an Agrarian Institute in the Cascine gardens, and a Chair of Agriculture in the *Liceo Fiorentino*.[3] He set up a commission to study the problem of primary education; he established an Inspectorate of Schools, and an Inspectorate of Parks and Gardens.[4] At the same time, he gave proof that Florence, restored to freedom, was not unmindful of her artistic and literary glories. He created a commission for conserving works of art,[5] he commissioned an unemployed advocate to write a history of Lucca,[6] and he delighted Tuscan sculptors by authorising them to erect in Tuscan cities a whole series of monuments to contemporary patriots.[7] Perhaps it was not his fault that all the monuments were very ugly. . . . Yet even in this field, Ricasoli did not leave Ridolfi a free hand. There were a number of chairs to be filled in the University of Pisa, and the President of the Ministry presented to his colleague a lengthy memorandum[8] which began with some platitudinous remarks on education, and ended with a nationalist discourse. A Professor, reasoned Ricasoli, must first of all be a man of upright life. Secondly, he must have a constant affection

---

[1] e.g. *XXV Lettere di B. R. a L. G.*, 15, 18, 17. Pamphlets by Galeotti, Peruzzi, Carletti, etc., were also intended for foreign consumption. In addition some of Ricasoli's speeches were published for immediate circulation. [2] *Atti*, III, 229. [3] *Ibid.* III, 248; IV, 317. [4] *Ibid.* I, 94, 113. [5] *Ibid.* VI, 69. [6] *Ibid.* II, 340. [7] *Ibid.* II, 250. These are only a few illustrations of Ridolfi's activities. Many others are recorded in the *Atti e Documenti*. ' He imagined Florence a great studio'. *Memorie di F. Ranalli*, p. 87. [8] *L. & D.*, III, 316–319.

for the Fatherland and for Liberty. Students, similarly, must learn from their professors not only dead knowledge, but also living maxims of conduct. They must be taught politics, not by 'fanatical orators', but by 'sapient professors'. There must be no divorce between the lecture-room and 'real life'. 'Let Youth, even in the *penetralia* of Knowledge, find the Fatherland, and listen to the voice of Liberty'. Perhaps Ricasoli had forgotten Professor Pigli, who in the bad old days of the 'Earthly Paradise' turned his lectures on physiology into patriotic orations, and, as Giusti said, found Italy in the pineal gland.

Ricasoli believed with a desperate sincerity that he stood, first and foremost, for the cause of Liberty. There was, perhaps, only one man in Florence who realised that Liberty was not indissolubly bound up with Nationality, and who doubted whether the nationalist party really cared for the freedom of the human spirit. This man, Ferdinando Ranalli,[1] held 'principles of liberty deduced from the books and the examples of the ancients', and as a result found himself continually in conflict with the tendency of his age. He was a sincere patriot who in 1848 had become attached—accidentally, it is true—to the more radical section, and who, after the revolution had been chastened, wrote one of the most balanced accounts of its vicissitudes.[2] 'To go with the majority', he declared in his memoirs, 'to make myself a sheep, is contrary to my nature'. He wished to contribute to the restoration of Italy's greatness, but his ideas were unorthodox; and though he had three books upon the Papal Index, the patriots threatened to burn in the piazza another of his writings which he published in 1859 upon the subject of Italian reform.[3] 'In a time of political changes', reflected Ranalli, 'it is extremely dangerous to publish a book of political science'. He was unorthodox, not only in his political, but in his literary opinions. His tastes were for

---

[1] E. Masi, *Memorie di F. Ranalli, passim.* [2] *Le Istorie Italiane dal 1846 al 1853.* Firenze, 1858. [3] *Del Riordinamento d'Italia.* Firenze, 1859. The author had not thought a revolution possible.

the classical style, and he did not care for Manzoni. This was considered almost treason, and it was reported that Ranalli had been pandering to the Austrians in the hope that they would give him a professorship. Ridolfi himself admitted that Ranalli's opinions with regard to Manzoni disqualified him from holding a chair in Pisa.[1] It is, indeed, doubtful whether Ranalli would have helped the Youth to ' find the Fatherland ' in the ' *penetralia* of Knowledge'; but he might have inspired them with some true ideas about freedom. His observations remain as a curious challenge to the enthusiastic proselytising of these years. He reflected, for example, that the various nations were becoming most like to each other at the very time when all were shouting most loudly about their nationality; and prophesied gloomily that before long it would be sufficient to see one country in order to gain a fairly accurate idea of all the others. He doubted whether teachers and professors could be turned out from training schools as goods are turned out from a factory, because he considered that teaching was ' a gift'. In later years, he would even have left Rome to the Pope, for he valued variety and intimacy in life above all things, and regarded capital cities as the worst tyrants of modern times. ' If I had to conspire for anything, I should conspire for the abolition of the capital'.[2]

Ranalli, contrasted with Ricasoli, represents detached intellectual sincerity as opposed to ardent, uncritical, moral sincerity. A mere statement of the conflicting points of view is sufficient to make it clear that the former could not hope to stem the triumphant proselytising of the latter. The questions of men like Ranalli do not even find listeners in times of crowd-excitement and moral exaltation; but they are not asked in vain, for they remain to suggest a criticism of the past when the minds of men have become more serene.

[1] E. Masi, *op. cit.* p. 89.   [2] Cf. p. 69 for Ranalli's reflections on the nationalist revolution in the days of its triumph. ' The Enterprise succeeded, and even more than could have been prophesied, but the effects were not such as a true and sincere lover of liberty could have wished'.

The crowds of the Tuscan cities had more fascinating literature than Ranalli could give to them. In these months Tuscany had also a 'low' propaganda, as once she had had a 'low' police. 'Prior Luca' was still hard at work enlightening 'vulgar intellects'. In his fourth 'Vigil', he recorded an imaginary letter from Pio Nono.[1] The Pope, instead of sending his Swiss to massacre the unfortunate citizens of Perugia,[2] informed them that he wished to possess, not their bodies, but their souls. They were therefore free to join the glorious new kingdom of Italy. Then the Holy Father turned to Cardinal Antonelli, and said sharply: 'Get thee behind me, Satan'. What would have been the result, demanded the writer of this imaginary letter, if the Pope had really composed and sent it? There would, he answered, have been no more schismatics and no more protestants. The Queen of England and the Emperor of Russia and the Sultan of Turkey would all have come—not for mere political reasons, but with a high moral purpose—to kiss the foot of the Pope. Then the priests, 'instead of being despised and hated, would be the idol and joy of the country'. The aim of the pamphlet was to prove that the government and its supporters were better friends of religion than was the Pope himself.

Unfortunately, the people for whom this pamphlet was intended were just as likely to read the comic papers. 'Three hundred and ninety-nine thousand and one', wrote one of these very papers, 'someone says; and we ask: Are you counting soldiers?—No, we are counting journals'.[3] There were in Florence alone more than a dozen comic papers which lent their support to the patriots with caricatures and humorous articles. Sometimes they became serious, like the *Piovano Arlotto*, which addressed the Tuscan clergy as follows: 'What devil stuck it in your

---

[1] *Confiteor. Veglie Quarta e Quinta del Prior Luca.* [2] The 'massacre' of Perugia, a favourite theme for propaganda, was grossly exaggerated. See *Archivio Storico Italiano*, V, 25, 301 *et seq.* (Letter of an eye-witness to Vieusseux). [3] G. Rondoni, *I Giornali Umoristici Fiorentini del Triennio Glorioso*. Firenze, 1914., p. 102.

head that it was good to have in the country a foreign race
to act the master, to tax, and hang us, drink our blood,
and befoul this beautiful land of ours. . . . God has in
hand the fortune of our land. . . . *He* knows what he is
about'.[1] Some of the caricatures were amusing and in-
offensive. *La Chiacchiera*, in January, printed a sketch
which showed Victor Emmanuel, with his coat and shoes
off, climbing up a greasy pole to plant upon it a bust of
Liberty. The reactionaries (in pig-tails) tried to climb up
after him and drag him down, but he shouted: ' If you
come on, you'll get a kick in the bread-basket'.[2] The
peasants may have laughed at this. But they shook their
heads when the new religion of patriotism took a blasphemous turn. *La Lenta* spoke of *Victor Emmanuel
Christus*, and published a sketch which pictured old Rome
as a she-wolf suckling twins, and modern Rome as a
wolf devouring children. It published, too, a new *Pater
Noster*. ' Our Father, which art in the Vatican, Hallowed
be Thy Name if Thou takest Thy Kingdom out of Italy,
and if Thou turnest Thy will more to heaven than to
earth'.[3] This was overshooting the mark, for though the
majority of the Florentines probably thought it extraordinarily funny, the simple people of the country were
shocked and alienated. ' Prior Luca', himself, who knew
better than most people what the peasants were thinking,
found it a difficult matter to explain away the more blasphemous or ungenerous caricatures. It was unkind to
caricature Leopold and the Pope, he said; for the Pope
had been so high, and now he was so low. As for Leopold,
it was a shame to laugh at his misery. Poor man! He had
no hope of returning to Tuscany, and could not even
possess ' internal consolations ' and the approval of his
own conscience.[4]

Capponi, who was almost alone among the liberals in
possessing a fine feeling for history, and who found time
to regret the past even when he believed it his duty to

[1] *Ibid*. 74. [2] *Ibid*. 116. *Se venite avanti, avrete il piede nella zucca.*
[3] *Ibid*. 28, 29. [4] *Confiteor, etc. (Veglia Quinta)*, p. 38.

applaud those who were assailing it, wrote to Ricasoli
imploring him to check these petty extravagances.

'For Pity's sake', he wrote, 'let it not be us who make the confusion.
It is we who to-day are the aggressors, I mean in the matter of the Temporal
Power; for it is in fact we who are in course of destroying the work of centuries, a work which to-day is bound up with evil. We must show that we
do not wish to overthrow the good together with the bad, nor to carry out
a work of mere destruction. . . .'[1]

Ricasoli was ready enough to listen to this plea. In an order
forbidding the publication of caricatures of the Pope,[2] he
had already insisted that the times demanded 'severity
and not frivolity'. He was too much of the aristocrat not
to hate cheap vulgarity, and was too conscientious to make
use of the thing he hated. Even so, it was hard to keep
the irreverent wit of Florentine journalists within bounds.
Their wit, after all, had done good service to the cause
during the years which preceded the triumphant revolution.

It would be difficult to over-estimate what Tuscany
and Italy gained through the leadership of Ricasoli. He
ennobled the nationalist movement by checking its extravagances, and by making it a reflection of his own rigid
morality. He refused to admit for a moment that it was
an affair of 'base interests'. Those generalisations which
explain every idealistic movement by referring to a direct
economic cause, conflict with all the facts of this period of
Tuscan history. It is of course true that the ideas of Democracy and Nationality were born from the rising power
of the 'Third Estate', and that they triumphed throughout
western Europe because they seemed to satisfy the peculiar
needs of this class. Ideas do not come to birth of themselves, but can only grow from a suitable economic and
social soil. But once they have been produced, they often
possess a reproductive power of their own. This was the
case in Tuscany. The direct economic impulse towards

[1] Capponi, Lettere, III, 333. Tabarrini, Capponi, 306.　　[2] Atti, III,
369. Cf. L. & D., III, 237 (August 31, 1859). Cf. Brolio MSS., 39,
22. He ordered the prefect of Florence to prevent small boys from
singing scandalous Stornelli in the streets (March 9, 1860).

unity with Piedmont was not an exceedingly strong one.[1] Tuscany exported very little. She had scarcely felt the need to raise foreign loans.[2] Her husbandry was almost entirely self-sufficing, and the great majority of her towns lived by local exchange. The men who had first become imbued with nationalist sentiment had been nobles like Capponi, Ridolfi, or Ricasoli, who owed their wealth to the land and increased it by paying intelligent attention to the land; or professors like Montanelli or Pigli, who were painfully ignorant of anything so concrete as economic fact; or lawyers with a literary bent, such as Guerrazzi and Salvagnoli; or poets with an interest in Italian history, such as Niccolini and Giuseppe Giusti. The bankers and manufacturers caught the new ideas from men like these; they did not catch them from the bankers and manufacturers. It is of course true that the people of the towns came at last to realise that union with a large state held forth all sorts of pleasant possibilities—loans, new industrial enterprises, and the like. This, however, was an afterthought—so much of an afterthought that it is very seldom referred to even in the propagandist literature of 1849–60. The economic motive was only one strand in a very complicated web of opinion.

As for Ricasoli, he was completely unconscious that the struggle had any other side save a moral one. And, while he checked the more vulgar manifestations of anti-clerical feeling, his principles inevitably led him into a conflict with the leaders of the Church. A few weeks before the plebiscite he wrote to Massari: ' We are at grips with the priests'.[3] The Church alone was capable of maintaining a degree of open opposition to the nationalist movement, and to a certain extent the plebiscite might be interpreted as a struggle in which government and priests fought for the possession of the peasants' votes.

[1] See Chapter 2. Leghorn may be regarded as an exception.   [2] The war and the revolution, however, changed this. The financial policy of Ricasoli's government was scorned by Cavour, and negotiations for a loan in Piedmont met serious difficulties.   [3] L. & D., IV, 320.

Ricasoli had offended the Church, first of all, by maintaining the principle of religious toleration. Belief in this principle had led him to give encouragement to the Jewish cult,[1] and to permit the opening in the Piazza dell' Indipendenza of an evangelical chapel presided over by the schismatic, Guicciardini. But the evangelicals caught the fashion of the times, and identified liberty with the right to proselytise; the chapel became the scene of demonstrations which were resented, not only by the clergy, but by moderate Catholics; the government was forced to discipline the gatherings, and Guicciardini left Florence in disgust.[2] Incidents such as this, however, expanded into disputes about principle. The Archbishop of Florence protested that the government was encouraging a revolt against Catholicism, and complained that it was stirring up suspicion against the clergy.[3] Ricasoli answered by asserting that he stood for complete religious liberty. ' This liberty, which is a right of every being who is responsible to God, which is a fact of the universal conscience and a principle of every civilised state, does not prevent the Catholic Church from being, if not the dominant, at least the prevailing, one'.[4] But the leaders of the Church wanted to keep what they held, and were not slow to realise that they were threatened by the new order.

While pamphleteers were trying to prove that the Catholic religion and Italian patriotism were not really opposed,[5] the two hostile powers of inclusive Catholicism and exclusive nationalism were gathering their forces, and indulging in preliminary skirmishes along the frontier. The government interfered with the discipline of ecclesiastical jurisdiction,[6] vetoed certain pamphlets which the clergy were distributing among the faithful,[7] prohibited

[1] *Atti*, IV, 245. It was given a yearly subsidy of 40,000 lire.   [2] Trollope, *op. cit.* letters of September 25, December 16. *L. & D.*, IV, 108, 125.   [3] Carletti, *op. cit.* 114–5.   [4] *Atti*, VI, 320.   [5] *e.g.* L. Crescioli, *Il Clero e la Nazione*. P. Pozzolini, *L'Italia e il partito clericale*. The argument is that all will be well so long as the clergy keep aloof from politics. —But the Church feels itself on the defensive.   [6] *e.g. Atti*, IV, 242.
[7] *Atti*, V, 293.

the introduction into Tuscany of *La Civiltà Cattolica* and
similar periodicals, and disapproved episcopal pastorals.[1]
Appealing to the legislation of the first Leopold, it abolished
the concordat which Leopold II had signed with the
Papacy.[2] Then Ricasoli, urged on by Salvagnoli, turned
his attention to the material position of the Church.
Ignoring warnings from men such as Capponi and Galeotti,
ignoring the protests of his own colleagues, he proceeded
with measures threatening *mortmain* and the property of
the ecclesiastical corporations.[3] While Ricasoli dreamed
of ' a new and great edifice, religious, economic, civil',
Galeotti protested against his proposals as ' illegitimate
spoliation'. But Ricasoli refused ' to creep, and pass for
a eunuch'. He was willing to postpone the execution of
the scheme till after the plebiscite had been held;[4] but he
had succeeded in thoroughly alarming the Church, and
other conservative interests as well.

The bishops, of course, resisted. They caused some
dismay by organising a sort of episcopal strike, refusing
to publish the usual indulgence for eating meat during
the season of Lent.[5] The Archbishop of Pisa involved
himself in trouble with the civil authorities by including in
his ecclesiastical calendar for 1860 the usual prayer for
Tuscany's sovereign.[6] In the end, Church and State were
arrayed openly against each other in their age-old conflict
of theory. The government called upon the Church to
' fulfil the ends of the Kingdom of Heaven, and not serve
things of the earth'.[7] The whole Tuscan hierarchy, on its
part, attacked the government's ecclesiastical policy in
point after point, and concluded by accusing the new
State of seeking to reduce the bishops to the level of its
own officials, and to make of religion a mere instrument
of politics. Ricasoli replied to these accusations on the very

---

[1] *Atti*, IV, 243.   [2] *Atti*, IV, 318.   [3] *Poggi*, II, 169 *et seq.*; III,
Doc. 108. Poggi more than once threatened resignation on this issue. For
Galeotti's opposition, *L. & D.*, IV, 276–7 and 279.   [4] The decree was
finally signed by four ministers only, on March 27. *Atti*, VI, 338.   [5] *Atti*,
V, 269.   [6] *Poggi*, II, 73–77.   [7] *Atti*, IV, 324.

day which followed the announcement of the plebiscite.[1]
He began by confessing frankly that he desired the abolition of the Temporal Power. This, he declared, would
help rather than hinder the spiritual work of the Church,
and would make possible a reconciliation between Rome
and Italy. He complained that the Church, ' in defiance of
the Laws and in open hostility to the sentiments of the
Nation', had left nothing undone to favour ' the hostile
faction'. Then he attacked the great questions of theory.
The Church, if it was a Divine Institution, in a sense
possessing a higher aim than the State, was also a Human
Institution, accepted by the State. Between Church and
State there must be a system of mutual non-interference.
The State must not interfere in questions of dogma: the
Church must obey the laws which the State had made for
the universal good of society. Ricasoli, in fact, anticipated
Cavour's famous slogan of a ' free Church in a free State'.

' The Church', he said, ' should remain, in the spiritual exercise of its
functions, entirely free from the State: as the State must remain free in the
temporal exercise of its rights'.

It was a doctrine easier to proclaim than to define to the
satisfaction of both sides. Ricasoli, for example, considered it a right of the State to censor ecclesiastical
literature. The Church, he said, should be thankful if the
State exercised this right, for then—' Its words of eternal
life directed to the flock will be accepted without any
suspicion, and hence will receive greater veneration'.
It is hardly surprising that the bishops were not convinced.
The Church demanded from its sons a larger allegiance
than the State would allow its citizens to yield. The bishops
saw clearly that the new Nationalist State was only the old
Despotic State writ large.

The government, since it was forced to regard the
priests as actual or potential enemies, took careful measures
to watch their activities. Individual patriots, among them
Ricasoli's own brother, helped the prefects in denouncing

[1] *Atti*, VI, 338–49 (March 16).

manifestations of clerical anti-nationalism.[1] But the police could not deal with the clergy as they could deal with the lay champions of the old dynasty. Supporters of the revolution were tormented by fears of a peasantry voting solidly at the instigation of its spiritual leaders, or at the very least, of discrediting the great cause by refusing to vote at all. An ardent nationalist wrote to Ricasoli that there was hardly a peasant who would take the trouble to vote, unless he were driven to the poll by the intrigues of the nationalists.[2] It is significant that 'Prior Luca', who understood very well what 'vulgar intellects' were prone to think, found it necessary to explain away some of Ricasoli's utterances with regard to ecclesiastical policy,[3] just as he had attempted to minimise the unfortunate impression caused by the anti-papal caricatures.

It was a difficult matter to counterbalance the influence of the priests, and to awaken in the country districts enthusiasm for the cause which had won its way in the towns. Ploughing between their vines with the oxen and the ploughs of Vergil's age, threshing their corn with the hand-flails of their Etruscan ancestors, the peasants of the more remote districts found the ideas of the nineteenth century as strange and as perplexing as its machinery. In 1799 the peasants of southern Tuscany had risen to fight for the Virgin Mary against the French, and in Siena had made of the Trees of Liberty a pyre for the burning of Jews and Jacobins.[4] In 1849 they had turned against the noisy patriots who were disturbing the even tenour of their existence, and had rallied to the cause of *Babbo*. In 1859 trusted agents of the government reported that the peasants of the south—notably of the department of Arezzo—were imbued with the same 'reactionary' spirit. Cambray-Digny, who was in charge of the state properties throughout Tuscany, reported that the spirit

---

[1] *Brolio MSS.*, 39, 44. Vicenzo Ricasoli reports that the clergy of San Felicità refuse to pray for the King. For similar denunciations *ibid.* 36, 71; 37, 10; 39, 44; 37, 25. [2] *L. & D.*, IV, 372.   [3] *Confiteor. Veglia Quinta di Prior Luca.* [4] See E. Masi. *Il Viva Maria.*

of the inhabitants of the Val di Chiana was bad, though he added that the government need not fear a rising.[1] The prefect wished Ricasoli to post in the district soldiers returned from Lombardy.[2] Another suggestion was that the government should arm ' chosen and upright citizens'. If the government gave to them old rifles and any kind of swords, it was claimed, the mere sight of them would be sufficient to keep the peasants in order.[3] This was in June 1859, and in October, when there were rumours of a plot, the prefect wrote that many ' good citizens ' were watching the enemy party, and that the infernal plot was petering out. The prefect assured Ricasoli that he himself would not sleep till the crisis was past.[4] After October, there were no more disquieting reports from Arezzo. The prefect and the ' good citizens ' between them completely gained the upper hand. In December, the prefect was granted an increased allowance for his expenses.[5] He used it to good purpose, and on March 4 he reported that he was ' neglecting nothing so that the approaching vote should respond worthily to the cares of the government and the expectation of the country'.[6] The 'good citizens' were equally active. The historian, Gualterio, wrote to Ricasoli from Cortona that he was working with Cambray-Digny ' in an agitation in the widest sense'. ' There has been nominated a commission for every single parish, and in order to make certain that the voting is not only good, but numerous, a committee remains in permanent sitting all the week'.[7]

The example of this province will serve to illustrate the activities directed by Ricasoli. The government claimed that the plebiscite was entirely free. The scrutiny was put into the hands of the judicial authorities,[8] and freedom of the Press was restored[9]—six days before the voting was to be held. In an official message to the country the govern-

---

[1] Brolio MSS., 32, 34. Cf. Cambray-Digny, Carteggio, 197.   [2] Ibid.
[3] Brolio MSS., 31, 48.   [4] Ibid. 34, 92.   [5] Ibid. 36, 127.   [6] L. & D.,
IV, 393.   [7] L. & D., IV, 396.   [8] Atti, V, 316–321. Decree for the
plebiscite, March 1.   [9] Ibid. V, 343.

ment reminded voters that they were under no restraint, that they were responsible to themselves and to God alone . . . then it congratulated them that, in a few days, they would have the satisfaction of being Italians under 'the Loyal and Magnanimous King VICTOR EMMANUEL'.[1] There was, indeed, no reason for doubt. 'Illumination' of the voters once again was proved to be a more satisfactory method of achieving the great end than constraining them. Patriotic propaganda reached its grand climax. In the last few weeks local committees had been stirring up a fever of enthusiasm by leading peasants into the towns to offer subscriptions for the purchase of 'a thousand rifles'. The press, every day, poured forth unanimous exhortations for a heavy poll in favour of the King. The *Nazione* distributed to all its subscribers numbers of voting-papers marked for the right cause, and exhorted the recipients to distribute the papers far and wide. The ladies of Florence wrote letters and circulars to their *fattori*, and to the peasants of their estates.[2] During the concluding weeks of the agitation a number of new pamphlets appeared—'Prior Luca' again to the fore[3]— and Ricasoli urged the prefects to spare no expense, to use all the men at their command, including the *carabinieri*, in order to distribute widely these little handbooks of patriotism.[4] On occasion, public-spirited prefects themselves undertook the task, and rode round the countryside as 'apostles of truth and paternal charity'.[5] In short, as Ricasoli explained to Cavour, there was 'an intelligent and decorous agitation'.[6] Ricasoli was determined that it should remain decorous. He insisted to the very end that his revolution should be sealed in that disciplined, Puritan spirit with which he had defended it. At the first signs of indisciplined and abusive agitation in Florence, he wrote to the prefect an indignant letter ordering him to prevent

---

[1] *Atti*, V, 339. [2] See *Della Torre*, p. 503. [3] *I due voti annessi e sconessi,Veglia VI.*Cf.C. Carfora, *L'Italia e le potenze Europee*. O. Orlandini, *Del suffraggio universale*, etc. [4] *L. & D.*, IV, 370. [5] *L. & D.*, IV, 393 (F. Doni, prefect of Siena). [6] *L. & D.*, IV, 400.

all such manifestations for the future. ' It is not with the importunate cry nor with plebeian shouting that Italians are made. Nations are made by firm will, by discipline, and by sacrifice'.[1]

The discipline of the plebiscite was modelled on that which the baron had made to prevail, long years ago, at Brolio. He marched the Tuscans to vote.

' The bailiffs at the head of their own administrations, the most influential peasant proprietor at the head of the men of his parish, the most authoritative citizen at the head of the inhabitants of one street, one quarter, etc. . . . will order and lead his voters in a troop, in a file more or less numerous, but always disciplined and marching in good order, to the urns of the Nation. The Italian flag will be at the head. Each one will lay in the urn his paper, and then retire, and at a fixed point the troop will be dissolved with that quiet and dignity, which comes from the consciousness of having performed a high duty'.[2]

Sometimes the leaders of these parties of voters pronounced a short discourse on their high duty before they led the march to the urns.[3] On March 11 the troops began to march; the voting continued that day and the next. The result was announced at midnight on the 15th. Of about 534,000 voters registered on the rolls, 386,445 had declared for union, 14,925 had declared for a separate Kingdom. Nearly 5,000 votes were declared null.[4]

Ricasoli had won the great triumph of his life. It was a victory of fervour and of discipline. Only one party of voters attempted to wreck the perfect order of this great national declaration. In the Chianti, some of Ricasoli's own peasants tried to knock over the voting urns. Who can tell what obscure thoughts, what blind, unreasoned feelings prompted this demonstration of peasants?[5]

[1] *L. & D.*, III, 393. Cf. 410. On the eve of the elections Ricasoli ordered the prefect of Florence to bring to order men who were crying out in the streets ' the confession of Leopold II'.   [2] *L. & D.*, III, 390. The voting-booths were beflagged, and the municipal officers were present to watch, ' helped by good patriots'. *Poggi*, II, 237.   [3] *Della Torre*, 509, mentions ' *Breve discorso e parole pronunziate alla Rotta presso Pisa, in occasione del suffragio Universale l*' 11 *marzo*, 1860.   [4] Supporters of the old dynasty could only abstain, as the voting formula gave them no opportunity of stating their will.
[5] *Poggi*, II, 239.

EPILOGUE

RICASOLI had fought the great battle of his life. He knew it himself; he felt himself to be a man of great occasions, and while he was fretting against every delay which stood between him and his victory, he almost feared the anti-climax which victory would bring. Italy free and Italy united meant a new, perplexing age of politics. Politics, he felt, were not for him. He would go away where he could be solitary; he would return to his 'hermit's exis-tence'.[1] He found that Italy could not spare him. He wrote to a friend: 'Can I not see that all the ideas of the time are in me, and find in me a free cultivator, without prejudice and without fanaticism of any sort? Can I not see that only the extreme parties, only the factious, the disturbers, the enemies of God and man, hate me and would wish to confound me?'[2] He told his daughter that he considered himself 'an instrument of Providence'.[3] He believed that he had divined the end which God willed for his age. Believing that, he could not shun the battle. The will of God would triumph, but only if God's instru-ments were ready to their Master's hand.

Italy, too, was an instrument of God. Ricasoli felt that the Italians were the Chosen People. They were destined, first of all, to complete their Nationhood. The revolution of Sicily and Naples succeeded that of central Italy; and Ricasoli, while he called upon Cavour to declare himself openly against ' the so-called public law of Europe, law divorced from Right, law of violence, law of material force, heritage of barbarous centuries',[4] fretted because he himself could not go forth as a soldier seeking victory or death.[5] Sicily was won; and with Sicily, Naples, Umbria, and the Marches. Yet to Ricasoli the work seemed un-finished. When he was Prime Minister in 1861, there hung in his room a map of Italy. Sometimes he would

---

[1] *L. & D.*, IV, 75, 199, 295, 312. *Poggi*, II, 49, 153-4. Pasolini, *Memorie*, 253. [2] *Trentacinque Lettere*, No. XXV. [3] Gotti, *Vita del Barone Bettino Ricasoli*, 395. [4] *L. & D.*, V, 132. [5] *L. & D.*, V, 101.

leave his desk and cross the room and gaze at the map, and think of Venice and Rome, invoking Italy to give him strength to persevere in 'the religion of the Father-land'.[1] The government of the King, he told Parliament, saw national territory to defend, to regain; it saw Rome, it saw Venice! 'Italy without Rome is nothing'.[2] But Venice came to Italy first; it came in 1866, in a manner which Ricasoli thought dishonouring, as the gift of vic-torious Prussia to a defeated ally. Ricasoli's 'religion of the Fatherland' tormented him with its unsatisfied aspira-tions. He had wished to let loose against the Hapsburgs a war of the nations, he was stirring up the Slavs, the Croats, the Hungarians.[3] His was a militant faith, driving him towards Istria, Dalmatia, and the Brenner Pass. He fumed against a peace which did not 'even speak of the Italian Tyrol, and of the other countries which belong to Italy.[4] . . .' More than sixty years were to pass before Italy won what Ricasoli had desired, and judged even this not enough, and governed aliens in the mountains of the Tyrol as the Austrians had ruled them in the plain of Lombardy. . . . But Rome came to Italy in 1870.

Ricasoli had already tried to win her. He had tried to win more than her body. That, indeed, would have been a triumph—to make peace between the new Nationalism and the age-old Universal spirit of Rome. Thus Italy would be ready to begin the moral conquest of the world. If Ricasoli believed that all the ideas of the time were in him, he believed also that this was the supreme idea of the time. He trembled when he thought that God might have destined him to bring it to fulfilment. He dedicated himself to the great task—but he failed.

Each failure came to him as a shock. 'Faith in wise principles', he thought, 'should create force to fight for them'.[5] Politics for him were nothing more than a branch of morals, and it was his prayer that Italy might prove this

[1] Finali, *op. cit.* Ch. IV. [2] *L. & D.*, V, 230. [3] *L. & D.*, VIII, 25.
[4] *L. & D.*, VIII, 42. [5] *Trentacinque Lettere*, p. 48.

truth to a wicked but repentant world.[1] When he discovered that even Italians regarded politics in the light
of expediency, of conflicting interests, of imperfect human
motives, of compromise, then he withdrew in disgust to
'disinfect himself'.[2] He failed to maintain the party and
the traditions of government which Cavour had handed
on to him, because he looked ever inward to the principles
which determined his own action, never outward to the
multiple motives, interests, prejudices, combinations, which
determined the actions of his supporters and his opponents.
Whenever Parliament turned against him, he believed that
there was something amiss with the moral order of the
world. 'They have made a game of my honesty, of my
resolution, of my dignity', he lamented when his first
ministry fell. 'Possessing these qualities, I have truly
embodied the essential character of the Italians'.[3] He
expected the Italians to exclaim: 'Thank God! Here is a
man who stands for all that is noblest in us. Let us trust
him' . . .! But perhaps the Italians were not as honest,
nor as resolute, nor as dignified as Ricasoli believed them
to be.

Thus it happened that he only ruled united Italy twice;
and that neither time did he rule long nor with great
success. But men honoured him, even when they did not
love him; and it was his dream that some day another
tempest might arise, a tempest which he alone could rule.
'If Italy demands from me a new sacrifice of my liberty
and inclinations I shall make it as in the past. . . . Now
Italy knows me, and knows where is the portal of my
house'.[4] He thought of himself as the 'most faithful
veteran' of Italy. If he was not called to be her general,
he was willing to serve her as a simple soldier; to serve
her in her Parliament, as an honourable deputy guarding

---

[1] *XII Lettere a Sansone D'Ancona*, p. 15.　[2] *Trentacinque Lettere*, No.
XXVII. Cf. *L. & D.*, V, 101–2. He considered himself 'too pure, too
untamed, too independent' to live in 'the putrid air' of politics. Cf. *L.
& D.*, VII, 17, 123.　[3] *L. & D.*, VII, 98.　[4] *XII Lettere a Sansone
D'Ancona*, p. 13 (April 1862, after the fall of his first ministry).

the morality of his countrymen in high places; to serve
her at his home in Tuscany, as a plain citizen attending to
his duties in that station of life to which it had pleased God
to call him.

When Italy rejected his leadership in 1862, he retired
to Brolio to take up again his old work after ' the little
digression of these three years'. The management of an
estate, he had once reflected, was as exacting and difficult
as the government of a nation; and he had never changed
his opinion. One maxim was sufficient either for the
landowner or for the prime minister: ' Do good for the
people who are entrusted to us'.[1] In 1866 he left Brolio to
practise this precept in a wider field; but he returned again.
In the evening of his life he divided his time between
Rome, and between his Tuscan estates. At Brolio, he
renewed all the practices of his strenuous youth. His
daughter had died, but she left two children whom he
loved to have about him, and to whom he made presents
of books, of maps, and of scientific instruments. He began
his days before four o'clock in the morning, and ended
them about eight, when he went to bed. The mornings
he spent in his writing-room; and every afternoon, even
under the blazing sun of August or amid the snow and rain
of February, he was in the saddle, making the rounds of
his estates. To the peasants it seemed as if he had never
left them. They knew that he had become great in the
world, for they had seen the King himself come to Brolio
to do him honour; but he had always been their master.
Now, as in the old days, he drove them, led them, ordered
them, pleaded with them. They must be hard-working,
pious, clean. They must rise early, teach their children the
Commandments and the Gospels, love their wives, love
God, love Italy.

In the evenings, Ricasoli would stand upon the ramparts
in front of the palace which he had built, looking over the
rough, beautiful country that was his, over the valley of

[1] *L. & D.*, IV, 119.

the Arbia, where his ancestors had fought upon a day fateful to Florence, over Siena, which once had been the enemy of his house, over the blue rolling hills which lifted themselves, far away to the south, into the great mass of Monte Amiata. One day in 1877 he stood there, mourning for the King whom he had helped to make; as he had mourned for his wife and for his daughter.[1] Soon there came to him news that Pius IX had died. He thought then of the great hopes of 1847 and 1848; he thought of his own hopes, how some of them had been realised, and some deceived; he thought of a future in which all would surely be realised, so that Rome and Italy, reconciled, might undertake together the moral conquest of the world.[2] His own powers were failing. In January of 1879 he wrote: ' My thought never ceases to offer prayers for the well-being of our Fatherland'.[3]

Within little more than a year, he too was dead.

L. & D., X, 414.   [2] *L. & D.*, X, 421.   [3] *XII Lettere a Sansone D'Ancona*, p. 23.

SELECTED BIBLIOGRAPHY

SECTION I. MATERIALS FOR THE BIOGRAPHY OF RICASOLI
TILL 1860.

(These also provide material for the history of the times)

MANUSCRIPT SOURCES

Essential to any study of Ricasoli are the documents in the *Archivio*, founded by Ricasoli himself, at Brolio. The *Archivio*, which has an excellent index, contains practically all the letters written to Ricasoli (he kept even begging letters) and many of those which he himself wrote. It contains also masses of memoranda, notebooks, diaries, etc., from which only a few selections have been published in the *Lettere e Documenti*. (See also *Ricordi Politici*, 1848, edited by G. Biagi, Firenze, 1908. An important extract from one of the diaries.) Apart from the Brolio Archives, the available manuscript sources are negligible. A search by the author in the *Carteggio Vieusseux* and the *Carteggio Lambruschini* in the Biblioteca Nazionale of Florence resulted in the discovery of some unpublished letters, but few of them are of any interest.

PRINTED SOURCES (ORIGINAL)

Most important are:

1. A. Gotti and M. Tabarrini, *Lettere e Documenti del Barone Bettino Ricasoli* (Firenze, Le Monnier 1887–1894. 10 volumes, and index). The collection is a splendid one, and by itself has served various writers as the sole source for a number of studies upon Ricasoli.

2. *Trentacinque lettere politiche . . . a Leopoldo Galeotti* (ed.: D. Zanichelli, Bologna, 1895). Especially valuable for 1859.

3. *XII Lettere a Sansone D'Ancona* (ed.: A. D'Ancona, Massa, 1913). Some interesting letters for 1859 and later.

4. *Lettere inedite di uomini illustri del secolo decimonono*. Some letters to T. Corsi in 1859. (Firenze, 1905).

Other stray letters are referred to in catalogues; but they have either been printed in the *Lettere e Documenti*, or are to be found in the various official collections mentioned in other parts of this bibliography, or are not sufficiently important to be cited here.

BIOGRAPHIES OF RICASOLI

1. A. Gotti, *Vita del Barone Bettino Ricasoli* (Firenze, 1894). Written by a contemporary who helped to edit the *Lettere e Documenti*, and who also used the *Brolio MSS*.

2. G. Finali, *La Vita politica di contemporanei illustri* (Torino, 1895). Contains information derived from a personal knowledge of Ricasoli and his family.

3. F. Dall' Ongaro, *Bettino Ricasoli*. (In series *I contemporanei Italiani*.)

A slight work, written in 1860, but Ricasoli's marginal notes in his own copy (at Brolio: Notes are reproduced in a Biblioteca Nazionale copy) give it autobiographical value.

ESSAYS AND STUDIES ON RICASOLI

They are numerous, but the only ones worth mentioning are: (1) L. Grottanelli, in *Rassegna Nazionale*, October 1, 1905. (2) G. Rondoni, *Un gran carattere*, Firenze, 1890. (3) M. Tabarrini in *Nuova Antologia*, serie 2, Vol. 24. (4) G. Gentile in *Gino Capponi* (Vallecchi, 1922). (5) A. Valle in *Studi Storici* (ed.: Crivelluci), Vols. 21, 22, 23. (6) D. Zanichelli in *Archivio Storico Italiano*, serie 5, Vol. 29 (and in collections of his writings).

For a list of numerous pamphlets and review articles dealing with Ricasoli, see *Firenze e Contorni* (Firenze, 1893. A bibliography).

SECTION 2.   PRINTED SOURCES FOR THE HISTORY OF TUSCANY TILL 1846.

Note.—Books dealing with the *Risorgimento* in general, or with non-Tuscan aspects of it—e.g. books by C. Tivaroni, I. Raulich, N. Bianchi, E. Masi, D. Zanichelli, A. Gori, Bolton King, etc.—are not cited here, in order that the bibliography may be kept within moderate length. For the same reason, many minor books, studies, or collections, cited only once or twice in the text, are not mentioned here. *Note also.* Books useful for the following section are marked (1); and books useful in later sections also are marked (2).

A. D'Ancona. *Ricordi ed affetti*. Milano, 1908. Well-written reminiscences, and studies of persons and episodes (2).

A. D'Ancona. *Ricordi storici del Risorgimento Italiano*. Firenze, 1914. Various studies, including a good one on Montanelli (2).

Atti dell' Accademia Reale dei Georgofili. A Florence periodical running into many volumes. Contains invaluable information on Tuscan agriculture, the economic theory of the time, educational aspirations, and similar subjects (2).

G. Baldasseroni. *Leopoldo II e i suoi tempi*. Firenze, 1871. A history and apology, written by an ex-minister of Leopold II. Contains some useful statistics (2).

G. Barbèra. *Memorie d'un editore*. Firenze, 1883. Contains information with regard to literary affairs. Barbèra was a liberal publisher (2).

N. Bianchi. *Carlo Matteucci e l'Italia del suo tempo*. Torino, 1874. Accurate life of a science professor, who became a diplomatist in 1859 (2).

Carlo Bini. *Scritti Editi e Postumi*. Livorno, 1843. Two volumes. Writings of a genial radical and romanticist, friend of Guerrazzi's.

Collodi. (Carlo Lorenzini.) *Occhi e Nasi*. Firenze, 1884. Humorous pictures of grand-ducal Florence (2).

G. Busoli. *F. D. Guerrazzi*. Firenze, 1912. Slight, but contains bibliography.

J. Bowring. *Report on the Statistics of Tuscany*. Parl. Papers, 1839, No. XVI. Contains very useful information.

L. Cappelletti. *Austria e Toscana*. Torino, 1918. A second-hand summary (2).

G. Capponi. *Lettere di G. C. e di altri a lui, raccolte . . . da A. Carraresi*. Firenze, 1877. Six volumes. Indispensable. Every letter good (2).

G. Capponi. *Scritti editi ed inediti di G. C. per cura di M. Tabarrini*. Firenze, 1877. Two volumes. Contains many interesting political writings, including a splendid account of Capponi's own ministry in 1848 (1).

G. Capponi. *Cinque Letture di Economia Toscana*. Firenze, 1845. Useful for the study of *mezzadria*.

V. Cian. *La prima Rivista Italiana*. Nuova Antologia 1/8/1906. A review of Prunas, giving some new facts.

E. Del Cerro. *Un Amore di Giuseppe Mazzini*. Milano, 1895. Illustrates skill and tolerance of the ' high police'.

E. Del Cerro. *Misteri di Polizia*. Firenze, 1899. Based on the papers of the department of *Buon-Governo*, in which Tuscany appears ' photographed in its shirt'.

G. Conti. *Firenze Vecchia*. Firenze, 1890. Excellent reconstruction of Florence in the first half of the nineteenth century.

G. Dupré. *Pensieri sull' Arte e Ricordi Autobiografici*. Firenze, 1899. Illustrates the artist's attitude to politics, and describes various historical episodes (2).

G. Fucini. *F. D. Guerrazzi*. Nuova Antologia, October, 1923. Throws some light on Guerrazzi's personality.

L. Galeotti. *Delle Leggi e dell' amministrazione della Toscana*. Firenze, 1847. A careful description of institutions, which are strongly criticised from the liberal point of view.

G. Gentile. *Gino Capponi e la coltura Toscano del secolo decimonono*. Firenze, 1922. Essays on Ricasoli, Capponi, Lambruschini, Centofanti, the revival of the cult of Savonarola, etc. Some of them good (2).

P. Giordani. *Epistolario edito ed inedito*. Firenze, 1854. Six volumes. Chiefly concerned with pure literature, but some letters deal with Tuscan conditions.

G. Giusti. *Epistolario edito ed inedito*. Firenze, 1904. Three volumes. Well edited by F. Martini, with notes. Liberal, witty, with pictures of Tuscany, judgments on events and personalities (1).

G. Giusti. *Memorie inedite*. Firenze, 1890. Again has excellent notes by F. Martini. Indespensable for tracing the beginnings of the revolution of 1848, and some of its problems (1).

G. Giusti. *Poesie*. Many editions. ' Satire is not history', but satires and patriotic verses help to make it.

G. Giusti. *Raccolta dei proverbi Toscani*. Two volumes. (Ed.: G. Capponi.) Illustrates the mentality of the peasants.

F. Gualterio. *Gli Ultimi Rivolgimenti Italiani.* Firenze, 1851. Four volumes. A narrative from the moderate-liberal point of view. Contains useful documents (1).

G. Guastalla. *La vita e le opere di F. D. Guerrazzi.* Rocca San Casciano, 1903. Critical and useful.

I. Grassi. *Il primo periodo della Giovine Italia in Toscana.* In Rivista Storica del Risorgimento Italiano, 1904. Gives the facts.

A. de Gubernatis. *Ricordi Biografici.* Firenze, 1873. For memories of Guerrazzi.

F. D. Guerrazzi. *L'Assedio di Firenze.* Many editions. The best illustration of literature turned to propaganda.

F. D. Guerrazzi. *Memorie.* Livorno, 1848. Story of his early life. Exaggerated.

F. D. Guerrazzi. *Note autobiografiche.* (Ed.: Guastalla.) The same.

F. D. Guerazzi. *Studii e Documenti.* Comitato Toscano per la storia del Risorgimento Italiano. Firenze, 1924. Useful information on the *Assedio di Firenze* and the police, on Guerrazzi's attitude to Gioberti, on the problem of order in 1848, etc.

[*Note.*—For Guerrazzi see also next section, and Vismara, *Bibliografia di F. D. G.* Milano, 1890. Also G. Stiavelli, *Guerrazzi.* Roma, 1904. Sketch bibliography.]

R. Lambruschini. *Elogii e Biografie.* Firenze, 1898. For an eulogy of Anna Ricasoli.

A. Linaker. *La vita e i tempi di Enrico Meyer.* Firenze, 1898. Two volumes. Useful documents. Life of a radical friend of Mazzini's, and an enthusiastic educationalist (2).

G. Marcotti. *Cronache segrete della polizia Toscana.* Firenze, 1898. Useful for Tuscan opinion after 1814.

A. Marradi. *Giuseppe Montanelli e la Toscana dal 1829 al 1859.* Firenze, 1909. Very uncritical, but contains some new documents (2).

A. Mangini. *F. D. Guerrazzi, Cenni e Ricordi.* Livorno, 1904. Publishes some forgotten writings of Guerrazzi's. Very friendly to him. The author's father had been the staunchest of Guerrazzi's supporters in Leghorn. There is a later edition of the book, largely changed (1).

A. Mangini. *Carlo Bini.* Nuova Antologia, 1907. p. 686 *et seq.* Sympathetic.

F. Martini. *Confessioni e Ricordi.* Firenze, 1922. The author recounts many events of which he was a witness. The sketches are well written, and based on an intimate knowledge of the period (2).

F. Martini. *Simpatie.* Firenze, 1909 (second edition). The sketches have the same merit as those above, and include an interesting study on Giusti and the Pisa University (2).

E. Masi. *Memorie di F. Ranalli.* Bologna, 1899. Excerpts from Ranalli's memoirs, with a running commentary. The memoirs are a useful criticism of all the assumptions of the time (2).

A. Manzoni. *Biografia di F. D. Guerrazzi*. Firenze, 1869. An eulogy.

E. Michel. *F. D. Guerrazzi e le cospirazioni in Toscana* (Bibl. Storica del Risorgimento, 1904). Accurate account of agitations in the 'thirties.

G. Montanelli. *Memorie sull' Italia, e specialmente sulla Toscana, dal 1814 al 1850.* Torino, 1850. Often untrustworthy, but contains interesting material, and has autobiographical value (1).

E. Montazio. Biographies of G. *Capponi*, G. *Giusti*, P. *Thouar, and Leopold II* (*L'Ultimo Granduca della Toscana*) in series *I contemporanei Italiani*. All slight and untrustworthy.

G. B. Niccolini. *Opere*. (Many editions.) Especially *Arnaldo da Brescia*. The popular dramatist of the age. Propagandist (2).

P. Prunas. *L'Antologia di Gian Pietro Vieusseux*. Roma, 1906. A most careful, accurate, and useful study of the *Antologia*.

P. Prunas. *N. Tommasèo e G. Capponi. Carteggio inedito dal 1834 al 1874.* New light on Capponi (2).

P. Puccini. *V. Salvagnoli*. Torino, 1861. Slight.

G. Rondoni. *Uomini e cose del Risorgimento . . . nel carteggio di G. P. Vieusseux*. Archivio Storico Italiano, *serie V. tomo* 22. A few new facts (2).

G. Rondoni. *G. P. Vieusseux*. Cenni biografici. *Ibid.* 1913. Slight.

Repetti. *Dizionario geografico-fisico-storico della Toscano*. Firenze, 1822–1846. A number of volumes, useful for reference.

A. von Reumont. *Gino Capponi e il suo secolo*. Milano, 1881. Written by a German scholar resident in Italy, and a friend of Capponi's (2).

E. Redi. *Ricordi Biografici di G. Montanelli*. Firenze, 1882. Slight.

L. Ridolfi. *Cosimo Ridolfi e gli istituti del suo tempo*. Firenze, 1900. Contains useful documents illustrating Ridolfi's ideas and career (2).

G. Scaramella. *Spirito publico, società segrete, e polizia in Livorno dal 1815 al 1821.* (Bibl. storica del Risorg., 1901.) Shows weakness of revolutionary movement in post-restoration Tuscany.

A. Salvagnoli. *Memorie economico-politiche sulle Maremme Toscane*. Firenze, 1858. Controversial from the technical point of view, but useful as illustrating the problem of the Maremme.

G. Stiavelli. *Antonio Guadagnoli e la Toscana etc., . . .* Torino, 1907. A vulgar and second-hand picture of Tuscany, with appraisement of a humorous poet (2).

N. Tommasèo. *Di G. P. Vieusseux . . . etc.*, Firenze, 1869. Contains first-hand information from one who owed much to Vieusseux. In the same volume is an eulogy written by Lambruschini.

M. Tabarrini. *Degli studii e delle vicende della Reale Accademia dei Georgofili*. Firenze, 1856. Useful for reference. Contains an index of the *Atti*, up to this date, by Ridolfi (2).

M. Tabarrini. *Gino Capponi, i suoi tempi, i suoi studii, i suoi amici*. Firenze, 1879. Elegantly written by one who knew and admired Capponi (2).

M. Tabarrini. *Vite e Ricordi d'Italiani illustri del secolo XIX* Firenze, 1884. Well-written sketches of various Tuscans, etc. Usually too laudatory (2).

La Toscana alla fine del granducato. Firenze, 1909. Various papers on persons, on professions, society, the press, etc. Some of them good (2).

La Vita Italiana del Risorgimento. Firenze, 1900. Contains articles on Giusti (by I. Del Lugno), and on the revolution of 1847–9 (by N. Nobili) (1).

A. Vannucci. *Ricordi della vita e delle opere di G. B. Niccolini.* Firenze, 1866. Two volumes. A good collection of documents and letters, with appreciative comments (2).

A. Zobi. *Memorie economico-politiche.* Firenze, 1860. Two volumes. Contains very useful information on the Tuscan economy. This is twisted to propaganda, the author's aim being to show how Tuscany has suffered from Austria (2).

A. Zobi. *Manuale Storico delle massime e degli ordinamenti economici vigenti in Toscana.* Firenze, 1858. Useful, and a little less propagandist (2).

A. Zobi. *Storia Civile della Toscana dal 1737 al 1848.* Firenze, 1859–1853. Five volumes. Volumes 4 and 5 are indispensable for nineteenth century Tuscany. The work is based on documents, official and otherwise, many of which are printed in the appendix. The point of view is moderate-liberal.

SECTION 3. PRINTED SOURCES FOR THE HISTORY OF TUSCANY FROM JUNE 1846 TILL APRIL 1849

(in addition to those marked with a numeral in the preceeding section)

Note—Books useful for the following section are marked (2)

Le Assemblee del Risorgimento. Atti raccolti e pubblicati per deliberazione della Camera dei Deputati. Roma, 1910. Vols. 3, 4, and 5 contain the Tuscan debates of 1848–9, and 1859, and also other documents concerning the Assemblies (2).

Atti del Governo Provvisorio Toscano, dal 8 Febbraio al 12 Aprile. Firenze, 1849. Copies of the proclamations, etc., posted up in the streets by the government of Guerrazzi.

G. Cambray-Digny. *Ricordi sulla commissione governativa Toscana.* Firenze, 1853. Tells the story of the attempt at a constitutional restoration from the point of view of those who attempted it. Contains all the most essential documents.

M. Carletti. *L'Aristocrazia Fiorentina nel 1848.* Firenze, 1848. Illustrates the democratic attack upon the moderates.

P. Cironi. *La Stampa nazionale Italiana, 1828–60.* Firenze, 1848. A short sketch of the patriotic press, written from the republican point of view (2).

Sir H. Codrington. *Selections from the Letters of Sir H. C., Admiral of the Fleet.* London, 1880. Codrington was stationed off Leghorn in 1848–9 as captain of the *Thetis.* His letters give a lively picture of how a liberal, efficient British officer was impressed by the personalities and methods of the Tuscan movement.

Correspondence respecting the affairs of Italy. State Papers, 1849 (1092), (1097), (1122), (1125). Illustrate English policy towards the liberal movement. Hamilton, the British envoy at Florence, makes very shrewd comments upon Tuscan affairs.

Collezione di documenti per servire alla storia della Toscana . . . ed alla difesa di F. D. Guerrazzi. (Corsi e Menichetti.) Firenze, 1853. Chooses and arranges the documents so as to show the work of Guerrazzi in the best possible light.

Documenti del Processo di Lesa Maestà, istituta . . . 1849–1850. Firenze, 1850. Documents collected to support the accusation against Guerrazzi and his contumacious associates.

Curtatone e Montanara. Pisa, 1899. Patriotic commemoration of the battle.

M. Gioli. *Il Rivolgimento Toscano e l'azione popolare,* 1847–60. Firenze, 1905. Full of useful material taken from the private records of the Marchese Bartolommei. The democratic-nationalist point of view (2).

A. Gennarelli. (1) *Epistolario Politico Toscano e atti diversi.* Firenze, 1860. (2) *Le Sventure d'Italia durante il pontificato di Pio Nono.* Firenze 1863. (3) *Atti e Documenti Diversi.* Firenze, 1863. All these books are first and foremost documents collected from the archives of Leopold II. They contain numerous letters illustrating how Leopold surrendered in 1849 to the pressure of Austria and of the Church; how this surrender prepared the reaction of the next ten years, and in what the reaction consisted. They are therefore very valuable, despite the extreme nationalist and antipapal bias of the collector (2).

L. Galeotti. (1) *Della Consulta di Stato.* Firenze, 1847. (2) *Osservazione sullo stato della Toscana nel Settembre* 1847. Firenze, 1847. Both pamphlets illustrate well the moderate liberal attitude.

F. D. Guerrazzi. *Apologia della sua vita politica.* Firenze, 1851. Tells the story of his part in the revolution, from the point of view of the advocate making his own defence.

F. D. Guerrazzi. *Appendice all' Apologia.* Firenze, 1853. Chiefly a reply to Pigli, who has contradicted parts of the *Apologia.*

F. D. Guerrazzi. *Scritti Politici.* Torino, 1862. Useful collection of his extreme democratic speeches, articles, etc. Very badly edited (2).

F. D. Guerrazzi. *Appendice agli Scritti Politici.* Torino-Melano, 1861. Contains his speech in his own defence.

L. Grottanelli. *I moti politici della Toscana.* Prato, 1902. Slight.

P. Jona. *I moti politici di Livorno,* 1848–1849. Milano, 1909. Full of useful information.

De Laugier. *Le Milizie Toscane nella guerra di Lombardia.* Pisa, 1849. The general of the Tuscan army puts the best light upon a campaign which, with the exception of one episode, was not creditable.

La Cecilia. *Cenno Storico dell' Ultima Rivoluzione Toscana.* Capolago, 1851. Extreme democratic point of view.

F. Martini. *Il Quarantotto in Toscana.* Firenze, 1918. Very useful. Gives the day-to-day diary of a ' good citizen', Conte L. Passerini de' Ricci, and fills in the gaps with excerpts from the newspapers, etc. Contains very erudite notes.

P. Miniati. *Il Carteggio di Guerrazzi durante la sua prigiona nel* 1848. Rassegna Storica del Risorgimento. Anno XI, Fasc. III. Shows that Guer-razzi had excellent treatment in prison.

P. Orsi. *Dispacci, Lettere, e Proclami di giorni assai agitati nella storia Toscana.* Nuova Antologia, October 1, 1923. Prints many new documents which illustrate the state of Tuscany and the work of Guerrazzi after the flight of the Grand-Duke.

G. Montanelli. *I scrittori e revisori dopo la legge Toscana del 6 Maggio,* 1847. Pisa, 1847. A statement of Montanelli's attitude at a time when he was still considered moderate.

G. Montanelli. *Schiarmenti nel processo politico, etc.* Firenze, 1852. A short defence of the democratic ministry.

G. Oxilia. *La Campagna Toscana del* 1848 *in Lombardia.* Firenze, 1904. The only full study on this campaign.

E. Passamonti. *Il Ministero Capponi e il tramonto del liberalismo Toscano.* Rassegna Storica del Risorg., 1919. Fasc. I and II. A careful and useful study.

E. Passamonti. *Militarismo ed anti-militarismo nel partito liberale Toscano* . . . 1848. Rassegna Storica del Risorg. Anno V, Fasc. III. A similar study.

Proclami, Decreti, Notificazioni e Circolari dal primo Gennaio al 8 Febbraio, e dal 12 *Aprile a tutto Giugno* 1849. Firenze, 1849. Copies of proclamations, etc., before the flight of Leopold and after his restoration.

C. Pigli. *Risposta all' Apologia di F. D. Guerrazzi.* Arezzo, 1852. Guerrazzi's old supporter replies to criticisms made in the *Apologia* with regard to his conduct in Leghorn.

F. Ranalli. *Le Istorie Italiane dal* 1846 *al* 1853. Firenze, 1858. Though Ranalli had been involved with the Tuscan democrats, he makes his account balanced and moderate.

T. A. Trollope. *Tuscany in* 1849 *and* 1859. London, 1859. Contrasts the two periods, to the advantage of the second. Pro-liberal, written by an *Inglese Italianizato* (2).

La Reazione Toscana e la carnificine di Livorno . . . *da un testimonio oculare.* Genova, 1849. Describes the Austrian bombardment and assault of Leghorn. Extreme nationalist and democratic bias. (Contrast Ricasoli's diary, when he was an eye-witness of the same event.)

G. Sforza. *La Cecilia e F. D. Guerrazzi.* Rassegna Storica del Risorg., Anno. I, Fasc. 5–6. Throws light on Guerrazzi's political methods.

V. Salvagnoli. *Discorso sullo stato politico della Toscana nel Marzo del* 1847. Lugano, 1847. Corresponds closely with the document presented by Ricasoli to Cempini.

SECTION 4. 1859–1860

(*Note*.—Most of the sources for the period of the restoration (1849–1859) have been already indicated in the previous sections by the numeral (2). The few additional works dealing with this period will be specifically noted. An excellent classified bibliography for the years 1859–1860 has been printed in R. Della Torre, *La Evoluzione del Sentimento Nazionale in Toscana* . . . 1859–60. (Biblioteca Storica del Risorg. Ital., 1916.) The existence of this bibliography has enabled the present one to be greatly curtailed.

A. *CONTEMPORARY SOURCES:* Letters and official acts, etc.

Atti e documenti editi ed inediti del Governo della Toscana dal 27 Aprile in poi. Firenze, 1860. Six volumes. This collection, together with the printed and manuscript sources for the life of Ricasoli, forms the essential groundwork for any study of the times.

L. G. De Cambray-Digny. *Carteggio politico di L. G. de C.-D.* With preface by G. Finali. Milano, 1913. These letters are as useful as those of Capponi for giving an insight into Tuscan opinion. The writer was at first sceptical with regard to Ricasoli's work, but later became an enthusiastic admirer.

Conte Camillo di Cavour. Volume 2 and volume 3 of Chiala's collection of his letters, together with the supplementary edition of E. Meyer, and the documents in N. Bianchi, *La politique du comte Camillo di Cavour* (Torino, 1885), and *Diplomazia*, are necessary for an understanding of the general situation as it affected Tuscany, and of Cavour's relations with the Tuscans.

Michelangelo Castelli. *Carteggio politico di M. C.* (Chiala). Torino, 1890. Similarly useful, Castelli being an intimate of Cavour's, as well as of Ricasoli's.

Correspondence concerning the affairs of Italy. (Several times continued.) Accounts and Papers, 1859; Sess. 2 (2524), (2527). Also 1860; (2636), (2638), (2656), (2660), (2702). Illustrating the diplomatic situation, and containing some scattered reports on Tuscany in particular.

G. La Farina. *Epistolario di La F. Giusseppe* (ed.: A. Franchi). Milano, 1869. Sheds light on the activities of the National Society in Tuscany before the revolution, and of La Farina's plans while it was in progress.

Lettere Politiche (ed.: S. Morpurgo and D. Zanichelli). Bologna, 1898. Letters of Ricasoli, Peruzzi, and Corsini, illustrating Tuscan opinion and diplomatic activities.

Il Monitore Toscano. Official news and propaganda.

La Nazione. Semi-official news and propaganda. (For the other newspapers see Della Torre, and G. Rondoni, cited below. Also remarks in the text of the present book.)

B. *CONTEMPORARY CHRONICLES*, etc.

M. Carletti. *Quattro mesi di storia Toscana* . . . Firenze, 1859. Written from the government point of view.

Theodosia Trollope. *Social Aspects of the Italian Revolution*. London, 1859. A collection of letters written from Florence to London by an enthusiastic and uncritical supporter of the revolution.

A. Zobi. *Cronaca di Avvenimenti d'Italia del* 1859. Florence, 1859–1860. This is a current history of the war and of politics, written as events succeeded each other, and based chiefly upon the documents made available by the governments. Liberal.

C. *CONTEMPORARY PAMPHLETS*, etc.

(*Note.*—Only a selection of the most important is given. A great many more are to be found in Della Torre. Many of them are mentioned in the text of the present book, and it may be assumed that they favour the nationalist cause in one way or another unless there is a note to the contrary. As far as possible, they are roughly arranged according to priority of appearance.)

L. Galeotti. *Considerazioni Politiche sulla Toscana*. Firenze, 1850. Sets out the attitude of the moderate liberals after the restoration of 1849.

T. Corsi. *Apologia delle leggi di giurisprudenza, amministrazione e polizie ecclesiastiche . . . sotto il regno di Leopoldo I*. Biblioteca civile dell' Italiano, Firenze, 1858.

L. Galeotti. *Parere per la verita*, etc. Firenze, 1858.

F. Ranalli. *Del Riordinamento d'Italia*. Firenze, 1859. Ranalli misjudged the tendencies of the time and was considered a reactionary.

Toscana ed Austria. Bibl. civ. dell' Italiano. Firenze, 1859.

V. Salvagnoli. *Dell' Indipendenza d'Italia*. Firenze, 1859.

B. Cini. *Sui danni recati dall' Austria alla Toscana*. Firenze, 1859.

N. Corsini. *Storia di quattro ore . . . del 27 Aprile*, 1859. Firenze, 1859.

C. Ridolfi. *Breve Nota a una Storia di quattro ore, etc*. Firenze, 1859.

Testamento dell' I. e R. casa di Lorena, ossia Atti e Rapporti ufficiali concernenti il Bombardamento di Firenze. Firenze, 1859.

300 vittime toscane dell' I. e R. casa Austro-lorenese. Firenze, 1859.

G. Montanelli. *Il 29 maggio in Toscana*. Livorno, 1859.

C. Matteucci. *Dello assestamento futuro d'Italia. Lettera a Lord Cowley*, etc. Torino, 1859.

Una conversazione del Curato Evangelico con i suoi popolani. Prato, 1859.

F. D. Guerrazzi. *Ritratto morale di Leopoldo II*. Livorno, 1859.

R. Volpi. *Allocuzione a tutti i sacerdoti italiani sulla guerra della indipenza nazionale*. Lucca, 1859.

E. Alberì. *La Toscana durante la guerra dell' indipendenza*. Firenze, 1859. (This pamphlet opposes the efforts of Ricasoli on behalf of 'fusion'.)

A. Conti. *Napoleone III o la norma degli italiani*. Lucca, 1859. (Shows a similar tendency.)

Lettura popolare. Le converazioni del villaggio . . . etc. Pistoia, 1859.

La Toscana nella nazionalita italiana. Firenze, 1859.

La Toscana dopo il 27 Aprile, 1859. Firenze, 1859.

M. Carletti. *La fusione*. Firenze, 1859.

F. Finocchietti. *Dell' Unificazione italiana.* Pisa, 1859.

A. De' Gori. *Confederazione.* Firenze, 1859. (This is the first important pamphlet published after the preliminaries of Villafranca.)

A. De' Gori. *Interesse della Toscana.* Firenze, 1859.

R. Volpi. *La Toscana, abbandonata da Leopold II, ha trovato un padrone migliore.* Lucca, 1859.

Per la decretata demolizione del forte di Belvedere. Bologna, 1859. (Rude songs about Leopold.)

Leopoldo II e la Toscana. Parole di un sacerdote al popolo. Firenze, 1859.

Poesie Nazionale di G. B. Niccolini . . . a profitto della guerra dell' indipendenza d'Italia. Firenze, 1859.

F. D. Guerrazzi. *La patria. Il Papa sarà presidente, etc.* Italia, 1859.

V. Masi. *Consigli di un esule a tutti i Toscani.* Livorno, 1859.

Non più Austriaci in Toscana. Parole al popolo. Firenze, 1859.

Delenda Cartago. Le fortezze erette dai tiranni per mitragliare i popoli. Firenze, 1859.

La pianeta dei morti. Veglia del Prior Luca. Firenze, 1859.

F. D. Guerrazzi. *Al popolo Toscano.* Torino, 1859.

I danni della pace; Napoleone III. . . . etc. Livorno, 1859.

L. Crescioli. *Il clero e la Nazione.* Firenze, 1859.

Come finirà? Firenze, 1859.

Dopo la guerra. Italia, 1859.

U. Peruzzi. *La Toscana e i suoi Granduchi Austriaci . . . etc.* Firenze, 1859. (Translated from French original.)

G. Toscanelli. *Pensieri dedicati ai rappresentanti del popolo toscano convocati per l' 11 Agosto, 1859.* Firenze, 1859.

Parole di un popolano. Ferdinando di Lorena e i suoi avvocati. Firenze, 1859.

L. Galeotti. *L'Assemblea Toscana.* Firenze, 1859.

G. Montanelli. *L' Impero, il Papato e la Democrazia in Italia.* Livorno, 1859.

E. Alberì. *La politica Napoleonica e il governo Toscano.* Paris, 1859. (Opposes union with Piedmont.)

Prior Luca. *Veglia del Ceppo. III.* Firenze, 1859.

M. Carletti. *Le elezioni comunali spiegate al popolo.* Firenze, 1859.

C. Boncompagni. *Considerazioni sull' Italia Centrale.* Torino, 1859.

Prior Luca. *Confiteor. Veglia IV e V.* Prato, 1860.

C. Collodi. *Il sig. Alberì ha ragione.* Firenze, 1859.

Il Papa e il Congresso. Firenze, 1859. (Translation.)

M. Carletti. *L'Italia centrale al congresso.* Firenze, 1860.

Unità italiana. Memorandum del popolo. Firenze, 1860.

C. Carfora. *L'Italia e le potenze europee.* Firenze, 1860.

Prior Luca. *I due voti, ossia annessi e sconnessi.* Firenze, 1860.

P. Cironi. *Al popolo dei cinque comuni di Prato.* Prato, 1860.

O. Orlandini. *Del suffragio universale.* Firenze, 1860.

D. *MEMOIRS, NARRATIVES, OR ESSAYS WRITTEN BY ACTORS IN THESE EVENTS OR BY OBSERVERS.*

Michelangelo Castelli. *Ricordi di M. C.* Torino, Roux. For an account of Cavour's ideas on Ricasoli and Tuscany.

I casi della Toscana nel 1859 *e* 1860 *narrati al Popolo da una compagnia di Toscani con note e documenti.* Firenze, 1864. Contains all the things which the supporters of the old dynasty would have said in 1859–60, if there had been no press censorship.

G. Cecconi. *Il* 27 *Aprile,* 1859. *Narrazione.* Firenze, 1892. An address delivered by an army officer who played a part in the events of that day.

G. Cecconi. *Il principe Napoleone in Toscana.* Roma, 1891. Contains, among other things, some reminiscences on the behaviour of the troops under the prince's commands.

L. Kossuth. *Souvenirs et Écrits de mon exil, periode de la guerre d'Italie* Paris, 1880. Kossuth professes to explain the Emperor's intentions in sending Prince Jerome to Tuscany.

Giusseppe Pasolini, 1815–1876. *Memorie raccolte da suo figlio.* Torino, 1887. Interesting as showing the attitude of the leaders in the Romagnas to the problem of central Italy, and as giving Pasolini's impressions of Ricasoli's work in Tuscany.

E. Poggi. *Memorie storiche del governo della Toscana nel* 1859–60. Pisa, 1867. The first two volumes give a narrative of these events by a member of the government, who inclined towards the opinions of Ridolfi rather than towards those of Ricasoli. The third volume contains useful documents, including the most important despatches of the Tuscan diplomatists.

E. Rubieri. *Storia intima della Toscana dal* 1 *Gennaio* 1859 *al* 30 *Aprile,* 1860. Prato, 1861. The radical-democrat point of view. Contains useful information, especially with regard to preparations for the movement.

Gustave de Reiset. *Mes Souvenirs.* Paris, 1903. The third volume has a chapter which throws light on the division of policy in France with regard to Tuscany, and which illustrates how Ricasoli profited by this division.

E. *MODERN STUDIES, BIOGRAPHIES,* etc.

Biografia di G. Dolfi. Firenze, 1861. Slight.

Baron Du Casse. *Le cinquième corps de l'armée d'Italie en* 1859. Revue Historique, 1898. LXVI., 301–23; LXVII, 36–58. Severely handled by J. Bicchierai in *Archivio Storico Italiano,* Serie V, Tomo XXII.

F. Carandini. *Manfredo Fanti, generale d' armata.* Verona, 1872. Illustrates relations between Farini, Ricasoli, Fanti, and Garibaldi in the autumn of 1859.

A. Commandini. *Il Principe Napoleone e l'Italia.* Torino, 1922. Contains hitherto unpublished letters of Jerome, showing beyond doubt that he had no designs on Tuscany before the peace of Villafranca.

Fanfulla della Domenica. 31 *Jan.*, 1892. Article on Cavour in February, 1859, giving information with regard to his relations with the Tuscan conservative nationalists.

Forzano. *Carrara dal 27 Aprile al 22 Agosto* 1859. Carrara, 1909. A short study with a nationalistic bias, illustrating the movement of opinion in a district bordering upon Tuscany.

E. Michel. *L'Ultimo moto Mazziniano.* Livorno, 1903. Describes a Mazzinian plot in Leghorn in 1857.

I. W. Mario. *G. Dolfi.* Firenze, 1866. Slight.

G. Rondoni. *Foglietti della clandestina alla vigiia del 27 Aprile in Toscana.* In Rassegna storica del risorg., 1908. I, 308, 312. A short notice which gives further evidence of the efforts made to secure an orderly demonstration.

G. Rondoni. *I Giornali Umoristici Fiorentini del Triennio Glorioso* (1859-61). Firenze, 1914. The author has performed the strenuous task of reading all the comic, patriotic papers, and re-producing their funniest passages. Reproduces also a number of caricatures.

A. Savelli. *Il moto nazionale nel* 1859-60 *in un comune di montagna della provincia di Firenze.* Rassegna storica del risorg., 1908. X, 135-164. A most careful and illuminating account of how opinion was made in an isolated district.

T. Signorini. *Caricaturisti e caricaturati al caffi Michelangiolo.* Firenze, 1893. An account of the bawdy society of liberal artists, etc., during the last decade of grand-ducal Florence. Illustrations.

V. Soldani. *Pasqua di Liberazione.* Firenze, 1907. An account of the revolution of April 1827, heavily biassed from the democratic standpoint.

A. Della Torre. *La Evoluzione del Sentimento Nazionale in Toscana dal Aprile* 1859 *al* 15 *Marzo,* 1860. (Bibl. Storica del Risorg. Ital., 1916.) Indispensable for reference and for comparing conclusions. A most careful, detailed, impartial study.

G. Valeggia. *G. Dolfi e la democrazia in Firenze,* 1859-60. Contains documents published here for the first time. The best account of Dolfi.

D. Zanichelli. *Studii politici e storici.* Bologna, 1893. Also, *Studii di storia costituzionale e politica del Risorgimento italiano.* Contain appreciative studies of Ricasoli, Peruzzi, and others.

INDEX

ACADEMY of the *Georgofili*; Ricasoli elected member of, 11; foundation and purposes of, 34; Ridolfi's interest in, 34, 35; Ridolfi increases government subsidy to, 277

Alba, the, 90

Antologia, the, founded by Vieusseux (1821), 37, 38; suppression of, 52

Apologia, the, of Guerrazzi, 50, 122, 150

Arese, 243, 246

Arms, the right to carry, conceded, 95

Austria; Tuscany, her jurisdiction in, 21, 22 26; aftermath of Carbonaro conspiracy (1820), 26; army of, sent through Tuscany to Naples, 27; *Antologia*, the, formal complaint, 38, and suppression of, 52; anti-Austrian demonstrations in Tuscany, 78, 95–99; revolution in Vienna (1849), 86, 113; army occupies Modena and Parma, 110, but retreats, 112, 113; *Salasco Armistice* (August 1848), 127, 146; Novara, Charles Albert of Sardinia defeated at, 155; invasion of Tuscany, 157; bombardment and capture of Leghorn, 158, and occupation of Florence, 158–181; social boycott of Austrians in Florence, 179; Florence vacated (1858), 181; Plombières (July 1858) Napoleon III and Cavour initiate Franco-Italian Alliance at, 184; Ultimatum to Victor Emmanuel (24th April 1859), 192; Ricasoli's press campaign against, 212; Magenta, defeated at (4th June), 221; Napoleon signs Armistice, 224; *Villafranca*, Treaty of (July), 227; European Congress, refuses to enter, 268

BALDASSERONI, G., 102, 176, 177, 180, 192, 193

Bandiera, E., 47

Bartolommei (Marchese) Ferdinando, organises demonstrations for the right to carry arms, 95, 96; puts forward Guerrazzi as leader of democrats, 96; is exiled for publishing clandestine sheets (1851), 185; forms National Party, 185–191; wins over the army (1859), 196, 197

Bianchi, Celestino, 183, 188, 191, 230, 232, 244, 276

Biblioteca Civile, the, 188, 191, 192

Bini, Carlo, 45, 48, 49, 91

Bonaccorsi, Anna, 9, 171, 172

Boncompagni, Carlo (Sardinian envoy at Florence), 186, 192, 198, 207, 220, 223, 233, 262–264

Borelli (President of Neapolitan parliament, 1820), 26, 27

Bossini (prefect of Florence, 1859), 223

British diplomacy, and Austrian intervention in Italy, 98 (footnote); guarantee to Tuscany, 127; refusal to intervene, 157; Anglo-French agreement (1860), 269

Brolio, home of Ricasoli family, 3, 4, 10, 11, 56–62; famous wine of, 11; Salvagnoli takes refuge at, 143; Ricasoli's retirement and death, see Epilogue

Buon-Governo, the (see Police)

Busacca (Tuscan Minister of Finance, 1859), 220

Byron, Lord, influence of, upon Guerrazzi, 45, 46, 152

CAIANO, Duke of, 96

Cambray-Digny, L. G. De, 94, 193, 218, 233, 241, 287, 288

Capponi (Marchese) Gino, on agricultural laws, 4; Carbonaro conspiracy, his implication in, 26; chafes under Tuscan ' somnambulism,' 28, 35; character of, 36, 126, 127; and Ricasoli, 68; and Salvagnoli, 70; denounces Papal government, 72; his relief at retirement of Fossombroni and Corsini, 73; his friendship with Guerrazzi, 92; his fear of Piedmont, 121, 218; succeeds Ridolfi in Ministry, 121; his programme, 127, 128; breaks off relations with Leghorn, 134; resigns office, 137; his confidence in Ricasoli, 233; he now counsels union with Piedmont, 243; letters of, 273, 274; protests to Ricasoli against extravagances of Florentine journalists, 281, 282

Carbonaro Conspiracy, the (1820), 26

Carducci, G., 276

Carignano, Prince of, 243, 255, 260–262

Castelli, M., 191, 261

Cavour, Count Camillo B. di, deprecates ' Songs of Freedom', 86; joins Ministry (1850), 175; discusses Franco-Italian Alliance with Napoleon III at Plombières (1858), 184; enlists support of the National Society, 186; prepares for war with Austria, 189–192; his conversations with Ricasoli, 189, 194 (footnote) 195; his policy, 195; objects to the Triumvirate of 1859, 205; and to presence of Jerome Napoleon in Florence, 216; vetoes creed of a ' United Italy' under sovereignty of Victor Emmanuel, 222; resigns after Treaty of Villafranca (1859) and nominates Ricasoli and Farini dictators of Tuscany and Piedmont respectively, 227, 228; his approval of Boncompagni, 262, 263; agrees to attend European Congress, 266; his return to power (1860) and programme of union, 268, 269; surrenders Savoy and Nice as price of French assistance, 271

Cempini, F., 72, 75, 80, 83, 102

Cempini, Leopoldo, 41, 179, 183

Centofanti, Prof., 40, 105, 107

Charles Albert (King of Sardinia) and Mazzini, 51; opens Lombardy campaign, 86; military errors of, 87; interviews with Ricasoli, 109, 110; defeated at Novara (24th March 1849), 155

Charles Louis (see Lucca, Duke of)

Chianti, the, 2, 3, 5, 171, 290

Children of Brutus, the, 48, 50

Cipriani, L., 131, 232, 249, 259

Circo Nazionale, the, 130
Cironi, P., 192
Clergy, the, attitude of, towards a United Italy, 204
Cobden, Richard, 11, 169
Colletta, History of Naples by, 37
Corriere Livornese, the, 91, 126
Corsi, T., 151, 190, 191, 206, 218
Corsini, Neri, 21, 26, 73, 96, 103, 133, 193, 198, 217, 230, 242, 246, 251, 260, 272
Curtatone, battle of (1848), 76, 115, 117
Custozza, battle of (1848), 115, 124

DABORMIDA, Piedmontese Minister for War (1859), 230, 263
Dall' Ongaro, F., biographer of Ricasoli, 159, 217, 273, 274
Dandrini, Triumvir in Florence (1859), 200
D'Aspré, Austrian General, 157, 158
D'Azeglio, Massimo, 72, 97, 138, 143, 189, 223, 227, 267, 268
De Boni, 258
De Laugier, Tuscan General, 95, 151, 152
Demidoff, Prince, 29, 178
de Reiset (see Reiset)
Digny (see Cambray-Digny)
Dolci, Carlo, 20
Dolfi, Giuseppe, leader of radical democrats (1859), 186, 187, 192; wins over the army, 196, 197; revolution planned in house of, 197; his address demanding United Italy, 222–224; organises National Guard, 236; protects Mazzini, 257
Donatello, 2

EDINBURGH REVIEW, the, 36
European Congress, the, 266

FABRIZI, Nicola, 260, 263
Fanti, General (Garibaldi's nominal chief), 249, 250, 259
Farini, Luigi C. (Dictator of Piedmont, 1859), 76, 93, 112, 120, 227, 228, 232, 245, 248–251, 255, 256, 259, 263
Fenzi, Carlo, 75, 187, 193
Ferdinand III of Tuscany, 18
Ferrara, Austrian occupation of, 95, 104
Firenzuola, Ricasoli's propaganda in, 202–204
Firidolfi branch of Ricasoli family, 3
Florence, description of, 1, 2; statues and monuments of, 2; cheap cost of living in, 29; feast-days and recreations of, 31–33; first gas illumination in, 35; federal demonstrations of 1848, 94–95; Austrian flag publicly burnt, 108; receive news of defeat at Custozza; Triumvirate elected (Montanelli, Guerrazzi and Manzoni), 150; tumults in, 153; Austrian

occupation of, 158; social boycott of Austrians in, and their withdrawal, 179; public hostility to Leopold, 180–183; streets crowded
with demonstrators, 198; collapse of municipal council and election
of provisional Triumvirate (Peruzzi, Malenchini and Dandrini), 200;
advent of Jerome Napoleon with army corps, 216; Ricasoli's propaganda in, 275; protest of Archbishop of, 284; Ricasoli condemns
abusive agitation in, 289, and triumphs at the polls (March 1860),
290

Food riots in Tuscany (1847), 78, 142
Foscolo, U., 28
Fossi, G. B., President of Chamber of Commerce in Florence, 193
Fossombroni, Vittorio, 21–27, 38, 47, 73, 74, 201
Francis of Modena (see Modena, Duke of)

GALEOTTI, L., 99, 101, 193, 242, 246, 276, 285
Garibaldi, leads Central Italian forces (1859), 249; Mazzini's influence
upon, 258; elected president of National Society, 259; prepares to
invade the Marches and Umbria, but resigns in November 1859,
259
Gavazzi, Father, 131
Ghibelline party, the, 3
Gioberti, Vincenzo, 40, 146, 147, 170
Giordani, Pietro, 17, 37
Giorgini, Prof., 187, 205, 208
Giusti, Giuseppe, 8, 14, 34, 36, 38, 49, 73, 75, 91, 93, 137, 139, 143, 275
278, 283
Gladstone, W. E., Italian sympathies of, 242
Goito, battle of (1848), 31
Gregory XVI, 76
Gualterio (historian), 288
Guelf party, the, 3
Guerrazzi, F. D., literary works of, 42, 45–47, 51, 100, 101, 119; parentage
and character of, 44–46, 91–93; sentenced to six months' seclusion
(1830) and visited by Mazzini, 48; the *apologia* of, 50, 122, 150;
his campaign, as leader of democrats, against anarchy (1848–1849),
87; negotiates for federation of Central Italy against Piedmont, 87;
stirs up agitation in Leghorn, 92, 93; his friendship with Cappon
92; his speech at Leghorn, 96; his pamphlet challenging the moderates,
100–102; is again imprisoned, 110, and released, 111; resumes attack
upon government, 118, 119, 122; and criticises the franchise, 125;
demands impeachment of Ridolfi, 126, and welcomes Capponi, 127;
outline of his policy, 130, 131; restores peace in Leghorn, but receiving no recognition from government makes way for Montanelli, 132–
134; takes office first as Minister of Interior, then as Triumvir and finally
as Dictator (1849), 138–156; his frantic efforts to stem anarchy,
142–144; obtains Leopold's signature to the *Constituent*, 148; his

quarrels with Mazzini, 152, 154; his trial and condemnation, 181, 206; counsels universal suffrage (August 1859), 238

Guerronière, La (see La Guerronière)

Guicciardini, 284

Guillotine, the, publicly burnt (1847); restored (1851); abolished (1859) and death penalty removed from penal code, 206

HAMILTON (British envoy at Florence), 75, 161, 181

ITALIA, the, 90, 104

Italian League, Ridolfi's hopes of an, defeated, 119, 120

Italy, Central, formation of defensive league between governments of, 249; Anglo-French agreement to occupation of, by Sardinian army, provided a plebiscite be taken, 269, 272

JESUITS, the, Montanelli's attack on, 75

LA CECILIA, 147, 258

La Farina, G., collaborator in the *Alba*, 90; Secretary of National Society, 185; exiled for one year, 185; his support enlisted by Cavour, 186, 188, 189, 191

La Guerronière, 184, 216, 267

La Marmora (President of Piedmont, 1859), 229, 243, 253

Lambruschini, R., 65–67, 107, 164–168, 178, 203, 208, 218, 223, 237

Landrini, 193

Lawley, Enrico, 197

Leghorn, importance of, 43, 44; Guerrazzi stirs up agitation in, 91, 92; punitive visit of Ridolfi to, 110; rebels against Florence, 131; nationalist fervour in, 196

Leopardi, Giacoma, and Mazzini, 37

Leopold II (Prince of Tuscany and Grand Duke of Austria), succeeds to throne of Tuscany, 17; character and early popularity of, 17–22; patronises science and literature, 20; his difficult position as an Austrian, 27, 28; waning influence of (1833), 52, 53; public outcry at his prosecution of Renzi, 74; issues proclamation, 94; receives warning note from Metternich, 97; refuses to grant Constitution and accept ' limited monarchy', and dismisses Neri Corsini, 103; compelled to grant Constitution he abdicates (1849), 148, 149; Guerrazzi's efforts to expel him from Tuscan soil, 150, 151; to deputation pleading for his return he denies duplicity in Austrian intervention; his letters to Emperor of Austria, 158, 159; hopeless attempt of his ministers to regain confidence of the people, and failure to balance budget by increased taxation, 175–177; his visit to Vienna with Baldasseroni (1850), 180; he abolishes Constitution (1852) and incurs public contempt, 182, 183; his fatal stand for neutrality, 192; he gives way and commissions Corsini to form a ministry, but on mutiny of army abdicates and flies to Vienna, 199

Leopold, Grand Duke Pietro, 17, 18, 25
Liberals, Tuscan, growing agitation of, against Leopold's government, 28, 36; and Academy of the *Georgofili*, 34; Cavour welcomed by, 175; chief members of, in 1859, 187; secure hold upon country, but find places for prominent moderates, 200; spread of propaganda to provinces, 201–205
Liechtenstein, Prince, 179–181
Louis Phillippe, 50
Luca, Prior (see ' Prior Luca ')
Lucca, demonstrations and disturbances in, 104, 105, 196; Treaty signed incorporating Lucca with Tuscany, 107; refusal of, to pay taxes, 142
Lucca, Charles Louis, Duke of, civic guard granted by, 96; forbids demonstrations and issues proclamation, 105, 106; abdicates but returns, 106; secretly cedes Lucca to Tuscany, 107
Lunigiana, ceded to Modena and Parma, 107, 122; strategic importance of, to Austria, 108

MACCHIAVELLI, 46, 100, etc.
Magenta, battle of (1859), 221
Malenchini (Triumvir in Florence, 1859), 200, 249
Mamiani, T., 115, 147
Manfredini, 185
Manin, Daniele, 185
Manzoni, A., 37, 279
Marliani, 250
Martini, F., 70
Massari, 189, 190, 194, 195, 232, 241, 250, 268–271, 283
Matteucci, 243, 246, 274
Mazzini, Giuseppe, contributes to the *Antologia*, 37; his appreciation of Guerrazzi, 49, and their quarrel, 152, 154; is expelled from Florence by Ricasoli, 257, 258
Medici, the, 3
Metternich, Prince (see also Austria), his warnings to Leopold II, 27, 28, 97, 158; his anger with Tuscan government, 27; Palmerston remonstrates with, 98
Meyer, Enrico, 37, 90, 114
Mezzadria, the (co-operative agricultural system in Tuscany), 12–15
Milan, rising in (1848), 86; Austrian army driven out of, 113
Minghetti, Marco, 115, 120, 194, 232, 250, 251, 255, 260–263
Modena, Francis, Duke of; his spies in Florence, 26; attacks the *Antologia*, 52, and throws in his lot with Austria, 53; ruins Ridolfi's project of a Customs League, 104; invades Fivizzano, 108; Austrians occupy Modena, 110
Monitore, the, 143, 157, 158, 167, 211, 222, 227, 239, 254
Montanara, battle of (1848), 115, 117

INDEX

Montanelli, Giuseppe, brilliant early career of, 40, 41; memoirs of, 50; starts reformist agitation in Pisa, 74; attacks Jesuits and distributes revolutionary pamphlets, 75; his faith in Pius IX, 77; publishes the *Italia*, 90; as lecturer, 105; favours entente with Rome and is hostile to Piedmontese annexation of Lombardy, 122; succeeds to Guerrazzi at Leghorn and presses for a *Constituent* to unite all Italy, 134–137; accepts invitation to form Ministry with Guerrazzi, 138; undoes good work of latter, 144–145; his Papal policy, 147; interviews Leopold at Siena, 149; proclaimed Triumvir with Guerrazzi and Manzoni (1849), 150; resigns, 155; elected deputy (August 1859), 241–244

Montazio, 153, 186

Mordini, 116

NAPLES, Ferdinand, King of, grants Constitution, 112; deserts Italian cause, 120

Napoleon III, consistent opposition of Ricasoli to policy of, 4, 5, 228–233, 271; Italian policy of, 184 (footnote), 207, 216, 222, 225 (footnote), 230, 242, 246; meets Cavour at Plombières, 184; signs preliminaries of peace at Villafranca, 227; debars Austria and Papal Government from entering European Congress, 267, 268; demands a plebiscite in Central Italy, 271

Napoleon, Jerome (Prince Imperial), 76, 184, 216, 242, also Appendix II (p. 225)

National Society, the, 185, 222, 259

Niccolini, G. B., 21, 42, 75, 77, 90, 183, 283

Nice, surrendered to France by Cavour (1860), 271

Nigra (Count) Constantino, 217, 219

Novara, battle of (final defeat of Charles Albert, 1849), 155

PALLAVICINO, Marchese, 185

Palmerston, Lord, intervenes with Austria, 98 (footnote); receives N. Corsini (1859), 242; counsels delay, 260 (see also Appendix I, pp. 84, 85)

Pamphlets, by Montanelli, 76; Galeotti, 99, 276; Guerrazzi, 100, 101, 119; La Guerronière, 184, 216, 267; in Ricasoli's campaign against Austria, 212; in election of August 1859, 239–241; by Bianchi and Tabarrini, 276; by 'Prior Luca', 280–289, and Roman Church, 281, 284

Papacy, the (see also Pius IX), Capponi denounces government of, 72; repudiates Italian nationalist programme, 120; Ricasoli's reluctance to quarrel with (1859–1860), 249; refusal of, to enter European Congress, 268; Ricasoli's propaganda against Roman Church, 283–287; pamphlets of, vetoed by Tuscan Government, 284

Paris, insurrection in (1848), 86

Parma, Duchess of, 241, 243

Parra, 244

Pasolini, 250, 251, 273

Patria, the, 88–90, 101–103, 108, 118, 126–129, 143

Pepoli, 230, 232

Peruzzi, Baldassare, 2, 188, 193, 200, 201, 211, 218, 241, 251, 262, 272

Piedmont, opinion of, in Florence, 1; Ricasoli urges Charles Albert of Sardinia to support Tuscan alliance with, 109; Constitution granted by King of, 112; alliance with Tuscany, Ridolfi's distrust of and Ricasoli's belief in, 109, 110, 172; and Tuscany, 127, 128; Gioberti's accession to power in, 146; Cavour aims at co-operation with Tuscany against Austria, 185; and Prince Carignano, 262; Napoleon's opposition to expansion of, 266; Cabinet of, overturned, 268; Cavour, restored to power, proclaims programme of union (January 1860), 269

Pigli, Prof., suspended at Pisa University for his revolutionary speeches, 39; Governor of Leghorn, 140–143, 151, 186, 278, 283

Pinelli, 127

Pisa, Montanelli starts reformist agitation in, 74; riots in, 107; report from, to Florence (1859), 196; Archbishop of, 285

Pisa University, 9, 38–40, 114, 206, 277, 279

Pius IX (see also the Papacy), elected Pope (1846), 76; publishes amnesty, but Tuscans remain sceptical of his liberalism, 77; Allocution of, against war with Austria, 120; threatens supporters of the *Constituent* with excommunication, 147, thus causing abdication of Leopold, 148; proclaims Rome centre of government, 148; Napoleon's note to, 268; caricatures of, published in Florence (1860), 281

Plombières, Cavour and Napoleon discuss Franco-Italian Alliance at (1858), 184; Ricasoli's ignorance thereof, 205

Poggi, Enrico (Minister of Justice and supporter of Ridolfi), 220, 233 234, 237, 254

Police, Tuscan (*buon-governo* and *sbirri*), 23–25, 48, 54, 76, 104, 209

Poniatowski, Prince, 97, 170

Prati, G., 143

Press, the, secret growth of, 75, 76; new press laws passed, 90, 93, 94; influence of (1848), 126; unbridled sedition of (1858), 183

' Prior Luca', 280–289

Public Meetings and placards, law disregarded prohibiting, 94

Puccini, Niccolo, 19, 46, 142, 183

RADETSKY, J. (Austrian General), 113, 159, 179

Railways, Ricasoli's belief in future of, 68; spread of, 73

Ranalli, Ferdinando, 278, 279

Rattazzi, Urbano (Piedmontese Minister of Interior) appointed 1859, 229, 246; converted to annexation of Tuscany, 268

Reiset, Comte de (French Ambassador to Florence, 1859), 231, 232

Renzi, hailed as ' martyr', 73, 74

Ricasoli (Baron), Benito, born 9th March, 1809, 6; austere character of 4, 8; his introspection and passion for principles, 63–65, 162–169 his strong views on education, 10; independence of, during schooldays, 6, 7; his diaries and notebooks, 7, 9, 11, 56, 163, 169, 194; his schemes for agricultural reform, 11, 55–57; his views on liberty, religion and free-trade, 161–166; his dislike of parliamentary life, 87, 167, 208, and of democracy, 102; his belief in future of railways, 68; administrates his family estates at age of 18, 7; marries Anna Bonaccorsi, 9; his daughter, Elisabetta, born (1831), 9; consecrates his life to her education, 10; preaches moral and religious precepts to his tenants, 57–63; Lambruschini, his friendship and correspondence with, 65–67; Salvagnoli, his influence upon, 70; visits France (1844), 68, and Switzerland (1849–1850) and England (1851), 164; death of his wife and marriage of daughter, 171, 172; retires to Brolio (1862) and dies 20th October, 1880 (Epilogue)

Ricasoli, public life of; embarks upon political career (1847), 72; Pius IX, is unenthusiastic at election of, 77; lectures Cempini, Leopold's Minister, upon his shortcomings, and hands him memorandum on causes of anarchy, 80–84; his anger against Austria, 83; Piedmont, stands almost alone in advocating alliance with, 87, 109, 110, 214–221; issues first number of the *Patria*, 88; his views on function of the press, 88; his duel with the Marchese Torriagini, 89; letter to Salvagnoli, 89; his proposals shelved by Government, 93; his mentality contrasted with that of Guerrazzi, 83; he praises the new Ministry, 103; pleads for artillery and munition factories, 108; is appointed ambassador to Charles Albert of Sardinia, and begs latter's support in alliance with Piedmont, 109; receives sinister title of 'Albertist', 110; appointed *gonfaloniere* of Florence, he makes his own terms with Ridolfi, 111, 112; his premature delight at repulse of Austrians, 113, 114; chafes at Government's incapacity and drifts into opposition, 118, 125, 126; is mobbed after battle of Custozza, 124; resigns, 138; elected member of governing commission (1849), 156; his interviews with Gioberti and Prince Poniatowski in Paris, 170; his doubts of Cavour, 175; initiates publishing propaganda, 188; interviews with Cavour and Massari at Turin, 189, 194 (footnote), 195; fails to secure support of Baldasseroni and is approached by the nationalists, 193; crystallizes 'national will' in the communes, 203; military levy, is warned against, 204; his work as Minister of Interior, 208–214; institutes press campaign against Austria, 212; Tuscan autonomists, his fundamental quarrel with, 214–221; urges Piedmont to incorporate Tuscan army; dictates to Boncompagni, his chief, 220, and compels Cabinet to pronounce the creed of unity, 221; his delight at public response to Dolfi's 'address', 224–225; is unmoved by disastrous Treaty of Villafranca, 228–230; his comments on Napoleon's opposition, 231; ignores threats of French Ambassador, 232; wins over Cambray-Digny, 233; becomes virtual Dictator, commissions Dolfi to organise a national guard, and renews propaganda for union with

Piedmont, 234–236; engineers elections of 1859, 237–240; scores signal success in Tuscan Assembly, 244, 245; wilfully misunderstands Victor Emmanuel and prematurely proclaims union with Piedmont, 247, 248; negotiates with trans-Apennine States, 249, 253; and regency question, 255, 256; his policy contrasted with that of Mazzini, whom he drives out of Tuscany, 256–258; his alarm at Garibaldi's activities, 259; Piedmont, his differences with, 261–264; European Congress, decides to send own envoy to, 267; welcomes Cavour's return to power (17th January, 1860), 268; publishes Constitution for 'first Italian Parliament' at Piedmont, 269; and Anglo-French proposal that Sardinians occupy Central Italy, 270; removes reactionaries from his path and intensifies propaganda, 274, 289; prohibits caricatures of Pope and other journalistic extravagances, 282, but launches campaign against Roman Church, 283–287; and disaffection of peasantry (June 1859), 287, 288; wins overwhelming victory at the polls, 15th March, 1860

Ricasoli family, history of, 2–4; their control of Chianti region, 3; supporters of the Medici, 3

Ricasoli, Elisabetta, 9, 10, 164–166

Ricasoli, Gaetano, 6

Ricasoli, Vincenzo, 6, 9, 72, 115, 117, 160, 170, 179, 194, 206, 218, 238, 286

Ricci, G., 95, 110

Ridolfi (Marchese), Cosimo, statue of, in Florence, 2; criticises Tuscan agricultural laws, 15; his character, municipal work and activities as president of Academy of Georgofili, 34, 35, 277; tutor of Leopold's heir, 35, 187; demands freedom of the press, 79; his fear of Piedmontese ambitions, 87, 121; proposes newspaper alliance with Ricasoli, 90; appeals for constitutional reform (1848), 99; appointed Minister of Interior, 102; plans Customs League and substitutes carabinieri for police force, 104; pays punitive visit to Leghorn and imprisons Guerrazzi, 110; his hopes of an Italian League quashed by the Pope, 119, 120; resigns after short span as Dictator (1848), 126; and Cavour, 190, 195; appointed Minister for Foreign Affairs (1859), 207; opposes fusion with Piedmont, 217, 233; resents high-handedness of Ricasoli, 220, 233; reproves Matteucci, 246

Rossi (Count), Pellegrini (Roman Minister), 128, 147; assassination of, 141

SALASCO ARMISTICE (August, 1848), 127, 146

Salvagnoli, Vincenzo, character of and friendship with Ricasoli, 70–72; champions Renzi, 74; contributes to the Patria, 88, 90, and to the Monitore, 211; and Lambruschini, 103; his letters to Ricasoli, 109; is denounced as an 'Albertist', 123; eloquence of, in Parliament, 125; his flight from Florence to Brolio, 143, and from Brolio to Turin, 160; unwisely hastens crisis with France, 215, 216; enters Cabinet in close co-operation with Ricasoli, 219–236, 263, 285; his diplomatic visit to Turin, 234; publicity work of, 244

Sardinia, King of (see Charles Albert)

Savoy, ceded by Cavour to France (1860), 271

Sbirri, the (see Police)

Serristori (Count), Luigi, Minister of Foreign Affairs and War (1847), 102; and Ricasoli, 109; resigns, 117; and Leopold II, 157, 158

Sicily, revolution in, 86, 120

Siena, 3, 5, 39, 75, 206

Solferino, battle of (1859), 230

Sterbini, 147

Strozzi, Prince, 275

TABARRINI, Marco, 211, 244, 276

Tartini, 134

Telegraph service, inauguration of, in Tuscany, 73

Tellini, C., 183

Thouar, P., 90

Thouvenel, succeeds to Walewski in Paris (1860), 268; repudiates Treaty of Villafranca, 269

Tommasèo, 37, 183

Torelli, 194

Triumvirate of 1849 (Montanelli, Guerrazzi and Manzoni), 150

Triumvirate of 1859 (Peruzzi, Malenchini and Dandrini), 200; Cavour's objection to, 205; administration of, 206, and resignation (9th May), 207

Tuscan army, 33, 116–118, 196–199, 206

Tuscany, soil of, 12; the *mezzadria* (agricultural system), 12, 13; conservatism of peasants of, 15, 16, 287, 290; proverbs of, 16; relations of, with Austria (1831), 21, 22; government of, under Leopold II, 22, 23; exiles (Carbonaro conspiracy of 1820) flock into, 26; population and industries of (1837), 30; negligible navy and army of, 31, 33; food-riots, anti-Austrian agitation, and embarrassment of Government (1846–1847), 78, 79, 94; widespread distrust of Piedmont, 87, 127; public demonstrations throughout, 93–97; futile committees draft codes of laws and council of state projected to discuss policy; laws prohibiting public meetings and posters flouted, 94, 95; fall of Government, 102; Austrian flag publicly burnt in Florence, 109; disintegration of Tuscan army, 117, 118; rioting and unemployment in, 142, 155, 156; and floods, bad crops and financial disaster, 177; chief political parties of (1858), 184–188; army mutinies (April 1859), 197; revolution spreads, 201, but peasants object to conscription, 204; Ricasoli's propaganda in, 222–224, 239; elections of August 1859, 237–240; Assembly votes for united Italy, legalises future powers of government, and is prorogued, 244–245; Mazzini banished from, 257, 258; Peace of Zurich well received in, 266; Cabinet resigns, 268; patriotic fervour throughout, 275–276

ULLOA, General, 206

VENICE, rising in, 86, 206; Austrians driven out of (1848), 113
Verdi's operas, popularity of, in Florence, 183
Victor Emmanuel, Tuscan patriots' hopes of, 181; Austrian Ultimatum sent to (24th April, 1859), 192; refuses dictatorship of Tuscany, 207; nominated 'National Sovereign' by Ricasoli, 222; signs Treaty of Villafranca, 227; equivocal reply of, to Tuscan delegation, 247; loyal demonstrations held, 275
Vienna (see Austria)
Vieusseux, Giampietro, 36–38, 52, 211, 218, 237
Villafranca, Treaty of, 1859 (Italy to be a Confederation under presidency of the Pope, Venetia to be left to Austria, and expelled Princes of Central Italy to be reinstated), consternation in Italy at terms of, 227–230; repudiation of, by France, 269

WALEWSKI (French Foreign Secretary), 232, 241, 266, 268, 272, 274
Wine, famous, of Brolio, 3

ZURICH, Peace of, 10th November, 1859 (federation of Central Italian States upheld but stipulation that expelled Princes return removed), 266

LIST OF BLACK AND WHITE
ILLUSTRATIONS
FULL PAGE PLATES

WILLIAM MORRIS (FROM A PHOTOGRAPH)   *Frontispiece*

Between pages 66–67

WINDOW IN ST. GILES, CAMBERWELL. FIGURE OF ST. PAUL

FIGURES OF ADAM AND EVE (FROM WINDOW BY MORRIS AND CO.), ST. MARTIN'S, SCARBOROUGH. DESIGNED BY FORD MADOX BROWN (double plate)

WINDOW IN JESUS COLLEGE CHAPEL, CAMBRIDGE. DESIGNED BY SIR EDWARD BURNE-JONES, BART.

VYNER MEMORIAL WINDOW (CHRISTCHURCH, OXFORD). DESIGNED BY SIR EDWARD BURNE-JONES, BART.

"PENELOPE." PAINTED GLASS IN SOUTH KENSINGTON MUSEUM. THE MEDALLION DESIGNED BY SIR EDWARD BURNE-JONES, BART.

HAND-PAINTED TILES, THE "DAISY" PATTERN

HAND-PAINTED TILES, THE "ROSE" PATTERN

Between pages 96–97

THE "DAISY" WALL PAPER

THE "TRELLIS" WALL PAPER. (THE BIRDS BY PHILIP WEBB.)

THE "MARIGOLD" WALL PAPER

THE "APPLE" WALL PAPER

THE "BRUGES" WALL PAPER

SILK AND WOOL TAPESTRY, "THE ANEMONE"

SILK AND WOOL TAPESTRY, "THE DOVE AND ROSE"

THE "HONEYSUCKLE" CHINTZ

THE "WANDLE" CHINTZ

THE "WEY" CHINTZ

SILK EMBROIDERY, "THE FLOWER-POT"

SKETCH DESIGN FOR THE "SMALL BARR" CARPET

SKETCH DESIGN FOR THE "LITTLE FLOWERS" CARPET

THE "BLACK TREE" CARPET

THE "LITTLE TREE" CARPET

THE "REDCAR" CARPET

SKETCH DESIGN FOR THE "BULLER'S WOOD" CARPET

Between pages 116–117

ARRAS TAPESTRY, "FLORA" AND "POMONA." THE FIGURES ARE BY SIR EDWARD BURNE-JONES, BART. (double plate)

DETAIL OF WATER-COLOUR PAINTING: "THE STAR OF BETHLEHEM," BY SIR E. BURNE-JONES, BART. (BY PERMISSION OF THE CORPORATION OF BIRMINGHAM)

DETAIL OF ARRAS TAPESTRY AT EXETER COLLEGE, OXFORD. "THE STAR OF BETHLEHEM," DESIGNED BY SIR E. BURNE-JONES, BART.

DETAIL OF ARRAS TAPESTRY AT STANMORE HALL. FROM "THE KNIGHTS DEPARTING ON THE QUEST OF THE HOLY GRAIL." DESIGNED BY SIR E. BURNE-JONES, BART.

NOTE—All the works illustrated, except those specially attributed, are designed by William Morris, and executed by Messrs. Morris and Co.

DETAIL OF ARRAS TAPESTRY AT STANMORE HALL. FROM "THE VISION OF THE HOLY GRAIL." DESIGNED BY SIR E. BURNE-JONES, BART.

ANGELS IN ADORATION. FROM CARTOONS BY WILLIAM MORRIS IN THE POSSESSION OF MR. C. FAIRFAX MURRAY (double plate)

ANGEL WITH SCROLL. (CARTOON BY WILLIAM MORRIS.) FROM THE ORIGINAL OWNED BY MR. C. FAIRFAX MURRAY

Between pages 378–379

GOLD-TOOLED LEATHER BINDING. MR. C. FAIRFAX MURRAY'S SKETCH BOOK

ILLUSTRATIONS IN THE TEXT

THE RED HOUSE. FROM THE GARDEN. FROM A DRAWING BY H. P. CLIFFORD   43
,,   ,,   THE WELL.   ,,   ,,   44
,.   ,,   STAIRCASE.   ,,   ,,   45
,,   ,,   EARLY MORRIS GLASS.   ,,   ,,   46
,,   ,,   ,,   ,,   ,,   ,,   47
,,   ,,   DINING ROOM BUFFET.   ,,   ,,   48
,,   ,,   LANDING.   ,,   ,,   50
MESSRS. MORRIS AND CO.'S WORKS AT MERTON ABBEY   .   126
KELMSCOTT MANOR. ENTRANCE FRONT. FROM A DRAWING BY C. M. GERE   185
,,   ,,   FROM THE GARTH. FROM A DRAWING BY R. J. WILLIAMS   186-7
,,   ,,   BACK OF THE HOUSE.   ,,   ,,   ,,
,.   ,,   THE GARRET.   ,,   ,,   ,,
,,   ,,   THE TAPESTRY ROOM.   ,,   ,,   ,,
,,   ,,   SEVENTEENTH CENTURY CARVED BEDSTEAD, WITH NEEDLEWORK HANGINGS DESIGNED AND WORKED BY MAY MORRIS   ,,   ,,   .   188
,,   ,,   FROM THE MEADOW AT THE BACK. FROM A DRAWING BY E. H. NEW   .   .   192
EXTERIOR OF HOUSE OCCUPIED IN PART BY THE KELMSCOTT PRESS. FROM A DRAWING BY H. P. CLIFFORD   .   394
KELMSCOTT PRESS. FIRST PAGE OF "POEMS BY THE WAY"   .   395
,,   ,,   PART OF PAGE OF "GODEFREY OF BOLOGNE"   399
,,   ,,   TITLE PAGE OF "A TALE OF OVER SEA".   402
,,   ,,   TITLE PAGE OF "HAND AND SOUL".   406
,,   ,,   PAGE FROM "THE WELL AT THE WORLD'S END"   407
KELMSCOTT PRESS MARK   413
,,   ,,   ,, ...   416

CORRIGENDA AND ADDENDA

Page 5, *line* 21 *from top.* Between the words "place" and "left" *insert* "under the headmastership of Dr. Gilderdale."

Page 17, *line* 2 *from bottom.* Between the words "performance" and "the," *insert* "the block of buildings comprising", and in the last line of the page, between the words "Street" and "it" *insert* "and the Strand."

Page 62, *line* 9 *from top.* Between the words "figures" and "Part" *insert* "Rossetti painted the subject of Gardening; the five others were the work of Burne-Jones."

Page 62, *line* 11 *from bottom.* For "Mr." *read* "Dr."

Pages 66 *and* 67. *Note.* Mr. Fairfax Murray has kindly pointed out, not, however, until the sheets had been printed off, and it was too late for correction, the mistake of attributing the design of the window of Adam and Eve to Rossetti, whereas it is actually the work of Madox Brown. On this point the present writer was misled by following M. Destrée and Mr. William Sharp, and also by what appeared to him to be the evidence of the glass itself, the face of Adam being an obvious portrait of Madox Brown's own features. The whole passage involving the error needs alteration to bring it into conformity with facts.

Page 234, *line* 17 *from top.* Between the words "Arts" and "In" *insert* "On September 14th, 1884, he lectured at Sheffield on 'Iceland and its Ancient Literature and History.'"

Page 247, *last line.* For "Æsthetic" *read* "Artistic."

THE ART OF WILLIAM MORRIS.
CHAPTER ONE: THE BEGINNING OF DAYS.

"WHAT are you?"
"I am an artist and a literary man, pretty well known, I think, throughout Europe."
It was on September 21st, 1885, when some few members of the Socialist League and others, having tried, on the previous day, to test the right of public speaking, were charged at the Thames Police Court with resisting the police whilst in the execution of their duty, and also with obstructing the highway. Mr. William Morris was present during the hearing of the case, and subsequently was placed at the bar for alleged disorderly behaviour in court. The prosecution failing to make out a case against him beyond the fact, which he himself confessed, that he had been carried away by his feelings so far as to exclaim "Shame!" on the passing of the sentences upon the prisoners, he was dismissed accordingly. The above is the description Mr. Morris gave of himself in the course of his examination by the magistrate on this same occasion. It is but just, however, to state that anything that savoured of self-assertion was entirely foreign to Morris's nature, and that the remark was wrung from him only at a moment when he was stung with an acute sense of the indignity of his position. In the daily press at the time there lacked not some ironical remarks about the artist's "European reputation." Nevertheless, Morris's was no empty boast; rather, his own estimate was considerably below the mark. For there needed not the past ten years to spread his fame so much more extensively, but that, had he so chosen, he might have claimed justly, even in 1885, to be known in the four continents. No quarter of the globe but contains either stained glass, carpets, tapestries, or other works of art from the firm of Morris and Co.; and as for Mr. Morris's numerous writings in prose and verse, their circulation is certainly not confined to the limits of the English-speaking peoples.

How widely his works are studied and esteemed in the

United States of America, the many articles that have
appeared in different periodicals and reviews in New York
and in Boston, in Baltimore, in Cambridge, Mass., and
in New Haven, bear witness.   While as to France,
which has so long assumed itself, and has by too many
amongst ourselves been accepted, as being the most
artistic nation in the world, there is a growing dissatisfac-
tion with its own performances, and a corresponding
recognition of the superiority of the English school of
decoration which had Mr. Morris for head.

In this regard a significant fact may be noted. A well-
known French critic, in a notice of the new postage stamp
and its designer, suggests that in the person of Eugène
Grasset a fitting object of artistic homage has now been
found nearer home than William Morris. Thus implicitly
does the writer treat it as beyond question that, but for
the genius discovered all too tardily in their midst, his
countrymen had been bound to concede the highest place
of honour to the English master before any of their own
people.

Of Welsh extraction, William Morris, the eldest son
of his parents, was born in Clay Street in the (then) village
of Walthamstow, Essex, on March 24th, 1834. " In his
own way," it has been said, " he was fond of . . . his
birthplace, as one or two stray references to it in 'News
from Nowhere' testify." The chief of these references are
as follows : "' I was born and bred on the edge of Epping
Forest, Walthamstow and Woodford, to wit.' 'A pretty
place, too, . . . a very jolly place, now that the trees have
had time to grow again since the great clearing of houses
in 1955.' " A few lines farther on Morris describes how
some one, in the romance, approached holding " some of
the plant that I used to call balm : its strong sweet smell
brought back to my mind my very early days in the kitchen-
garden at Woodford, and the large blue plums which grew
on the wall beyond the sweet-herb patch,—a connection of
memories which all boys will see at once. . . . 'When I
was a boy, and for long after, except for a piece about
Queen Elizabeth's Lodge, and for the part about High

Beech, the forest was almost wholly made up of pollard hornbeams mixed with holly. . . . I have not seen the place now for many years, except once. . . . I was very much shocked then to see how it was built over and altered. . . . What you were saying about the building being stopped and the trees growing is only too good news.'" In the same work Morris recalls with lingering regret the pleasantness of the meadows by "'the lovely river Lea (where old Isaak Walton used to fish . . . about the places called Stratford and Old Ford.'"

Moreover, though it is as representative of the Society for the Protection of Ancient Buildings that he writes in "The Nineteenth Century" in 1889, there is personal feeling in Mr. Morris's expression of gratitude to Mr. Shaw-Lefevre for the latter's "successful efforts to save the poor remains of Epping Forest from complete destruction." The matter indeed was one very near to Morris's heart. As recently as 1895 he wrote two letters to "The Daily Chronicle" on the subject of tree-felling in Epping Forest. "I was born and bred in its neighbourhood," he says in the first letter, dated April 22nd, ". . . and when I was a boy and young man, knew it yard by yard from Wanstead to the Theydons, and from Hale End to the Fairlop Oak. In those days it had no worse foes than the gravel stealer and the robbing fence maker, and was always interesting and often very beautiful." He goes on to say that the forest, being composed of pollard hornbeams "interspersed in many places with holly thickets," forms a "very curious and characteristic wood such as can be seen nowhere else." He pleads earnestly for the preservation of these trees, and urges that not a single one of them ought to be felled unless it be necessary for the growth of its neighbours, lest irreparable damage be done and "the essential character of one of the greatest ornaments of London disappear." Morris's statements having been controverted, he took the trouble to go down for a long day's inspection of the place, visiting in turn Loughton, Monk Wood, Theydon Woods, Chingford by way of Fair Mead Bottom and lastly Bury Wood. He then assured himself that he had not been mistaken, and wrote again to " The Daily Chronicle " to that effect on May 8th. He showed, on the evidence of what he had seen on the spot with his own eyes, and from passages in a report of one of the official conservators, that the steps proposed on the part of those who had charge of this " strange, unexampled and most romantic " forest were, by getting rid of the hornbeams, to alter its special and native aspect. And he maintains that his claim on behalf of the trees still standing is timely and useful at that juncture while yet, " in spite of all disfigurements, the northern part of the forest, from Sewardstone Green to beyond Epping, is still left to us, not to be surpassed in interest by any other wood near a great capital." Morris was thus to the last warmly attached to his old home scenes. It has also been recorded of him that " as a boy of nine, with a pony of his own, he rode half Essex over in search of old churches." Such was the practical beginning of his artistic researches, and so firm a hold did they take upon his mind that, after many years' interval, he could remember the details of a building he had not seen since his boyhood.

As many a one besides himself must own with thankfulness to having done, Morris imbibed his first impressions, acquired his first taste for art and romance, from Sir Walter Scott. For this writer he always cherished an enthusiastic admiration, wherein he would not submit to be outdone even by Mr. Ruskin. William Morris could not recall a time when he was unable to read, and, by the early age of seven, had read the greater part, if not indeed every word, of Scott's works. From Scott it was, in the first place, that he learned to love Gothic architecture, though not, certainly, to apologize for loving it, as Scott felt himself obliged to do to the pedantry of his generation. " It is curious," remarks Morris, " as showing how sometimes one art will lag behind another in a revival, that the man who wrote the exquisite and wholly unfettered naturalism of the ' Heart of Midlothian,' for instance, thought himself continually bound to seem to feel ashamed of, and to excuse himself for " his instinctive love of

Gothic architecture. For his part, Morris's association of ideas will be conveyed best in his own words : " How well I remember as a boy," he says, " my first acquaintance with a room hung with faded greenery at Queen Elizabeth's Lodge, by Chingford Hatch, in Epping Forest, and the impression of romance that it made upon me ! a feeling that always comes back on me when I read, as I often do, Sir Walter Scott's 'Antiquary,' and come to the description of the green room at Monkbarns, amongst which the novelist has with such exquisite cunning of art imbedded the fresh and glittering verses of the summer poet Chaucer."

Elsewhere Mr. Morris speaks of other pleasant reminiscences, when, referring to the late Dr. Neale's carol of " Good King Wenceslas," he says, " The legend itself is pleasing and a genuine one, and the Christmas-like quality of it, recalling the times of my boyhood, appeals to me at least as a happy memory of past days." On the other hand, the stress of the officialism that bore upon him in his public school career, previously to which he had been sent to Forest School in his native place, left a less agreeable if not less enduring impression. "I was educated at Marlborough under clerical masters, and I naturally rebelled against them." It is said however that the lax discipline of the place in those days allowed him ample opportunity for cultivating his individual tastes and pursuits. One experience of his public school days may be gathered from an incidental allusion which, years afterwards, he made in an address to a South London audience. The man, he observed, must be hard to move who could look without emotion upon Stonehenge, and that although the stones that remained then, in 1894, were much fewer than they were at the time when Morris was yet at school at Marlborough.

" The Captain of our Dormitory, who was much more fond of out-of-door life than of study," writes an old schoolfellow of Morris's in "The Marlburian," "made great friends with Morris—not that their tastes were at all similar, but that the former having a passion for listening to tales of romance.... found quite a repertoire of them in Morris. 'Such wonderful stories,' he would say, 'that fellow Morris is able to tell one.' But Morris was not always in such favour with his friend ; for at other times the friend, in the height of indignation, his own conservative instincts taking great offence, would be inveighing against the extraordinary opinions to which Morris had been giving utterance." Thus it was evident, remarks the writer, "that 'the boy was father of the man.'"

William Morris was not above fourteen years old when, about the year 1845, according to his own reckoning, " the first general appearance of the Pre-Raphaelites before the public" took place. But the time for him to come under their influence was not yet. On the contrary he considered the early training that was provided for him to have been that of a layman in the matter of painting and the other arts, notwithstanding the fact that he used, in his young days, to be taken to see the Royal Academy. " I remember distinctly myself," he says, "as a boy, that when I had pictures offered to my notice I could not understand what they were about at all. I said, 'Oh, well, that is all right. It has got the sort of thing in it which there ought to be in a picture. There is nothing to be said against it, no doubt. I cannot say I would have it other than that, because it is clearly the proper thing to do.' But really I took very little interest in it, and I should think that would be the case with nine hundred and ninety-nine out of every thousand of those people who had not received definite technical instruction in the art, who were not formally artists."

However, with his undergraduate days Mr. Morris was destined to undergo a great development. The 2nd June, 1852, the date of his matriculation at Exeter College, Oxford, must be regarded as marking one of the most momentous events in his life. True, neither in his own time at the University, nor yet for a considerable number of years later, was there any sort of æsthetic tradition with regard to decoration of the rooms or the surroundings of the men. But for all that the genius of the place was more powerful in that pre-æsthetic period of the early fifties, to leave a lasting impress on the sympathetic and receptive than, as Mr. Morris never ceased to regret, it is now or probably ever will be again. The early zeal of the Tractarian movement had scarcely had time to cool, or to become diverted into side issues; the University Commission, the Gaul within the gates, had not begun to carry out their reforming work. And as for the old city itself, it was still, comparatively speaking, untouched by modern "improvements," in the shape of new college buildings and new schools. His own college did not present a new front to the Broad, neither had its homely old chapel been replaced by a bran-new travesty of St. Louis's thirteenth-century "Sainte Chapelle." Magdalen Bridge had not yet been widened; neither did tramcars, only less obnoxious in such a place than steamers on the Grand Canal at Venice, desecrate the High. Mr. Morris has on more than one occasion expressed his opinion quite candidly on the subject: " It is a grievous thing to have to say, but say it I must, that the one most beautiful city in England, the city of Oxford, has been ravaged for many years past, not only by ignorant tradesmen, but by the University and College authorities. Those whose special business it is to direct the culture of the nation have treated the beauty of Oxford as if it were a matter of no moment, as if their commercial interests might thrust it aside without consideration." The result is that the Oxford of to-day is " a lamentable example of all kinds of architectural errors and mistakes, and crimes, I might almost say. There, some time ago, when they were roofing the new buildings, which I am very sorry to say they built there, like Exeter College Chapel, they roofed them with stone slates." The stone slates decaying, the roofs were stripped and covered with green Westmoreland slates, which " on a grey stone building in Oxford . . . look absolutely horrible." Lecturing in 1883 in Oxford, " amidst sights and memories which we older men, at least," observed Morris, " regard with nothing short of love," he told his audience how sorely the changed aspect of the place distressed him. " Go through Oxford streets," said he, " and ponder on what is left us there unscathed by the fury of the thriving shop and the progressive college. .... *Must* I speak to you of the degradation that has so speedily befallen this city, still the most beautiful of" all our finest and most ancient cities?—"a city which, with its surroundings, would, if we had had a grain of common sense, have been treated like a most precious jewel, whose beauty was to be preserved at any cost. . . . I am old enough to know how we have treated that jewel—as if it were a common stone kicking about on the highway. . . . When I remember the contrast between the Oxford of to-day and the Oxford which I first saw thirty years ago, I wonder I can face the misery (there is no other word for it) of visiting it." The passage previously quoted continues: "There are many places in England where a young man may get as good book-learning as in Oxford; not one where he can receive the education which the loveliness of the grey city used to give us. Call this sentiment if you please, but you *know* that it is true." In another lecture he records how, while an undergraduate at Oxford, he "first saw the city of Rouen, then still in its outward aspect a piece of the Middle Ages: no words can tell you how its mingled beauty, history and romance took hold on me; I can only say that, looking back on my past life,"—after a lapse, that is, of between thirty and forty years—"I find it was the greatest pleasure I have ever had: and now it is a pleasure which no one can ever have again: it is lost to the world for ever." At the time when a "restoration" of Rouen Cathedral was in prospect, Morris, in vigorous language, opposed it in "The Daily Chronicle;" deprecating any such measures which, in the generally understood sense of the word "restoration," "*must* mean serious and lasting injury" to the building, "and *may* mean the destruction of all interest and beauty in it." "It would be impossible," so he wrote, "to over-estimate the interest of this most beautiful monument of art, which, taking it altogether, is second to none in the two great architectural countries, France and England. And though visitors to the ancient Norman capital are most often captivated by the extraordinary elegance of St.

Ouen, and in consequence somewhat neglect the ca....ural, the latter has both more interest and more special beauty than the former." The proposed scheme necessarily implied the re-doing of detail "into a mere modern imitation of the ancient work. This has been done for some years now " (1895) "in the case of the Palais de Justice in Rouen, which is, in consequence, no longer a beautiful Late Gothic building, as I first saw it in 1853, but a lifeless modern 'study in Gothic' prepared in the architect's office, and carried out slavishly by the workman reduced to a mere machine." "It is now thirty years ago," writes Morris in 1884, "since I first saw Rouen, then almost entirely a mediæval city, and more romantic and beautiful than words can convey; I wonder how many beautiful houses have been wantonly or commercially destroyed in those thirty years, leaving no record behind them."

"Though not so astounding, so romantic, or at first sight so mediæval as the Norman city, Oxford in those days still kept a good deal of its earlier loveliness; and the memory of its grey streets as they were has been an abiding influence and pleasure in my life, and would be greater still if I could only forget what they are now—a matter of far more importance than the so-called learning of the place could have been to me in any case, but which, as it was, no one tried to teach me, and I did not try to learn." In another place Mr. Morris supplies further autobiographical details relating to the same period. "Not long ago,"—it was in February, 1856, that these words appeared—"Not long ago I saw for the first time some of the churches of North France; still more recently I saw them for the second time; and, remembering the love I have for them and the longing that was in me to see them, during the time that came between the first and second visit, I thought I should like to tell people of some of those things I felt when I was there." However, as a matter of fact, he does not describe in detail any church beside that named in the sub-title of his article, viz., " Shadows of Amiens," wherein, by many years, he anticipated strikingly Mr. Ruskin's "Bible of Amiens." It was by the northernmost door of the great triple porch of the west front that Mr. Morris passed into the building for the first time. " I think I felt inclined to shout when I first entered Amiens Cathedral; it is so free and vast and noble, I did not feel in the least awestruck or humbled by its size and grandeur. I have not often felt thus when looking on architecture, but have felt, at all events at first, intense exultation at the beauty of it ; that, and a certain kind of satisfaction in looking on the geometrical tracery of the windows, on the sweeping of the huge arches, were, I think, my first feelings in Amiens Cathedral." Proceeding to describe the magnificent choir-stalls and the figure subjects sculptured upon them, he says that those he remembers best are the scenes of the history of Joseph, and in particular that which represents the dream of Pharaoh. " I think the lean kine about the best bit of carving I have seen yet, . . . the most wonderful symbol of famine ever conceived. I never fairly understood Pharaoh's dream till I saw the stalls at Amiens."

But to return to Oxford. It was surely something more than mere chance that there should have matriculated on the very same day at the same college with William Morris the man whose name must ever be associated with his, viz., Edward Burne-Jones, " of whom indeed," said Mr. Morris, in 1891, at Birmingham, the native place of the former, " I feel some difficulty in speaking as the truth demands, because he is such a close friend of mine." The two freshmen quickly became acquainted, and, discovering how many tastes and aspirations they had in common, were drawn together in intimate comradeship, a bond which continued steadfast and unbroken to the day of Morris's death. They shared one another's profound enthusiasm, it is scarcely necessary to say, for the art and literature of the Middle Ages. Morris, so Mr. Herbert Horne says, " had come to Oxford with a great admiration for the writings of Mrs. Browning ; at college he became acquainted not only with the works of Browning and Tennyson, but also with some older writers, with Froissart's Chronicle, and especially with a book which was